Microsoft® Official Academic Course

Microsoft® Project 2010

WILEY

Credits

EDITOR	Bryan Gambrel
DIRECTOR OF SALES	Mitchell Beaton
EXECUTIVE MARKETING MANAGER	Chris Ruel
MICROSOFT STRATEGIC RELATIONSHIPS MANAGER	Merrick Van Dongen of Microsoft Learning
EDITORIAL PROGRAM ASSISTANT	Jennifer Lartz
CONTENT MANAGER	Micheline Frederick
PRODUCTION EDITOR	Amy Weintraub
CREATIVE DIRECTOR	Harry Nolan
COVER DESIGNER	Jim O'Shea
PHOTO EDITOR	Sheena Goldstein
TECHNOLOGY AND MEDIA	Tom Kulesa/Wendy Ashenberg

Cover Photo Credit: Tetra Images/Getty Images, Inc.

This book was set in Garamond by Aptara, Inc. and printed and bound by Bind Rite Robbinsville. The covers were printed by Bind Rite Robbinsville.

Microsoft, ActiveX, Excel, InfoPath, Microsoft Press, MSDN, OneNote, Outlook, PivotChart, PivotTable, PowerPoint, SharePoint, SQL Server, Visio, Windows, Windows Mobile, and Windows Server are either registered trademarks or trademarks of Microsoft Corporation in the United States and/or other countries. Other product and company names mentioned herein may be the trademarks of their respective owners.

The example companies, organizations, products, domain names, e-mail addresses, logos, people, places, and events depicted herein are fictitious. No association with any real company, organization, product, domain name, e-mail address, logo, person, place, or event is intended or should be inferred.

The book expresses the author's views and opinions. The information contained in this book is provided without any express, statutory, or implied warranties. Neither the authors, John Wiley & Sons, Inc., Microsoft Corporation, nor their resellers or distributors will be held liable for any damages caused or alleged to be caused either directly or indirectly by this book.

Founded in 1807, John Wiley & Sons, Inc. has been a valued source of knowledge and understanding for more than 200 years, helping people around the world meet their needs and fulfill their aspirations. Our company is built on a foundation of principles that include responsibility to the communities we serve and where we live and work. In 2008, we launched a Corporate Citizenship Initiative, a global effort to address the environmental, social, economic, and ethical challenges we face in our business. Among the issues we are addressing are carbon impact, paper specifications and procurement, ethical conduct within our business and among our vendors, and community and charitable support. For more information, please visit our website: www.wiley.com/go/citizenship.

ISBN 978-0-470-63888-0

Printed in the United States of America

10 9 8 7 6 5 4 3 2 1

Foreword from the Publisher

Wiley's publishing vision for the Microsoft Official Academic Course series is to provide students and instructors with the skills and knowledge they need to use Microsoft technology effectively in all aspects of their personal and professional lives. Quality instruction is required to help both educators and students get the most from Microsoft's software tools and to become more productive. Thus our mission is to make our instructional programs trusted educational companions for life.

To accomplish this mission, Wiley and Microsoft have partnered to develop the highest quality educational programs for Information Workers, IT Professionals, and Developers. Materials created by this partnership carry the brand name "Microsoft Official Academic Course," assuring instructors and students alike that the content of these textbooks is fully endorsed by Microsoft, and that they provide the highest quality information and instruction on Microsoft products. The Microsoft Official Academic Course textbooks are "Official" in still one more way—they are the officially sanctioned courseware for Microsoft IT Academy members.

The Microsoft Official Academic Course series focuses on *workforce development*. These programs are aimed at those students seeking to enter the workforce, change jobs, or embark on new careers as information workers, IT professionals, and developers. Microsoft Official Academic Course programs address their needs by emphasizing authentic workplace scenarios with an abundance of projects, exercises, cases, and assessments.

The Microsoft Official Academic Courses are mapped to Microsoft's extensive research and job-task analysis, the same research and analysis used to create the Microsoft Office Specialist (MOS) exams. The textbooks focus on real skills for real jobs. As students work through the projects and exercises in the textbooks, they enhance their level of knowledge and their ability to apply the latest Microsoft technology to everyday tasks. These students also gain resume-building credentials that can assist them in finding a job, keeping their current job, or in furthering their education.

The concept of lifelong learning is today an utmost necessity. Job roles, and even whole job categories, are changing so quickly that none of us can stay competitive and productive without continuously updating our skills and capabilities. The Microsoft Official Academic Course offerings, and their focus on Microsoft certification exam preparation, provide a means for people to acquire and effectively update their skills and knowledge. Wiley supports students in this endeavor through the development and distribution of these courses as Microsoft's official academic publisher.

Today educational publishing requires attention to providing quality print and robust electronic content. By integrating Microsoft Official Academic Course products, *WileyPLUS*, and Microsoft certifications, we are better able to deliver efficient learning solutions for students and teachers alike.

Joe Heider
General Manager and Senior Vice President

Preface

Welcome to the Microsoft Official Academic Course (MOAC) program for Microsoft Project 2010. MOAC represents the collaboration between Microsoft Learning and John Wiley & Sons, Inc. publishing company. Microsoft and Wiley teamed up to produce a series of textbooks that deliver compelling and innovative teaching solutions to instructors and superior learning experiences for students. Infused and informed by in-depth knowledge from the creators of Microsoft Project and Windows, and crafted by a publisher known worldwide for the pedagogical quality of its products, these textbooks maximize skills transfer in minimum time. Students are challenged to reach their potential by using their new technical skills as highly productive members of the workforce.

Because this knowledgebase comes directly from Microsoft, creator of Microsoft Project 2010, you are sure to receive the topical coverage that is most relevant to students' personal and professional success. Microsoft's direct participation not only assures you that MOAC textbook content is accurate and current; it also means that students will receive the best instruction possible to enable their success in the workplace.

■ The Microsoft Official Academic Course Program

The *Microsoft Official Academic Course* series is a complete program for instructors and institutions to prepare and deliver great courses on Microsoft software technologies. With MOAC, we recognize that, because of the rapid pace of change in the technology and curriculum developed by Microsoft, there is an ongoing set of needs beyond classroom instruction tools for an instructor to be ready to teach the course. The MOAC program endeavors to provide solutions for all these needs in a systematic manner in order to ensure a successful and rewarding course experience for both instructor and student—technical and curriculum training for instructor readiness with new software releases; the software itself for student use at home for building hands-on skills, assessment, and validation of skill development; and a great set of tools for delivering instruction in the classroom and lab. All are important to the smooth delivery of an interesting course on Microsoft software, and all are provided with the MOAC program. We think about the model below as a gauge for ensuring that we completely support you in your goal of teaching a great course. As you evaluate your instructional materials options, you may wish to use the model for comparison purposes with available products.

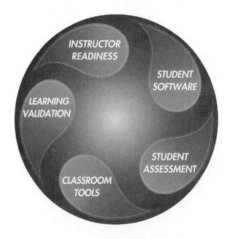

www.wiley.com/college/microsoft or call the MOAC
Toll-Free Number: 1+(888) 764-7001 (U.S. & Canada only)

■ Pedagogical Features

Many pedagogical features have been developed specifically for *Microsoft Official Academic Course* programs. Unique features of our task-based approach include a Lesson Skill Matrix, Workplace Ready, and Internet Ready exercises; and three levels of increasingly rigorous lesson-ending activities: Competency, Proficiency, and Mastery Assessment.

Presenting the extensive procedural information and technical concepts woven throughout the textbook raises challenges for the student and instructor alike. The Illustrated Book Tour that follows provides a guide to the rich features contributing to *Microsoft Official Academic Course* program's pedagogical plan. Following is a list of key features in the lessons, which are designed to prepare students for success on the certification exams and in the workplace:

- Each lesson begins with a **Lesson Skill Matrix**. This feature outlines all the topics covered in the lesson.

- Each lesson features a real-world **business case** scenario that places the software skills and knowledge to be acquired in a real-world setting.

- Every lesson includes a **Software Orientation**. This feature provides an overview of the software features students will be working with in the lesson. The orientation will detail the general properties of the software or specific features, such as a ribbon or dialog box, and it includes a large, labeled screen image.

- Concise and frequent **Step-by-Step** instructions teach students new features and provide an opportunity for hands-on practice. Numbered steps give detailed instructions to help students learn software skills. The steps also show results and screen images to match what students should see on their computer screens.

- **Illustrations:** Screen images provide visual feedback as students work through the exercises. The images reinforce key concepts, provide visual clues about the steps, and allow students to check their progress.

- **Button images:** When the text instructs a student to click a particular button, an image of that button is shown in the margin or in the text.

- **Key Terms:** Important technical vocabulary is listed at the beginning of the lesson. When these terms are used later in the lesson, they appear in bold italic type and are defined. The Glossary contains all of the key terms and their definitions.

- Engaging point-of-use **Reader aids**, located throughout the lessons, tell students why this topic is relevant (*The Bottom Line*), provide students with helpful hints (*Take Note*), show alternate ways to accomplish tasks (*Another Way*), or point out things to watch out for or avoid (*Troubleshooting*). Reader aids also provide additional relevant or background information that adds value to the lesson.

- Each lesson ends with a **Skill Summary** recapping the skills covered in the lesson.

- **Knowledge Assessment:** Provides a total of 20 questions from a mix of True/False, Fill-in-the-Blank, Matching, or Multiple Choice, testing students on concepts learned in the lesson.

- **Competency, Proficiency, and Mastery Assessment:** Provide three progressively more challenging lesson-ending activities.

- **Internet Ready.** Projects combine the knowledge that students acquire in a lesson with Web-based task research.

- **Circling Back:** These integrated projects provide students with an opportunity to renew and practice skills learned in previous lessons.

- **Workplace Ready.** These new features preview how Microsoft Project 2010 is used in real-world situations.

- **Online files:** The student companion website contains the data files needed for each lesson. These files are indicated by the @ icon in the margin of the textbook.

■ Lesson Features

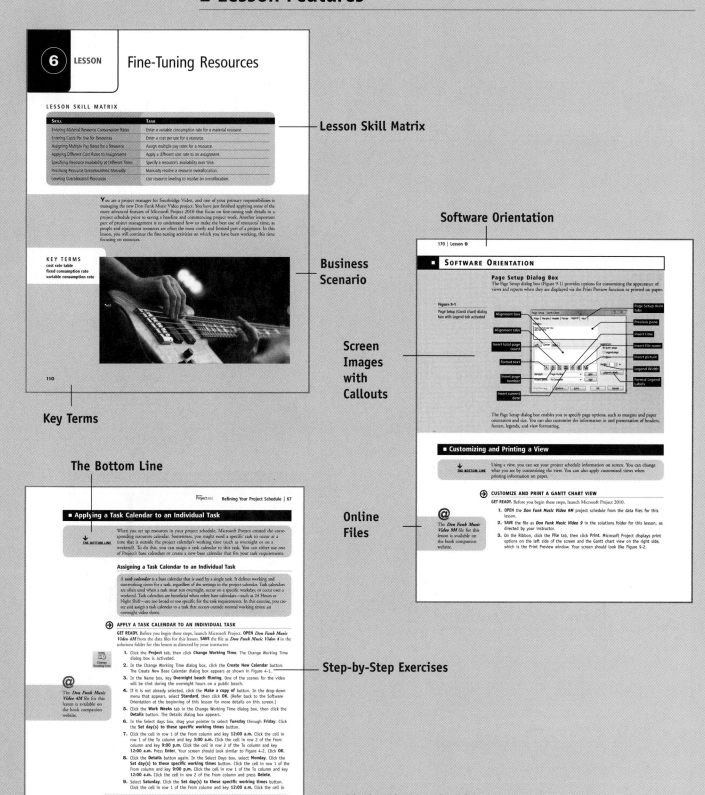

Lesson Skill Matrix

Software Orientation

Business Scenario

Key Terms

Screen Images with Callouts

The Bottom Line

Online Files

Step-by-Step Exercises

Troubleshooting Reader Aid

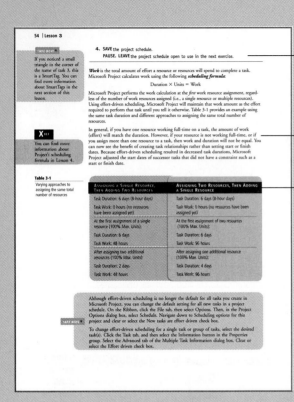

Take Note Reader Aid

Cross Reference Reader Aid

Easy-to-Read Tables

Another Way Reader Aid

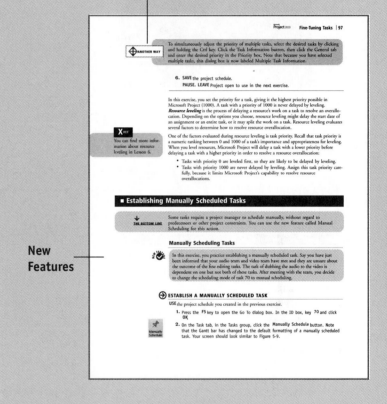

New Features

Summary Skill Matrix

60 | Lesson 3

SKILL SUMMARY

IN THIS LESSON, YOU LEARNED:	TASK
To assign work resources to tasks.	Make individual resource assignments.
	Assign multiple resources simultaneously.
To add more resource assignments to tasks.	Add resources to a task.
	Use SmartTags to assign resources to tasks.
To assign material resources to tasks.	Assign a material resource to a task.
To assign cost resources to tasks.	Assign a cost resource to a task.

■ Knowledge Assessment

Fill in the Blank

Complete the following sentences by writing the correct word or words in the blanks provided.

1. A(n) _____ is the matching of a specific resource to a particular task to do work.

2. Assigning a(n) _____ or _____ resource to a task will not affect the duration of the task.

3. In Microsoft Project, when you assign a human or equipment resource to a task, the result is _____.

4. _____ is the number of work periods you expect a task to take to complete.

5. If a resource is assigned to do more work than can be done within the normal work capacity of the resource, it is _____.

6. The capacity of a resource to work is measured in _____.

7. In Microsoft Project, Duration × Units = Work is known as the _____.

8. Effort-driven scheduling adjusts a task's duration only if you add or remove _____ from a task.

9. When you assign _____ to tasks, you can track their consumption and cost.

10. According to the scheduling formula in Microsoft Project, 20 hours task duration × 200% assignment units ≈ _____ hours work.

Multiple Choice

Select the best response for the following statements.

1. If you assign a resource to a task with more units than the resource has available, then the resource is:
   a. maximized.
   b. overutilized.
   c. compromised.
   d. overallocated.

Knowledge Assessment Questions

Competency Assessment Projects

Project 2010   Customizing and Printing Project Information | 179

■ Competency Assessment

Project 9-1: Printing a Gantt Chart View

You are preparing to print and distribute a copy of your project schedule to your team. You need to make several format changes to the printed version of the Gantt chart view before you distribute it.

GET READY. Launch Microsoft Project 2010 if it is not already running.
OPEN *Don Funk Music Video 9-1* from the data files for this lesson.

@ The *Don Funk Music Video 9-1* file for this lesson is available on the book companion website.

1. On the Ribbon, click the File tab. Select Print to view the print preview.
2. Under Settings, click the Page Setup hyperlink.
3. Click the Header tab, then click the Center tab in the alignment area.
4. In the alignment area, click to position your cursor at the end of &[Company]. Press Enter.
5. Key 2345 Main Street and press Enter. Then key New York, NY 11223.
6. Click the Footer tab.
7. In the alignment box, click to position your cursor at the end of &[Page].
8. Key of (note that there is a space before and after the word "of"). Click the Insert Total Page Count button.
9. Click the Legend tab. Then, in the alignment area, click the Left tab.
10. In the alignment box, click to position your cursor at the end of &[Date]. Press Enter.
11. Click the Insert Current Time button.
12. Click OK.
13. Click Close on the Print Preview toolbar.
14. SAVE the project schedule as *Don Funk Printing Gantt View* and CLOSE the file.
   LEAVE Project open to use in the next exercise.

Project 9-2: HR Interview Schedule

For your HR Interview project schedule, you want to print a report that displays the resources' workload for each two-week period. You will customize an existing report to meet your requirements.

OPEN *HR Interview Schedule 9-2* from the data files for this lesson.

@ The *HR Interview Schedule 9-2* file for this lesson is available on the book companion website.

1. Click the Project tab, then click the Reports button in the Reports group.
2. Click the Workload button, then click the Select button.
3. Click the Resource Usage button, then click the Edit button.
4. On the Definition tab, change the column to reflect every 2 weeks.
5. Click the Details tab. In the date format, select the option that shows the project information in the following format: Week1, Week2 ....(From Start).
6. Click OK, then click Select.
7. SAVE the project schedule as *HR Interview Custom Critical Task Report*, then CLOSE the file.
   LEAVE Project open to use in the next exercise.

Proficiency Assessment Projects

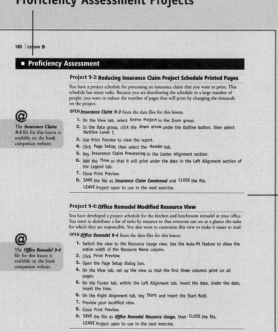

180 | Lesson 9

■ Proficiency Assessment

Project 9-3: Reducing Insurance Claim Project Schedule Printed Pages

You have a project schedule for processing an insurance claim that you want to print. This schedule has many tasks. Because you are distributing the schedule to a large number of people, you want to reduce the number of pages that will print by changing the timescale on the project.

OPEN *Insurance Claim 9-3* from the data files for this lesson.

@ The *Insurance Claim 9-3* file for this lesson is available on the book companion website.

1. On the View tab, select Entire Project in the Zoom group.
2. In the Data group, click the down arrow under the Outline button, then select Outline Level 1.
3. Use Print Preview to view the report.
4. Click Page Setup, then select the Header tab.
5. Key Insurance Claim Processing in the Center Alignment section.
6. Add the Time so that it will print under the date in the Left Alignment section of the Legend tab.
7. Close Print Preview.
8. SAVE the file as *Insurance Claim Condensed* and CLOSE the file.
   LEAVE Project open to use in the next exercise.

Project 9-4: Office Remodel Modified Resource View

You have developed a project schedule for the kitchen and lunchroom remodel at your office. You want to distribute a list of tasks by resource so that everyone can see at a glance the tasks for which they are responsible. You also want to customize this view to make it easier to read.

OPEN *Office Remodel 9-4* from the data files for this lesson.

@ The *Office Remodel 9-4* file for this lesson is available on the book companion website.

1. Switch the view to the Resource Usage view. Use the Auto-fit feature to show the entire width of the Resource Name column.
2. Click Print Preview.
3. Open the Page Setup dialog box.
4. On the View tab, set up the view so that the first three columns print on all pages.
5. On the Footer tab, within the Left Alignment tab, insert the date. Under the date, insert the time.
6. On the Right Alignment tab, key Start, and insert the Start field.
7. Preview your modified view.
8. Close Print Preview.
9. SAVE the file as *Office Remodel Resource Usage*, then CLOSE the file.
   LEAVE Project open to use in the next exercise.

Mastery Assessment Projects

Project 2010   Customizing and Printing Project Information | 181

■ Mastery Assessment

Project 9-5: Don Funk Music Video Calendars

You would like to print a report to show the different calendars that are being used in the production of the Don Funk Music Video.

OPEN *Don Funk Music Video 9-5* from the data files for this lesson.

1. Using the Reports dialog box, review the predefined reports that are available for this project. You would like to print a report that shows the different calendars that have been defined for this project so that you can quickly refer to them when needed. Identify the report that meets this need.
2. In a separate Word document, write a short paragraph detailing the steps you took to be able to preview this report.
3. Save the Word document as *Don Funk Music Video Calendars*. Save the Project file as *Don Funk Music Video Calendars*. CLOSE both files.
   LEAVE Project open to use in the next exercise.

Project 9-6: HR Interview Custom Network Diagram

You want to view and print your HR Interview Schedule as a Network Diagram, as well as customize some of the fields for printing.

OPEN *HR Interview Schedule 9-6* from the data files for this lesson.

1. Change the view to the Network Diagram view.
2. Hide the summary tasks.
3. Activate the Page Setup dialog box.
4. In the Page Setup dialog box, make the following custom changes:
   - Increase the width of the Legend to 3 inches
   - Add the time to the left side of the Legend, under the date
   - Key Start and insert the Start field on the right side of the Legend
   - Add the title "HR Interview Network Diagram" to the center of the header
   - Change the font of the title to Arial Bold 10pt, with color blue
   - Add your name to the second line of the header, under the project title
   - Have the legend print only on one page
5. Check your changes to make sure they appear correctly.
6. SAVE the file as *HR Interview Network Diagram* and CLOSE the file.
   CLOSE Project.

The *Don Funk Music Video 9-5* file for this lesson is available on the book companion website.

The *HR Interview Schedule 9-6* file for this lesson is available on the book companion website.

Internet Ready Project

146 | Lesson 7

Project 7-6: Costs and Durations for Hiring a New Employee

You want to compare the cost of tasks that have the same duration in your project schedule to hire a new employee. You therefore need to set up a custom group in order to group the data by duration and then by cost.

OPEN *Hiring New Employee 7-6* from the data files for this lesson.

1. Switch to the Task Usage view.
2. Use the Duration group to set up a new custom group called Duration-Cost.
3. Set up the new group so that it groups by descending duration and then descending cost.
4. Apply the Duration-Cost group.
5. SAVE the project schedule as *Hiring Duration Cost Group* and CLOSE the file.
   CLOSE Project.

The *Hiring New Employee 7-6* file for this lesson is available on the book companion website.

INTERNET READY

Over the last seven lessons, you have become familiar with the basics of Microsoft Project: tasks, resources, assignments, constraints, and resource allocation. You have learned that even the best project schedule is only as good as the information you can get out of it.

Search the Internet for current events in your city or state, and locate a story about a project that has not gone according to schedule (construction of a road or building, production of a new product, opening of a restaurant, etc.). Review the article; then, using what you have learned about Microsoft Project so far, write a short paragraph on what you believe went "wrong" with the project you selected. Make suggestions on how these problems could be avoided in the future. If necessary, perform additional Internet research on your selected current event.

■ WORKPLACE READY

Using Microsoft Project Templates

Suppose you are the conversion project manager at a company that processes electronic payments. You manage the "conversion" of new clients onto your data processing systems. Your manager has been impressed with your hard work and attention to detail, so he gives you a new project responsibility that is not in your range of experience–developing the project schedule for your company's upcoming move to a new office location. Although you are glad that your manager has confidence in you, you are a bit nervous because you are unfamiliar with the tasks involved in the process. You know that an office move involves more than just relocating furniture, phones, and computers, but where do you go from there?

Microsoft Project 2010 provides access to a number of templates at www.office.microsoft.com that are ready for you to download and customize for your specific project needs. Upon opening Microsoft Project 2010, a new blank project schedule is automatically opened. If you click the File tab and then click New, the Available Templates screen opens. Microsoft Project 2010 no longer provides templates built into the software. The templates at Microsoft Office.com are always being updated, and going directly to the source will ensure you get the latest template. Microsoft Office.com provides several different options for starting a new project, as shown in Figure 7-14.

Workplace Ready

Circling Back Exercises

Project 2010   Circling Back 2 | 197

■ Circling Back 2

Mete Goktepe is a project management specialist at Woodgrove Bank. He has put together the initial components of a project plan for a Request for Proposal (RFP) process to evaluate and select new commercial lending software. This process entails determining needs, identifying vendor, requesting proposals, reviewing proposals, and selecting the software.

Now that Mete has established the foundation of the project plan, he begins to put the plan into action.

Project 1: Setting Deadlines and Establishing Multiple Pay Rates

Acting as Mete, you need to set a deadline for one of the tasks in the project. You then need to establish and apply multiple pay rates for a resource.

GET READY. Launch Microsoft Project if it is not already running.

OPEN *RFP Bank Software Schedule* from the data files for this lesson.

1. In the Task Name column, click the name of task 11, RFP ready to release.
2. On the Task tab, click the Information button in the Properties group.
3. On the Advanced tab, in the drop-down date box next to Deadline, key or select 5/27/11.
4. Close the Task Information dialog box.
5. Scroll the Gantt bar chart to the right of task 11 to view the deadline marker.
6. On the Ribbon, click the View tab, then click Resource Sheet.
7. In the Resource Name column, double-click the name of resource 9, Marc J. Ingle. Because Marc J. Ingle's rate differs depending on whether he is doing document preparation or meeting facilitation, you need to enter a second rate for him.
8. In the Resource Information dialog box, click the Costs tab, if it is not already selected.
9. Under Cost rate tables, click the B tab.
10. Select the default entry of $0.00/h in the field directly below the Standard Rate column heading, key 1200/w, and press Enter. Click OK.
11. On the View tab, click the Task Usage button.
12. On the Ribbon, click the Tables button, then select the Cost table.
13. Under task 5, double-click Marc J. Ingle to activate the Assignment Information dialog box.
14. Click the General tab, if it is not already selected.
15. In the Cost rate table box, key or select B, then click OK.
16. SAVE the project plan as *RFP Bank Software Multiple Rates* in the solutions folder for this lesson, as directed by your instructor.
    PAUSE. LEAVE Project and the project plan open to use in the next exercise.

Project 2: Formatting and Printing the Project Plan

Acting as Mete, you need to change the appearance of some of your data before sharing it with stakeholders. You then need to prepare to print the project plan for distribution.

USE the project schedule from the previous exercise.

1. SAVE the schedule as *RFP Bank Software Formatted*.
2. Click the View tab, then click Gantt chart.
3. Click the Format tab, then click the check box next to Project Summary Task in the Show/Hide group.

The *RFP Bank Software Schedule* file for this lesson is available on the book companion website.

Conventions and Features Used in This Book

This book uses particular fonts, symbols, and heading conventions to highlight important information or to call your attention to special steps. For more information about the features in each lesson, refer to the Illustrated Book Tour section.

CONVENTION	MEANING
CLOSE	Words in all capital letters indicate instructions for opening, saving, or closing files or programs. They also point out items you should check or actions you should take.
TAKE NOTE*	Reader aids appear in shaded boxes found in your text. *Take Note* provides helpful hints related to particular tasks or topics.
ANOTHER WAY	*Another Way* provides an alternative procedure for accomplishing a particular task.
X REF	These notes provide pointers to information discussed elsewhere in the textbook or describe interesting features that are not directly addressed in the current topic or exercise.
Alt + Tab	A plus sign (+) between two key names means that you must press both keys at the same time. Keys that you are instructed to press in an exercise will appear in the font shown here.
A ***shared printer*** can be used by many individuals on a network.	Key terms appear in bold italic.
Key **My Name is.**	Any text you are asked to key appears in blue.
Click **OK.**	Any button on the screen you are supposed to click on or select will also appear in color.
OPEN *BudgetWorksheet1*	The names of data files will appear in bold, italic font for easy identification.

Instructor Support Program

The *Microsoft Official Academic Course* programs are accompanied by a rich array of resources that incorporate the extensive textbook visuals to form a pedagogically cohesive package. These resources provide all the materials instructors need to deploy and deliver their courses. Resources available online for download include:

- The **Instructor's Guide** contains solutions to all the textbook exercises as well as chapter summaries and lecture notes. The Instructor's Guide and Syllabi for various term lengths are available from the Instructor's Book Companion site (www.wiley.com/college/microsoft).

- The **Solution Files** for all the projects in the book are available online from our Instructor's Book Companion site (www.wiley.com/college/microsoft).

- The **Test Bank** contains hundreds of questions organized by lesson in multiple-choice, true-false, short answer, and essay formats and is available to download from the Instructor's Book Companion site (www.wiley.com/college/microsoft). A complete answer key is provided.

  This title's test bank is available for use in Respondus' easy-to-use software. You can download the test bank for free using your Respondus, Respondus LE, or StudyMate Author software.

  Respondus is a powerful tool for creating and managing exams that can be printed to paper or published directly to Blackboard, WebCT, Desire2Learn, eCollege, ANGEL, and other eLearning systems.

- **PowerPoint Presentations and Images**. A complete set of PowerPoint presentations is available on the Instructor's Book Companion site (www.wiley.com/college/microsoft) to enhance classroom presentations. Tailored to the text's topical coverage and Skills Matrix, these presentations are designed to convey key Microsoft Project concepts addressed in the text.

  All figures from the text are on the Instructor's Book Companion site (www.wiley.com/college/microsoft). You can incorporate them into your PowerPoint presentations, or create your own overhead transparencies and handouts.

  By using these visuals in class discussions, you can help focus students' attention on key elements of Microsoft Project and help them understand how to use it effectively in the workplace.

- The **MSDN Academic Alliance** is designed to provide the easiest and most inexpensive developer tools, products, and technologies available to faculty and students in labs, classrooms, and on student PCs. A free 3-year membership is available to qualified MOAC adopters.

- The **Student Data Files** are available online on both the Instructor's Book Companion Site and for students on the Student Book Companion Site.

WFN

- When it comes to improving the classroom experience, there is no better source of ideas and inspiration than your fellow colleagues. The Wiley Faculty Network connects teachers with technology, facilitates the exchange of best practices, and helps to enhance instructional efficiency and effectiveness. Faculty Network activities include technology training and tutorials, virtual seminars, peer-to-peer exchanges of experiences and ideas, personal consulting, and sharing of resources. For details visit www.WhereFacultyConnect.com.

MSDN ACADEMIC ALLIANCE—FREE 3-YEAR MEMBERSHIP AVAILABLE TO QUALIFIED ADOPTERS!

The Microsoft Developer Network Academic Alliance (MSDN AA) is designed to provide the easiest and most inexpensive way for universities to make the latest Microsoft developer tools, products, and technologies available in labs, classrooms, and on student PCs. MSDN AA is an annual membership program for departments teaching Science, Technology, Engineering, and Mathematics (STEM) courses. The membership provides a complete solution to keep academic labs, faculty, and students on the leading edge of technology.

Software available in the MSDN AA program is provided at no charge to adopting departments through the Wiley and Microsoft publishing partnership.

As a bonus to this free offer, faculty will be introduced to Microsoft's Faculty Connection and Academic Resource Center. It takes time and preparation to keep students engaged while giving them a fundamental understanding of theory, and the Microsoft Faculty Connection is designed to help STEM professors with this preparation by providing articles, curriculum, and tools that professors can use to engage and inspire today's technology students.

Note: Microsoft Project 2010 Professional can be downloaded from MSDN AA for use by students in this course.

Contact your Wiley rep for details.

For more information about the MSDN AA program, go to:

msdn.microsoft.com/academic/

Important Web Addresses and Phone Numbers

To locate the Wiley Higher Education Representative in your area, go to the following Web address and click on the "*Who's My Rep?*" link at the top of the page:

www.wiley.com/college

Or call the MOAC toll-free number: 1 + (888) 764-7001 (U.S. & Canada only).

To learn more about becoming a Microsoft Certified Professional and exam availability, visit www.microsoft.com/learning/mcp.

Student Support Program

Book Companion Web Site (www.wiley.com/college/microsoft)

The students' book companion site for the MOAC series includes any resources, exercise files, and Web links that will be used in conjunction with this course.

Wiley Desktop Editions

Wiley MOAC Desktop Editions are innovative, electronic versions of printed textbooks. Students buy the desktop version for 50% off the U.S. price of the printed text, and get the added value of permanence and portability. Wiley Desktop Editions provide students with numerous additional benefits that are not available with other e-text solutions.

Wiley Desktop Editions are NOT subscriptions; students download the Wiley Desktop Edition to their computer desktops. Students own the content they buy to keep for as long as they want. Once a Wiley Desktop Edition is downloaded to the computer desktop, students have instant access to all of the content without being online. Students can also print out the sections they prefer to read in hard copy. Students also have access to fully integrated resources within their Wiley Desktop Edition. From highlighting their e-text to taking and sharing notes, students can easily personalize their Wiley Desktop Edition as they are reading or following along in class.

CourseSmart

CourseSmart goes beyond traditional expectations—providing instant, online access to the textbooks and course materials you need at a lower cost option. You can save time and hassle with a digital eTextbook that allows you to search for the most relevant content at the very moment you need it. To learn more, go to: www.coursesmart.com.

Microsoft Software

As an adopter of a MOAC textbook, your school's department is eligible for a free three-year membership to the MSDN Academic Alliance (MSDN AA). Through MSDN AA, full versions of Microsoft Project 2010 Professional and Microsoft Visual Studio are available for your use with this course. See your instructor for details.

Student Data Files

All of the practice files that you will use as you perform the exercises in the book are available for download on our student companion site. By using the practice files, you will not waste time creating the samples used in the lessons, and you can concentrate on learning how to use Microsoft Office 2010. With the files and the step-by-step instructions in the lessons, you will learn by doing, which is an easy and effective way to acquire and remember new skills.

Copying the Practice Files

Your instructor might already have copied the practice files before you arrive in class. However, your instructor might ask you to copy the practice files on your own at the start of class. Also, if you want to work through any of the exercises in this book on your own at home or at your place of business after class, you may want to copy the practice files.

OPEN Internet Explorer.

1. In Internet Explorer, go to the student companion site: www.wiley.com.
2. Search for your book title in the upper-right corner.
3. On the Search Results page, locate your book and click the **Visit the Companion Sites** link.
4. Select **Student Companion Site** from the pop-up box.
5. In the left-hand column, under "Browse by Resource" select **Student Data Files**.
6. Now select **Student Data Files** from the center of the screen.
7. In the File Download dialog box, select **Save** to save the data files to your external drive (often called a ZIP drive, a USB drive, or a thumb drive) or a local drive.
8. In the Save As dialog box, select from the left-hand panel a local drive that you'd like to save your files to; again, this should be an external drive or a local drive. Remember the drive name that you saved your files to.

Acknowledgments

We'd like to thank the many reviewers who pored over the manuscript, providing invaluable feedback in the service of quality instructional materials.

Access 2010 Reviewers

Tammie Bolling, Tennessee Technology Center—Jacksboro
Mary Corcoran, Bellevue College
Trish Culp, triOS College—Business Technology Healthcare
Jana Hambruch, Lee County School District
Aditi Mukherjee, University of Florida—Gainesville

We would also like to thank Lutz Ziob, Jason Bunge, Ben Watson, David Bramble, Merrick Van Dongen, Don Field, Pablo Bernal, and Wendy Johnson at Microsoft for their encouragement and support in making the Microsoft Official Academic Course program the finest instructional materials for mastering the newest Microsoft technologies for both students and instructors. Finally, we would like to thank Lorna Gentry of Content LLC for development editing and Jeff Riley and his team at Box Twelve Communications for technical editing.

Excel 2010 Reviewers

Tammie Bolling, Tennessee Technology Center—Jacksboro
Mary Corcoran, Bellevue College
Trish Culp, triOS College—Business Technology Healthcare
Dee Hobson, Richland College
Christie Hovey, Lincoln Land Community College
Ralph Phillips, Central Oregon Community College
Rajeev Sachdev, triOS College—Business Technology Healthcare

Outlook 2010

Mary Harnishfeger, Ivy Tech State College—Bloomington
Sandra Miller, Wenatchee Valley College
Bob Reeves, Vincennes University
Lourdes Sevilla, Southwestern College—Chula Vista
Phyllis E. Traylor, St. Philips College

PowerPoint 2010

Natasha Carter, SUNY—ATTAIN
Dr. Susan Evans Jennings, Stephen F. Austin State University
Sue Van Lanen, Gwinnett Technical College
Carol J. McPeek, SUNY—ATTAIN
Michelle Poertner, Northwestern Michigan College
Tim Sylvester, Glendale Community College (AZ)

Project 2010

Tatyana Pashnyak, Bainbridge College
Debi Griggs, Bellevue College

Word 2010

Portia Hatfield, Tennessee Technology Center—Jacksboro
Terri Holly, Indian River State College
Pat McMahon, South Suburban College
Barb Purvis, Centura College
Janet Sebesy, Cuyahoga Community College

Author Credits

Gregg Richie

Gregg D. Richie, PMP, MCTS is a Senior Project Manager at Key Consulting, Inc., which provides consulting and training in PM techniques, including advanced usage of Microsoft Project. He teaches the project planning and risk management sections for the University of Washington's Project Management Certificate Program, Microsoft Project for Bellevue College, and other PM topics at colleges in Western Washington on a part-time basis.

He has more than 30 years of experience in the field of project management, working on projects on almost every continent. He joined the US Navy in 1979 and is a 20-year veteran of the SEABEES, which is the self-sustained, combat-trained construction force for the US Navy. It was here that his love for both teaching and project management was discovered and developed. He began instructing in 1983 and has taught more than five thousand people, in classroom environments, and publicly spoken to groups as large as a thousand. His education includes two technical degrees; one in computer programming and the other in civil engineering and architectural drafting; he also holds a Bachelor of Science from Southern Illinois University in Workforce Education and Development, and a Master's Certificate from Villanova University in Applied Project Management.

www.wiley.com/college/microsoft or call the MOAC
Toll-Free Number: 1+(888) 764-7001 (U.S. & Canada only)

Brief Contents

Contents

**www.wiley.com/college/microsoft or call the MOAC
Toll-Free Number: 1+(888) 764-7001 (U.S. & Canada only)**

Lesson 16: Working with Resource Pools 288

Lesson 17: Customizing Microsoft Project 308

Project Basics

LESSON SKILL MATRIX

SKILL	TASK
Starting Microsoft Project	Start Microsoft Project.
Creating a Project Schedule	Open a new project schedule.
	Specify a start date.
	Save the project schedule.
Defining Project Calendars	Define the project calendar.
Entering Tasks and Task Details	Enter tasks.
	Enter task durations.
	Create a milestone.
Organizing Tasks into Phases	Create summary tasks.
Linking Tasks	Link two tasks.
	Link several tasks at once.
	Link milestone tasks.
Documenting Tasks	Enter a task note.
Reviewing the Project Schedule's Duration	Check the project's duration.

Southridge Video is a video production and editing agency that works primarily with clients in the music industry to produce promotional videos for tours and full-length music videos for television play. The company's video production managers must identify the production tasks, plan and manage the schedule, and communicate project information to all the members of the production team. Microsoft Project 2010 is the perfect tool for managing a project such as this. In this lesson, you will learn how to create a new project schedule in Microsoft Project 2010; enter tasks, durations, and milestones into that schedule; and organize the tasks in the schedule.

KEY TERMS

base calendar
bottom-up planning
calendar
deliverable
dependency
duration
elapsed duration
Gantt chart view
link
milestone
note
phase
predecessor

project calendar
project schedule
resource calendar
Ribbon
risk
sequence
subtasks
successor
summary task
task
task calendar
Task ID
top-down planning

■ SOFTWARE ORIENTATION

Microsoft Project's Opening Screen and the New Fluent User Interface (UI)

Before you begin using Microsoft Project 2010, you need to become familiar with the new user interface, also known as the *Ribbon*. As in other Office 2010 applications, commands in Project 2010 are no longer driven by menu commands on the menu bar. Instead, project commands are collected in tabs, such as the File, Task, Resource, Project, and View tabs. Selecting any of these tabs activates the Ribbon. Within the Ribbon for each tab, individual commands are organized into groups, and each command has its own button, which you activate by clicking with the mouse. This new user interface makes it easy to find the commands you need more quickly.

Figure 1-1

Project's opening screen

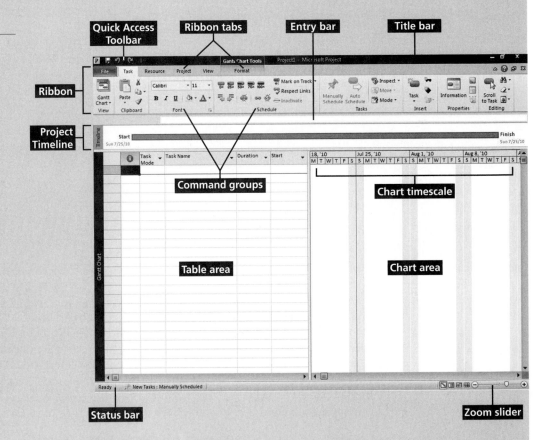

When you first launch Microsoft Project, you will see a screen similar to that shown in Figure 1-1. The features and options on this screen are those typically seen when starting Microsoft Project. However, your screen may be different if the program's default settings have been changed or if other preferences have been set. Use this figure as a reference for this lesson and throughout the rest of this book.

■ Starting Microsoft Project

Microsoft Project is a tool used by project managers to manage project schedules; it is not the actual process of project management. A **_project schedule_** is a model of a real project—including what you want to happen or what you think will happen throughout the project. The schedule contains all the tasks, resources, time frames, and costs that might be associated with the project. You can modify this schedule (or any other project template) to fit your specific needs. Later in this lesson, you will learn how to create a project schedule from a blank template. But first, you must know how to launch Microsoft Project and how to open a template.

Starting Microsoft Project

In this exercise, you learn how to start Microsoft Project and open a template. Notice that when you launch Project, the **_Gantt Chart View_** appears.

⊕ **START MICROSOFT PROJECT**

GET READY. Before you begin these steps, be sure to turn on or log on to your computer.

1. On the Windows taskbar, click the **Start** button. The Start menu appears.
2. On the Start menu, point to **All Programs**, then point to **Microsoft Office**, and then click **Microsoft Project 2010**. Microsoft Project opens.
3. Click the **File** tab to open Backstage view, then click **New**. This launches the New Project screen, as shown in Figure 1-2. This screen allows you to create a new file from various templates, including a blank project template; create a new file from an existing Project file, Excel workbook, or SharePoint list; or create a file from a template available at www.office.microsoft.com.

Figure 1-2

New Project screen

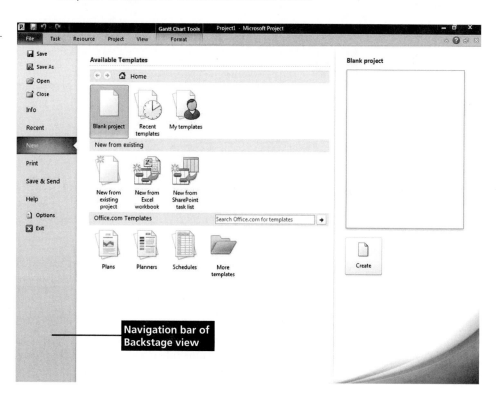

Navigation bar of Backstage view

4. In the Office.com section of the New Project screen, click in the **Search Office.com** box, then key **Customer Feedback Monitoring**. The Customer Feedback Monitoring template is displayed, and a preview appears on the right side of the screen, as in Figure 1-3.

Figure 1-3

Preview of the Customer Feedback Monitoring template from Office.com

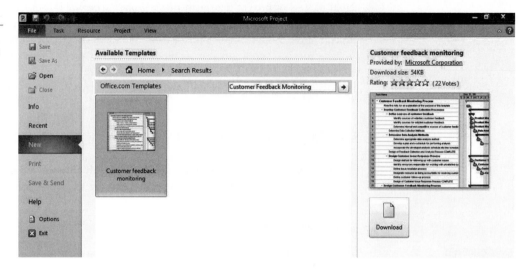

5. Click the **Download** button. The template is downloaded to your system, a new project based on the Customer Feedback Monitoring template opens in the Gantt chart view, and the New Project screen closes. Your screen should look similar to Figure 1-4.

Figure 1-4

Project created from the Customer Feedback Monitoring template

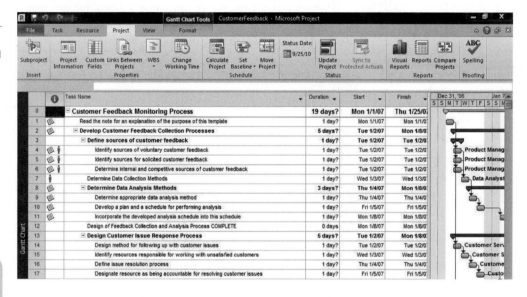

TAKE NOTE✱

As you create your own templates, Project stores them by default in the tab called Personal Templates.

6. Close the Customer Feedback Monitoring project schedule by clicking the small white **X** in the upper-right corner of your screen. Click **No** when prompted to save the file.
PAUSE. LEAVE Microsoft Project open for the next exercise.

In the preceding exercise, you opened a project schedule from a template in Microsoft Project. Recall that a project schedule is a model of a real project, including the associated tasks, resources, time frames, and costs. You don't need a template to create a new project schedule, however. As shown in the following exercise, you can also create a new project schedule "from scratch."

■ Creating a Project Schedule

Microsoft Project 2010 is an active scheduling tool; accordingly, you should perform all the planning processes associated with your organization's project management methodology before entering any information into the program. Then, when you're ready to create a new schedule in Project, one of your first tasks should be to set a start date for the project.

Opening a New Project Schedule

Instead of using a project schedule template, you may opt to create a new, blank project schedule that you can fine-tune to your specific needs. In this exercise, you learn how to open this type of file.

⊖ OPEN A NEW PROJECT SCHEDULE

GET READY. Microsoft Project should be open.

1. On the Ribbon, click the **File** tab, then click **New**. The New Project screen appears.

2. On the right side of the screen, under Blank Project, click the **Create** button. A new blank project schedule appears, and you are briefly notified that new tasks will be created in the new Manually Scheduled Mode (which is discussed in greater detail in the Appendix). Your screen will look like Figure 1-5.

Figure 1-5

Manual scheduling notification

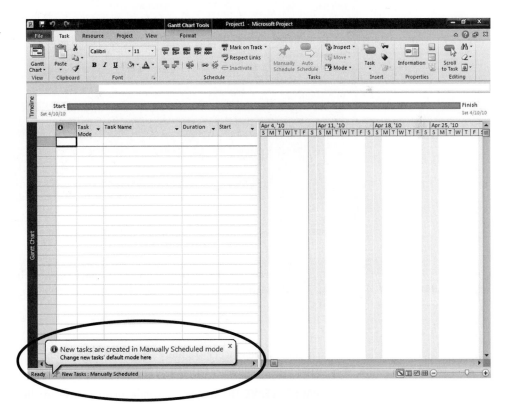

3. In the Status Bar at the bottom of the screen, click **New Tasks: Manually Scheduled**, then click the **Auto Scheduled** option from the pop-up menu that appears.

PAUSE. LEAVE the project schedule open to use in the next exercise.

In this exercise, you created a new, blank project schedule. Now you will begin to add details to the project schedule, such as a start date, tasks, and calendars. This book presents a process for ensuring that such information is entered into the software in the proper order. Entering information out of sequence could result in inaccurate information or re-entry of data.

Specifying the Project's Start Date

The first step in creating a new project schedule is to specify the start date for the project. In this exercise, you enter a start date for the new project you created in the previous activity.

→ SPECIFY A START DATE

USE the project schedule you opened in the previous exercise.

Project Information

1. On the Ribbon, click the **Project** tab. Then, in the Properties group, click the **Project Information** button. The Project Information dialog box appears.

2. Click the **arrow** in the Start Date text box. A small monthly calendar appears. For this exercise, you will change the project start date to January 10, 2011.

3. Click the calendar's **left** or **right arrow** until January 2011 is displayed, as shown in Figure 1-6.

TAKE NOTE*

By default, Microsoft Project uses the current date as the project start date.

Figure 1-6

Setting a project's start date

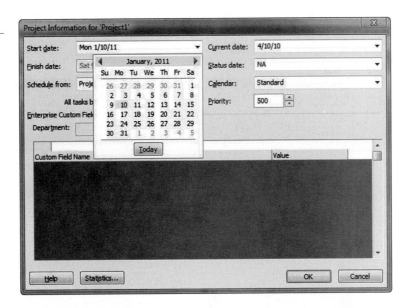

ANOTHER WAY

You can also quickly set the start date in the Project Information dialog box by highlighting the current date in the Start Date box and keying your desired start date in month/day/year format.

4. In the calendar, click **January 10**.
5. Click **OK** at the bottom of the pane.

PAUSE. LEAVE the project schedule open to use in the next exercise.

In this exercise, you specified a start date for your project. You can schedule a project from either its start date or its end date, but not both. Most projects should be scheduled from their start date. Scheduling from a start date causes all tasks to begin as soon as possible, and it gives you the greatest scheduling flexibility. However, scheduling from a finish date can be helpful in determining when a project must start if the finish date is fixed.

Saving the Newly Created Project Schedule

Once you have created a new project schedule and specified the start date, you need to save the file.

⊕ SAVE THE PROJECT SCHEDULE

USE the project schedule you created in the previous exercise.

1. On the Ribbon, click the **File** tab, then click the **Save** button. Because you have not previously saved the project schedule, the Save As dialog box appears. By default, the My Documents folder is displayed.
2. Locate and select the solutions folder for this lesson as directed by your instructor.
3. In the File name box, key **Don Funk Music Video 1**.
4. Click **Save**. The Save As dialog box closes, and the project schedule is saved as *Don Funk Music Video 1*.

   PAUSE. LEAVE the project schedule open to use in the next exercise.

In this exercise, you named and saved your project file. It is important to get into the habit of saving your files frequently so that minimal information is lost should you experience a software or hardware malfunction.

TAKE NOTE *   You can also have Microsoft Project save a project schedule at specified intervals. Under the File tab, click Options in the navigation bar, then select Save. In the Save Options dialog box, under Save Projects, select the Auto Save Every check box and then specify the time interval at which you want Microsoft Project to automatically save your file.

■ Defining Project Calendars

↓
THE BOTTOM LINE   In Microsoft Project, calendars determine how tasks and the resources assigned to these tasks are scheduled. You can set a project calendar to reflect the working days and hours of your project, as well as nonworking times such as evenings, weekends, and holidays.

Defining Project Calendars

In this exercise, you define the calendar for your project and set up exception time (here, a holiday).

⊕ DEFINE THE PROJECT CALENDAR

USE the project schedule you created in the previous exercise.

Change
Working Time

1. On the Ribbon, click the **Project** tab. In the Properties group, select the **Change Working Time** button. The Change Working Time dialog box is displayed.
2. Click the **For Calendar** drop-down arrow; in the menu that appears, select **Standard**, if it is not already selected.
3. Using the scroll control at the right of the calendar, navigate until the calendar displays January 2011. Click the date box for **January 17**.
4. In the **Exceptions** tab, click the first **Name** field and key **Martin Luther King Jr. Day**.
5. Click the first **Start** field. The date **1/17/2011** is displayed. Also note that the finish date is automatically entered. Your screen should look similar to Figure 1-7.

Change Working Time dialog box

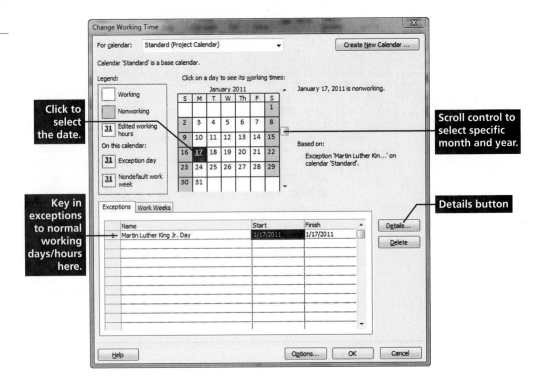

Change Working Time dialog box

6. Click the **Details** button. The Details dialog box appears. Under Recurrence Pattern, click **Yearly.**

7. Click the **The** button, and use the arrows next to each selection box to select **Third, Monday,** and **January.**

8. Under Range Of Recurrence, change the date in the **End by** box to **Mon 1/21/15.**

9. Click **OK** to close the Details dialog box, then click **OK** to close the Change Working Time dialog box.

10. SAVE the project schedule.

PAUSE. LEAVE the project schedule open to use in the next exercise.

In this exercise, you both defined the calendar for this project and set up exception time (a holiday). A *calendar* is a scheduling tool that determines the standard working time and nonworking time (such as evenings or holidays) for a project and its associated resources and tasks. Calendars are used to determine how tasks and the resources assigned to these tasks are scheduled. Project 2010 uses four types of calendars:

- A *base calendar* specifies default working and nonworking times for a set of resources. It can serve as a project calendar or a task calendar. Microsoft Project provides three base calendars: Standard, 24-Hours, and Night Shift.
- A *project calendar* is the base calendar that is used for an entire project. It defines the normal working and nonworking times.
- A *resource calendar* defines working and nonworking times for an individual work resource.
- A *task calendar* is the base calendar used for individual tasks to manage the scheduling of these tasks. A task calendar defines working and nonworking times for a task, regardless of the settings in the project calendar.

X REF

You'll learn more about base calendars, project calendars, and resource calendars in Lesson 2. You'll learn more about task calendars in Lesson 4.

Base calendars can be created and assigned to a project, a resource, or a task. Project, resource, and task calendars are all used in scheduling tasks. For instance, if resources are assigned to a task, the task is scheduled based upon the resource calendar. If a task calendar is used to schedule a task and the assigned resources do not work during the task calendar's working hours, you will receive a warning about an assignment mismatch.

■ Entering Tasks and Task Details

↓
THE BOTTOM LINE

Tasks represent the actual individual work activities that must be completed to accomplish a project's final goal, or *deliverable*. In Project, the tasks you define contain details about each activity or event that must occur in order for your project to be completed. These details include the order and duration of tasks, critical tasks, and resource requirements.

Entering Tasks

Once you have created and saved a new project schedule and defined the project's working times, you can begin to enter tasks. Tasks are the basic building blocks of any project schedule. In this exercise, you will enter a single task in each row of the Entry table.

⊕ **ENTER TASKS**

USE the project schedule you created in the previous exercise.

1. Click the first blank cell directly below the Task Name column heading.
2. Key **Review screenplay** and press **Enter**. Your screen should look similar to Figure 1-8.

Figure 1-8

First task for Don Funk Music Video 1

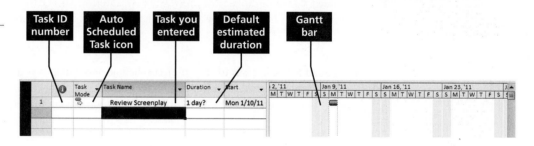

3. Enter the following task names below the Review screenplay task name. Press **Enter** after each task name:

   Develop scene and blocking schedule

   Develop production layouts

   Identify and reserve locations

   Book musicians

   Book dancers

   Reserve audio recording equipment

   Reserve video recording equipment

4. As you enter new tasks, they are assigned a default duration of one day, and they are not linked. Your screen should look similar to Figure 1-9.

Figure 1-9

Task list for Don Funk Music
Video 1

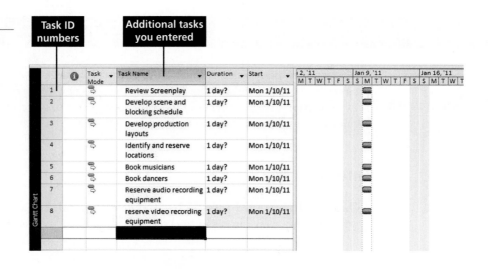

5. SAVE the project schedule.

PAUSE. LEAVE the project schedule open to use in the next exercise.

TAKE NOTE *
The question mark behind the duration of the task (1 day?) indicates that this is an estimated duration. You can remove this by entering an actual duration, or you can remove it in the Task Options dialog box, as discussed later in the lesson.

You just added eight tasks to your project schedule. Note that as you entered a task on each row of the Entry table, Microsoft Project assigned a Task ID (see Figure 1-8). The *Task ID* is a unique number that is assigned to each task in a project. It appears on the left side of the task's row.

■ SOFTWARE ORIENTATION

Calendar Options

Microsoft Project uses standard values of minutes and hours for durations: one minute equals 60 seconds, and one hour equals 60 minutes. However, you can redefine the duration of days, weeks, and months for your project. To do so, click the **File** tab, click the **Schedule** option, and then look under Calendar options for this project (see Figure 1-10).

Figure 1-10

Calendar options

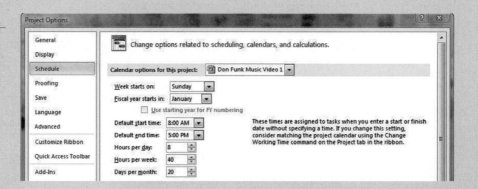

CALENDAR OPTION	FUNCTION
Week starts on	Changes the day on which the project week starts
Fiscal year starts in	Changes the month in which the project fiscal year begins
Default start time	Changes the default start time for scheduled tasks
Default end time	Changes the default end time for scheduled tasks
Hours per day	Changes how many hours are scheduled for one day
Hours per week	Changes how many hours are scheduled for one week
Days per month	Changes how many days are scheduled for one month

Entering Task Durations

A task's **duration** is the amount of working time required to complete that task. Because different tasks usually take different amounts of time to complete, each task is assigned a separate duration. Do not confuse duration with elapsed time or work effort. For example, a task's duration may be two weeks, but the task may require only 20 hours of effort to complete. In contrast, another task could have four work resources assigned to it and equate to 24 hours of effort in a single eight-hour work day.

⊕ ENTER TASK DURATIONS

USE the project schedule you created in the previous exercise.

1. Click the first cell in the Duration column, next to task 1, **Review screenplay**. The Duration field for task 1 is selected.
2. Key **3w** and press **Enter**. The value 3 wks appears in the Duration field.
3. Enter the following durations for the remaining tasks:

TASK ID	TASK NAME	DURATION
2	Develop scene and blocking schedule	1w
3	Develop production layouts	1mo
4	Identify and reserve locations	5w
5	Book musicians	2w
6	Book dancers	2w
7	Reserve audio recording equipment	5d
8	Reserve video recording equipment	8d

Your screen should look similar to Figure 1-11.

Figure 1-11

Gantt chart showing task durations

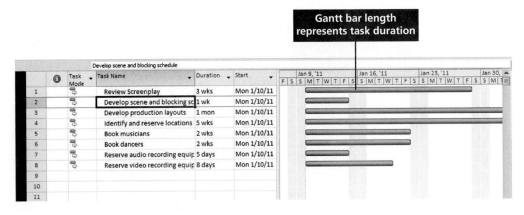

4. **SAVE** the project schedule.

   PAUSE. LEAVE the project schedule open to use in the next exercise.

Recall that when you set up your project calendar in the previous exercise, the working times for your project were Monday through Friday from 8:00 a.m. to 5:00 p.m., with an hour off for lunch each day. Microsoft Project differentiates between working and nonworking time, so the duration of a task doesn't always correspond to elapsed time. For example, if you estimate that a task will take 24 hours of working time, you would enter its duration as 3d to schedule the task over three eight-hour workdays. If this task were to start at 8:00 a.m. on Thursday, it would not be completed until 5:00 p.m. on Monday. Remember, no work is scheduled on evenings or weekends because these have been defined as nonworking times.

You can also schedule tasks to occur over both working and nonworking time by assigning an elapsed duration to a task. *Elapsed duration* is the total length of working and nonworking time you expect it will take to complete a task. Suppose you own an automobile body shop. In the process of repainting a car, you have the tasks "Apply rustproof undercoat" and "Apply first color overcoat." You also need a task called "Wait for undercoat to dry" because you cannot apply the color paint until the undercoat has cured. The task "Wait for undercoat to dry" will have an elapsed duration because the undercoat will dry over a continuous range of hours, whether they are working or nonworking. If the undercoat takes 24 hours to cure, you would enter the duration for this task as 1ed (or 1 elapsed day). If you scheduled this task to start at 11 a.m. on Wednesday, it would be complete at 11 a.m. on Thursday.

Table 1-1 shows the abbreviations and meanings for both actual and elapsed times in Microsoft Project.

Table 1-1

Abbreviations and meanings for actual and elapsed times

IF YOU ENTER THIS ABBREVIATION	IT APPEARS LIKE THIS	AND MEANS
m	min	Minute
h	hr	Hour
d	day	Day
w	wk	Week
mo	mon	Month
em	emin	Elapsed minute
eh	ehr	Elapsed hour
ed	eday	Elapsed day
ew	ewk	Elapsed week
emo	emon	Elapsed month

For most projects, you will use task durations of hours, days, and weeks. When estimating task durations, think carefully about the level of detail you want to apply to your project's tasks. If you have a multiyear project, it is probably not practical or even possible to track tasks that are measured in minutes or hours. You should measure task durations at the lowest level of detail or control necessary, but no lower.

Although you are supplied with task durations for the exercises in this book, you will have to estimate these durations in most real-world projects. There are a number of sources of task duration estimates, including:

- Information from previous similar projects
- Estimates from the people who will actually complete the tasks
- Recommendations from people who have managed similar projects
- Information from professional or industry organizations that deal with the project's subject matter

For any project, one major source of risk is inaccurate task duration estimates. **_Risk_** is an event or condition that, if it occurs, will have an impact on your project, either positive or negative. Risk decreases the likelihood of completing a project on time, within budget, and to specification. Making good estimates is therefore worth the time and effort it requires.

Creating a Milestone

A **_milestone_** represents a major event or a significant point in a project. Milestones can be imposed upon the project by the project sponsor, or they can be set by the project team to monitor the project's progress. In Microsoft Project, milestones are represented as a task with zero duration.

⊕ CREATE A MILESTONE

USE the project schedule you created in the previous exercise.

1. In the Task Name column, click the empty cell below the name of task 8, **Reserve video recording equipment**.
2. Key **Pre-production complete** and press **Tab** to move to the Duration field.
3. Key **0** for the duration.
4. In the Task Name column, click the name of task 1, **Review screenplay**.
5. Click the **Task** tab; then, in the Insert group, click **Task**. Microsoft Project inserts and numbers a new task (1). Notice that the other tasks after the new task insertion point are renumbered.

ANOTHER WAY

You can also press Insert to add a new task above a selected task. To insert multiple new tasks, select a number of existing tasks equal to the number of new tasks you want to add, then press Insert. For instance, if you want to add three new tasks, select three existing tasks; then, when you press Insert, three blank tasks will appear above the existing tasks you selected.

6. Key **Pre-production begins** and press the **right arrow** key to move to the Duration field.
7. Key **0** for the duration and press **Enter**. Your screen should look similar to Figure 1-12.
8. **SAVE** the project schedule.
    PAUSE. LEAVE the project schedule open to use in the next exercise.

Figure 1-12

Gantt chart showing milestones

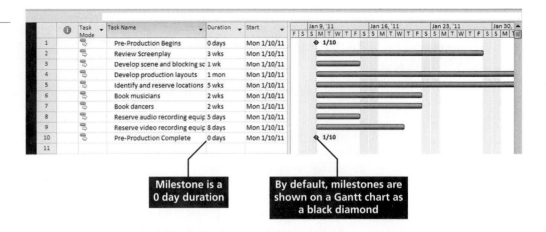

Milestone is a 0 day duration

By default, milestones are shown on a Gantt chart as a black diamond

■ Organizing Tasks into Phases

THE BOTTOM LINE

During the planning portion of a project, many teams create a tool called a work breakdown structure (WBS) to ensure no work is missed. A simple WBS for the project you've been working with is shown in Figure 1-13, which shows "Don Funk Music Video" as the name of the project. It includes three phases named Pre-Production, Production, and Post-Production, all of which are summary tasks.

Create Summary Tasks

After you enter tasks in a project, it can be helpful to organize your project by grouping related tasks into *phases*, or groups of closely related tasks that encompass a major section of your project. In Microsoft Project, these phases are represented by summary tasks. A *summary task* consists of and summarizes all the tasks within its hierarchical structure, which could also include other summary tasks, detail tasks, or *subtasks* that fall below it. You cannot directly edit a summary task's duration, start date, or other calculated values. In this exercise, you organize your project's tasks into summary tasks to identify the project's phases.

Figure 1-13

Typical graphical work breakdown structure (WBS)

→ CREATE SUMMARY TASKS

USE the project schedule you created in the previous exercise.

1. Click the name of task 1, **Pre-production begins**.
2. Press the **Insert** key. A new row is inserted, and the subsequent tasks are shifted down and renumbered.
3. In the Task Name field for the new task, key **Pre-production** and press **Enter**.

4. Key the following task names below task 11, Pre-production complete. Press **Enter** after each task name:

Production

Post-production

5. Click the name of task 13, **Post-production,** and press **Insert** twice. Two blank tasks are inserted above the Post-production task.

6. Key the following task names and durations below task 12, Production:

Task Name	Duration
Production begins	**0d**
Production complete	**0d**

7. Key the following task names and durations below task 15, Post-production:

Task Name	Duration
Post-production begins	**0d**
Post-production complete	**0d**

8. Click and hold the name for task 2, **Pre-production begins**. While holding down the mouse button, drag your cursor to task 11, **Pre-production complete**, to highlight and select tasks 2 through 11.

To quickly select a range of tasks to be indented under a summary task, click the name of the first task to be indented, hold down the Shift key, then click the name of the last task to be indented. All the tasks between the two you clicked will be selected.

9. On the Ribbon, click the **Task** tab; then, in the Schedule group, click the **Indent** button. Tasks 2 through 11 are indented, and task 1 becomes a summary task.

10. Click the name of task 13, **Production begins**. While holding down the mouse button, drag your cursor to the name of task 14, **Production complete**. Tasks 13 and 14 are highlighted and selected.

11. On the Ribbon, click the **Task** tab; then, in the Schedule group, click the **Indent** button. Tasks 13 and 14 are indented, and task 12 becomes a summary task.

12. Click the name of task 16, **Post-production begins**. While holding down the mouse button, drag your cursor to the name of task 17, **Post-production complete**. Tasks 16 and 17 are highlighted and selected.

13. Hold down **Ctrl + Shift + Right Arrow**. Tasks 16 and 17 are indented, and task 15 becomes a summary task. Your screen should look similar to Figure 1-14.

TAKE NOTE★

The Production and Post-production summary tasks appear as milestones because they have no subtasks with a positive duration below them (only milestones with zero duration). The appearance of the Production and Post-production summary tasks will change when you add additional tasks in later lessons.

Figure 1-14

Gantt chart showing summary and indented tasks

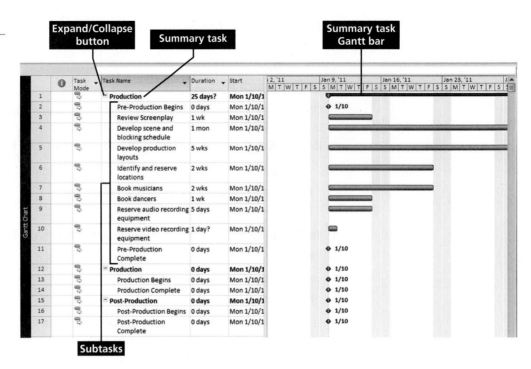

14. SAVE the project schedule.

PAUSE. LEAVE the project schedule open to use in the next exercise.

You have just organized your tasks into phases. Working with phases and tasks in Microsoft Project is similar to working with an outline in Microsoft Word. You can create phases by indenting and "outdenting" tasks, and you can collapse an entire task list into its phase components.

Most complex projects require a combination of both top-down and bottom-up planning in order to create accurate tasks and phases:

- *Top-down planning* develops a project schedule by identifying the highest-level phases or summary tasks before breaking them into lower-level components or subtasks. This approach works from general to specific.
- *Bottom-up planning* develops a project schedule by starting with the lowest-level tasks before organizing them into higher-level phases or summary tasks. This approach works from specific to general.

■ Linking Tasks

THE BOTTOM LINE

You can create task relationships by creating **links** between two or more tasks. In Auto Scheduled mode, the links create a sequential dependency in which one task depends on the start or completion of another task in order to begin or end.

Linking Two Tasks

When you created your project, all of the tasks in the project schedule were scheduled to start on the same date—the project start date. As you fill out your project schedule, you must link (or create a relationship between) various tasks to correctly reflect the order in which work must be completed. In this exercise, you will link two tasks to reflect the actual order in which they will occur.

⊕ LINK TWO TASKS

USE the project schedule you created in the previous exercise.

1. Select the names of tasks 2 and 3.
2. On the Ribbon, click the **Task** tab. Next, click the **Link Tasks** button in the Schedule group.
3. Tasks 2 and 3 are now linked with a finish-to-start relationship.
4. Select the names of tasks 3 and 4.
5. Press **Ctrl + F2**. Microsoft Project changes the start date of task 4 to the next working day following the completion of task 3. Note that because January 17 was a nonworking day (the Martin Luther King Jr. holiday you set up earlier), task 3 does not finish until January 24 and task 4 does not start until January 25. If necessary, scroll the Gantt chart to January 24 so that the link you just created is visible.
6. **SAVE** the project schedule.

PAUSE. LEAVE the project schedule open to use in the next exercise.

When you started the exercise in this section, all of the tasks in the project schedule were scheduled to start on the same date—the project start date. Then, in the exercise, you linked two tasks to reflect the actual order in which they will occur. A link is a logical connection between two or more tasks that controls their sequence and defines their relationship.

The two tasks that you linked in this exercise have a finish-to-start relationship. The first task is called the *predecessor*, a task whose start or end date determines the start or finish of another task or tasks. Any task can be a predecessor for one or more tasks. The second task is called the *successor*, a task whose start or finish is driven by another task or tasks. Again, any task can be a successor to one or more predecessor tasks. The second task occurs after the first task. This is called a *sequence*, or the chronological order in which tasks must occur. Tasks can have only one of four types of task relationships, as shown in Table 1-2.

Table 1-2

The four types of task relationships

TASK RELATIONSHIP	DESCRIPTION	APPEARANCE IN THE GANTT CHART	EXAMPLE
Finish-to-start (FS)	The finish date of the predecessor task determines the start date of the successor task.		A music track must be recorded before it can be edited.
Start-to-start (SS)	The start date of the predecessor task determines the start date of the successor task.		Booking musicians and Booking dancers are related tasks and can occur simultaneously.
Finish-to-finish (FF)	The finish date of the predecessor task determines the finish date of the successor task.		Tasks that require the use of specific equipment must end when the equipment rental ends.
Start-to-finish (SF) (This relationship type is rarely used.)	The start date of the predecessor task determines the finish date of the successor task.		The time when the production sound studio becomes available determines when rehearsals must end.

Do not get task relationships in Microsoft Project confused with task dependencies in project management. A **_dependency_** is a need or a condition that exists between two elements. Knowing dependencies is an important factor in defining the task relationships. Dependencies come in three types:

- **Mandatory:** Also known as a hard logic dependency. Here, the first task *must* be done before the second task (e.g., you must construct the walls of a house before you can build the roof). Dependencies of this type usually have relationships of FS, but they can also be SS with a lag applied. (Lags are described in a later lesson.)

- **Discretionary:** Also known as a soft logic or preferred dependency. Here, the first task *doesn't necessarily* have to be done in order to complete the second task (e.g., you do not have to paint the walls before you lay the carpet). It is preferred that the first task be finished first, but it is not absolutely necessary. Dependencies of this type can have any type of task relationship.

- **External:** Here, something from outside the project is driving the task (e.g., you cannot paint the walls until the vendor delivers the paint). Dependencies of this type can have any type of task relationship.

Linking Several Tasks

In the previous exercise, you linked only two tasks. In this exercise, you use Microsoft Project to link several tasks at once.

 LINK SEVERAL TASKS AT ONCE

USE the project schedule you created in the previous exercise.

1. Select the names of tasks 4 through 11.

2. On the Ribbon, click the **Task** tab; then click the **Link Tasks** button in the Schedule group. Tasks 4 through 11 are now linked with a finish-to-start relationship. Click the minus sign on the zoom slider two or three times to see less detail in the Gantt chart. Your screen should look similar to Figure 1-15.

Figure 1-15

Gantt chart showing tasks 4 through 11 linked with a finish-to-start relationship

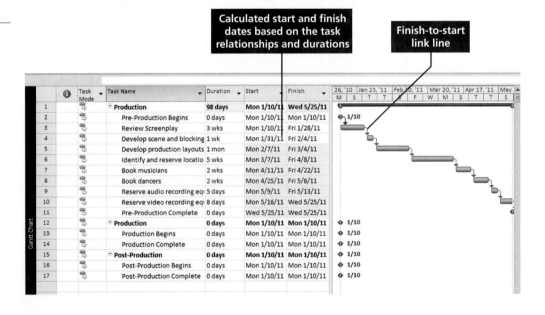

 **ANOTHER WAY**   You can also set finish-to-start links using the Task Information dialog box. Start by clicking the name of the task you wish to set as the successor. Next, on the Task tab, click the Information button, then click the Predecessors tab. Click the first cell in the Task Name column, and then click the arrow to select the task you wish to set as the predecessor.

3. **SAVE** the project schedule.

PAUSE. LEAVE the project schedule open to use in the next exercise.

Linking Milestones

Now that you've linked multiple tasks in the project schedule, it's time to link milestones across summary tasks. Linking milestones to one another reflects the sequential nature of the project's phases.

→ LINK MILESTONE TASKS

USE the project schedule you created in the previous exercise.

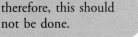

It is considered poor practice to link summary tasks; therefore, this should not be done.

1. Select the name of task 11, **Pre-production complete**, and, while holding down the **Ctrl** key, select the name of task 13, **Production begins**. (This is the general method for selecting nonadjacent tasks in a table in Microsoft Project.)
2. On the **Task** tab, in the Schedule group, click the **Link Tasks** button. Tasks 11 and 13 are linked with a finish-to-start relationship.
3. Select the name of task 14, **Production complete**, and, while holding down the **Ctrl** key, select the name of task 16, **Post-production begins**.
4. On the **Task** tab, in the Schedule group, click the **Link Tasks** button. Tasks 14 and 16 are linked with a finish-to-start relationship.
5. Scroll the chart section of the Gantt chart view to the right until the later portion of the project schedule is visible. Your screen should look similar to Figure 1-16.

Figure 1-16

Gantt chart showing milestones linked with finish-to-start relationships

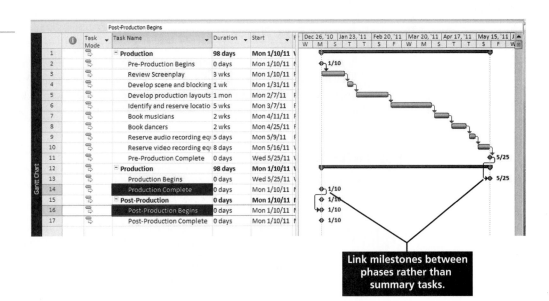

TAKE NOTE ★ Because you have not yet entered and linked actual tasks under the Production and Post-production summary tasks, the milestones for these phases (tasks 13, 14, 16, and 17) remain at the beginning (left end) of the Gantt bar chart. They will move to the right side of the Gantt bar chart once you add and link more subtasks in a future lesson.

    6. **SAVE** the project schedule.

ANOTHER WAY You can also create finish-to-start relationships between tasks directly in the Gantt chart. Point to the predecessor task until the pointer changes to a four-arrow star. Then drag the pointer up or down to the task bar of the successor task. Microsoft Project will link the two tasks. Notice that while you are dragging, the pointer image changes to a chain link. Be aware, however, that this method requires precise mouse control.

    PAUSE. LEAVE the project schedule open to use in the next exercise.

In this exercise, you linked milestones across summary tasks. When you link milestones, you set up the natural flow of the project—when one phase finishes, the next phase begins. In this particular project, you have not yet entered all of the subtasks for the Production and Post-production phases, so the graphical representation of the milestones and links on the Gantt chart may look a bit strange. Once you begin to enter and link these tasks, the project will begin to look more like the Pre-production section of the Gantt chart.

■ Documenting Tasks

↓ **THE BOTTOM LINE** You should keep the tasks in a project schedule simple and specific. Any additional task information that is important to the project can be recorded in a note. You can also provide more information about a task by linking it to another file, an intranet page, or an Internet page through a hyperlink.

Entering Task Notes

A *note* is supplemental text that you can attach to a task, resource, or assignment. Attaching a note to a task in a project schedule allows you to document important information while keeping your project schedule succinct. In this exercise, you enter a task note.

⊕ **ENTER A TASK NOTE**

USE the project schedule you created in the previous exercise.

    1. Select task 7, **Book musicians**, by clicking the task number (7).
    2. On the **Task** tab, in the Properties group, click the **Task Notes** icon. The Task Information dialog box appears with the Notes tab displayed.
    3. In the Notes box, key **Call Andy Teal for the mandolin** and click **OK.** A note icon appears in the Indicators column for task 7.

ANOTHER WAY You can also add a note by right-clicking the task name and selecting Notes from the shortcut menu that appears.

4. Point to the note icon. The note appears in a ScreenTip. For longer notes or to see other task information, you can double-click the note icon and the Task Information box will display the full text of the note. The note icon and a ScreenTip are shown in Figure 1-17.

Figure 1-17

Task note displayed as a tool tip.

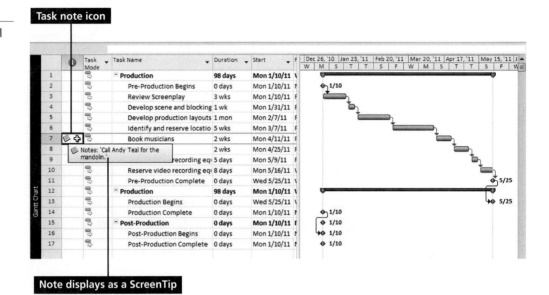

5. **SAVE** the project schedule.

PAUSE. LEAVE the project schedule open to use in the next exercise.

If you add photos or videos to your Project file, the file size can become quite large.

As you saw in this activity, you enter and review task notes on the Notes tab in the Task Information dialog box. Project also allows you to enter a wide variety of additional information to help clarify or enhance your project schedule. You can also attach a file, paste text and graphics from other Microsoft programs, insert sound or video files, or add photos (to link faces with resource names), company logos, PowerPoint slides, or organizational charts.

■ Reviewing a Project Schedule's Duration

↓
THE BOTTOM LINE

Microsoft Project calculates both the current duration and the scheduled finish date of a project based on the task durations and relationships you enter. To review these values, you can either view the project statistics or look at the Gantt chart for the entire project.

Checking Project Duration

In this exercise, you practice using the Project Information dialog box to view and check a project's duration.

⊕ **CHECK A PROJECT'S DURATION**

USE the project schedule you created in the last exercise.

Project Information

1. Click the **Project** tab, then click **Project Information** in the Properties group. The Project Information dialog box appears, as shown in Figure 1-18.

Figure 1-18

Project Information dialog box

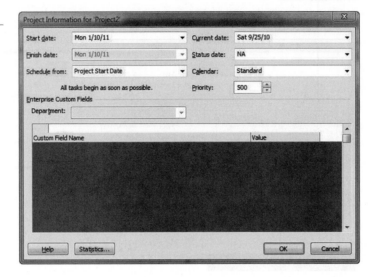

2. Click the **Statistics** button. The Project Statistics dialog box appears and displays information including the project start and finish dates and duration.

3. Click the **Close** button to close the Project Statistics dialog box.

4. Click the **View** tab, then click the **Zoom Entire Project** button in the Zoom group.

5. The graphical portion of the Gantt chart is now compressed so that the entire project is visible onscreen. Your screen should appear similar to Figure 1-19.

Figure 1-19

Gantt chart view of an entire project

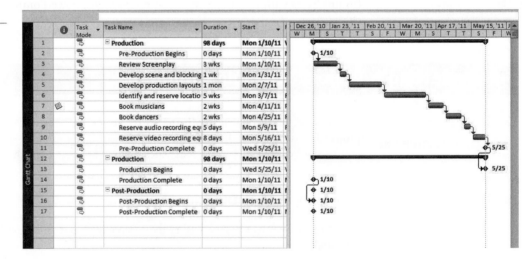

6. **SAVE** and **CLOSE** the *Don Funk Music Video 1* file.

   PAUSE. If you are continuing to the next lesson, keep Project open. If you are not continuing to additional lessons, close Project.

SKILL SUMMARY

IN THIS LESSON, YOU LEARNED:	TASK
To start Microsoft Project.	Start Microsoft Project.
To create a project schedule.	Open a new project schedule.
	Specify a start date.
	Save the project schedule.
To define project calendars.	Define the project calendar.
To enter tasks and task details.	Enter tasks.
	Enter task durations.
	Create a milestone.
To organize tasks into phases.	Create summary tasks.
To link tasks.	Link two tasks.
	Link several tasks at once.
	Link milestone tasks.
To document tasks.	Enter a task note.
To review a project schedule's duration.	Check the project's duration.

■ Knowledge Assessment

Fill in the Blank

Complete the following sentences by writing the correct word or words in the blanks provided.

1. A(n) _____ is a model of a real project—including what you want to happen or what you think will happen.

2. A(n) _____ is a logical connection between tasks that controls sequence and dependency.

3. A group of closely related tasks that encompass a major section of a project is a(n) _____.

4. A(n) _____ is a scheduling tool that determines the standard working time and nonworking time for the project, resources, and tasks.

5. _____ is the total length of working and nonworking time you expect will be needed to complete a task.

6. A(n) _____ is supplemental text that you can attach to a task, resource, or assignment.

7. A(n) _____ is added to the project calendar to denote something different from the standard working times.

8. A task whose start or end date determines the start or finish of another task or tasks is a(n) _____.

9. A(n) _____ represents a significant event reached within the project or imposed upon the project.

10. A(n) _____ represents the actual individual work activities that must be done to accomplish the final goal.

True/False

Circle T if the statement is true or F if the statement is false.

T | F   **1.** It is always best to schedule a project from a finish date.

T | F   **2.** When you initially enter tasks into Project, they are linked in a finish-to-start relationship that can be changed later.

T | F   **3.** The task note field can contain only words and not pictures.

T | F   **4.** A milestone can be imposed on a project or developed and used by the project team to track progress.

T | F   **5.** An estimated duration of three weeks for a task would be shown as 3ew.

T | F   **6.** A task calendar defines working and nonworking times for an individual work resource.

T | F   **7.** A summary task is derived from all of the detail tasks that fall below it.

T | F   **8.** Once you have entered all of the tasks and durations for a project, the project duration does not change.

T | F   **9.** Tasks that are indented below a summary task are called successors.

T | F **10.** For tasks that are linked in a finish-to-start relationship, the finish date of the predecessor task determines the start date of the successor task.

■ Competency Assessment

Project 1-1: Adding Production Tasks

Using the project schedule you created in this lesson, you will add several tasks and their durations under a summary task.

GET READY. Launch Microsoft Project if it is not already running.

OPEN *Don Funk Music Video 1-1* from the data files for this lesson.

1. Click the name of task 14, **Production complete**. Drag your cursor so that five rows are highlighted, including the row for task 14.

2. On the Ribbon, in the Insert group, click **Task**.

3. Click the blank Task Name field for task 14. Starting in this field, enter the following tasks and durations:

Task	Duration
Scene 1 setup	2d
Scene 1 rehearsal	6h
Scene 1 vocal recording	1d
Scene 1 video shoot	2d
Scene 1 teardown	1d

4. Select tasks 14 through 18.

5. On the Ribbon, in the Schedule group, click the **Indent Task** button.

The *Don Funk Music Video 1-1* file for this lesson is available on the book companion website.

6. SAVE the project as *Don Funk Scene 1* in the solutions folder for this lesson. CLOSE the file.

   LEAVE Project open for the next exercise.

Project 1-2: Adding Notes

In this activity, you will add a note to a project schedule to remind you of the information that must be given to new employees.

GET READY. Launch Microsoft Project if it is not already running.

OPEN *New Employee 1-2* from the data files for this lesson.

The *New Employee 1-2* file for this lesson is available on the book companion website.

1. Double-click the name of task 9, **Take picture for employee ID**.
2. In the Task Information dialog box, on the Notes tab, key **Remember to use blue backdrop for digital pics**.
3. Click **OK**.
4. Click the name of task 22, **Complete health insurance paperwork**.
5. In the Task Information dialog box, key the note **Verify all insurance needs and any other insurance carriers**.
6. Click **OK**.
7. SAVE the project schedule as *New Employee Orientation* in the solutions folder for this lesson, then CLOSE the file.

   LEAVE Project open for the next exercise.

■ Proficiency Assessment

Project 1-3: Hiring a New Employee

In this activity, you will create a project schedule for the process of hiring a new employee for your department.

OPEN a new blank project schedule.

1. Set the project start date to be October 24, 2011.
2. Change the scheduling mode to Auto-scheduled.
3. Enter the following tasks and durations:

Task	Duration
Write job description	2d
Notify departmental recruiter	1d
Post job internally	5d
Post job externally	5d
Collect resumes	10d
Review resumes	5d
Set up interviews	3d
Conduct interviews	8d
Select candidate	1d
Make offer	milestone

4. Assign a finish-to-start relationship to all the tasks.
5. Change the dependency between tasks 3 and 4 to a start-to-start relationship.
6. Use the Project Information dialog box to determine the current project duration.

7. **SAVE** the project schedule in the solutions folder for this lesson as *Hiring Employee xxd*, where the *xx* in the filename is the duration (in days) of the project. (For example, if the project is 13 days long, save the file as *Hiring Employee 13d*.) **CLOSE** the file.

LEAVE Project open for the next exercise.

Project 1-4: Changing Task Dependencies

After reviewing your project schedule, you decide that some of the tasks could be linked in a different way to make your project more efficient. You therefore decide to change some of your task relationships.

OPEN *Don Funk Music Video 1-4* from the data files for this lesson.

The *Don Funk Music Video 1-4* file for this lesson is available on the book companion website.

1. Change tasks 9 and 10 so they have a start-to-start relationship.
2. Change tasks 7 and 8 so they have a start-to-start relationship.
3. Adjust the Gantt bar section of your screen so that the Gantt bars for these new relationships are visible.
4. **SAVE** the project schedule as *Don Funk Revised Links* in the solutions folder for this lesson, then **CLOSE** the file.

LEAVE Project open to use in the next exercise.

■ Mastery Assessment

Project 1-5: Setting Up a Home Office

You are ordering equipment and setting up a home office—but first, you want to create a schedule to minimize the amount of time it takes to complete this process.

OPEN *Home Office 1-5* from the data files for this lesson.

The *Home Office 1-5* file for this lesson is available on the book companion website.

1. Set tasks 6, 9, 10, and 14 as milestones.
2. Assign a start-to-start relationship for tasks 1, 2, and 3.
3. Assign a finish-to-start relationship for tasks 1 and 6, 3 and 9, and 2 and 10.
4. Assign a finish-to-start relationship for tasks 4, 5, 7, and 8.
5. Assign a finish-to-start relationship for tasks 10 through 14.
6. **SAVE** the project schedule as *Home Office* in the solutions folder for this lesson, then **CLOSE** the file.

LEAVE Project open for the next exercise.

Project 1-6: Entering and Organizing Production Tasks

You need to enter and organize the tasks for producing the four scenes in the Don Funk music video.

OPEN *Don Funk Music Video 1-6* from the data files for this lesson.

The *Don Funk Music Video 1-6* file for this lesson is available on the book companion website.

1. Insert a new row after task 13. Name this new task **Scene 1**.
2. Indent tasks 15 through 21 under the Scene 1 summary task you just created.
3. Add two more sets of summary tasks and subtasks (including durations) for Scenes 2 and 3 under the Production summary task. They will be identical to the Scene 1 tasks and durations except for the scene number.
4. Assign the subtasks for Scenes 2 and 3 finish-to-start relationships.

5. Assign a finish-to-start relationship between the Scene 1 complete milestone and the Scene 2 begin milestone. Assign a finish-to-start relationship between the Scene 2 complete milestone and the Scene 3 begin milestone.

6. Link the Scene 3 complete milestone and the Production complete milestone with a finish-to-start dependency.

7. Link the Production complete milestone and the Post-production begins milestone with a finish-to-start dependency.

8. **SAVE** the project schedule as *Don Funk 3 Scenes* in the solutions folder for this lesson, then **CLOSE** the file.

CLOSE Project.

INTERNET READY

Many companies trace their beginnings to an entrepreneur who had an idea for a product or service that satisfied a customer need. Use Web search tools to find information about the basics of starting your own business. Identify 15 to 20 tasks you would need to complete to begin setting up your own business. Develop a simple project plan with these tasks, and include a start date, working times, task durations, and task dependencies. Add notes where appropriate.

2 LESSON

Establishing Resources

LESSON SKILL MATRIX

SKILL	TASK
Establishing People Resources	Establish individual people resources.
	Establish a resource that represents multiple people.
Establishing Equipment Resources	Establish equipment resources.
Establishing Material Resources	Establish material resources.
Establishing Cost Resources	Establish cost resources.
Establishing Resource Pay Rates	Enter resource cost information.
Adjusting Resource Working Times	Establish nonworking times for an individual resource.
	Establish a specific work schedule for a resource.
Adding Resource Notes	Attach a note to a resource.

Now that Southridge Video has laid out the initial project schedule for Don Funk's latest music video, the next step for the video production manager is to identify the people, equipment, and materials needed to complete the tasks in this project. He must also determine when these resources are available, how much work they can do, and their cost. One of the most powerful tools in Microsoft Project 2010 is the ability to manage resources effectively. In this lesson, you will learn how to set up basic resource information for people, equipment, and materials; how to set up cost information for a resource; and how to change a resource's availability for work.

KEY TERMS
availability
base calendar
cost
cost resource
material resource
maximum units
resource calendar
resources
work resource

Microsoft Project's Resource Sheet View

You have several views available when working in Microsoft Project. One view you will use in this lesson is the Resource Sheet view, as shown in Figure 2-1.

Figure 2-1

Resource Sheet view

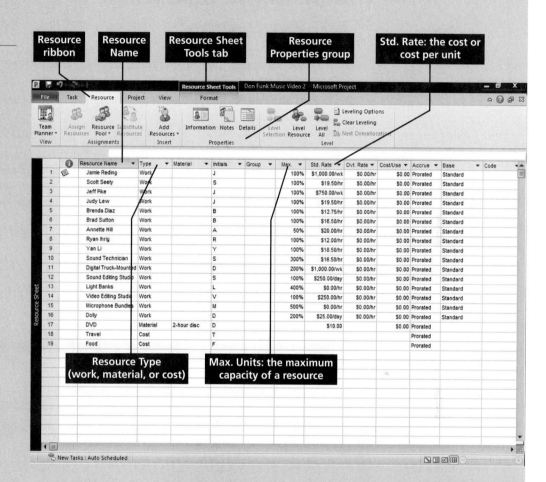

In this lesson, you will work on establishing your project *resources*—the people, equipment, materials, and money used to complete the tasks in the project. Some of the features you will use in this lesson are depicted in Figure 2-1. Note, however, that your screen may appear somewhat different if your default settings have been changed or if other preferences have been set. Use this figure as a reference for this lesson.

■ Establishing People Resources

THE BOTTOM LINE

When you set up people resources in Microsoft Project, you are able to track who is available to work, the type of work they can do, and when they are available to do it. In this section, you learn how to establish and enter people resources in Project 2010.

Establishing Individual People Resources

People resources can be in the form of individuals, individuals identified by their job function or title, or groups of individuals with a common skill. In this exercise, you practice setting up resource information for the individual people who will perform the tasks in a project.

 ESTABLISH INDIVIDUAL PEOPLE RESOURCES

GET READY. Before you begin these steps, launch Microsoft Project and **OPEN** *Don Funk Music Video 2A* from the data files for this lesson.

1. Click the **View** tab, then in the Resource Views group, select **Resource Sheet** to open the Resource Sheet view.

2. In the Resource Sheet view, click the empty cell directly below the Resource Name column heading.

 If your resource information for your own project exists on your network, such as in a Microsoft Outlook address book, you can quickly import this information into Microsoft Project. Importing saves the time and effort of retyping information and reduces the possibility of data entry errors.

3. Key **Jamie Reding** and press **Enter**. Microsoft Project adds Jamie Reding as a work resource and automatically enters additional default information. Your screen should look similar to Figure 2-2.

Figure 2-2

Resource Sheet with newly entered resource

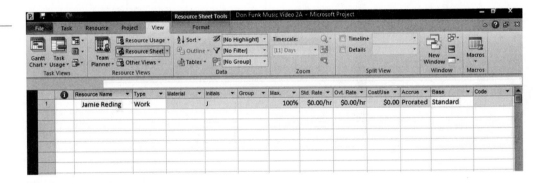

4. Add the remaining names to the Resource Sheet. Enter the first column of names (Scott Seely, Jeff Pike, etc.), then enter the second column:

Scott Seely	**Brad Sutton**
Jeff Pike	**Annette Hill**
Judy Lew	**Ryan Ihrig**
Brenda Diaz	**Yan Li**

Your screen should look similar to Figure 2-3.

Figure 2-3

Resource Sheet with additional resources added

	ⓘ	Resource Name ▼	Type ▼	Material ▼	Initials ▼	Group ▼	Max. ▼	Std. Rate ▼	Ovt. Rate ▼	
1		Jamie Reding	Work		J		100%	$0.00/hr	$0.00/hr	
2		Scott Seely	Work		S		100%	$0.00/hr	$0.00/hr	
3		Jeff Pike	Work		J		100%	$0.00/hr	$0.00/hr	
4		Judy Lew	Work		J		100%	$0.00/hr	$0.00/hr	
5		Brenda Diaz	Work		B		100%	$0.00/hr	$0.00/hr	
6		Brad Sutton	Work		B		100%	$0.00/hr	$0.00/hr	
7		Annette Hill	Work		A		100%	$0.00/hr	$0.00/hr	
8		Ryan Ihrig	Work		R		100%	$0.00/hr	$0.00/hr	
9		Yan Li	Work		Y		100%	$0.00/hr	$0.00/hr	

5. SAVE the file as *Don Funk Music Video 2*.

PAUSE. LEAVE the project schedule open to use in the next exercise.

In this exercise, you began to set up some of the basic resource information for the people who will work on this project. As you continue entering this information, keep in mind two important aspects of resources: availability and cost. *Availability* determines when a resource can be assigned to work on tasks and for how long it can be assigned. *Cost* refers to how much money will be needed to pay for a resource. Although setting up resource information in Microsoft Project may take a little extra time and effort, entering this data will provide you with more control over your project.

You will work with three types of resources in Microsoft Project: work resources, material resources, and cost resources. *Work resources* are the people and equipment that do work to accomplish the tasks of a project. (You will learn about material resources and cost resources later in the lesson.) Work resources use time to accomplish tasks, and these resources can take many different forms:

WORK RESOURCE	EXAMPLE
Individual people	Yan Li; Jeff Pike
Individual people identified by job title or function	Editor; camera person
Groups of people with a common skill	Sound technician; dancer
Equipment	Keyboard; digital recorder

When establishing your resources, use resource names that will make sense to you and to anyone else who uses the project schedule.

Establishing a Group Resource

In the previous exercise, you set up resources that were individuals. Now, you will set up a single resource that represents multiple people, sometimes called a generic resource.

 ESTABLISH A RESOURCE THAT REPRESENTS MULTIPLE PEOPLE

USE the worksheet you created in the previous exercise.

1. Click the blank **Resource Name** field below the last resource, key **Sound Technician**, and then press **Tab**.

TAKE NOTE *

Maximum units refers to the maximum capacity of a resource to accomplish tasks. For example, specifying that a resource has 75% maximum units means that 75% of the resource's time is available to work on the tasks assigned to it. The default value for maximum units is 100%. Microsoft Project will warn you if you assign a resource to more tasks than it can accomplish at its maximum units.

2. In the Type field, make sure that Work is selected. Press **Tab** four times to move to the Max. Units field.

3. In the Max. Units field for the sound technician, key or select **300%** to indicate that you will have three sound technicians devoting 100% of their working time to this project. Then, press **Tab**.

ANOTHER WAY

When you tab into or click a numeric field, up and down arrows appear in the field. You can simply click these arrows to scroll to the number you want displayed.

4. Click the Max. Units field for Annette Hill, key or select **50%**, then press **Enter**. This indicates that Annette is only available part-time on this project. Your screen should look similar to Figure 2-4.

Figure 2-4

Resource Sheet with a part-time resource and a group resource

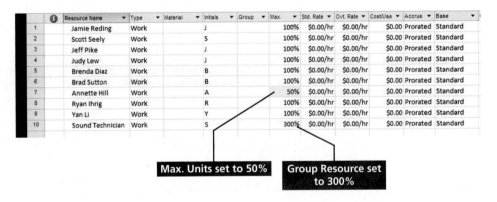

ANOTHER WAY

You can also enter maximum units as a decimal rather than a percentage. To change to this format, on the Ribbon, click File, then click Options, and then select the Schedule option. In the Show assignment units as a box, select Decimal.

5. SAVE the project schedule.

PAUSE. LEAVE the project schedule open to use in the next exercise.

In this exercise, you established a group resource. The resource named Sound Technician does not represent a single person—it actually represents a group of people called sound technicians. By setting the Max. Units for this resource at 300%, you indicated that three sound technicians will be available to work full time on every workday. You might not know specifically who the sound technicians will be at this point, but you can still proceed with more planning. Keep in mind if you use a group resource, a single resource calendar will be assigned to that resource name. Therefore, it is beneficial to have all of the people represented by the resource name work the same hours.

■ Establishing Equipment Resources

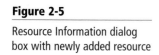

THE BOTTOM LINE

Setting up equipment resources in Microsoft Project is similar to setting up people resources. There are key differences, however, in the ways that equipment resources can be scheduled.

Establishing Equipment Resources

You don't need to track every piece of equipment that will be used in your project. It is helpful, though, to track equipment resources when you need to schedule and track equipment costs, or when equipment might be needed by multiple people at the same time. In this exercise, you learn how to establish the equipment resources for a project.

⊖ ESTABLISH EQUIPMENT RESOURCES

USE the project schedule you created in the previous exercise.

1. In the Resource Sheet, click the next empty cell in the Resource Name column.
2. Click the **Resource** tab, then click the **Resource Information** button in the Properties group. The Resource Information dialog box appears.

ANOTHER WAY

You can also activate the Resource Information dialog box by clicking the Resource Information button on the Standard toolbar, or by double-clicking a resource name or an empty cell in the Resource Name column.

3. If it is not already displayed, click the **General** tab in the Resource Information dialog box.
4. In the Resource Name field, key **Digital Truck-Mounted Video Camera**.
5. In the Type field, select **Work** from the drop-down menu. Your screen should look similar to Figure 2-5. Notice that the Resource Information dialog box contains many of the same fields as the Resource Sheet.

Figure 2-5

Resource Information dialog box with newly added resource

Resource name field

Resource type field

(Resource Information dialog box)

6. Click **OK**. The Resource Information dialog box closes and the Resource Sheet is visible. Notice that Microsoft Project has automatically wrapped the text in the Resource Name field. Also note that Max. Units is set to the default of 100%.

7. In the Max. Units field for the Digital Truck-Mounted Video Camera, key **200** or press the arrows until the value shown is 200%; then press **Tab**. This indicates that you will have two truck cameras available every workday.

8. Add the following additional equipment resources to the project schedule. You can use the Resource Sheet or the Resource Information dialog box to enter your information. Make sure that **Work** is selected in the Type field for each resource:

Resource Name	Max. Units
Sound Editing Studio	100%
Light Banks	400%
Video Editing Studio	100%
Microphone Bundles	500%
Dolly	200%

Your screen should look similar to Figure 2-6.

Figure 2-6

Resource Sheet showing additional equipment resources

	①	Resource Name	Type	Material	Initials	Group	Max.	Std. Rate	Ovt. Rate	Cost/Use	Accrue	Base	Code
1		Jamie Reding	Work		J		100%	$0.00/hr	$0.00/hr	$0.00	Prorated	Standard	
2		Scott Seely	Work		S		100%	$0.00/hr	$0.00/hr	$0.00	Prorated	Standard	
3		Jeff Pike	Work		J		100%	$0.00/hr	$0.00/hr	$0.00	Prorated	Standard	
4		Judy Lew	Work		J		100%	$0.00/hr	$0.00/hr	$0.00	Prorated	Standard	
5		Brenda Diaz	Work		B		100%	$0.00/hr	$0.00/hr	$0.00	Prorated	Standard	
6		Brad Sutton	Work		B		100%	$0.00/hr	$0.00/hr	$0.00	Prorated	Standard	
7		Annette Hill	Work		A		50%	$0.00/hr	$0.00/hr	$0.00	Prorated	Standard	
8		Ryan Ihrig	Work		R		100%	$0.00/hr	$0.00/hr	$0.00	Prorated	Standard	
9		Yan Li	Work		Y		100%	$0.00/hr	$0.00/hr	$0.00	Prorated	Standard	
10		Sound Technician	Work		S		300%	$0.00/hr	$0.00/hr	$0.00	Prorated	Standard	
11		Digital Truck-Mounted Video Camera	Work		D		200%	$0.00/hr	$0.00/hr	$0.00	Prorated	Standard	
12		Sound Editing Studio	Work		S		100%	$0.00/hr	$0.00/hr	$0.00	Prorated	Standard	
13		Light Banks	Work		L		400%	$0.00/hr	$0.00/hr	$0.00	Prorated	Standard	
14		Video Editing Studio	Work		V		100%	$0.00/hr	$0.00/hr	$0.00	Prorated	Standard	
15		Microphone Bundles	Work		M		500%	$0.00/hr	$0.00/hr	$0.00	Prorated	Standard	
16		Dolly	Work		D		200%	$0.00/hr	$0.00/hr	$0.00	Prorated	Standard	

9. **SAVE** the project schedule.

   PAUSE. LEAVE the project schedule open to use in the next exercise.

There's an important difference between scheduling equipment resources and scheduling people resources: Equipment resources tend to be more specialized than people resources. For example, a microphone can't be used as a video recorder, but an audio technician might be able to fill in as an "extra" in a video shoot. Also, some equipment resources might work 24 hours a day, but most people resources don't work more than 8 or 12 hours in a day.

■ Establishing Material Resources

THE BOTTOM LINE

Just as you established people and equipment resources in your project schedule, you can also set up material resources to track the rate of use of a particular resource and the related cost. Depending on the depth of your planning, Microsoft Project can provide an accurate bill of material (BOM) for your project's material resources.

Establishing Material Resources

Material resources are consumable items that are used up as the tasks in a project are completed. Unlike work resources (including human resources and equipment resources), material resources have no effect on the total amount of work scheduled to be performed on a task. For your music video project, DVDs are the consumable that interests you most. In this exercise, you practice entering material resources for your project.

→ ESTABLISH MATERIAL RESOURCES

USE the project schedule you created in the previous exercise.

1. In the Resource Sheet, click the next empty cell in the Resource Name column.
2. Key **DVD** and press **Tab**.
3. In the Type field, click the arrow and select **Material**, then press **Tab**.
4. In the Material Label field, key **2-hour disc** and press **Enter**. This means you will use two-hour discs as the unit of measure to track consumption during the project. Your screen should look similar to Figure 2-7.

Figure 2-7

Material resource added to the Resource Sheet

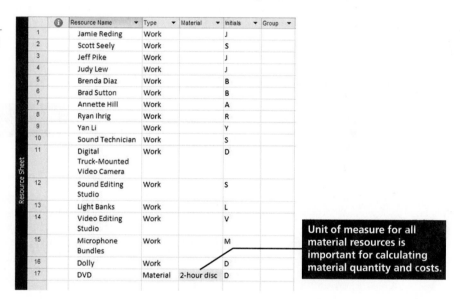

		Resource Name	Type	Material	Initials	Group
1		Jamie Reding	Work		J	
2		Scott Seely	Work		S	
3		Jeff Pike	Work		J	
4		Judy Lew	Work		J	
5		Brenda Diaz	Work		B	
6		Brad Sutton	Work		B	
7		Annette Hill	Work		A	
8		Ryan Ihrig	Work		R	
9		Yan Li	Work		Y	
10		Sound Technician	Work		S	
11		Digital Truck-Mounted Video Camera	Work		D	
12		Sound Editing Studio	Work		S	
13		Light Banks	Work		L	
14		Video Editing Studio	Work		V	
15		Microphone Bundles	Work		M	
16		Dolly	Work		D	
17		DVD	Material	2-hour disc	D	

Unit of measure for all material resources is important for calculating material quantity and costs.

5. **SAVE** the project schedule.

   PAUSE. LEAVE the project schedule open to use in the next exercise.

■ Establishing Cost Resources

THE BOTTOM LINE

Cost resources are financial obligations to your project. A cost resource enables you to apply a cost to a task by assigning a cost item (such as travel) to that task. The cost resource has no relationship to the work assigned to the task, but assigning cost resources gives you more control when applying various types of costs to tasks within your project.

Establishing Cost Resources

A *cost resource* is a resource that doesn't depend on the amount of work in a task or the duration of the task. Unlike fixed costs, you can apply as many cost resources to a task as necessary. In this exercise, you add cost resources to the Resource Sheet for your project.

➔ ESTABLISH COST RESOURCES

USE the project schedule you created in the previous exercise.

1. In the Resource Sheet, click the next empty cell in the Resource Name column.
2. Key **Travel** and press **Tab**.
3. In the Type field, click the arrow and select **Cost**. The travel resource has now been established as a cost resource.
4. In the Resource Name field below Travel, key **Food** and press **Tab**.
5. In the Type field, select **Cost** and press **Tab**. Your screen should look like Figure 2-8.

Figure 2-8

Resource Sheet with cost resource added

	ⓘ	Resource Name ▾	Type ▾	Material ▾	Initials ▾	Group ▾	
1		Jamie Reding	Work		J		
2		Scott Seely	Work		S		
3		Jeff Pike	Work		J		
4		Judy Lew	Work		J		
5		Brenda Diaz	Work		B		
6		Brad Sutton	Work		B		
7		Annette Hill	Work		A		
8		Ryan Ihrig	Work		R		
9		Yan Li	Work		Y		
10		Sound Technician	Work		S		
11		Digital Truck-Mounted Video Camera	Work		D		
12		Sound Editing Studio	Work		S		
13		Light Banks	Work		L		
14		Video Editing Studio	Work		V		
15		Microphone Bundles	Work		M		
16		Dolly	Work		D		
17		DVD	Material	2-hour disc	D		
18		Food	Cost		F		

Cost resources added on Resource Sheet

TAKE NOTE ✱   Cost resources differ from fixed costs in that cost resources are created as a type of resource and then assigned to a task. Also, unlike work resources, cost resources cannot have a calendar applied to them and therefore do not affect the scheduling of a task. In addition, the dollar value of cost resources doesn't depend on the amount of work done on the task to which they are assigned.

6. **SAVE** the project schedule.

PAUSE. LEAVE the project schedule open to use in the next exercise.

■ Establishing Resource Pay Rates

THE BOTTOM LINE   Although you might not track costs on small or personal projects, managing cost information is a key part of most project managers' job descriptions. When you enter the cost information for resources, tracking the finances of a project becomes a more manageable task.

Entering Resource Cost Information

Knowing resource cost information will help you take full advantage of the cost management features of Microsoft Project. In this exercise, you practice entering cost information for both work and material resources.

→ ENTER RESOURCE COST INFORMATION

USE the project schedule you created in the previous exercise.

1. In the Resource Sheet, click the **Std. (Standard) Rate** field for resource 1, Jamie Reding.

2. Key **1000/w** and press **Enter**. Jamie's standard weekly rate of $1,000 per week appears in the Std. rate column.

3. In the Std. Rate column for resource 2, Scott Seely, key **19.50/h** and press **Enter**. Scott's standard hourly rate of $19.50 appears in the Std. Rate column. Your screen should look similar to Figure 2-9.

Figure 2-9

Resource Sheet with standard rates for two resources

		Resource Name	Type	Material	Initials	Group	Max.	Std. Rate	Ovt. Rate	Cost/Use	Accrue	Base	Code
	1	Jamie Reding	Work		J		100%	$1,000.00/wk	$0.00/hr	$0.00	Prorated	Standard	
	2	Scott Seely	Work		S		100%	$19.50/hr	$0.00/hr	$0.00	Prorated	Standard	
	3	Jeff Pike	Work		J		100%	$0.00/hr	$0.00/hr	$0.00	Prorated	Standard	
	4	Judy Lew	Work		J		100%	$0.00/hr	$0.00/hr	$0.00	Prorated	Standard	
	5	Brenda Diaz	Work		B		100%	$0.00/hr	$0.00/hr	$0.00	Prorated	Standard	
	6	Brad Sutton	Work		B		100%	$0.00/hr	$0.00/hr	$0.00	Prorated	Standard	
	7	Annette Hill	Work		A		50%	$0.00/hr	$0.00/hr	$0.00	Prorated	Standard	
	8	Ryan Ihrig	Work		R		100%	$0.00/hr	$0.00/hr	$0.00	Prorated	Standard	
	9	Yan Li	Work		Y		100%	$0.00/hr	$0.00/hr	$0.00	Prorated	Standard	
	10	Sound Technician	Work		S		300%	$0.00/hr	$0.00/hr	$0.00	Prorated	Standard	
	11	Digital Truck-Mounted Video Camera	Work		D		200%	$0.00/hr	$0.00/hr	$0.00	Prorated	Standard	
	12	Sound Editing Studio	Work		S		100%	$0.00/hr	$0.00/hr	$0.00	Prorated	Standard	
	13	Light Banks	Work		L		400%	$0.00/hr	$0.00/hr	$0.00	Prorated	Standard	
	14	Video Editing Studio	Work		V		100%	$0.00/hr	$0.00/hr	$0.00	Prorated	Standard	
	15	Microphone Bundles	Work		M		500%	$0.00/hr	$0.00/hr	$0.00	Prorated	Standard	
	16	Dolly	Work		D		200%	$0.00/hr	$0.00/hr	$0.00	Prorated	Standard	
	17	DVD	Material	2-hour disc	D			$0.00		$0.00	Prorated		
	18	Food	Cost		F						Prorated		

4. Enter the following standard pay rates for the remaining resources:

Resource Name	Standard Rate
Jeff Pike	750/w
Judy Lew	19.50/h
Brenda Diaz	12.75/h
Brad Sutton	16.50/h
Annette Hill	20.00/h
Ryan Ihrig	12.00/h
Yan Li	18.50/h
Sound Technician	16.50/h
Digital Truck-Mounted Video Camera	1000/w
Sound Editing Studio	250/d
Light Banks	0/h
Video Editing Studio	250/d
Microphone Bundles	0/h
Dolly	25/d
DVD	10

5. Widen the Std. Rate column by moving the mouse pointer to the vertical divider line between the Std. Rate column and the Ovt. Rate column. Double-click the divider line. Your screen should look similar to Figure 2-10.

Figure 2-10

Resource Sheet with standard rates for all resources

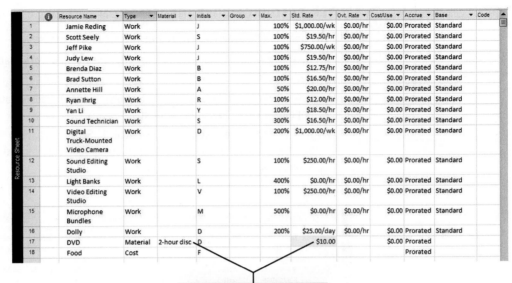

	ⓘ	Resource Name	Type	Material	Initials	Group	Max.	Std. Rate	Ovt. Rate	Cost/Use	Accrue	Base	Code
1		Jamie Reding	Work		J		100%	$1,000.00/wk	$0.00/hr	$0.00	Prorated	Standard	
2		Scott Seely	Work		S		100%	$19.50/hr	$0.00/hr	$0.00	Prorated	Standard	
3		Jeff Pike	Work		J		100%	$750.00/wk	$0.00/hr	$0.00	Prorated	Standard	
4		Judy Lew	Work		J		100%	$19.50/hr	$0.00/hr	$0.00	Prorated	Standard	
5		Brenda Diaz	Work		B		100%	$12.75/hr	$0.00/hr	$0.00	Prorated	Standard	
6		Brad Sutton	Work		B		100%	$16.50/hr	$0.00/hr	$0.00	Prorated	Standard	
7		Annette Hill	Work		A		50%	$20.00/hr	$0.00/hr	$0.00	Prorated	Standard	
8		Ryan Ihrig	Work		R		100%	$12.00/hr	$0.00/hr	$0.00	Prorated	Standard	
9		Yan Li	Work		Y		100%	$18.50/hr	$0.00/hr	$0.00	Prorated	Standard	
10		Sound Technician	Work		S		300%	$16.50/hr	$0.00/hr	$0.00	Prorated	Standard	
11		Digital Truck-Mounted Video Camera	Work		D		200%	$1,000.00/wk	$0.00/hr	$0.00	Prorated	Standard	
12		Sound Editing Studio	Work		S		100%	$250.00/hr	$0.00/hr	$0.00	Prorated	Standard	
13		Light Banks	Work		L		400%	$0.00/hr	$0.00/hr	$0.00	Prorated	Standard	
14		Video Editing Studio	Work		V		100%	$250.00/hr	$0.00/hr	$0.00	Prorated	Standard	
15		Microphone Bundles	Work		M		500%	$0.00/hr	$0.00/hr	$0.00	Prorated	Standard	
16		Dolly	Work		D		200%	$25.00/day	$0.00/hr	$0.00	Prorated	Standard	
17		DVD	Material	2-hour disc	D			$10.00		$0.00	Prorated		
18		Food	Cost		F						Prorated		

Material resource cost will be the per unit cost, listed in the Material Label column

TAKE NOTE*

Notice that you didn't enter a rate (weekly, hourly, or daily) for the cost of the DVD. For a material resource, the standard rate is per unit of consumption. For this exercise, that is a two-hour DVD. Also note that you did not assign a cost to the cost resources; this is done when the cost resources are assigned to a task (covered in Lesson 3).

6. **SAVE** the project schedule.

PAUSE. LEAVE the project schedule open to use in the next exercise.

In the real world, it is often difficult to get cost information for people resources because that information is usually considered confidential. As a project manager, it is important that you are aware of the limitations of your project schedule because of the information that is not available to you, and that you communicate these limitations to your project team and management. Some suggested methods of inserting costs without using actual pay rates are as follows:

- Use publicly available salary data, such as that from the Federal Bureau of Labor Statistics
- Ask for an average salary rate from the accounting department for workers with various skill sets (e.g., electricians, administrative assistants, etc.)

As a project manager, tracking and managing cost information may be a significant part of your responsibilities. Understanding the cost details of your project will allow you to stay on top of such key information as:

- The expected total cost of the project
- Resource costs over the life of the project
- Possible cost savings from using one resource versus another
- The rate of spending in relation to the length of the project

These and other cost limits often drive the scope of your project and may become critical to the project decisions you make.

■ Adjusting Resource Working Times

THE BOTTOM LINE

Project 2010 uses resource working and nonworking times to schedule tasks. You should define these times prior to assigning them to tasks. Resource working times apply only to people and equipment (work) resources—not to material resources. Now that you have entered resources and their associated pay rates in your project schedule, you can specify the working and nonworking times for some of these resources.

Establishing Nonworking Times

When you establish work resources in your project schedule, a *resource calendar* is created for each resource to define the resource's working and nonworking time. The resource calendar provides default working times for an entire project. Typically, you will need to make changes to individual resource calendars to reflect vacation, flextime work schedules, or conference attendance. In this exercise, you establish nonworking times for your individual work resources.

⊕ ESTABLISH NONWORKING TIMES FOR AN INDIVIDUAL WORK RESOURCE

USE the project schedule you created in the previous exercise.

Change
Working Time

X REF

Refer back to Lesson 1 for a quick refresher on the types of calendars used by Microsoft Project.

1. Click the **Project** tab, then click **Change Working Time**. The Change Working Time dialog box appears.
2. In the For Calendar box, select **Jamie Reding**. Jamie Reding's resource calendar appears in the Change Working Time dialog box.
3. Slide the button next to the calendar until the calendar displays January 2011.
4. Select the dates **January 27** and **January 28**.
5. In the first Name field on the Exceptions tab, key **Vacation Days**.
6. Click the first field in the Start column. The Start field displays 1/27/2011 and the Finish field displays 1/28/2011. Microsoft Project will not schedule Jamie Reding to work on these two days. Your screen should look similar to Figure 2-11.

Figure 2-11

Change Working Time dialog box showing exception dates for Jamie Reding

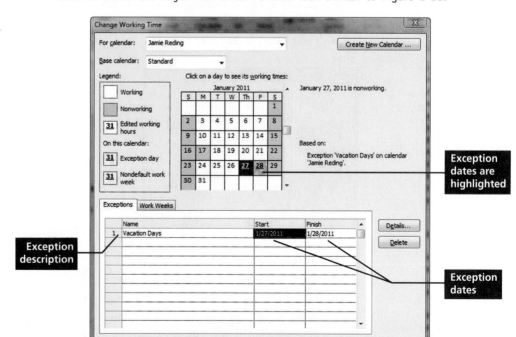

7. Click **OK** to close the Change Working Time dialog box.

8. **SAVE** the project schedule.

   PAUSE. LEAVE the project schedule open to use in the next exercise.

 Keep in mind that when you make changes to a project calendar, the changes are reflected in all resource calendars that are based on that project calendar. However, any changes you have made to the working times of an individual resource are not changed.

Establishing Specific Work Schedules

In addition to specifying exception times for resources, you can also set up a specific work schedule for any given resource. To practice establishing working times for your project's work resources, in this exercise, you make a change to the resource calendar for an individual resource.

⊕ ESTABLISH A SPECIFIC WORK SCHEDULE FOR A RESOURCE

USE the project schedule you created in the previous exercise.

1. Click the **Project** ribbon, and then click **Change Working Time** to open the Change Working Time dialog box.

2. Slide the button next to the calendar until the calendar displays January 2011.

3. In the For Calendar box, select **Scott Seely**.

4. Click the **Work Weeks** tab, and then click the **Details** button. The Details dialog box appears.

5. In the Select Day(s) box, click and drag to select **Monday** through **Thursday**.

6. Select **Set day(s) to these specific working times**.

7. On line 1 of the Working Times box, click the **8:00 am** box and replace it with **7:00 am**.

8. On line 2 of the Working Times box, click the **5:00 pm** box and replace it with **6:00 pm**.

9. Press **Enter** to set your changes. Your screen should look similar to Figure 2-12.

Figure 2-12

Details dialog box showing modified working times for Scott Seely

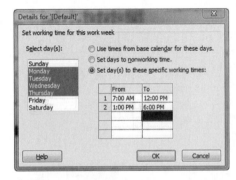

10. In the Select Day(s) box, click **Friday**.

11. Select **Set days to nonworking time**.

12. Click **OK** to close the Details dialog box. Microsoft Project can now schedule Scott Seely to work as early as 7:00 am and as late as 6:00 pm on Monday through Thursday, but it will not schedule him to work on Friday. Your screen should look similar to Figure 2-13.

Figure 2-13

Change Working Time dialog
box showing the modified
resource calendar for Scott
Seely

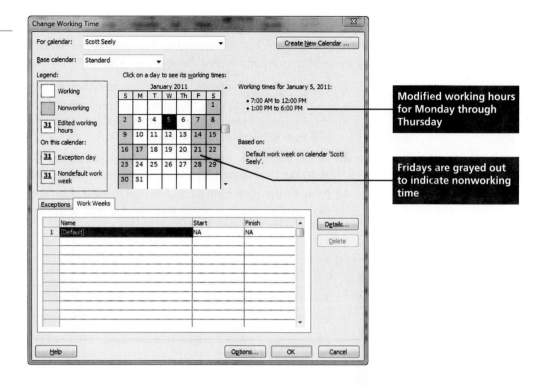

13. Click **OK** to close the Change Working Time dialog box.
14. **SAVE** the project schedule.
      PAUSE. LEAVE the project schedule open to use in the next exercise.

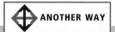
ANOTHER WAY

You can also change a
resource's base calendar
in Resource Sheet view
by clicking the arrow in
the Base Calendar field
of that resource.

If you need to edit several resource calendars in the same way (to handle a flex-time schedule
or night shift, for example), you might find it easier to assign a different base calendar to this
group of resources. A ***base calendar*** can be used as a task calendar, project calendar, or
resource calendar, and it specifies default working and nonworking times. Assigning a
different base calendar is quicker than editing each individual resource calendar, and it allows
you to make future project-wide changes to a single base calendar (rather than editing each
resource calendar again). You can change a resource's base calendar by opening the Change
Working Time dialog box from the Project ribbon. In the For Calendar box, select the desired
resource, and then in the Base Calendar box, select the desired base calendar. For a group of
resources that will be using the same calendar, you can change the calendar directly in the
Base Calendar column of the Entry table in Resource Sheet view. Microsoft Project includes
three base calendars: Standard, 24 Hours, and Night Shift. You can customize these or use
them as a basis for your own base calendar.

■ Adding Resource Notes

THE BOTTOM LINE

At times, you may want to provide details regarding how (and why) a resource is
scheduled the way it is. You can add this additional information about a resource by
attaching a note.

Attaching a Note to a Resource

In this exercise, you learn how to attach a scheduling note to a resource in Project 2010.

⊕ ATTACH A NOTE TO A RESOURCE

USE the project schedule you created in the previous exercise. Make sure you are still in the Resource Sheet view of the *Don Funk Music Video 2* file.

Notes

1. In the Resource Name column, select the name of resource 1, **Jamie Reding**.
2. On the Ribbon, click the **Resource** tab, then click the **Resource Notes** button in the Properties command group. The Resource Information dialog box is displayed with the Notes tab visible.
3. In the Notes box, key **Jamie on vacation Jan 30 and 31; available for consult at home if necessary** and click **OK**. A note icon appears in the indicator column.
4. Point to the note icon on the Resource Sheet. The note appears in a ScreenTip (double-click the icon to display the full text of longer notes). Your screen should look similar to Figure 2-14.

Figure 2-14

Resource note displayed as a ScreenTip

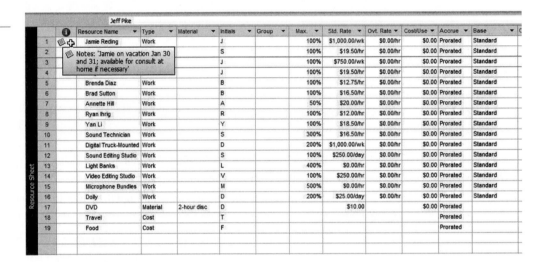

5. **SAVE** the project schedule.
6. **CLOSE** the *Don Funk Music Video 2* file.

   PAUSE. If you are continuing to the next lesson, keep Project open. If you are not continuing to additional lessons, **CLOSE** Project.

SKILL SUMMARY

IN THIS LESSON, YOU LEARNED:	TASK
To establish people resources.	Establish individual people resources.
	Establish a resource that represents multiple people.
To establish equipment resources.	Establish equipment resources.
To establish material resources.	Establish material resources.
To establish cost resources.	Establish cost resources.
To establish resource pay rates.	Enter resource cost information.
To adjust resource working times.	Establish nonworking times for an individual resource.
	Establish a specific work schedule for a resource.
To add resource notes.	Attach a note to a resource.

■ Knowledge Assessment

Matching

Match the term in column 1 to its description in column 2.

Column 1	Column 2
1. Resource calendar	**a.** The maximum capacity of a resource to accomplish tasks
2. Max. Units	**b.** Specifies default working and nonworking times for a resource, project, or task
3. Material resource	**c.** When and how much of a resource's time can be assigned to work on tasks
4. Project calendar	**d.** The people and equipment that do work to accomplish the tasks of a project
5. Cost resource	**e.** The people, equipment, money, and materials used to complete the tasks in a project
6. Work resource	**f.** A way of documenting information about resources, tasks, and assignments
7. Base calendar	**g.** Consumable items that are used up as the tasks in a project are accomplished
8. Availability	**h.** A resource that doesn't depend on the amount of work in a task or the duration of a task
9. Resources	**i.** The base calendar that provides default working times for an entire project
10. Note	**j.** The working and nonworking time for an individual resource

Multiple Choice

Select the best response for each of the following statements.

1. Which of the following is NOT an example of a work resource?
   a. Yan Li
   b. Keyboard
   c. DVD disc
   d. Electrician
2. It is helpful to assign a base calendar to a group of resources when they all:
   a. have the same pay rate.
   b. work night shift.
   c. have the same Max. Units.
   d. do the same job function.
3. A resource calendar does not apply to:
   a. material resources.
   b. people resources.
   c. equipment resources.
   d. work resources.

4. You can view information for the individual people who will perform the tasks in a project in the:

   a. Calendar view.

   b. Gantt chart view.

   c. Task Usage view.

   d. Resource Sheet view.

5. You can provide additional information about how a resource is scheduled by:

   a. changing the Max. Units.

   b. establishing a project calendar.

   c. adding a resource note.

   d. setting constraints.

6. For which of the following resources is the standard rate listed per unit of consumption?

   a. Material

   b. Equipment

   c. People

   d. All of the above

7. If you have four electricians who can each work part-time (four hours rather than eight), what value should you assign to Max. Units for the resource "Electrician"?

   a. 50%

   b. 25%

   c. 100%

   d. 200%

8. If you assign a resource to more tasks than it can accomplish at its maximum units, the resource is:

   a. maxed out.

   b. overallocated.

   c. constrained.

   d. in default.

9. To add vacation days to the calendar for an individual work resource, which dialog box would you use?

   a. Resource Information

   b. Resource Notes

   c. Change Working Time

   d. None of the above

10. It is often difficult to get cost information for people resources because:

    a. the information is confidential.

    b. the information is too complex to calculate.

    c. the information changes too frequently.

    d. the costs are large in comparison with other resource costs.

■ Competency Assessment

Project 2-1: Hiring a New Employee

In the previous lesson, you entered the tasks of a project schedule for hiring a new employee. Now you need to add some of the people resources that will be responsible for performing those tasks.

GET READY. Launch Microsoft Project if it is not already running.

OPEN *Hire New Employee 2-1* from the data files for this lesson.

1. Click the **View** tab; then, in the Resource Views group, select **Resource Sheet**.
2. In the Resource Sheet view, click the empty cell directly below the Resource Name column heading.
3. Enter the following resource names into the Resource Sheet:
   Gabe Mares
   Barry Potter
   Amy Rusko
   Jeff Smith
4. **SAVE** the project as *Hire New Employee*, then **CLOSE** the file.
   LEAVE Project open for the next exercise.

The *Hiring New Employee 2-1* file for this lesson is available on the book companion website.

Project 2-2: Entering Pay Rates for an Office Remodel

You are in charge of the remodeling project for the kitchen and lunchroom at your office. Your facilities manager has just provided you with the resource pay rates for this project. You need to enter these pay rates in the project schedule.

OPEN *Office Remodel 2-2* from the data files for this lesson.

1. Select the **Resource Sheet** view.
2. For the Drywall resource, click the **Type** field drop-down arrow, select **Material**, then press **Tab**. For the Nails resource, click the **Type** field drop-down arrow, select **Material**, then press **Tab**.
3. In the Resource Sheet, click the **Std. Rate** field for resource 1, Toby Nixon.
4. Key **500/w** and press **Enter**.
5. Enter the following standard pay rates for the remaining resources:

Resource Name	Standard Rate
Lori Kane	500/w
Run Liu	20/h
Electrician	30/h
Plumber	30/h
Drywall	11
Nails	5
John Emory	450/w
Scaffolding	50/d
Table saw	35/d

6. **SAVE** the project as *Remodel-2*, then **CLOSE** the file.
   LEAVE Project open for the next exercise.

The *Office Remodel 2-2* file for this lesson is available on the book companion website.

■ Proficiency Assessment

Project 2-3: Adding a Resource Note for Hiring New Employee

You have created a project schedule for hiring a new employee. Now you need to add a note to one of the resources in the project.

OPEN *Hiring Empl-Note 2-3* from the data files for this lesson.

1. Select the name of resource 3, **Amy Rusko**.
2. On the Ribbon, click the **Resource Notes** button in the Properties command group.
3. Add the following note: **Amy will be at the SHRM conference on July 20-22. Not available for any interviews**.
4. Close the Resource Information box.
5. Select the name of resource 4, **Jeff Smith**.
6. Click the **Resource Notes** button.
7. Add the following note: **Jeff will be at the SHRM conference on July 20-21. Available for interviews on July 23**.
8. Close the Resource Information box.
9. **SAVE** the project schedule as *Hiring Empl-Note,* then **CLOSE** the file.

   LEAVE Project open for the next exercise.

The *Hiring Empl-Note 2-3* file for this lesson is available on the book companion website.

Project 2-4: Adding Equipment Resources for New Employee Orientation

You have already developed a project schedule for new employee orientation in your department. Now you need to add several equipment resources to make sure that your schedule flows smoothly.

OPEN *Employee Orientation 2-4* from the data files for this lesson.

1. Change to Resource Sheet view.
2. Add the following equipment resources to the project schedule:

Resource Name	Max. Units
DVD/TV Combo	100%
Digital Camera	50%
Laminating Machine	50%
Laptop Computer	600%
Large Conference Room	100%

The *Employee Orientation 2-4* file for this lesson is available on the book companion website.

3. **SAVE** the project schedule as *Employee Orientation Resources,* then **CLOSE** the file.

   LEAVE Project open for the next exercise.

■ Mastery Assessment

Project 2-5: Changing Work Times for a Resource on Office Remodel

You have just been told that one of your resources on your office remodel project is planning to take a week of vacation. You need to add this information to your project schedule.

The *Office Remodel 2-5* file for this lesson is available on the book companion website.

OPEN *Office Remodel 2-5* from the data files for this lesson.

1. Open the Change Working Time dialog box.
2. Change Lori Kane's resource calendar to reflect her vacation from August 22 to August 26, 2011.
3. **SAVE** the project schedule as *Office Remodel Vacation,* then **CLOSE** the file.
   LEAVE Project open to use in the next exercise.

Project 2-6: Don Funk Music Video Problems

A student who is interning with your company made some updates to the music video project schedule. Unfortunately, he is still learning about Microsoft Project and has entered some information incorrectly. You need to correct the problems with the project schedule before distributing it to your team.

OPEN *Don Funk Incorrect 2-6* from the data files for this lesson.

1. Review the Resource Sheet for this project schedule.
2. Based on what you learned in this lesson about Resource Types, Maximum Units, and Standard Rates, find the resource errors in this project schedule and correct them. (Hint: There are three resource errors in the project schedule.)
3. Study the last three resources on the sheet. If dry ice is a material resource and bottled water is a cost resource, make corrections to the information given for these resources (estimate the rate if necessary).
4. **SAVE** the project schedule as *Don Funk Corrected,* then **CLOSE** the file.
   CLOSE Project.

The *Don Funk Incorrect 2-6* file for this lesson is available at the book companion website.

INTERNET READY

Search the Internet for information on summer camps for children. Review locations, facilities, equipment, activities, and staffing for several well-developed camp programs. Based on your research, develop a Resource table in Microsoft Project of the resources (people, equipment, cost, and material) that are necessary for running a summer camp. Include at least 20 resources. For each resource, include the type, maximum units, standard rate, and material label if appropriate. (Make estimates of the maximum units and standard rate.)

3 LESSON

Resource and Task Assignments: Fundamentals

LESSON SKILL MATRIX

SKILL	TASK
Assigning Work Resources to Tasks	Make individual resource assignments.
	Assign multiple resources simultaneously.
Adding More Resource Assignments to Tasks	Add resources to a task.
	Use SmartTags to assign resources to tasks.
Assigning Material Resources to Tasks	Assign a material resource to a task.
Assigning Cost Resources to Tasks	Assign a cost resource to a task.

As the production manager at Southridge Video, you are working on a new music video for Don Funk, an up-and-coming singer/songwriter. You first mapped out the initial tasks in the project, then identified the resources needed to complete these tasks. Now you must put the two together. When you make assignments (i.e., when you link resources and tasks), Microsoft Project 2010 can provide several key pieces of information, including who is working on what tasks and when; whether you have adequate resources; whether the resources are available when you need them; and more. In this lesson, you will learn how to assign work, material, and cost resources to a task; how to manipulate resources to fine-tune a project; and how to use SmartTags.

KEY TERMS
assignment
effort-driven scheduling
scheduling formula
SmartTag
units
work

■ SOFTWARE ORIENTATION

Microsoft Project's Assign Resources Dialog Box

In Microsoft Project, when you assign work or material resources to a task, you use the Assign Resources dialog box. You activate the Assign Resources dialog box via the Assign Resources button located in the Assignments group on the Resource tab. Your Assign Resources dialog box should look similar to Figure 3-1 or Figure 3-2, depending upon whether the Resource List options are collapsed or expanded.

Figure 3-1

Assign Resources dialog box with Resource List options collapsed

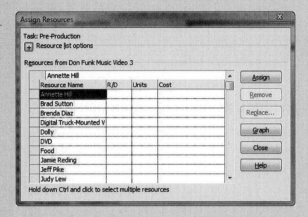

Figure 3-2

Assign Resources dialog box with Resource List options expanded

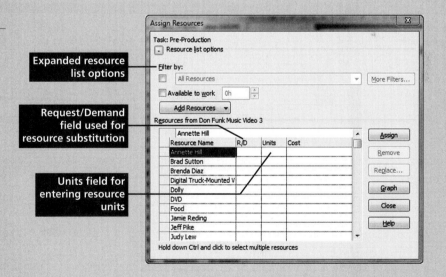

You can expand the Resource List options by clicking the button marked with a plus sign next to the Resource List Options heading. You can then collapse the expanded list by clicking the button, now marked with a minus sign, once again.

■ Assigning Work Resources to Tasks

THE BOTTOM LINE

Microsoft Project provides you with various options for assigning resources to tasks. You can assign individual resources to a task or multiple resources to a task. Once assigned, you can track the resources working on the task. Microsoft Project also enables you to see whether resource assignments affect task duration.

Making Individual Resource Assignments

An *assignment* is the matching of a specific resource to a particular task to do work. Depending on your perspective, you might call it a resource assignment, or you might call it a task assignment. In previous lessons, you mapped out tasks and resources for your project schedule. In this exercise, you learn how to assign those resources to the tasks they will perform.

⊕ MAKE INDIVIDUAL RESOURCE ASSIGNMENTS

GET READY. Before you begin these steps, launch Microsoft Project. **OPEN** *Don Funk Music Video 3M* from the data files for this lesson. **SAVE** the file as *Don Funk Music Video 3*.

1. Click the **Resource** tab, then click the **Assign Resources** button in the Assignments group. The Assign Resources dialog box appears.

2. If the Assign Resources dialog box is covering the task name column, drag the dialog box to the lower-right corner of the screen. Your screen should look similar to Figure 3-3.

Figure 3-3

Gantt chart view with Assign Resources dialog box open

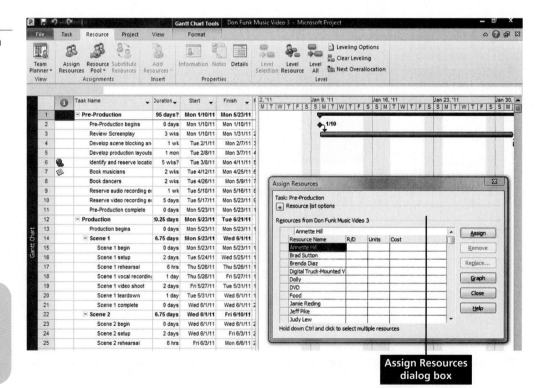

Assign Resources dialog box

The *Don Funk Music Video 3M* file for this lesson is available on the book companion website.

3. In the Task Name column of the Gantt chart, click the name of task 3, **Review screenplay.**

4. In the Resource Name column of the Assign Resources dialog box, scroll down and click **Scott Seely**, then click the **Assign** button. A check appears next to Scott Seely's name, indicating that you have assigned him to the task of reviewing the screenplay. Your screen should look similar to Figure 3-4.

Figure 3-4

Gantt chart showing names of resources assigned

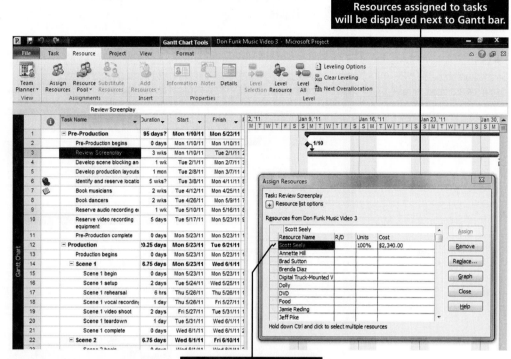

5. In the Task Name column, click the name of task 5, **Develop production layouts**.
6. In the Assign Resources dialog box, click **Jeff Pike**, then click the **Assign** button. A check appears next to Jeff's name to show that you have assigned him to task 5.
7. **SAVE** the project schedule.

   PAUSE. LEAVE the project schedule open to use in the next exercise.

Assigning Multiple Resources Simultaneously

You just assigned a single resource to a task. In this exercise, you practice assigning multiple resources to a task simultaneously.

ASSIGN MULTIPLE RESOURCES SIMULTANEOUSLY

USE the project schedule you created in the previous exercise.

1. In the Task Name column, click the name of task 4, **Develop scene blocking and schedule**.
2. In the Assign Resources dialog box, scroll down and click **Scott Seely**. Next, scroll up or down in the list until the name Judy Lew is visible. Hold down **Ctrl**, click **Judy Lew**, and then click the **Assign** button. Checkmarks appear next to Scott Seely's and Judy Lew's names, indicating that you assigned them both to task 4.

3. In the Task Name column, click the name of task 6, **Identify and reserve locations**.

4. In the Assign Resources dialog box, click **Jeff Pike**. Next, scroll up or down in the list until the name Yan Li is visible. Hold down **Ctrl**, click **Yan Li**, and then click the **Assign** button. Checkmarks appear next to Jeff Pike's and Yan Li's names, indicating that you assigned them both to task 6. Your screen should look similar to Figure 3-5.

Figure 3-5

Gantt chart showing two resources assigned to task 6

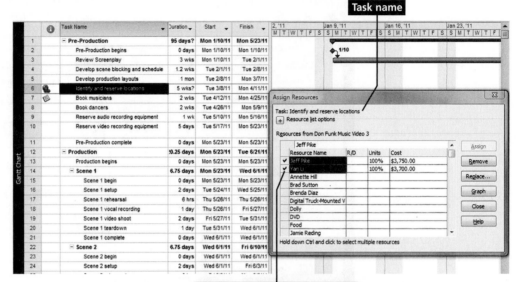

5. SAVE the project schedule.

PAUSE. LEAVE the project schedule open to use in the next exercise.

X REF | Recall that in Lesson 2, you learned that Max. Units refers to the maximum capacity of a resource to accomplish tasks.

You may have noticed that the duration of task number 4 changed from 1 week to 1.2 weeks when you assigned both Scott and Judy to the task. Bear in mind that Microsoft Project is using the resource calendars to schedule the tasks. Here, the duration is extended by 0.2 weeks (one day) due to the fact that Scott works Monday through Thursday. Therefore, the last eight hours of his portion of the work will not be completed until the following week.

The capacity of a resource to work when you assign that resource to a task is measured in *units*. Units are recorded in the Max. Units field on the Resource Sheet view. One full-time resource has 100% (or 1.0) resource units. As you are assigning resources, you need to be careful that you do not overallocate a resource by assigning it more work than can be done within its normal work capacity. This may happen if you assign a resource to a task with more units than the resource has available. Another possibility is that you assign the resource to multiple tasks with schedules that overlap and with combined units that exceed those of the resource. Keep in mind that Microsoft Project assumes all of a resource's work time can be allotted to an assigned task unless you specify otherwise. If a resource has less than 100% maximum units, Microsoft Project assigns the value of the resource's maximum units.

■ Adding More Resource Assignments to Tasks

↓ THE BOTTOM LINE

Microsoft Project has the ability to apply a scheduling method called effort-driven scheduling when you assign resources to or remove resources from tasks. With *effort-driven scheduling*, a task's initial work value remains constant, no matter how many additional resources are assigned. The most obvious effect of effort-driven scheduling is that as you add or remove resources, a task's duration either decreases or increases.

Adding Resources to a Task

In the previous exercise, you started to define resource assignments for several tasks in your project schedule. Now you want to assign additional resources to those tasks. To view work information in each task, you will use a split view. As you complete the following exercise, pay close attention to the results in relation to task duration and work in the split view.

⊕ ADD RESOURCES TO A TASK

USE the project schedule you created in the previous exercise.

1. Click the **View** tab. In the Split View group, select the **Details** check box. The Task Form view appears in the bottom part of your screen.
2. Click the name of task 3, **Review screenplay**. In the Task Form pane at the bottom of the screen, take note of the Work field.
3. In the Assign Resources dialog box, click **Jeff Pike**, then click the **Assign** button. Microsoft Project assigns Jeff Pike to task 3.

   Notice that Microsoft Project changes the work (effort) that each individual is now assigned for this task, and it also automatically highlights all items that change as a result of your most recent change. This helps you gain a better understanding of the effects of your choices. Your screen should look similar to Figure 3-6.

Figure 3-6

Split window view with Gantt chart (top) and Task Form (bottom) views

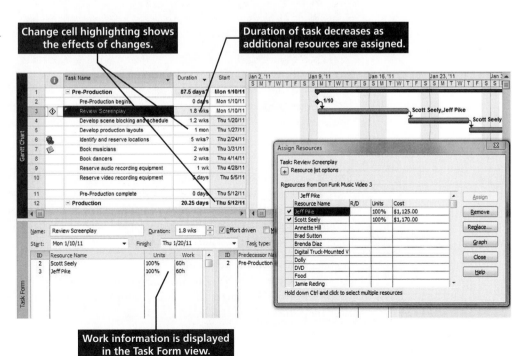

TAKE NOTE*

If you noticed a small triangle in the corner of the name of task 3, this is a SmartTag. You can find more information about SmartTags in the next section of this lesson.

X REF

You can find more information about Project's scheduling formula in Lesson 4.

Table 3-1

Varying approaches to assigning the same total number of resources

4. **SAVE** the project schedule.

PAUSE. LEAVE the project schedule open to use in the next exercise.

Work is the total amount of effort a resource or resources will spend to complete a task. Microsoft Project calculates work using the following *scheduling formula*:

$$Duration \times Units = Work$$

Microsoft Project performs the work calculation at the *first* work resource assignment, regardless of the number of work resources assigned (i.e., a single resource or multiple resources). Using effort-driven scheduling, Microsoft Project will maintain that work amount as the effort required to perform that task until you tell it otherwise. Table 3-1 provides an example using the same task duration and different approaches to assigning the same total number of resources.

In general, if you have one resource working full-time on a task, the amount of work (effort) will match the duration. However, if your resource is not working full-time, or if you assign more than one resource to a task, then work and duration will not be equal. You can now see the benefit of creating task relationships rather than setting start or finish dates. Because effort-driven scheduling resulted in decreased task durations, Microsoft Project adjusted the start dates of successor tasks that did not have a constraint such as a start or finish date.

ASSIGNING A SINGLE RESOURCE, THEN ADDING TWO RESOURCES	ASSIGNING TWO RESOURCES, THEN ADDING A SINGLE RESOURCE
Task Duration: 6 days (8-hour days)	Task Duration: 6 days (8-hour days)
Task Work: 0 hours (no resources have been assigned yet)	Task Work: 0 hours (no resources have been assigned yet)
At the first assignment of a single resource (100% Max. Units):	At the first assignment of two resources (100% Max. Units):
Task Duration: 6 days	Task Duration: 6 days
Task Work: 48 hours	Task Work: 96 hours
After assigning two additional resources (100% Max. Units):	After assigning one additional resource (100% Max. Units):
Task Duration: 2 days	Task Duration: 4 days
Task Work: 48 hours	Task Work: 96 hours

TAKE NOTE*

Although effort-driven scheduling is no longer the default for all tasks you create in Microsoft Project, you can change the default setting for all new tasks in a project schedule. On the Ribbon, click the File tab, then select Options. Then, in the Project Options dialog box, select Schedule. Navigate down to Scheduling options for this project and clear or select the New tasks are effort driven check box.

To change effort-driven scheduling for a single task or group of tasks, select the desired task(s). Click the Task tab, and then select the Information button in the Properties group. Select the Advanced tab of the Multiple Task Information dialog box. Clear or select the Effort driven check box.

Using a SmartTag to Assign Resources

Now that you have assigned multiple resources to several tasks, in this exercise you will learn how to use SmartTags to assign additional resources to a task. A *SmartTag* is an indicator that signals the user of a change, additional information, formatting options, and so on. In Project 2010, SmartTags are mainly used for changes to durations, work, and units. SmartTags appear at each change in one of these elements and remain available only until you perform your next action.

⊘ USE A SMARTTAG TO ASSIGN RESOURCES TO TASKS

USE the project schedule you created in the previous exercise.

1. Click the name of task 5, **Develop production layouts**. Jeff Pike is the only resource currently assigned to this task. You want to assign an additional resource and reduce the task's duration.

2. In the Resource Name column of the Assign Resources dialog box, click **Brenda Diaz**, then click the **Assign** button. Brenda Diaz is assigned to task 5. In addition, a small triangle appears in the top-left corner of the Task Name cell. This means there is a SmartTag activated for this task.

3. Click again on the name of task 5, **Develop production layouts**. The SmartTag Actions button appears in the Indicators column for task 5.

4. Click the **SmartTag Actions** button. A list of options for handling this additional resource is displayed. Your screen should look similar to Figure 3-7.

Figure 3-7

SmartTag options list

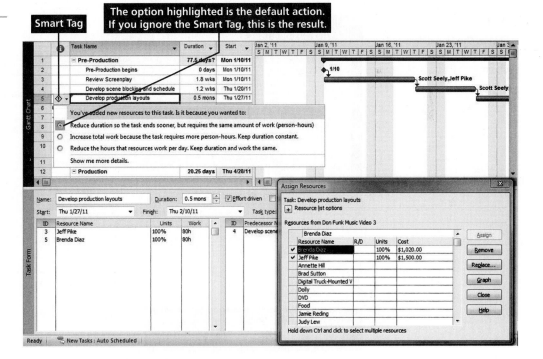

TAKE NOTE* Although Microsoft Project assumes that you want to use effort-driven scheduling, the SmartTag Actions list lets you choose the scheduling option you need. You can change the task's duration, the resource's work, or the assignment units. The default setting in the SmartTag Actions list is to reduce the task's duration.

5. You want to reduce the task's duration. Because this option is already selected, you do not need to make any changes. Click the **SmartTags Action** button again to close the list.

6. Click the name of task 6, **Identify and reserve locations**.

7. In the Resource Name column of the Assign Resources dialog box, click **Annette Hill**.

8. Scroll down until Ryan Ihrig's name is visible. Hold down **Ctrl**, click **Ryan Ihrig**, and then click the **Assign** button.

   Microsoft Project assigns Annette and Ryan to the task. Because effort-driven scheduling is the default, Microsoft Project also reduces the task duration and adjusts the start date of all successor tasks. However, you do not want the additional resources to change the task's duration. You have determined that the original scope of this task was underestimated and that Annette and Ryan must perform additional work on this task. Take note of the work data in the Task Form pane.

9. Select **task 6** again. Your screen should look similar to Figure 3-8.

Figure 3-8

Split view showing details of task information after resource addition

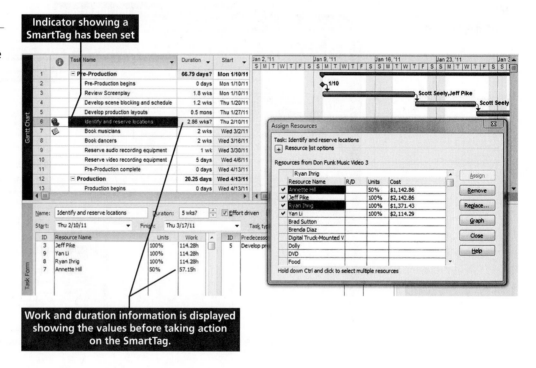

Indicator showing a SmartTag has been set

Work and duration information is displayed showing the values before taking action on the SmartTag.

10. Click the **SmartTag Actions** button. In the SmartTag Actions list, select **Increase total work because the task requires more person-hours. Keep duration constant**. Microsoft Project changes the task's duration back to five weeks and adjusts the start dates of successor tasks. It also resets the work values back to the values that the initially assigned resources had, resulting in an increase in total work on the task. Your screen should look similar to Figure 3-9.

Figure 3-9

Split view showing that duration remains the same but total work increases

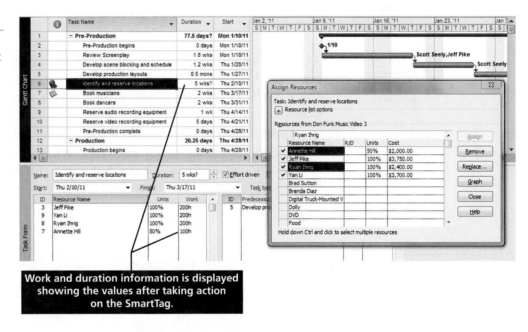

Work and duration information is displayed showing the values after taking action on the SmartTag.

Exercise caution when determining the extent to which effort-driven scheduling should apply to the tasks in your project. Although applying more resources to your tasks may reduce their duration on paper, this may not be possible in a real-world situation. For example, if one resource could complete a task in 20 hours, could 20 resources complete the task in one hour? What about 40 resources in 30 minutes? In reality, the resources would probably get in each other's way, and productivity might even decrease. Additional coordination might be needed. For complex tasks, a resource might need specialized training before they can be productive. There is no exact rule about when you should or should not apply effort-driven scheduling. As a project manager, you need to review the requirements of your project tasks and use your best reasoning.

11. Click the **Close** button in the Assign Resources dialog box.
12. **SAVE** the project schedule.

PAUSE. LEAVE the project schedule open to use in the next exercise.

It is important to remember that effort-driven scheduling adjusts task duration only if you add or delete resources from a task. For example, if you initially assign a resource to a task with a duration of 16 hours and later add a second resource, effort-driven scheduling will cause Microsoft Project to schedule each resource to work eight hours at the same time, resulting in 16 hours of work on the task. However, if you initially assign two resources to a task with a duration of 16 hours, Microsoft Project schedules each resource to work 16 hours, for a total of 32 hours of work on the task. Keep this in mind as you are assigning resources.

■ Assigning Material Resources to Tasks

THE BOTTOM LINE

In this exercise, you assign material resources to tasks. Most projects use at least some material resources. When you assign material resources to tasks, Microsoft Project can track their consumption and cost.

⊕ ASSIGN A MATERIAL RESOURCE TO A TASK

USE the project schedule you created in the previous exercise.

Assign
Resources

1. Click the **Resource** tab, then click the **Assign Resources** button in the Assignments group. The Assign Resources dialog box appears.
2. In the Task Name column, click the name of task 6, **Identify and reserve locations**.
3. In the Assign Resources dialog box, click the **Units** field for the DVD resource.
4. Key **8**, then click the **Assign** button. Scroll the Gantt bar portion of your screen so that the right end of the bar for task 6 is visible. You will use eight DVDs while identifying locations for this video. Remember that a DVD is a material resource and cannot do work, so assigning it to a task does not affect the task's duration. Your screen should look similar to Figure 3-10.

Figure 3-10

Standard rates for all resources added to the Resource Sheet

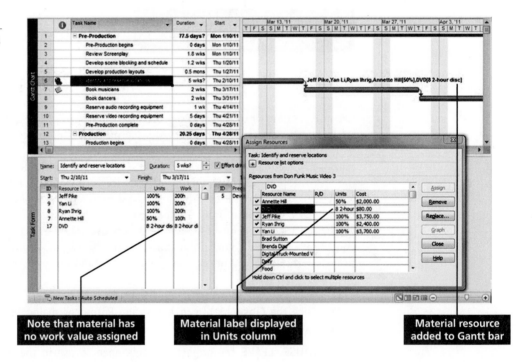

Note that material has no work value assigned

Material label displayed in Units column

Material resource added to Gantt bar

5. In the Assign Resources dialog box, click **Close**.
6. **SAVE** the project schedule.

PAUSE. LEAVE the project schedule open to use in the next exercise.

When you assign a material resource to a task, there are two ways in which you can handle its consumption and cost:

- Assign a fixed-unit quantity of the material resource. This is what you did in the preceding exercise. Microsoft Project then multiplied the unit cost of the resource by the number of units to calculate the total cost.
- Assign a variable-rate quantity of the material resource. For example, if two DVDs will be used per day, you would enter 2/day as the assignment unit. Microsoft Project will adjust the quantity and cost of the resource as the duration of the task changes. You will assign a material resource using this method in lesson six.

■ Assigning Cost Resources To Tasks

THE BOTTOM LINE A cost resource is another type of resource that you can assign to a task. A cost resource represents a financial obligation to your project. Once you assign the cost resource to the task, you can then assign the cost for the resource.

Assigning a Cost Resource to a Task

In this exercise, you assign a cost resource to an individual task.

ASSIGN A COST RESOURCE TO A TASK

USE the project schedule you created in the previous exercise.

1. Click the **Resource** tab, then click the **Assign Resources** button in the Assignments group. The Assign Resources dialog box appears.
2. In the Task Name column, click the name of task 17, **Scene 1 rehearsal.**
3. In the Resource Name column of the Assign Resources dialog box, click **Food**, then click the **Assign** button.
4. In the Cost column for the Food resource, key **500** and press **Enter.** During the Scene 1 rehearsal, $500 of food will be used to feed the crew and performers working on this task.
5. Click the name of task 25, **Scene 2 rehearsal.**
6. In the Resource Name column of the Assign Resources dialog box, click **Food**, then click the **Assign** button.
7. In the Cost column for the Food resource, key **500** and press **Enter.**
8. In the Assign Resources dialog box, click **Close.**
9. **SAVE** and then **CLOSE** the ***Don Funk Music Video 3*** file.

   PAUSE. If you are continuing to the next lesson, keep Project open. If you are not continuing to additional lessons, **CLOSE** Project.

SKILL SUMMARY

In This Lesson, You Learned:	Task
To assign work resources to tasks.	Make individual resource assignments.
	Assign multiple resources simultaneously.
To add more resource assignments to tasks.	Add resources to a task.
	Use SmartTags to assign resources to tasks.
To assign material resources to tasks.	Assign a material resource to a task.
To assign cost resources to tasks.	Assign a cost resource to a task.

■ Knowledge Assessment

Fill in the Blank

Complete the following sentences by writing the correct word or words in the blanks provided.

1. A(n) _____ is the matching of a specific resource to a particular task to do work.

2. Assigning a(n) _____ or _____ resource to a task will not affect the duration of the task.

3. In Microsoft Project, when you assign a human or equipment resource to a task, the result is _____.

4. _____ is the number of work periods you expect a task to take to complete.

5. If a resource is assigned to do more work than can be done within the normal work capacity of the resource, it is _____.

6. The capacity of a resource to work is measured in _____.

7. In Microsoft Project, Duration $\times$ Units = Work is known as the _____.

8. Effort-driven scheduling adjusts a task's duration only if you add or remove _____ from a task.

9. When you assign _____ to tasks, you can track their consumption and cost.

10. According to the scheduling formula in Microsoft Project, 20 hours task duration $\times$ 200% assignment units = _____ hours work.

Multiple Choice

Select the best response for the following statements.

1. If you assign a resource to a task with more units than the resource has available, then the resource is:

   a. maximized.

   b. overutilized.

   c. compromised.

   d. overallocated.

2. The _____ lets you choose the scheduling option you need.

   a. SmartTag Action list

   b. scheduling formula

   c. Assign Resources dialog box

   d. effort-driven scheduler

3. A task plus a resource equals:

   a. work.

   b. an assignment.

   c. overallocation.

   d. duration.

4. If, after an initial assignment, you assign more resources to a task, the task's duration will:

   a. double.

   b. decrease.

   c. be reduced by half.

   d. increase.

5. Where do you normally record the dollar value of the cost resources for a project?

   a. On the Resource Sheet in the Cost column

   b. On the Resource Sheet in the Std. Rate column

   c. In the Assign Resources dialog box when the cost resource is assigned

   d. In a separate Excel spreadsheet

6. If, on the first task assignment, you assign two resources at the same time, each at 100% assignment units, to a task with 24 hours' duration, then each resource will work on the task for:

   a. 12 hours.

   b. 24 hours.

   c. 36 hours.

   d. 48 hours.

7. To assign more than one resource to a task using the Assign Resources dialog box, click the first resource name, then hold down the _____ key while clicking the second resource name, and then click Assign.

   a. Alt

   b. Shift

   c. Ctrl

   d. None of the above

8. Which of the following is an advantage of assigning resources to tasks?

   a. You can see if the resource assignment affects task duration.

   b. You can track the progress of the resource in working on the task.

   c. You can track resource and task costs.

   d. All of the above

9. If you assign a(n) _____ quantity of a material resource to a task, Microsoft Project will adjust the quantity and cost of the resource as the task's duration changes.

   a. variable-rate

   b. open-ended

   c. fixed-unit

   d. declining-rate

10. With effort-driven scheduling, if you initially assign multiple resources to a task and later remove one of those resources from the task, the amount of work for the task:

    a. decreases.

    b. increases.

    c. stays constant.

    d. The answer cannot be determined with the information provided.

■ Competency Assessment

Project 3-1: Hiring a New Employee–Resource Assignments

You have a project schedule for hiring a new employee that contains both tasks and resources. Now you will assign some of the resources to perform specific tasks.

GET READY. Launch Microsoft Project if it is not already running. **OPEN** *Hiring Employee 3-1* from the data files for this lesson.

1. Click the **Resource** tab, then click the **Assign Resources** button in the **Assignments** group.
2. In the Task Name column, click name of task 1, **Write job description**.
3. In the Resource Name column of the Assign Resources dialog box, click **Amy Rusko**, then click **Assign**.
4. In the Task Name column, click the name of task 6, **Review resumes**.
5. In the Resource Name column of the Assign Resources dialog box, click **Barry Potter**, then click **Assign**.
6. Click **Close** in the Assign Resources dialog box.
7. **SAVE** the project as *Hiring Employee-Resources*, then **CLOSE** the file.

    LEAVE Project open for the next exercise.

The *Hiring Employee 3-1* file for this lesson is available on the book companion website.

Project 3-2: Office Remodel

You are in charge of the remodel for the kitchen and lunchroom of your office. You need to assign resources to tasks. In fact, it is necessary to simultaneously assign several of these resources to a single task.

OPEN *Office Remodel 3-2* from the data files for this lesson.

1. Click the **Assign Resources** button in the **Assignments** group on the Resource tab.
2. In the Task Name column, click the name of task 5, **Remove drywall from main walls**.
3. In the Assign Resources dialog box, select **John Emory** and **Toby Nixon**, then click **Assign**.
4. In the Task Name column, click the name of task 12, **Paint walls and woodwork**.
5. In the Assign Resources dialog box, select **Run Liu** and **Toby Nixon**, then click **Assign**.
6. Click **Close** in the Assign Resources dialog box.
7. **SAVE** the project as *Office Remodel Multiple Resources*, then **CLOSE** the file.

    LEAVE Project open for the next exercise.

The *Office Remodel 3-2* file for this lesson is available on the book companion website.

■ Proficiency Assessment

Project 3-3: Office Remodel Material Resources

You now need to assign material resources to tasks in your office remodel project schedule.

OPEN *Office Remodel 3-3* from the data files for this lesson.

1. Open the Assign Resources dialog box using the appropriate button on the Resource tab.
2. Select task 9, **Install drywall**.
3. In the Assign Resources dialog box, assign **drywall** as a resource, then assign **50** units for the drywall resource.
4. In the Assign Resources dialog box, assign **nails** as a resource, then assign **5** units for the nails resource.
5. Close the Assign Resources dialog box.
6. **SAVE** the project as *Office Remodel Material Resources*, then **CLOSE** the file.
   LEAVE Project open for the next exercise.

The *Office Remodel 3-3* file for this lesson is available on the book companion website.

Project 3-4: Don Funk Video–Assigning Resources Using a SmartTag

Although you have already assigned most of the resources for your music video, you now realize that you need to assign additional resources for a few of the tasks. You can use a SmartTag to do this.

OPEN *Don Funk Music Video 3-4* from the data files for this lesson.

1. Select task 7, **Book musicians**.
2. Activate the Assign Resources dialog box.
3. Click **Brenda Diaz**, then assign her to the task.
4. Use the SmartTag to indicate that you want to increase the total work for this task.
5. Close the Assign Resources dialog box.
6. **SAVE** the project schedule as *Don Funk Smart Tag*, then **CLOSE** the file.
   LEAVE Project open to use in the next exercise.

The *Don Funk Music Video 3-4* file for this lesson is available on the book companion website.

■ Mastery Assessment

Project 3-5: Don Funk Cost Resources

In this exercise, you will assign cost resources for the Don Funk Music Video.

OPEN *Don Funk Music Video 3-5* from the data files for this lesson.

1. Open the Assign Resources dialog box.
2. For task 6, Identify and reserve locations, assign **Travel** as a resource at a cost of **5000**.
3. For task 18, Scene 1 vocal recording, assign **Food** as a resource at a cost of **250**.
4. Close the Assign Resources dialog box.
5. **SAVE** the project schedule as *Don Funk Cost Resources*, then **CLOSE** the file.
   LEAVE Project open for the next exercise.

The *Don Funk Music Video 3-5* file for this lesson is available on the book companion website.

Project 3-6: Hiring a New Employee–Additional Resources

You have just learned of a change in scope for some of the tasks in your project schedule for hiring a new employee. One task will require more work than originally estimated, and for another task, the assigned resources must work fewer hours.

OPEN *Hiring New Employee 3-6* from the data files for this lesson.

The *Hiring New Employee 3-6* file for this lesson is available on the book companion website.

1. For the task Review resumes, assign **Gabe Mares** and **Jeff Smith** to assist. Set their assignments so that the total work is increased and the duration is kept constant.

2. For the task Conduct interviews, assign **Gabe Mares**. Set his assignment so that for this task, the resources work fewer hours per day, but the work and task duration remain constant.

3. Close the Assign Resources dialog box.

4. **SAVE** the project schedule as *New Employee Adding Resources*, then **CLOSE** the file.

   CLOSE Project.

INTERNET READY

There are many Internet resources that offer advice or solutions to the challenges that arise during any given project implementation. Microsoft's website is one such resource. Search the Microsoft website for Work Essentials—a subsite that provides information on how to perform daily work functions more efficiently in a wide variety of occupations. Browse the occupations and select one that relates to project managers. Explore the resources provided to find information on managing project scope changes. Write a short paragraph highlighting the best practices of change management.

Refining Your Project Schedule

LESSON SKILL MATRIX

SKILL	TASK
Applying a Task Calendar to an Individual Task	Apply a task calendar to an individual task.
Changing Task Types	Change scheduling formula values to change task types.
	Change a task type using the Task Information dialog box.
Splitting a Task	Split a task.
Establishing Recurring Tasks	Set up a recurring task.
	Assign resources to a recurring task.
Applying Task Constraints	Apply a Start No Earlier Than constraint to a task.
Reviewing a Project's Critical Path	Review a project's critical path.
Viewing Resource Allocations Over Time	Explore resource allocations.

As Southridge Video's production manager, you have been working on the project schedule for a new music video for Don Funk. You have developed the three key building blocks for the project: tasks, resources, and assignments. By setting up tasks and resources and then assigning one to the other, you helped the schedule take shape. Now, you need to fine-tune your schedule to reflect some of the details of and exceptions to these building blocks. For instance, some tasks cannot occur during normal working hours, other tasks will have interruptions, and still others will repeat on a regular basis throughout the project. There are also tasks that have limits on when or by whom they can be performed. In this lesson, you will learn how to create task calendars, change task types, split tasks, set up and apply resources to recurring tasks, apply constraints, and identify the critical path of your project.

KEY TERMS

allocation	noncritical tasks
constraint	overallocated
critical path	recurring task
fixed duration	semi-flexible
fixed units	constraint
fixed work	slack
flexible constraint	split
float	task calendar
free float	task type
free slack	total float
fully allocated	total slack
inflexible constraint	underallocated
negative slack	

■ SOFTWARE ORIENTATION

Microsoft Project's Change Working Time and Create New Base Calendar Dialog Boxes

When working in Microsoft Project 2010, there may be instances when you want specific tasks to occur at times that are outside the project calendar's working time. To do this, you need to create a new base calendar—a function that is accessed through the Change Working Time dialog box.

Figure 4-1

Change Working Time dialog box, with Create New Base Calendar dialog box open

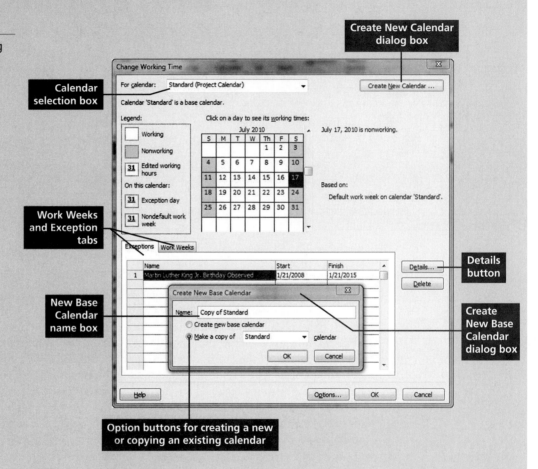

The Create New Base Calendar dialog box is accessed by clicking the Create New Calendar button in the Change Working Time dialog box, which is opened from the Project tab. The Create New Base Calendar dialog box enables you to name a new calendar, create a totally new calendar, or make a copy of an existing calendar on which to base a new calendar.

■ Applying a Task Calendar to an Individual Task

THE BOTTOM LINE

When you set up resources in your project schedule, Microsoft Project created the corresponding resources calendar. Sometimes, you might need a specific task to occur at a time that is outside the project calendar's working time (such as overnight or on a weekend). To do this, you can assign a task calendar to this task. You can either use one of Project's base calendars or create a new base calendar that fits your task requirements.

Assigning a Task Calendar to an Individual Task

A *task calendar* is a base calendar that is used by a single task. It defines working and nonworking times for a task, regardless of the settings in the project calendar. Task calendars are often used when a task must run overnight, occur on a specific weekday, or occur over a weekend. Task calendars are beneficial when other base calendars—such as 24 Hours or Night Shift—are too broad or too specific for the task requirements. In this exercise, you create and assign a task calendar to a task that occurs outside normal working times: an overnight video shoot.

 APPLY A TASK CALENDAR TO AN INDIVIDUAL TASK

GET READY. Before you begin these steps, launch Microsoft Project. **OPEN** *Don Funk Music Video 4M* from the data files for this lesson. **SAVE** the file as *Don Funk Music Video 4* in the solutions folder for this lesson as directed by your instructor.

Change Working Time

1. Click the **Project** tab, then click **Change Working Time**. The Change Working Time dialog box is activated.

The *Don Funk Music Video 4M* file for this lesson is available on the book companion website.

2. In the Change Working Time dialog box, click the **Create New Calendar** button. The Create New Base Calendar dialog box appears as shown in Figure 4-1.

3. In the Name box, key **Overnight beach filming**. One of the scenes for the video will be shot during the overnight hours on a public beach.

4. If it is not already selected, click the **Make a copy of** button. In the drop-down menu that appears, select **Standard**, then click **OK**. (Refer back to the Software Orientation at the beginning of this lesson for more details on this screen.)

5. Click the **Work Weeks** tab in the Change Working Time dialog box, then click the **Details** button. The Details dialog box appears.

6. In the Select days box, drag your pointer to select **Tuesday** through **Friday**. Click the **Set day(s) to these specific working times** button.

7. Click the cell in row 1 of the From column and key **12:00 a.m.** Click the cell in row 1 of the To column and key **3:00 a.m.** Click the cell in row 2 of the From column and key **9:00 p.m.** Click the cell in row 2 of the To column and key **12:00 a.m.** Press **Enter**. Your screen should look similar to Figure 4-2. Click **OK**.

8. Click the **Details** button again. In the Select Days box, select **Monday**. Click the **Set day(s) to these specific working times** button. Click the cell in row 1 of the From column and key **9:00 p.m.** Click the cell in row 1 of the To column and key **12:00 a.m.** Click the cell in row 2 of the From column and press **Delete**.

9. Select **Saturday**. Click the **Set day(s) to these specific working times** button. Click the cell in row 1 of the From column and key **12:00 a.m.** Click the cell in

TROUBLESHOOTING

Microsoft Project will not allow you to set a timeframe that spans two days. For instance, you cannot specify a working time for Monday of 9 p.m. through 3 a.m. because 3 a.m. is on Tuesday. Instead, you must set the time intervals for each specific day, as you did in this exercise.

Figure 4-2

Details dialog box showing
evening working times

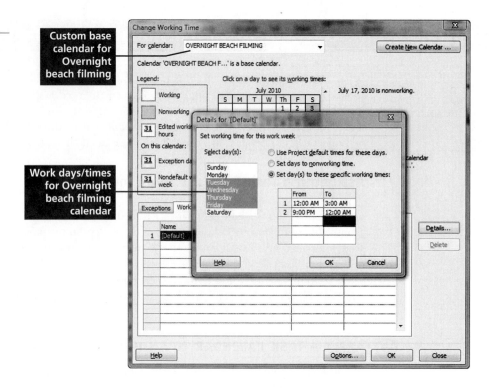

row 1 of the To column and key **3:00 a.m.** Press **Enter**. You have now set the
working times for this calendar from 9:00 p.m. to 3:00 a.m. from Monday night
through Friday night (Saturday morning). Click **OK** to close the Details dialog box.
Click **OK** to close the Change Working Time dialog box.

10. Select the name of task 35, **Scene 3 video shoot**. If the Gantt bar of this task is
    not visible, click the **Scroll To Task** button on the Task tab.

TROUBLESHOOTING If the Scroll To Task button is not visible on your Standard toolbar, click Toolbar
Options to display a list of additional buttons, then click the Scroll To Task button to
add it to your Standard toolbar.

Information

11. Click the **Task** tab, then click the **Task Information** button in the **Properties**
    group. The Task Information dialog box appears.

12. Click the **Advanced** tab of the Task Information dialog box.

13. In the Calendar box, select **Overnight beach filming** from the drop-down list. Click
    the **Scheduling ignores resource calendars** check box. Your screen should look like
    Figure 4-3.

14. Click **OK** to close the Task Information dialog box. Microsoft Project applies the
    Overnight beach filming calendar to task 35, and a calendar icon appears in the
    Indicators column. Because you chose to ignore resource calendars, the resources
    for this task will be scheduled at times that would usually be nonworking times for
    them.

TAKE NOTE* Notice that a small red human icon appears in the Indicators column. This is a new
feature in Microsoft Project 2010 that notifies the user of a resource overallocation, as
described later in this chapter.

Figure 4-3

Advanced tab of the Task
Information dialog box

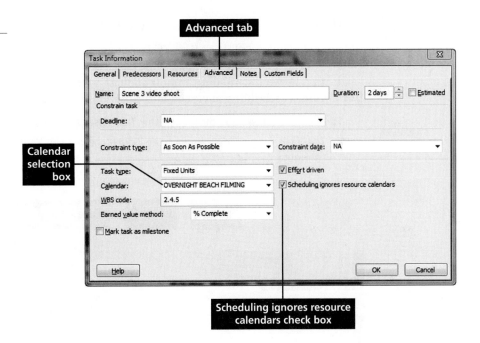

15. SAVE the project schedule.

PAUSE. LEAVE the project schedule open to use in the next exercise.

You have just created and assigned a task calendar to a task that occurs outside normal working times—specifically, an overnight video shoot. For tasks that have both a task calendar and resource assignments (and therefore a resource calendar), Microsoft Project will schedule work in the working time that is common between the task and resource calendar(s). If there is no common time, Project will alert you when you assign a resource to the task or when you apply the task calendar. As you saw in this exercise, you can explicitly choose to ignore resource calendars.

■ Changing Task Types

THE BOTTOM LINE

As you learned in Lesson 3, Microsoft Project uses the scheduling formula of Duration × Units = Work. The *task type* specifies which value in the scheduling formula remains fixed if the other two values change. The three available task types are fixed units, fixed duration, and fixed work. To determine which task type is the right one to apply to each task in your project schedule, you must determine how you want Project to schedule those tasks.

Using the Scheduling Formula to Change Task Types

As previously mentioned, there are three task types in Project 2010: fixed units, fixed duration, and fixed work. The default task type is *fixed units*, a task type in which the units value does not change. With the fixed units task type, if you change a task's duration, Microsoft Project recalculates work. Similarly, if you change work, duration is recalculated. A *fixed duration* task is one in which the duration value is fixed. Thus, if you change the task's work or units value, Project recalculates the other value. Finally, a *fixed work* task is one in which the work value is held constant. Here, you can change the duration or units and Project will determine the other value. Project has a bias toward changing duration first. If it cannot change duration, it will change work and then units.

CHANGE SCHEDULING FORMULA VALUES TO CHANGE TASK TYPES

In Lesson 3, you learned that Microsoft Project uses the scheduling formula (Duration × Units = Work) to determine a task's work value. In this exercise, you examine the relationship between scheduling formula and task type.

USE the project schedule you created in the previous exercise.

Task
Usage ▾

1. Click the **View** tab, then click the **Task Usage** button in the Task Views group.

2. The Task Usage view replaces the Gantt chart view. Your screen should look similar to Figure 4-4.

Figure 4-4

Task Usage view

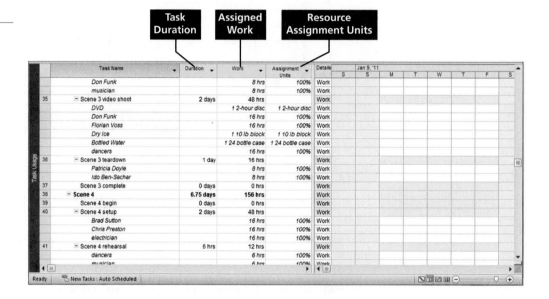

3. Press the **F5** key. In the ID box, key **4**, then click **OK**. Microsoft Project shifts the project schedule so that task 4, Develop scene blocking and schedule, and its assignments are visible.

4. Auto-fit the Task Name Column and move the center divider to the right until you can see the Start column. To auto-fit a column, place the pointer on the right dividing line of the column name and double-click.

5. Right-click the **Start** column heading, then select **Insert Column**. From the drop-down list that appears, locate and click **Assignment Units**.

   Note that task 4 has a total work value of 80 hours, 40 work hours, 100% resource units for each of two resources, and a duration of 1.2 weeks. Your team has determined that this task's duration should be two weeks, but the work necessary to complete the task should remain the same.

6. In the Duration field for task 4, select or key **2w** and press **Enter**. Microsoft Project changes the duration of task 4 to two weeks and increases the work for each resource. However, you want to increase the duration but keep the work the same.

7. Point to the Duration field for task 4, then click the **SmartTag** button. Your screen should look similar to Figure 4-5. Review the options in the SmartTag list.

   The task type for task 4 is fixed units (the default task type), so the default selection in the SmartTag is to increase work as duration increases. Based on your team's discussions, you want to keep the work value constant and decrease assignment units for the task's new duration.

> **TAKE NOTE** *
>
> If a task type is fixed, this doesn't mean that its units, work, or duration values are unchangeable. You can change any value for any task type.

Figure 4-5

SmartTag actions list for task 4

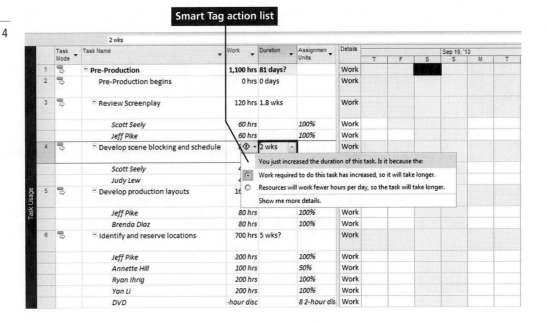

8. Click **Resources will work fewer hours per day, so the task will take longer** in the SmartTag actions list. The total work on the task is still 80 hours, but the assignment units value of each resource decreases. Another way to think of this is to say that the resources will put in the same total effort over a longer period of time. Figure 4-6 shows the adjusted scheduling formula values for task 4.

Figure 4-6

Adjustments made after the SmartTag action on task 4

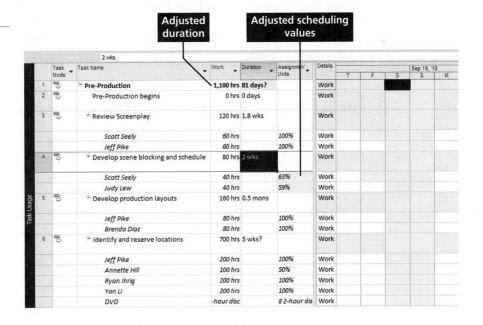

9. **SAVE** the project schedule.

   PAUSE. LEAVE the project schedule open to use in the next exercise.

Table 4-1 highlights the effects of changing any scheduling formula variable for any task type.

As you fine-tune your project schedule, keep in mind that you cannot turn off effort-driven scheduling for a fixed work task.

Table 4-1

Task types and scheduling formula values

IF THE TASK TYPE IS....	AND YOU CHANGE THE...		
	Duration	Units	Work
Fixed duration	Project recalculates work	Project recalculates units	Project recalculates work
Fixed units	Project recalculates work	Project recalculates duration	Project recalculates duration
Fixed work	Project recalculates units	Project recalculates duration	Project recalculates duration

TAKE NOTE* To see the task type of a task you have selected, click the Information button on the Task tab, then click the Advanced tab in the Task Information dialog box. You can also see the task type when you are in Gantt chart view via the Task Form. On the View tab, click Details in the Split View group. The Task Form will appear in the lower portion of your screen.

Using the Task Information Dialog Box to Change a Task Type

In the previous exercise, you changed the task type using SmartTag actions. In this exercise, you change the task type using the Task Information dialog box.

 CHANGE A TASK TYPE USING THE TASK INFORMATION DIALOG BOX

USE the project schedule you created in the previous exercise.

1. Switch back to the Gantt chart view by clicking the **Gantt Chart** button in the View tab.
2. Press the **F5** key. In the ID box, key **6**, then click **OK**.
3. Double-click **task 6**. The Task Information dialog box appears.
4. Click the **Advanced** tab if it is not already selected. Note that in the Task type box, the task has a Fixed Units task type. You will adjust this task's resources but leave its duration fixed at five weeks.
5. Select **Fixed Duration** from the drop-down menu in the Task type box.
6. Click the **Resources** tab in the Task Information dialog box.
7. In the Units column, set the units value for Jeff Pike to **50%** and the units value for Ryan Ihrig to **75%**. Your screen should look similar to Figure 4-7.

TAKE NOTE* You cannot change the task type on a summary task—it is always fixed duration. This is the case because the summary task is based on the earliest start date and the latest finish date of its subtasks.

Figure 4-7

Task Information dialog box
showing adjusted resource
units

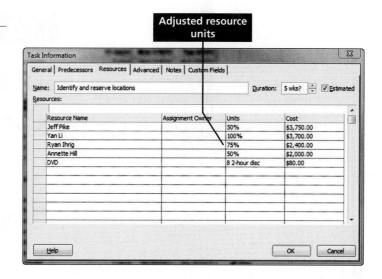

8. Click **OK** to close the Task Information dialog box. Note that the duration of the task did not change.

9. **SAVE** the project schedule.

PAUSE. LEAVE the project schedule open to use in the next exercise.

As you are fine-tuning your project schedule, keep in mind that it is easy to confuse task type and effort-driven scheduling. They are similar in that they both affect work, duration, and units values. The key difference is that effort-driven scheduling affects your schedule only when you add or remove resources from tasks, whereas modifying the task type affects only the resources that are assigned to the task when the change is made.

■ Splitting A Task

THE BOTTOM LINE   Sometimes, work on certain tasks in a project schedule will stop and then start again; these interruptions may be planned or unplanned. In Microsoft Project, you split a task to show that work has been interrupted and restarted.

Splitting a Task

A *split* is an interruption in a task, represented in Project's Gantt bar by a dotted line between the two segments of the task. In this exercise, you practice splitting a task to represent some nonworking time in the middle of the task.

⊕ **SPLIT A TASK**

USE the project schedule you created in the previous exercise.

1. Select the name of task 5, **Develop production layouts**.

2. Click the **Task** tab, then click the **Scroll to Task** button in the Editing group.

Scroll
to Task

3. Microsoft Project brings the Gantt bar of task 5 into view. Your screen should look similar to Figure 4-8. (You may have to zoom in or out to display days.) You have just been told that work on this task will be interrupted from February 7 to February 10; no work will occur on these days.

Figure 4-8

Gantt chart view of task 5

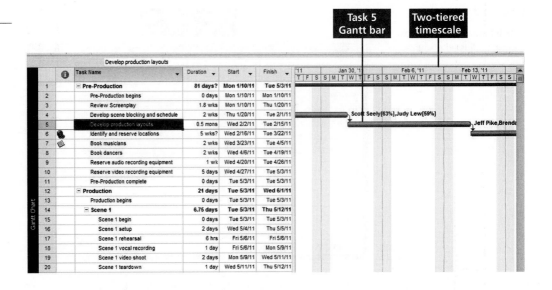

TAKE NOTE *

The timescale at the top of the right half of the Gantt chart (above the graphical bars) determines at what level of time (months, weeks, days, etc.) you can split a task. The calibration of the bottom tier of the timescale is the smallest increment into which you can split a task. In this exercise, you can split the task into one-day increments because days are on the bottom tier. If you wanted to split the task at the hourly level, you would need to adjust the tiers via the Timescale option on the Format tab.

4. On the Ribbon, click the **Split Task** button in the Schedule group. A ScreenTip appears and the mouse pointer changes to a double vertical line with an arrow to the right.

5. Move the mouse pointer over the Gantt bar of task 5. Watch the ScreenTip as you move the pointer—the date changes. The ScreenTip reflects the date on which you will begin to split the task. Your screen should look similar to Figure 4-9.

Figure 4-9

ScreenTip for splitting a task

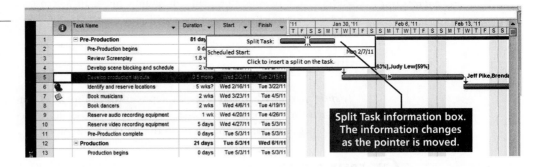

6. Move (but don't click the mouse pointer) over the Gantt bar until the Start date of Monday, 2/7/11, appears in the ScreenTip.

7. Click and drag the mouse pointer to the right until the Start date of Friday, 2/11/11, appears in the ScreenTip, then release the mouse button. Microsoft Project inserts a task split between the two parts of the task. The split, or interruption in work, is represented by a dotted line in the Gantt chart, as shown in Figure 4-10.

Figure 4-10

Gantt chart view with a split in task 5

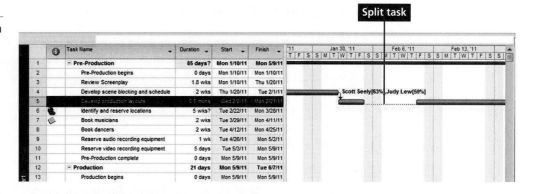

Splitting tasks using the mouse pointer takes a little practice. If you split a task on the wrong date, there are two ways you can correct the error. First, you can click the Undo button on the menu bar to remove the incorrect split. Alternatively, you can point to the second segment of the task again, and when the mouse pointer changes to a circle with four arrows, you can drag the segment to the correct start date. Note that you can drag a segment multiple times.

TROUBLESHOOTING

> **8. SAVE** the project schedule.
>
> **PAUSE. LEAVE** the project schedule open to use in the next exercise.

Keep the following points in mind when splitting a task:

- You can split a task into as many parts as necessary.
- You can drag a segment of a split task either right or left to reschedule the split.
- The time of the actual task split, represented by the dotted line, does not count in the duration of the task unless the task type is fixed duration. Work does not occur during the split.

XREF

Resource leveling or manually contouring assignments can also cause tasks to split. You will find out more about resource leveling in Lesson 6 and about contouring assignments in Lesson 13.

- If the duration of a split task changes, the last segment of the task is lengthened or shortened.
- If a split task is rescheduled, the whole task, including the splits, is rescheduled. The same pattern of segments and splits is preserved.

■ Establishing Recurring Tasks

↓ THE BOTTOM LINE

Many projects require repetitive tasks, such as attending status meetings or cleaning the production line. Even though these may seem like negligible tasks, you should account for them in your project schedule because they require time from project resources.

Setting Up a Recurring Task

A *recurring task* is a task that is repeated at specified intervals, such as daily, weekly, or monthly. When you create a recurring task, Microsoft Project creates a series of tasks with Start No Earlier Than constraints, no task relationships, and effort-driven scheduling turned off. In this exercise, you learn how to set up a task that will repeat at specified intervals during the project.

⊕ SET UP A RECURRING TASK

USE the project schedule you created in the previous exercise.

1. Select the name of task 11, **Pre-production complete**. You want to insert the recurring tasks as the last items in the Pre-Production phase.
2. On the **Task** tab, in the Insert group, click the **downward arrow** under the Task button. Select **Recurring Task**. The Recurring Task Information dialog box appears.
3. In the Task Name box, key **Status Meeting**.
4. In the Duration box, key **1h**.
5. Under Recurrence Pattern, make sure that **Weekly** is selected, then select the **Monday** check box.
6. In the Start box, key or select **1/17/11**. The first occurrence of your weekly meeting will be on January 17, 2011.

Timescale:
Days

TAKE NOTE* Microsoft Project schedules a recurring task to start at the Default Start Time value you established at the beginning of your project. To schedule a recurring task to begin at a different time, enter that time along with the start date in the Start box of the Recurring Task Information dialog box. For instance, if you want the status meeting to start at 9 a.m. on January 17, you would enter 1/17/11 9 a.m. in the Start box.

7. Under Range of Recurrence, select **End after**, then key or select **15** occurrences. Your screen should look like Figure 4-11.

Figure 4-11

Recurring Task Information dialog box with all task information

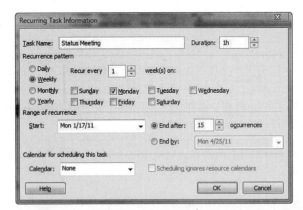

8. Click **OK** to create the recurring task. A Microsoft Project dialog box appears to notify you that one of the instances of the recurring task will occur during nonworking times (the holiday on January 17).
9. Review the options presented in the dialog box. You want to skip the status meeting for this particular week. Click **No** to not schedule this occurrence of the task. Microsoft Project inserts the recurring tasks within the Pre-production phase. A recurring task icon appears in the Indicators column, as shown in Figure 4-12.

Figure 4-12

Gantt chart with recurring task icon

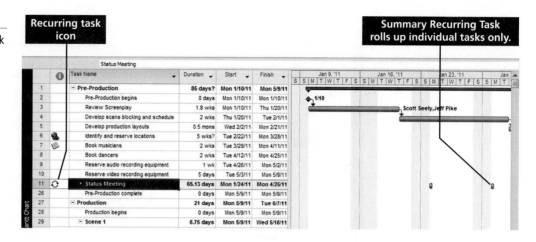

10. Click the name of task 11, **Status meeting**, then click the **Scroll to Task** button in the Editing group on the Task tab. The Gantt chart displays the first occurrences of the recurring meeting's Gantt bars. Notice that the summary Gantt bar for the recurring task shows only the individual occurrences of the tasks.

11. **SAVE** the project schedule.

PAUSE. LEAVE the project schedule open to use in the next exercise.

Assigning Resources to a Recurring Task

In the previous exercise, you established a recurring task in your project schedule. In this exercise, you assign resources to the task.

➔ ASSIGN RESOURCES TO A RECURRING TASK

USE the project schedule you created in the previous exercise.

1. If it is not already selected, click the name of task 11, **Status meeting**.
2. Click the **Resource** tab. In the Assignments group, click **Assign Resources**.
3. In the Assign Resources dialog box, click **Brad Sutton**. Then hold down **Ctrl** while clicking **Chris Preston**, **Eva Corets**, **Jamie Reding**, **Jane Clayton**, and **Judy Lew**.
4. Click **Assign**, then click **Close**. Microsoft Project assigns the selected resources to the recurring task.
5. Click the **plus sign (+)** next to task 11's title to expand and show the subtasks. Your screen should look similar to Figure 4-13.
6. Click the **minus sign (–)** next to task 11's title to collapse the subtasks under the summary task.

Figure 4-13

Gantt chart displaying resource assignments on a recurring task

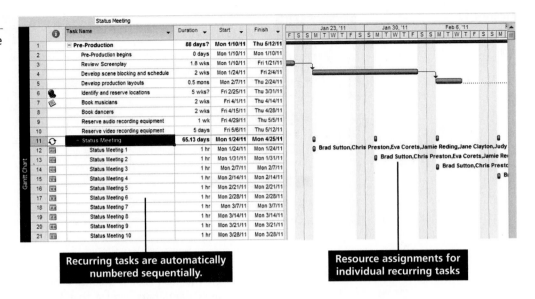

Recurring tasks are automatically numbered sequentially.

Resource assignments for individual recurring tasks

7. **SAVE** the project schedule.

PAUSE. LEAVE the project schedule open to use in the next exercise.

Keep the following points in mind when establishing a recurring task:

- Always use the Assign Resources dialog box when assigning resources to recurring tasks. If you enter resource names in the Resource Name field of the summary task, the resources will be assigned only to the summary task, not to the individual occurrences.
- If you schedule a recurring task to end on a specific date, Microsoft Project will suggest the current project end date. If you select the project end date, you will need to manually change this setting later if the project end date changes.
- As you saw in this exercise, Microsoft Project will alert you if an occurrence of a recurring task will take place during nonworking time. You can choose either to skip that occurrence or to schedule it for the next working day.

■ Applying Task Constraints

↓
THE BOTTOM LINE

Every task that you enter into your project schedule has some type of limit, or constraint, applied to it. The *constraint* controls the start or finish date or the extent to which the task can be adjusted. There are three categories of constraints, and each has very different effects on the scheduling of tasks. A *flexible constraint* gives Project the ability to change start and finish dates (this is the default type). An *inflexible constraint* forces a task to begin or end on a specific date, and it should be used only when necessary. A *semi-flexible constraint* gives Project the ability to change task start and finish dates (but not duration) within one date boundary.

Table 4-2 shows the eight types of task constraints within Project's three constraint categories.

Applying a Constraint to a Task

In this exercise, you apply a constraint to a task in Microsoft Project.

Table 4-2

Constraint categories and types

CONSTRAINT CATEGORY	CONSTRAINT TYPE	PROPERTIES
Flexible	As Soon As Possible (ASAP)	Project will schedule a task to occur as soon as it can happen. This is the default constraint type applied to new tasks when scheduling from the project start date.
	As Late As Possible (ALAP)	Project will schedule a task to occur as late as it can happen. This is the default constraint type applied to all new tasks when scheduling from the project finish date.
Semi-Flexible	Start No Earlier Than (SNET)	Project will schedule a task to start on or after the specified constraint date. Use this type of constraint to make sure a task will not start before a specific date.
	Start No Later Than (SNLT)	Project will schedule a task to start on or before the specified constraint date. Use this type of constraint to make sure a task will not start after a specific date.
	Finish No Earlier Than (FNET)	Project will schedule a task to finish on or after the specified constraint date. Use this type of constraint to ensure a task will not finish before a specific date.
	Finish No Later Than (FNLT)	Project will schedule a task to finish on or before the specified constraint date. Use this type of constraint to ensure that a task will not finish after a specific date.
Inflexible	Must Start On (MSO)	Project will schedule a task to start on the specified constraint date. Use this type of constraint to ensure that a task will begin on an exact date.
	Must Finish On (MFO)	Project will schedule a task to finish on the specified constraint date. Use this type of constraint to ensure that a task will end on an exact date.

APPLY A START NO EARLIER THAN CONSTRAINT TO A TASK

USE the project schedule you created in the previous exercise.

1. Select task 38, **Scene 2 begin**. This scene will be shot at a location that is not available until May 26, 2011.

2. On the Task tab, click the **Scroll to Task** button, located in the Editing group. The Gantt bars for this task come into view.

Scroll to Task

3. Double-click **task 38**. The Task Information dialog box appears.

4. Click the **Advanced** tab. In the Constrain task section, next to Constraint Type, select **Start No Earlier Than** from the drop-down box.

5. In the Date box, key or select **May 26, 2011**. Your screen should look similar to Figure 4-14.

Figure 4-14

Task Information dialog box
with Start No Earlier Than
constraint and constraint date
entered

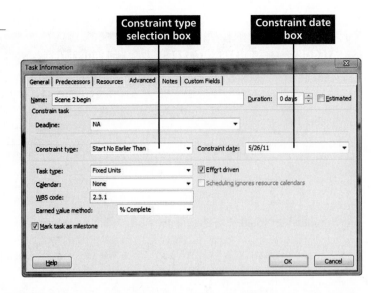

TAKE NOTE*

Unless you specify otherwise, Microsoft Project schedules the start or finish time of a constraint date using the Default Start Time or Default End Time value you established at the beginning of your project (on the File tab, click Options, then click the Schedule section).

6. Click **OK**. Note the highlighted cells showing the effect of this change. Widen the table as necessary to view additional data columns.

7. The constraint is applied and a constraint icon appears in the Indicators column. When you point to the icon, constraint details are shown in a ScreenTip. The task is rescheduled to start on May 26, and all other tasks that depend on task 38 are also rescheduled.

8. **SAVE** the project schedule.

   PAUSE. LEAVE the project schedule open to use in the next exercise.

TROUBLESHOOTING

Avoid entering task start and finish dates unless absolutely necessary. When you enter start or finish dates, Project applies semi-flexible constraints such as Start No Earlier Than or Finish No Earlier Than, which prevents the project manager from taking advantage of the Microsoft Project scheduling engine.

Keep the following points in mind when setting constraints for tasks:

• To remove a constraint, click Project on the menu bar, then click Task Information. In the Task Information dialog box, click the Advanced tab. In the Constraint Type box, select As Soon As Possible (if scheduling from the start date) or As Late As Possible (if scheduling from the finish date).

• If you try to apply inflexible or semi-flexible constraints to tasks in addition to task links, you might create what is known as ***negative slack***—the amount of time that tasks overlap due to a conflict between task relationships and constraints. For example, a task with a Must Start On (MSO) constraint for April 24 and a finish-to-start relationship to another task will always be scheduled for April 24, no matter when its predecessor finishes. To set Microsoft Project to honor relationships over constraints, select the File tab, click Options, and then click the Schedule option. Under Schedule Options for this project, clear the Tasks will always honor their constraint dates check box.

- Some constraint behaviors change if you must schedule a project from a finish date rather than a start date. For instance, the ALAP constraint type becomes the default for new tasks, rather than ASAP. Pay close attention to the constraints you apply in this case to make sure the results are what you expect.

A new feature in Microsoft Project 2010 that is helpful in reviewing constraints, assignments, and dependencies is the Task Inspector. You can use the Task Inspector to determine the factor(s) driving the start date of a task or to follow a chain of factors to find the cause of a delay. You can access the Task Inspector by clicking the Task tab, then clicking Inspect in the Tasks group. The Task Inspector pane will appear on the left side of your screen. Figure 4-15 shows the Task Inspector pane activated for task 50.

Figure 4-15

Task Inspector activated for task 50

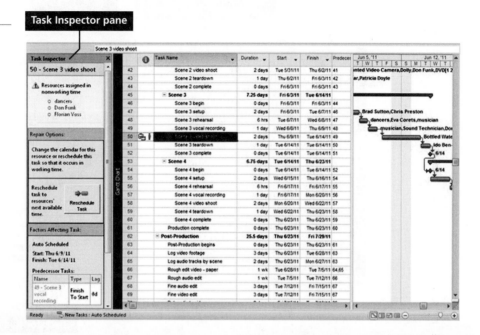

■ Reviewing the Project's Critical Path

THE BOTTOM LINE

In every project, there is a series of tasks, known as the *critical path*, that directly affect the finish date of the project. If the start or completion of any one of these tasks is delayed, the finish date of the entire project will be delayed.

Reviewing the Project's Critical Path

The term "critical" refers not to the importance of the tasks in the critical path, but rather to the impact that the scheduling of these tasks has on the finish date of the project. One of the best ways to shorten the overall duration of a project is to shorten its critical path. In Project 2010, you can review your project's critical path, including any existing *free slack*—the amount of time a task can be delayed before it will delay another task. In this exercise, you review your project's critical path.

REVIEW THE PROJECT'S CRITICAL PATH

USE the project schedule you created in the previous exercise.

1. Click the **Task** tab, then click the **downward arrow** under the Gantt chart button; the view list appears. Select **More Views**.

2. In the More Views dialog box, select **Detail Gantt**, then click the **Apply** button. The project schedule is displayed in the Detail Gantt view.

3. Press the **F5** key. The Go To dialog box appears. In the ID box, key **51**, then click **OK**. The view shifts so that the Gantt bar for task 51 is visible. Scroll down so that most of the tasks after task 51 are visible and you can see more of the critical path. Your screen should look similar to Figure 4-16. Almost all of the tasks that fall after task 50, Scene 3 video shoot, are on the critical path, which is shown in red. Noncritical tasks are displayed in blue and also show free slack. (Total slack is shown as the thin bar that extends to the right of the task bar.)

Figure 4-16

Gantt chart showing critical path tasks from task 51 onward

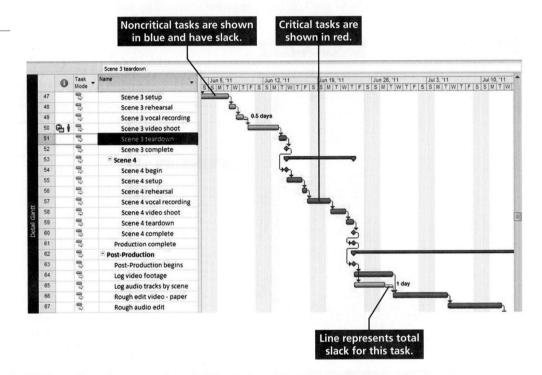

4. **SAVE** the project schedule.

PAUSE. LEAVE the project schedule open to use in the next exercise.

To fully understand the critical path concept, there are a few other terms with which you need to be familiar. Microsoft Project uses the term *slack* in place of the term *float*. **Float** or **slack** is the amount of time a task can be delayed without causing a delay to another task or to the overall project. *Free Float* (or *Free Slack*) is the amount of time a task can be delayed before it will delay another task. *Total Float* (or *Total Slack*) is the amount of time a task can be delayed without delaying the project end date. A task is usually considered to be on the critical path if its total float is zero (or occasionally, less than some specified amount). Conversely, *noncritical tasks* have float greater than zero. Their start or finish dates can vary within their slack amounts without affecting the finish date of the project.

■ Viewing Resource Allocations Over Time

THE BOTTOM LINE

As a project manager, you are responsible for distributing work among the people and equipment resources of the project. *Allocation* is the portion of a resource's capacity devoted to work on a specific task. Allocation is how you manage resources and their assignments over time.

Reviewing Resource Allocations

You need to be able to review each resource's allocation, identify any problems that are evident, and adjust allocations as needed. In this exercise, you review your resources to identify allocation issues.

→ REVIEW RESOURCE ALLOCATIONS

USE the project schedule you created in the previous exercise.

1. On the Task tab, in the View group, click the **downward arrow** under the Gantt Chart button. Select **More Views**.

2. In the More Views dialog box, locate and select the **Resource Allocation** view. Click **Apply**. A split view appears: the Resource Usage view is on the top, and the Leveling Gantt Chart view is on the bottom. Your screen should look similar to Figure 4-17.

Figure 4-17

Split view, with Resource Usage view on top and Leveling Gantt view on the bottom

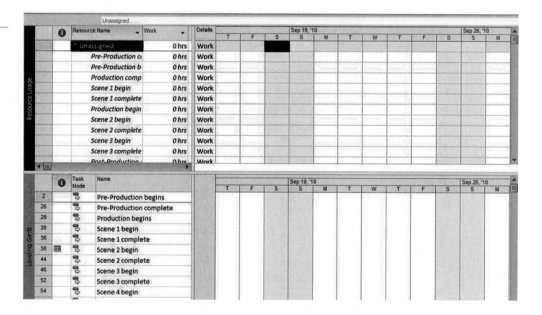

On the left side of the Resource Usage view is the Usage table, which shows assignments grouped by resource, the total work assigned to each resource, and the work for each assignment. The table's outline format can be expanded and collapsed. The right side of the view contains assignment details (default setting is work) displayed on a timescale.

3. In the Usage table, click the **Resource Name** column heading.

 Outline ▾

4. Click the **View** tab. In the Data group, click the **Outline** button, then select **Hide Subtasks**. Microsoft Project collapses the Resource Usage view. The resources' total work values over the project timescale appear in the grid on the right. In the Resource Name column, click **Unassigned**. Your screen should look similar to Figure 4-18.

TAKE NOTE *

Don't worry if you see a resource group titled Unassigned. Sometimes there are tasks that have no specific resources assigned to them. These tasks are grouped together in this view and listed as a resource named Unassigned.

Scroll
to Task

5. In the Resource Name column, click the name of resource 3, **Jeff Pike**.

6. Click the **Task** tab, then click the **Scroll to Task** button. Project scrolls the grid to show Jeff Pike's earliest assignment: eight hours on Monday, January 10. At the bottom of the screen, the Gantt chart view shows the actual tasks to which Jeff is assigned.

Figure 4-18

Collapsed Resource usage view

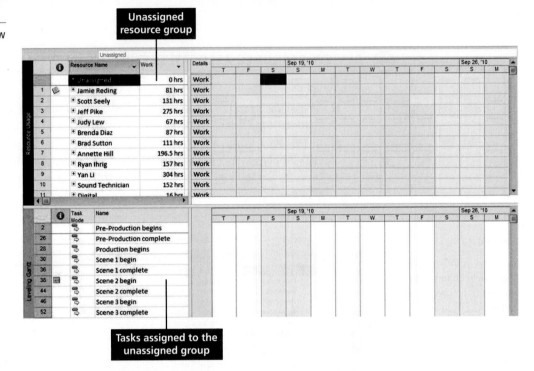

7. Click the **View** tab. In the Zoom group, click the **downward arrow** next to the Timescale units box and select **Months**. The timescaled grid now shows work values per month. Your screen should look similar to Figure 4-19.

Figure 4-19

Timescaled grid showing monthly work assignment values

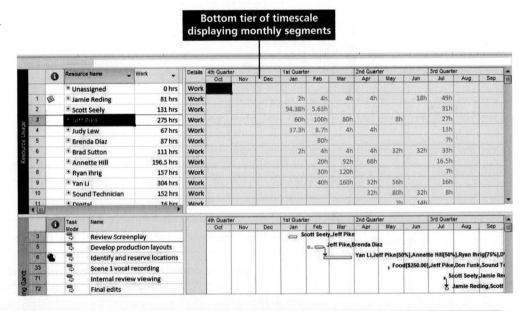

ANOTHER WAY

Instead of using the Timescale command (or Timescale units box) to change the tiers of the timescale, you can click the zoom slider located in the lower right of your screen. If this method doesn't provide the level of detail you need, then you can use the Timescale command.

8. SAVE the project schedule. **CLOSE** the project schedule.

PAUSE. If you are continuing to the next lesson, keep Project open. If you are not continuing to additional lessons, close Project.

As the project manager, the decisions you make regarding task assignments affect the workloads of the resources on the project. Every resource is said to be in one of three states of allocation:

1. *Underallocated:* Here, the work assigned to a resource is less than the resource's maximum capacity. For example, a full-time resource that has only 20 hours of work assigned in a 40-hour work week is underallocated.

2. *Fully allocated:* This describes the condition of a resource when the total work of its task assignments is exactly equal to its work capacity. For example, a full-time resource that is assigned to work 40 hours per week is fully allocated.

3. *Overallocated:* Here, the work assigned to a resource is more than the resource's maximum capacity. For example, a full-time resource that has 55 hours of work assigned in a 40-hour work week is overallocated.

Allocating resources takes a combination of skill and common sense. It might seem straightforward to say that all resources should be fully allocated all of the time, but this is not always possible, practical, or even desirable. There are situations in which overallocation or underallocation is quite acceptable. As the project manager, you must learn how to identify allocation problems and how to handle them.

You might also want to keep the following points in mind when reviewing resource allocation:

- In the Resource Usage view, the default table is the Usage table. You can display other table views by clicking the View tab, then clicking Usage in the Table command group and selecting the table you want to display.

- Work values are the default in the timescaled grid of the Resource Usage view. To display other assignment values, such as cost, click the Format tab, then click Details and select the value you want to display.

SKILL SUMMARY

IN THIS LESSON, YOU LEARNED:	TASK
To apply a task calendar to an individual task.	Apply a task calendar to an individual task.
To change task types.	Change scheduling formula values to change task types.
	Change a task type using the Task Information dialog box.
To split a task.	Split a task.
To establish recurring tasks.	Set up a recurring task.
	Assign resources to a recurring task.
To apply task constraints.	Apply a Start No Earlier Than constraint to a task.
To review a project's critical path.	Review a project's critical path.
To view resource allocations over time.	Explore resource allocations.

■ Knowledge Assessment

Matching

Match the term in column 1 with its description in column 2.

Column 1	Column 2

1. critical path   **a.** The amount of time a task can be delayed before it will delay another task

2. free slack   **b.** A restriction that controls the start or finish date of a task

3. split   **c.** The condition of a resource when the total work of its task assignments is exactly equal to its work capacity

4. underallocated   **d.** The amount of time a task can be delayed without delaying the project end date

5. recurring task   **e.** The series of tasks whose scheduling directly affects the project's finish date

6. fixed units   **f.** A restriction that forces a task to begin or end on a certain date, completely preventing the rescheduling of a task

7. constraint   **g.** An interruption in a task

8. fully allocated   **h.** The condition of a resource when the work assigned to the resource is less than the resource's maximum capacity

9. inflexible constraint   **i.** A task that is repeated at specific intervals

10. total slack   **j.** A task type in which the units value does not change

True/False

Circle T if the statement is true or F if the statement is false.

T | F **1.** It is always best to enter a start or finish date for every task.

T | F **2.** By default, critical path tasks are shown in red in the Detail Gantt view.

T | F **3.** It is never acceptable to have an overallocated resource.

T | F **4.** It is not possible to split a task over a weekend.

T | F **5.** Effort-driven scheduling and changing a task type both affect all resources in the same way.

T | F **6.** You cannot change the task type for a summary task.

T | F **7.** You can use a task calendar to schedule a task that will occur during a time that is not on the project calendar.

T | F **8.** It is acceptable to have a resource group named Unassigned.

T | F **9.** It is not possible to set a specific time of day for a recurring task.

T | F **10.** You can split a task only three times.

■ Competency Assessment

Project 4-1: Adjusting Working Time for Office Remodel

You are in charge of the kitchen and lunchroom remodel for your office. Based on feedback from your associates, you have decided to schedule the drywall installation after working hours because of noise concerns. You need to set up a task calendar that reflects the different working hours.

GET READY. Launch Microsoft Project if it is not already running. **OPEN** *Office Remodel 4-1* from the data files for this lesson.

1. Click the **Project** tab, then click **Change Working Time**.
2. In the Change Working Time dialog box, click **Create New Calendar**.
3. In the Name box, key **Evening Drywall Install**.
4. If it is not already selected, click the **Make a copy of** button. In the drop-down menu, select **Standard**, then click **OK**.
5. Click the **Work Weeks** tab in the Change Working Time dialog box, then click the **Details** button.
6. In the Select Days box, drag your pointer to select **Monday** through **Friday**. Click the **Set day(s) to these specific working times** button.
7. Click the cell in row 1 of the From column and key **4:00 p.m.** Click the cell in row 1 of the To column and key **12:00 a.m.** Click the cell in row 2 of the From column and press **Delete**. Click **OK**. Click **OK** again to close the Change Working Time dialog box.
8. Double-click task 9, **Install drywall**. The Task Information dialog box appears.
9. Click the **Advanced** tab.
10. In the Calendar box, select **Evening Drywall Install** from the drop-down list.
11. Click the **Scheduling ignores resource calendars** check box, then click **OK**.
12. **SAVE** the project schedule as *Office Remodel Drywall Install*, then **CLOSE** the file. **LEAVE** Project open for the next exercise.

The *Office Remodel 4-1* file for this lesson is available on the book companion website.

Project 4-2: Weekly Meeting for Hiring a New Employee

You have developed a project schedule for hiring a new employee. You now need to add a recurring weekly status meeting to your tasks.

OPEN *Hiring New Employee 4-2* from the data files for this lesson.

1. Select the name of task 5, **Collect resumes**.
2. Click the **Task** tab. In the Insert group, click the **downward arrow** under the Task button, then select **Recurring Task**.
3. In the Task Name box, key **Status Meeting**.
4. In the Duration box, key **1h**.
5. Under Recurrence pattern, select **Daily**.
6. In the Every box, key or select **3** and then select **workdays**.
7. In the Start box, key or select **11/1/11**.
8. Under Range of Recurrence, select **End after**, then key or select **10** occurrences.
9. Click **OK**.
10. **SAVE** the project schedule as *Hiring New Employee Recurring*, then **CLOSE** the file. **LEAVE** Project open for the next exercise.

The *Hiring New Employee 4-2* file for this lesson is available on the book companion website.

■ Proficiency Assessment

Project 4-3: Splitting a Task for Setting Up a Home Office

You are in the process of setting up a home office, and you have just been notified that you will need to be out of town from Wednesday, October 12, through Friday, October 14, for a training session. You need to adjust your project schedule to reflect this out-of-town time.

OPEN *Home Office 4-3* from the data files for this lesson.

The *Home Office 4-3* file for this lesson is available on the book companion website.

1. Change the view to Gantt chart view.
2. Select the name of task 13. Scroll to the bar chart view for this task.
3. Use the Split Task Button to shift the task from Wednesday, October 12, to Monday, October 17 (because you will not be in town from Wednesday through Friday).
4. **SAVE** the project schedule as *Home Office Split Task*, then **CLOSE** the file.

   LEAVE Project open to use in the next exercise.

Project 4-4: Setting a Constraint for the Don Funk Music Video

You have just been informed that Don Funk is not available for the formal approval viewing until July 20, 2011. You need to set a constraint for this task so that it cannot start until July 20.

OPEN *Don Funk Music Video 4-4* from the data files for this lesson.

The *Don Funk Music Video 4-4* file for this lesson is available on the book companion website

1. Select the name of task 73. Scroll the Gantt bars to this task.
2. Click the **Task** tab. Select the **Information** button in the Properties group.
3. Click the **Advanced** tab and set a Start No Earlier Than constraint with a date of **July 21, 2011**.
4. **SAVE** the project schedule as *Don Funk Constraint*, then **CLOSE** the file.

   LEAVE Project open to use in the next exercise.

■ Mastery Assessment

Project 4-5: Hiring a New Employee–Adding Resources to the Recurring Status Meeting

Earlier, in Project 4-2, you established a recurring status meeting for the Hiring a New Employee project schedule. Now you will add resources to that task.

OPEN *Hiring New Employee Recurring 4-5* from the data files for this lesson.

The *Hiring New Employee Recurring 4-5* file for this lesson is available on the book companion website.

1. Assign the resources Amy Rusko, Barry Potter, Gabe Mares, and Jeff Smith to the Status Meeting recurring task.
2. Expand the subtasks for the recurring task to visually confirm that the resources have been assigned.
3. **SAVE** the project schedule as *Hiring New Employee Recurring Resources*, then **CLOSE** the file.

   LEAVE Project open to use in the next exercise.

Project 4-6: Don Funk Music Video Overallocated Resources

Review the resource allocations for the Don Funk Music Video. Pay close attention to any overallocated resources.

OPEN *Don Funk Music Video 4-6* from the data files for this lesson.

The *Don Funk Music Video 4-6* file for this lesson is available on the book companion website.

1. Use the Resource Usage view to review resource assignments for this project.

2. Locate Yan Li, then review his task assignments for the weeks of April 17 and April 24, 2011.

3. In a separate Word document, write a brief paragraph detailing Yan Li's assignments for those weeks. Include any times that he is overallocated, and discuss whether you think the overallocation is critical or can be left as is.

4. **SAVE** the project schedule as *Don Funk-Yan Li*, then **CLOSE** the file. **SAVE** the Word document as *Don Funk-Yan Li Discussion*, then **CLOSE** that file as well.

   CLOSE both Project and Word.

INTERNET READY

Many sites on the Internet provide Microsoft Project templates for public use. You can download a template that someone else has created and modify it to fit your specific needs. You will find a large variety of templates at Microsoft Office Online.

Open Microsoft Project. Click File, then click New. In the Office.com Templates section, click the Search Office.com for templates box. Then search Microsoft Office Online for a Project template that is of some personal interest to you. Download the template. Using the skills you learned in this lesson, change the view so that you can review the critical path of the project. Study how the tasks are linked and why some tasks are not on the critical path. Make changes to some of the start dates to see the effects of your changes on the critical path.

5 LESSON

Fine-Tuning Tasks

LESSON SKILL MATRIX

SKILLS	TASKS
Managing Task Constraints and Relationships	Explore the effects of constraints and relationships on task scheduling.
Setting Deadline Dates	Set a deadline date for a task.
Establishing Task Priorities	Establish task priorities.
Establish Manually Scheduled Mode Tasks	Establish manually scheduled tasks.

You are a project manager for Southridge Video, and recently, one of your primary responsibilities has been to manage the new Don Funk Music Video project. So far, you have learned most of the basics for building a project schedule, communicating project data to shareholders, and tracking work. In this lesson, you will learn some of the more advanced features of Microsoft Project 2010 that focus on fine-tuning the details in a project schedule prior to saving a baseline and commencing work.

KEY TERMS
deadline
manually scheduled tasks
resource leveling
task priority

■ SOFTWARE ORIENTATION

Microsoft Project's Task Information Dialog Box—General Tab

The General tab of the Task Information dialog box provides general information about a selected task, and it allows you to make changes and updates to the task. On the General tab, you can edit the task name, update the duration and the percent complete, change the priority, and modify the start and finish dates.

Figure 5-1

General tab of the Task Information dialog box

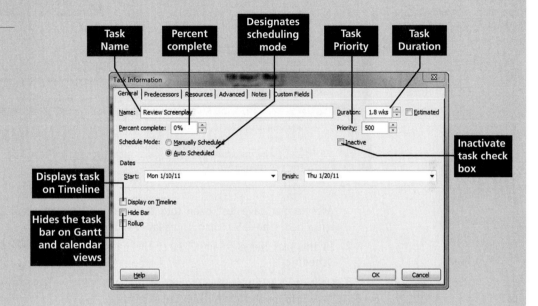

■ Managing Task Constraints and Dependencies

THE BOTTOM LINE

As you build a project schedule, you will usually use both task relationships and constraints within the schedule. You can control how Microsoft Project schedules these elements. Recall that Project alerts you to conflicts between relationships and constraints so that you can maintain control over the rules that the software follows. It is important to understand the effects of the constraints you apply on the overall project schedule—not just on the specific tasks to which you apply the constraints.

Exploring Effects of Constraints and Dependencies

In this exercise, you review two basic elements of scheduling—constraints and task relationships—and learn how to control the actions of Microsoft Project when there is a conflict between a constraint and a task relationship. Note that Project always honors constraint dates over task relationships by default, even if this causes negative float (slack).

The *Don Funk Music Video 5M* file for this lesson is available on the book companion website.

GET READY. Before you begin these steps, launch Microsoft Project. **OPEN** the *Don Funk Music Video 5M* project schedule from the data files for this lesson. **SAVE** the file as *Don Funk Music Video 5* in the solutions folder for this lesson as directed by your instructor.

1. In the Gantt chart view, review the start-to-finish dependency between tasks 3 and 4. Your screen should look similar to Figure 5-2.

Figure 5-2

Gantt chart view with start-to-finish relationship between tasks 3 and 4

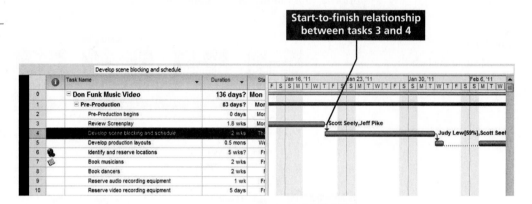

Assume you have just been told that task 4, Develop scene blocking and schedule, must begin no later than Thursday, January 13, 2011.

2. In the Task Name column, select the name of task 4, **Develop scene blocking and schedule**.

3. On the Task tab, in the Properties group, click the **Task Information** button. The Task Information dialog box appears.

4. Click the **Advanced** tab.

5. In the Constraint Type box, select **Start No Later Than**. In the Constraint Date box, key or select **January 13, 2011**.

6. Click **OK** to close the dialog box. The Planning Wizard appears, notifying you of a scheduling conflict between the constraint you just applied to task 4 and the existing task dependency between tasks 3 and 4. Your screen should look similar to Figure 5-3.

Figure 5-3

Planning Wizard dialog box

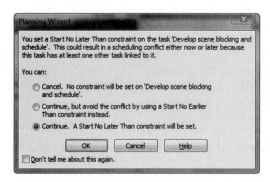

7. In the You Can selection list, click **Continue. A Start No Later Than constraint will be set.**

8. Click **OK**.

9. A second alert appears. Click **Continue**. **Allow the scheduling conflict**, then click **OK**. Microsoft Project applies the SNLT constraint to task 4 and reschedules it to start on Thursday, as shown in Figure 5-4.

Figure 5-4

Gantt chart with SNLT constraint applied

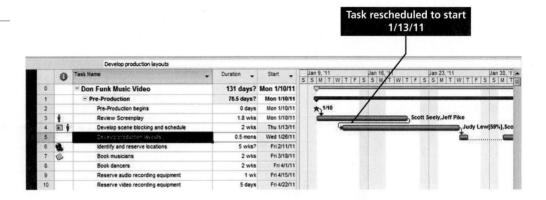

Microsoft Project would reschedule task 4 to avoid the negative slack between tasks 3 and 4, but this SNLT constraint prevents the software from doing so.

TAKE NOTE*   Note that the red human icon appears in the indicators column, notifying you that this action causes a resource overallocation on both tasks.

10. Click the **File** tab, then click **Options**.

11. Select the **Schedule** options, then navigate to the **Scheduling options for this project** section. Your screen should look similar to Figure 5-5.

Figure 5-5

Scheduling Options dialog box

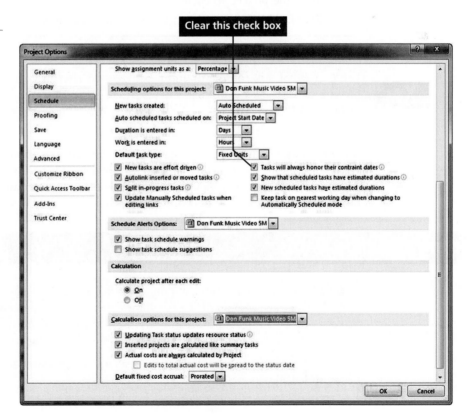

12. Clear the **Tasks will always honor their constraint dates** check box, then click **OK**. A calendar alert icon appears in the indicators column for task 4.

13. Rest the mouse pointer on the calendar alert icon in the indicators column. A ScreenTip appears. Now Microsoft Project honors the task relationship over the constraint. Microsoft Project preserves the constraint information, but it does not honor the constraint. If the scheduling conflict is removed (by a change in task duration, for example), Microsoft Project would then honor the constraint. Your screen should look similar to Figure 5-6.

Figure 5-6

Calendar alert and ScreenTip

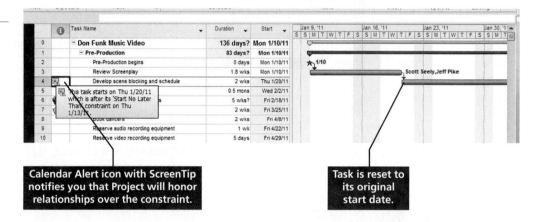

Calendar Alert icon with ScreenTip notifies you that Project will honor relationships over the constraint.

Task is reset to its original start date.

14. Click the **File** tab again, then click **Options**. Select the **Schedule** options, then navigate to the **Scheduling options for this project** section.

15. Click the **Tasks will always honor their constraint dates** check box on the Schedule tab, then click **OK**. This restores the default behavior to Microsoft Project, and task 4 is rescheduled to honor its constraint date.

16. **SAVE** the project schedule.

PAUSE. LEAVE Project open to use in the next exercise.

For a review of task constraints and negative slack, refer to Lesson 4. The best way to prevent negative slack is through the use of leads and lags, which are discussed in detail in Lesson 13.

It is a good idea to develop a consistent strategy for using constraints and relationships in your projects. One recommendation is to use the default behavior of honoring constraint dates. As you learned in previous lessons, you should always set task relationships in your projects, then apply semi-flexible or inflexible constraints only when truly necessary.

■ Setting Deadline Dates

THE BOTTOM LINE

A *deadline* is a date value you enter for a task that indicates the latest date by which you want the task to be completed. The deadline date itself does not constrain the task. When you enter a deadline date, Microsoft Project displays a deadline marker on the Gantt chart and alerts you if the task's finish date moves beyond the deadline.

Assigning a deadline date to a task, rather than a semi-flexible or inflexible constraint, allows the most flexibility in scheduling tasks.

Setting Task Deadline Dates

Rather than using semi-flexible or inflexible constraints, a better approach to scheduling is to use the default As Soon As Possible (ASAP) constraint and then enter a deadline for the task. In this exercise, you enter a deadline date for a task rather than entering a constraint.

⊖ SET A DEADLINE DATE FOR A TASK

USE the project schedule you created in the previous exercise.

1. Press the **F5** key; the Go To dialog box appears.
2. In the ID box, key **26**, then click **OK**. Microsoft Project displays task 26. You want to make sure that the pre-production tasks conclude by May 4, 2011, so you will enter a deadline date for this milestone.
3. Double-click the task name of task 26, **Pre-production complete**. The Task Information dialog box appears.
4. Click the **Advanced** tab.
5. In the drop-down date box next to Deadline, key or select **5/4/11**, then click **OK**. Microsoft Project inserts a deadline marker in the chart portion of the Gantt chart view. Your screen should look similar to Figure 5-7.

Figure 5-7

Gantt chart view with deadline indicator on task 26

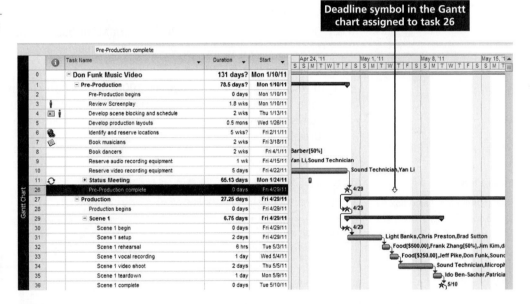

If the scheduled completion of a task moves past the deadline date, Microsoft Project displays a missed deadline indicator in the indicators column. To remove a deadline from a task, clear the Deadline field on the Advanced tab of the Task Information dialog box.

6. Double-click the name of task 27, **Production**. The Task Information dialog box appears. Click the **Advanced** tab.
7. In the drop-down date box next to Deadline, key or select **6/10/11**, then click **OK**. Microsoft Project inserts a deadline date marker for the summary task. Scroll the chart portion of the Gantt chart view to the right to view the marker.

TAKE NOTE*

A deadline date will cause Microsoft Project to notify you if the scheduled completion of a task exceeds its deadline date. Entering a deadline date has no effect on the scheduling of a summary task or subtask, except in one situation, which involves slack. When any task is assigned a deadline date, its slack will not extend beyond the deadline date.

8. **SAVE** the project schedule.

PAUSE. LEAVE Project open to use in the next exercise.

■ Establishing Task Priorities

THE BOTTOM LINE

Task priority is a numeric ranking between 0 and 1000 of a task's importance. Microsoft Project uses task priorities to determine which tasks can be delayed in order to resolve periods of resource overallocation. The default task priority Microsoft Project assigns is 500.

➔ ESTABLISH TASK PRIORITIES

USE the project schedule you created in the previous exercise.

1. In the Task Name column, select the name of task 6, **Identify and reserve locations**.

2. On the Task tab, click the **Task Information** button, located in the Properties group. The Task Information dialog box appears.

3. Click the **General** tab.

4. In the Priority box, key or select **1000**. Your screen should look similar to Figure 5-8. Note that there is a message at the bottom of the Task Information dialog box that states the task will not be moved through either Resource Leveling or the Prevent Overallocations mode.

Figure 5-8

Task Information dialog box for task 6 with Priority set to 1000

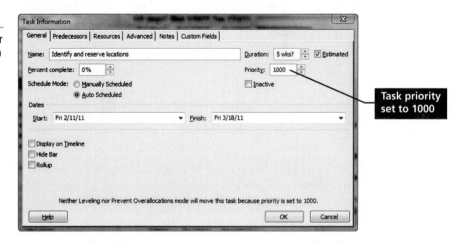

5. Click **OK** to close the dialog box. Microsoft Project adjusts the task's priority. Note that there is no visual indicator for the adjusted priority, and the effect of the new task's priority is only apparent after resource leveling.

ANOTHER WAY

To simultaneously adjust the priority of multiple tasks, select the desired tasks by clicking and holding the Ctrl key. Click the Task Information button, then click the General tab and enter the desired priority in the Priority box. Note that because you have selected multiple tasks, this dialog box is now labeled Multiple Task Information.

6. SAVE the project schedule.

PAUSE. LEAVE Project open to use in the next exercise.

In this exercise, you set the priority for a task, giving it the highest priority possible in Microsoft Project (1000). A task with a priority of 1000 is never delayed by leveling. *Resource leveling* is the process of delaying a resource's work on a task to resolve an overallocation. Depending on the options you choose, resource leveling might delay the start date of an assignment or an entire task, or it may split the work on a task. Resource leveling evaluates several factors to determine how to resolve resource overallocation.

You can find more information about resource leveling in Lesson 6.

One of the factors evaluated during resource leveling is task priority. Recall that task priority is a numeric ranking between 0 and 1000 of a task's importance and appropriateness for leveling. When you level resources, Microsoft Project will delay a task with a lower priority before delaying a task with a higher priority in order to resolve a resource overallocation:

- Tasks with priority 0 are leveled first, so they are likely to be delayed by leveling.
- Tasks with priority 1000 are never delayed by leveling. Assign this task priority carefully, because it limits Microsoft Project's capability to resolve resource overallocations.

■ Establishing Manually Scheduled Tasks

THE BOTTOM LINE

Some tasks require a project manager to schedule manually, without regard to predecessors or other project constraints. You can use the new feature called Manual Scheduling for this action.

Manually Scheduling Tasks

NEW FEATURE

In this exercise, you practice establishing a manually scheduled task. Say you have just been informed that your audio team and video team have met and they are unsure about the outcome of the fine editing tasks. The task of dubbing the audio to the video is dependent on one but not both of these tasks. After meeting with the team, you decide to change the scheduling mode of task 70 to manual scheduling.

⊕ ESTABLISH A MANUALLY SCHEDULED TASK

USE the project schedule you created in the previous exercise.

Manually
Schedule

1. Press the **F5** key to open the Go To dialog box. In the ID box, key **70** and click **OK**.

2. On the Task tab, in the Tasks group, click the **Manually Schedule** button. Note that the Gantt bar has changed to the default formatting of a manually scheduled task. Your screen should look similar to Figure 5-9.

Figure 5-9

Gantt chart view with task 70 set to manually scheduled mode

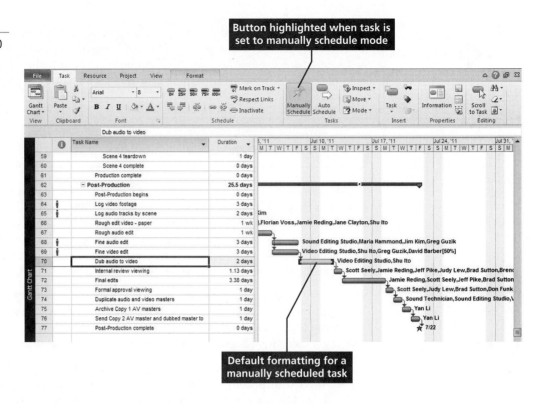

Button highlighted when task is set to manually schedule mode

Default formatting for a manually scheduled task

3. Click in the **Duration** cell of task 69, **Fine video edit**. You have just been informed that this task will now take five days instead of three. Key **5d** and press **Enter**. Notice that task 70 did not move from its original start date. Your screen should look like Figure 5-10.

Figure 5-10

Manually scheduled task that does not honor its relationship with its predecessor task

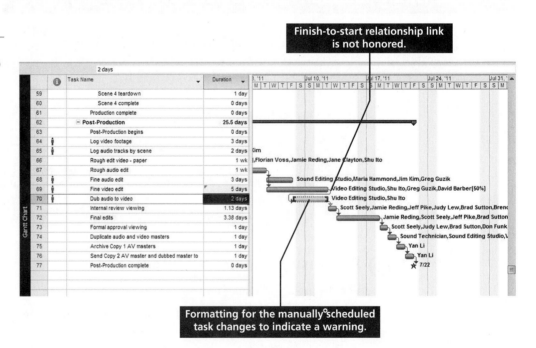

Finish-to-start relationship link is not honored.

Formatting for the manually scheduled task changes to indicate a warning.

4. Position the mouse pointer over the Gantt bar of the manually scheduled task. Notice that it displays a warning. Right-click the Gantt bar of the manually scheduled task and select **Fix in Task Inspector**. Your screen should look like Figure 5-11.

Figure 5-11

Task Inspector pane visible to make repairs to task 70

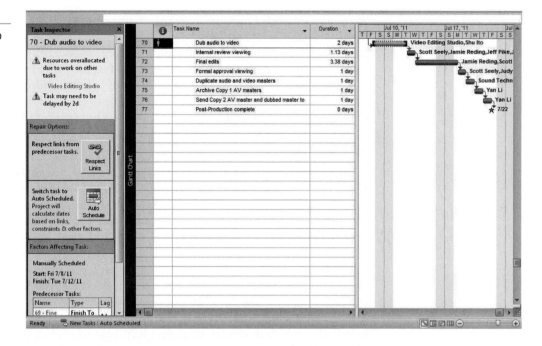

You can also activate the Task Inspector by selecting the Inspect button on the Task ribbon.

5. Review the various options and information in the Task Inspector pane. After reviewing this information, you decide that manually scheduling this task is not the best option. Thus, in the Task Inspector pane, under the Repair Options section, click the **Auto Schedule** button. Microsoft Project returns the task to auto-scheduled mode. Your screen should look like Figure 5-12.

Figure 5-12

Task 70 returned to auto-scheduled mode

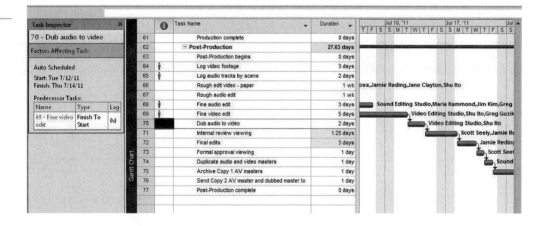

6. **DO NOT SAVE** the project schedule; **CLOSE** the file.

   PAUSE. If you are continuing to the next lesson, keep Project open. If you are not continuing to additional lessons, **CLOSE** Project.

Manually scheduled tasks are tasks that must be manually scheduled, calculated, and set by the operator. Such tasks may be needed at certain points in your project, and they require much more attention by the project manager. Manually scheduled tasks can allow you more scheduling flexibility, but they should be used sparingly. Microsoft Project treats manually scheduled tasks much differently from auto-scheduled tasks. In fact, certain features that are available with auto-scheduled tasks are not available with manually scheduled tasks. For example, Overtime, Actual Overtime, and Remaining Overtime cannot be tracked with manually scheduled tasks. You also cannot use task constraints or work contouring.

When using manually scheduled tasks, Microsoft Project treats nonworking times differently. If you use a manually scheduled task during normal working hours and on normal working days, you will not notice a difference. However, if you start a manually scheduled task on a non-work day, outside of normal, non-work hours, you will quickly see the difference. In essence, the system creates an exception on the calendar to close the gap between the manually scheduled task's start and the next working time. In the first release of Microsoft Project 2010, the leveling engine does not recognize work for a resource on any day that has this elapsed time exception. Therefore, it is recommended that you fully understand all the pros and cons of using manually scheduled tasks before employing them in your schedules. To better understand the differences between automatic and manual scheduling, visit http://office.microsoft.com/en-us/project-help/how-scheduling-works-in-project-HA010373148.aspx.

SKILL SUMMARY

IN THIS LESSON, YOU LEARNED:	TASK
To manage task constraints and relationships.	Explore the effects of constraints and relationships on task scheduling.
To set deadline dates.	Set a deadline date for a task.
To establish task priorities.	Establish task priorities.
To set manually scheduled mode tasks.	Establish manually scheduled tasks.

■ Knowledge Assessment

Fill in the Blank

Complete the following sentences by writing the correct word or words in the blanks provided.

1. A numeric ranking of a task's importance and appropriateness for leveling is called _____ .

2. A better approach to scheduling tasks is to use a deadline date rather than a(n) _____ .

3. When you link the tasks in a project schedule, you establish a(n) _____ between the tasks.

4. _____ is the process of delaying a resource's work on a task to resolve an overallocation.

5. Microsoft Project honors constraint dates over task relationships, even if this causes _____.

6. Tasks with a priority of _____ are leveled first.

7. When you enter a deadline date, Microsoft Project alerts you if the task's _____ moves beyond the deadline.

8. A(n) _____ is a value you enter for a task that indicates the latest date by which you want the task to be completed.

9. The default task priority value for all tasks is _____.

10. Tasks with a priority of _____ are never delayed by leveling.

Multiple Choice

Select the best response for the following statements.

1. Microsoft Project uses _____ to determine which tasks can be delayed in order to resolve periods of resource overallocation.
   a. load balancing
   b. random selection
   c. task priorities
   d. task deadlines

2. The numeric ranking range for task priority is:
   a. 1 to 100.
   b. 0 to 100.
   c. 1 to 500.
   d. 0 to 1000.

3. Entering a deadline date has no effect on the scheduling of a summary task or subtask, except when the task involves:
   a. slack.
   b. the critical path.
   c. dependencies.
   d. a priority equal to 0.

4. Which of the following is *not* a semi-flexible constraint?
   a. Start No Earlier Than
   b. Must Start On
   c. Finish No Earlier Than
   d. Start No Later Than

5. Depending on options you choose, resource leveling might:
   a. delay the start date of a specific resource's assignment.
   b. delay the start date of an entire task.
   c. split the work on a task.
   d. All of the above

6. What must you do to remove a deadline from a task?
   a. Delete the deadline indicator from the bar chart portion of the Gantt chart.
   b. Slide the deadline indicator off the active portion of the Gantt chart.
   c. Clear the Deadline field on the Advanced tab of the Project Information dialog box.
   d. Change the deadline date to 00/00/00.
7. Which of the following is *not* a type of task relationship?
   a. Finish to Start
   b. Finish to Finish
   c. Start to Start
   d. Start No Earlier Than
8. A deadline date:
   a. is the due date of the project.
   b. does not constrain a task.
   c. is not indicated on the Gantt chart.
   d. is a semi-flexible constraint.
9. Which of the following allows the most flexibility in scheduling a task?
   a. A semi-flexible constraint
   b. A deadline date
   c. An inflexible constraint
   d. None of the above
10. By default, Microsoft Project honors:
    a. constraint dates over dependencies.
    b. deadline dates over dependencies.
    c. dependencies over constraint dates.
    d. negative slack over dependencies.

■ Competency Assessment

Project 5-1: Setting a Constraint for Insurance Claim Processing

You are managing an insurance claim processing process, and you have just been informed that the repairer, Chris Gray, will not be available for work after June 7, 2011, for several days. You need to set a constraint on one of his tasks to reflect this information, even if it causes a conflict with existing task relationships.

GET READY. Launch Microsoft Project if it is not already running. **OPEN** *Insurance Claim Processing 5-1* from the data files for this lesson.

1. Click the name of task 16, **Repairer notifies adjuster**.
2. On the Task tab, click the **Task Information** button, located in the **Properties** group. Then click the **Advanced** tab.

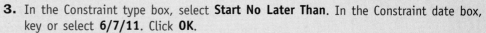

The *Insurance Claim Processing 5-1* file for this lesson is available on the book companion website.

3. In the Constraint type box, select **Start No Later Than**. In the Constraint date box, key or select **6/7/11**. Click **OK**.

4. In the Planning Wizard dialog box that appears, select the **Continue. A Start No Later Than constraint will be set**. option. Click **OK**.

5. In the next Planning Wizard dialog box that appears, select the **Continue. Allow the scheduling conflict** option, then click **OK**.

6. **SAVE** the project schedule as *Insurance Claim Processing Constraint,* then **CLOSE** the file.

   PAUSE. LEAVE Project open to use in the next exercise.

Project 5-2: Don Funk Music Video Deadlines

You have just received additional information about scheduling on the Don Funk Music Video, and you need to add some deadline dates to the project schedule.

OPEN *Don Funk Music Video 5-2* from the data files for this lesson.

1. Select the name of task 9, **Reserve audio recording equipment**.

2. On the Task tab, click the **Scroll to Task** button, located in the Editing group.

3. Double-click the task name cell of **task 9**. Then, click the **Advanced** tab.

4. In the Deadline box, key or select **5/6/11**. Click **OK**.

5. Select the name of task 61, **Production complete**. Click the **Scroll to Task** button.

6. On the Task tab, click the **Information** button, located in the Properties group.

7. Click the **Advanced** tab.

8. In the date box, key or select **6/22/11**, then click **OK**.

9. **SAVE** the project schedule as *Don Funk Deadlines,* then **CLOSE** the file.

   PAUSE. LEAVE Project open to use in the next exercise.

The *Don Funk Music Video 5-2* file for this lesson is available on the book companion website.

■ Proficiency Assessment

Project 5-3: Establishing Task Priorities for the HR Interview Schedule

You are making some changes and adjustment to your HR Interview project schedule, and you have decided to establish task priorities for some tasks in case there are resource allocation issues later.

OPEN *HR Interview 5-3* from the data files for this lesson.

1. Select the name of **task 21**.

2. Open the Task Information dialog box. Select the **General** tab.

3. Key or select a priority of **800**. Click **OK**.

4. Select the names of **tasks 13** and **14**.

5. Open the Task Information dialog box and select the **General** tab.

6. Key or select a priority of **400** for these two tasks. Click **OK**.
7. **SAVE** the project schedule as *HR Interview Priorities,* then **CLOSE** the file.
   PAUSE. **LEAVE** Project open to use in the next exercise.

Project 5-4: Setting Deadline Dates for the Office Remodel

You would like to keep a closer eye on some of the tasks for the office lunchroom remodel project you are managing. You decide it is a good idea to add some deadline dates to several tasks. You know that Microsoft Project will alert you if a task's finish date moves beyond the deadline.

OPEN *Office Remodel 5-4* from the data files for this lesson.

1. Select the name of **task 7**.
2. Open the Task Information dialog box. Select the **General** tab.
3. Set a deadline date of **11/4/11**.
4. Select the name of **task 14**.
5. Open the Task Information dialog box and select the **General** tab.
6. Set a deadline date of **11/25/11**.
7. **SAVE** the project schedule as *Office Remodel Deadlines,* then **CLOSE** the file.
   PAUSE. **LEAVE** Project open to use in the next exercise.

■ Mastery Assessment

Project 5-5: Changing Default Handling for Task Relationships/Constraints on Insurance Claim Processing

After a meeting with your project team, you decide to honor task relationships over constraints for the Insurance Claim schedule from Project 5-1. Another repairer has agreed to fill in for Chris Gray if necessary. Thus, you need to revise your project schedule to change the default method by which Microsoft Project handles dependencies and constraints.

OPEN *Insurance Claim Processing 5-5* from the data files for this lesson.

1. Review the task list.
2. Open the Options dialog box from the File tab.
3. Select **Schedule**.
4. Clear the check box so that tasks do not always honor their constraint dates.
5. Close the dialog box.
6. Review the task list and locate the task that has been affected by this change. In a separate Microsoft Word document, state the information that is contained in the calendar alert icon for this task, and briefly explain how your change affected the task.
7. **SAVE** the project schedule as *Insurance Claim No Default.* **SAVE** the Word document as *Insurance Claim No Default.* **CLOSE** both files.
   PAUSE. **LEAVE** Project open to use in the next exercise.

Project 5-6: Removing, Adding, and Changing Deadlines

You just finished reviewing the Don Funk Music Video project schedule, and you decide to make some changes and additions to the deadlines on this project.

OPEN *Don Funk Music Video 5-6* from the data files for this lesson.

The *Don Funk Music Video 5-6* file for this lesson is available on the book companion website.

1. Remove the deadline for **task 9**.
2. Change the deadline for **task 61** to **June 24, 2011**.
3. Add a deadline of **May 20, 2011** for **task 36**.
4. **SAVE** the project schedule as *Don Funk Revised Deadlines*, then **CLOSE** the file. **CLOSE** Project.

■ Circling Back 1

Mete Goktepe is a project management specialist at Woodgrove Bank. The management at Woodgrove has recently decided that the eight-year-old commercial lending software currently in use is outdated and needs to be replaced. Mete has been assigned as the project manager for the Request for Proposal (RFP) process to evaluate and select new software. This process entails determining needs, identifying vendors, requesting proposals, reviewing proposals, and selecting the software.

⊙ Project 1: Entering Tasks

Acting as Mete, you first need to enter project information, then enter and organize the tasks for this project.

GET READY. Launch Project if it is not already running.

1. In the status bar, click **New tasks: Manually Scheduled**, then click **Auto Scheduled—Tasks dates are calculated by Microsoft Project**.
2. Click the **Project** tab, then click **Project Information**. Set the start date as **May 2, 2011**.
3. **SAVE** the project plan as *RFP Bank Software Tasks*.
4. In the Properties group on the Ribbon, click the **Change Working Time** button.
5. Add the following exception dates:
   - Memorial Day to begin on May 30, 2011, and to occur yearly on the last Monday of May for two occurrences
   - Independence Day to begin on July 4, 2011, and to occur yearly on July 4 for two occurrences
   - Labor Day to begin on September 5, 2011, and to occur the first Monday of September for two occurrences
   - Veterans' Day to begin on November 11, 2011, and to occur on November 11 for two occurrences
   - Thanksgiving Day to begin on November 24, 2011, and to occur on the fourth Thursday of November for two occurrences
   - Christmas Day to occur on December 25, 2011, and to occur on December 25 for two occurrences
   - Christmas Holiday to occur on December 26, 2011
6. Close the Change Working Time dialog box.
7. In the Gantt chart view, enter the following task names (in order) and durations (enter all tasks, even if no duration is listed). (This is a partial list of tasks in the project plan. Additional data will be available in future exercises.)

TASK NAME	DURATION
RFP Solicitation Process	
RFP Solicitation Process Begins	0d
RFP Creation	
RFP creation begins	0d
Document software requirements	8d
Define evaluation criteria	2d
Identify evaluation team	1d
Draft RFP	5d
Review RFP with management and commercial lending representatives	1d
Refine RFP	1d
RFP ready to release	0d
RFP Release	
RFP release begins	0d
Identify software suppliers	5d
Determine deadline dates for vendor responses	2h
Finalize RFP with timeframes and points of contact	6h
Release RFP to target companies	2d
Conduct RFP briefing	1d
RFP release complete	0d
RFP Solicitation Process Complete	0d

8. **SAVE** the project plan.

9. Click the **Task** tab. Using the outline structure in the previous table, indent and outdent tasks as necessary to organize the tasks into phases.

10. **SAVE** the project plan.

11. Select **tasks 2, 4 through 11**, and **13 through 20**. Link them with a finish-to-start relationship.

12. **SAVE** the project plan.

    PAUSE. LEAVE Project and the project schedule open to use in the next exercise.

➔ Project 2: Establishing Resources

You now need to establish the resources that will perform the work on the tasks in this project plan.

USE the schedule you created in the previous exercise.

1. **SAVE** the project plan as *RFP Bank Software Resources*.

2. Change the view to the Resource Sheet.

3. Enter the following resource information on the Resource Sheet.

NAME	TYPE	INITIALS	GROUP	MAX UNITS	STD. RATE
Syed Abbas	Work	SA	CL Mgmt	100	2000/w
Eli Bowen	Work	EB	CL Mgmt	100	1850/w
Nicole Caron	Work	NC	IT Mgmt	100	2200/w
Aaron Con	Work	AC	IT Mgmt	100	2000/w
Andrew Dixon	Work	AD	IT	50	25/h
JoLynn Dobney	Work	JD	IT	100	1400/w
Mete Goktepe	Work	MG	IT	100	1250/w
Nicole Holliday	Work	NH	CL	50	20/h
Marc J. Ingle	Work	MJI	CL	100	1300/w
Kevin Kennedy	Work	KK	CL	100	1200/w
Dan Moyer	Work	DM	SR Mgmt	100	3000/w
Misty Shock	Work	MS	SR Mgmt	100	3500/w
Nate Sun	Work	NS	CL Ops	100	20/h
Tai Yee	Work	TY	CL Ops	100	19.50/h
Frank Miller	Work	FM	CL Ops	100	18/h
Jo Brown	Work	JB	CL Ops Mgmt	100	1850/w
Mike Tiano	Work	MT	CL Ops Mgmt	100	1900/w
CL Usergroup	Work	CLUG	CL	600	100/h
Digital Projector	Work	DP	Equip	200	0
Large Conference Room	LCR	Location	100	0	
Small Conference Room	SCR	Location	400	0	
Food/Catering	Cost	FOOD	Cost		
Travel	Cost	TRVL	Cost		

4. **SAVE** the project plan.

    PAUSE. LEAVE Project and the project schedule open to use in the next exercise.

 Project 3: Assigning Resources to Tasks

Finally, you need to assign the resources to the tasks in your project plan.

USE the schedule you created in the previous exercise.

1. **SAVE** the project plan as *RFP Bank Software Assignments*.
2. Switch to the Gantt chart view.
3. Click the **Resource** tab, then activate the Assign Resources dialog box.
4. Select the name of task 5, **Document software requirements**.
5. In the Assign Resources dialog box, select the following resources: **JoLynn Dobney**, **Nicole Holliday**, and **CL Usergroup**. Click the **Assign** button.
6. Select the name of task 6, **Define evaluation criteria**.
7. In the Assign Resources dialog box, select the following resources: **Mete Goktepe**, **Syed Abbas**, **Nicole Caron**, and **Mike Tiano**. Click the **Assign** button.

8. Using the same process that you used in steps 4–7, assign the following resources to the corresponding tasks.

Task #	Task Name	Resource Names to Assign
7	Identify evaluation team	Syed Abbas, Nicole Caron, Jo Brown
8	Draft RFP	Mete Goktepe, Kevin Kennedy
9	Review RFP with management	Mete Goktepe, Kevin Kennedy, Eli Bowen, Large Conference Room
10	Refine RFP	Mete Goktepe, Kevin Kennedy
14	Identify software suppliers	Mete Goktepe, Kevin Kennedy
15	Determine deadline dates	Eli Bowen, Mete Goktepe, Aaron Con
16	Finalize RFP with timeframes	Kevin Kennedy
17	Release RFP to target companies	Mete Goktepe, Kevin Kennedy
18	Conduct RFP briefing	Mete Goktepe, Kevin Kennedy, Nicole Caron, Small Conference Room

9. Select the name of task 5, **Document software requirements**.

10. In the Assign Resources dialog box, select the following resources: **Marc J. Ingle**, **Kevin Kennedy**, and **Andrew Dixon**. Assign these resources to the task.

11. In the Smart Tag Actions button that appears in the Indicators column, select **Reduce the hours that resources work per day. Keep duration and work the same**.

12. Select the name of task 9, **Review RFP with management and commercial lending representatives**.

13. In the Assign Resources dialog box, select the following resources: **Marc J. Ingle**, **Nicole Holliday**, and **Mike Tiano**. Assign these resources to the task.

14. In the Smart Tag Actions button that appears in the Indicators column, select **Increase total work because the task requires more person hours. Keep duration constant**.

15. Select the name of task 18, **Conduct RFP briefing**.

16. In the Assign Resources dialog box, select the following resources: **Eli Bowen** and **Jo Brown**. Assign these resources to the task.

17. In the Smart Tag Actions button that appears in the Indicators column, select **Reduce the hours that resources work per day. Keep duration and work the same**.

18. Click **Close** in the Assign Resources dialog box, then click **Done** in the Assign Resources pane.

19. **SAVE** and **CLOSE** the project schedule.

CLOSE Microsoft Project.

6 LESSON

Fine-Tuning Resources

LESSON SKILL MATRIX

SKILL	TASK
Entering Material Resource Consumption Rates	Enter a variable consumption rate for a material resource.
Entering Costs Per Use for Resources	Enter a cost per use for a resource.
Assigning Multiple Pay Rates for a Resource	Assign multiple pay rates for a resource.
Applying Different Cost Rates to Assignments	Apply a different cost rate to an assignment.
Specifying Resource Availability at Different Times	Specify a resource's availability over time.
Resolving Resource Overallocations Manually	Manually resolve a resource overallocation.
Leveling Overallocated Resources	Use resource leveling to resolve an overallocation.

You are a project manager for Southridge Video, and one of your primary responsibilities is managing the new Don Funk Music Video project. You have just finished applying some of the more advanced features of Microsoft Project 2010 that focus on fine-tuning task details in a project schedule prior to saving a baseline and commencing project work. Another important part of project management is to understand how to make the best use of resources' time, as people and equipment resources are often the most costly and limited part of a project. In this lesson, you will continue the fine-tuning activities on which you have been working, this time focusing on resources.

KEY TERMS
cost rate table
fixed consumption rate
variable consumption rate

■ Entering Material Resource Consumption Rates

 THE BOTTOM LINE   In order to accurately calculate the cost of a material resource, you need to know the resource's consumption rate, or how quickly it is used up.

ENTER A VARIABLE CONSUMPTION RATE FOR A MATERIAL RESOURCE

The *Don Funk Music Video 6M* file for this lesson is available on the book companion website.

Assign Resources

GET READY. Before you begin these steps, launch Microsoft Project. **OPEN** the *Don Funk Music Video 6M* project schedule from the data files for this lesson. **SAVE** the file as *Don Funk Music Video 6* in the solutions folder for this lesson as directed by your instructor.

1. Press the **F5** key. The Go To dialog box appears. Key **34** in the ID box, then click **OK**. Microsoft Project displays task 34, Scene 1 video shoot.

   This is the first of several scenes that require DVDs to be recorded. You have determined that the initial estimates for DVD consumption were incorrect. Because for each hour of work you will only record 30 minutes of material, you determine that the correct consumption rate for the DVD resource is 0.25 DVD/hour. (Remember, each DVD holds two hours of material.)

2. Click the **Resource** tab, then click the **Assign Resources** button. The Assign Resources dialog box appears.

3. In the Assign Resources dialog box, click the **Units** field for DVD. Key **0.25/h** and press **Enter**. Microsoft Project changes the consumption rate of DVDs for this task to 0.25 per hour.

4. Double-click the **column divider** between the Units and Cost columns to expand the Units column. The Assign Resources dialog box should look similar to Figure 6-1.

Figure 6-1

Assign Resources dialog box displaying consumption rate for DVDs

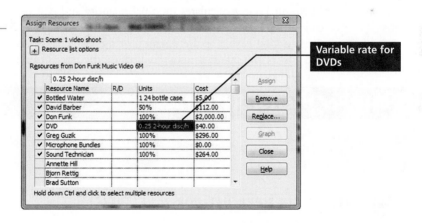

Team Planner ▾

5. Click the **Close** button in the Assign Resources dialog box. You will now verify the cost and work values of the DVD assignment to task 34.

6. On the Ribbon, click the **downward arrow** under the Team Planner button. Click **Task Usage**.

7. Double-click the **DVD resource assignment** under task 34, Scene 1 video shoot. The Assignment Information dialog box appears.

8. Select the **General** tab, if it is not already selected. Note the Work, Units, and Cost fields. The Assignment Information box should look similar to Figure 6-2.

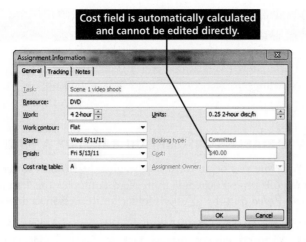

Cost field is automatically calculated
and cannot be edited directly.

9. Click **OK** to close the Assignment Information dialog box.
10. **SAVE** the project schedule.

> **PAUSE. LEAVE** Project open to use in the next exercise.

In this exercise, you assigned a variable consumption rate to a material resource. As you have seen, in Microsoft Project, you can assign two types of consumption rates:

- A *fixed consumption rate* means that an absolute quantity of the resources will be used, no matter the duration of the task to which the material is assigned. For example, filling a swimming pool requires use of a fixed amount of water.
- A *variable consumption rate* means that the amount of the material resource consumed is dependent upon the duration of the task. For instance, when shooting DVDs (as in this exercise), you will use more DVDs in six hours of shooting than in four. After you enter a variable consumption rate for a material resource's assignment, Microsoft Project calculates the total quantity and cost of the material resource consumed, based on the task's duration. An advantage of using a variable rate of consumption is that as the duration of the task changes, so do the calculated amount and cost of the material resource, because the rate is tied to the task's duration.

■ Entering Costs Per Use for Resources

THE BOTTOM LINE

In addition to its pay or consumption rate, a resource can also have a cost associated with each use.

 ENTER A COST PER USE FOR A RESOURCE

USE the project schedule you created in the previous exercise.

Team
Planner ▾
View

1. On the Resource tab, click the **downward arrow** under the Team Planner button, then select **Resource Sheet**.
2. On the Resource Sheet, select resource 11, **Digital Truck-Mounted Video Camera**.
3. On the Ribbon, click the **Resource Information** button, located in the Properties group. The Resource Information dialog box appears.

Information

4. Select the **Costs** tab.
5. Under Cost rate tables, select the **A(default)** tab if it is not already selected. The Digital Truck-Mounted Video Camera has a $100 maintenance fee for each time you use it.

6. In the first row under the Per Use Cost column, key **100**, then press **Enter**.

7. Select **End** from the Cost accrual drop-down menu. Your screen should look similar to Figure 6-3.

Figure 6-3

Resource Information dialog box displaying cost per use for the resource

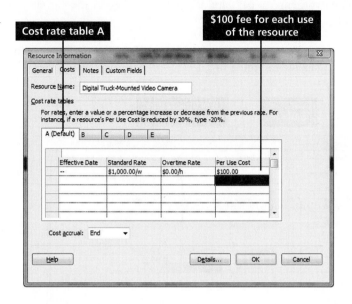

8. Click **OK** to close the Resource Information dialog box.

9. **SAVE** the project schedule.

   PAUSE. LEAVE Project open to use in the next exercise.

In this exercise, you entered a per-use cost for a material resource. Any resource can have a cost per use, either in place of or in addition to the costs derived from its pay rate (for a work resource) or its consumption rate (for a material resource). You can also specify whether the per-use cost should accrue at the beginning or the end of the task to which the resource is assigned.

■ Assigning Multiple Pay Rates for a Resource

THE BOTTOM LINE

Sometimes, the same work resource may perform different tasks with different pay rates. Microsoft Project enables you to enter multiple pay rates for a single resource.

 ASSIGN MULTIPLE PAY RATES FOR A RESOURCE

USE the project schedule you created in the previous exercise. Because Yan Li's rate differs depending on whether he is working on sound production tasks or administrative tasks, you need to enter a second rate for him.

1. In the Resource Sheet view, click the name of resource 9, **Yan Li**.

2. On the Ribbon, click the **Resource Information** button. The Resource Information dialog box appears.

Information

ANOTHER WAY

You can also double-click the Resource Name field to activate the Resource Information dialog box.

3. Click the **Costs** tab, if it is not already selected. Each tab of the cost rate table corresponds to one of the five pay rates a resource can have.

4. Under Cost rate tables, click the **B** tab.

5. Select the default entry of $0.00/h in the field directly below the Standard Rate column heading, key **15/h**, and press **Enter**.

 TAKE NOTE * When you enter a pay rate, if you do not key in the currency symbol, Microsoft Project will supply it for you.

6. In the Overtime Rate field, key **22.50/h**, then press **Enter**. Your screen should look similar to Figure 6-4.

Figure 6-4

Resource Information dialog box showing the second rate table for Yan Li

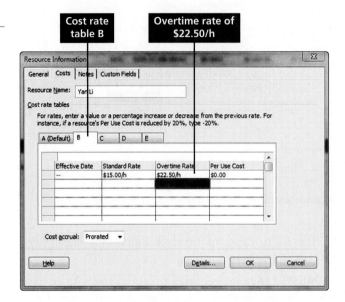

7. Click **OK** to close the Resource Information dialog box. Note that on the Resource Sheet, Yan Li's standard pay rate is still $18.50 per hour. This was the value in Rate Table A, the default rate table. This value will be used for all of Yan Li's task assignments unless you specify a different rate table.

8. **SAVE** the project schedule.

PAUSE. LEAVE Project open to use in the next exercise.

In this exercise, you entered a second cost rate table for a resource. A ***cost rate table*** consists of the resource pay rates that are stored on the Costs tab of the Resource Information dialog box. For a given resource, you can enter up to five cost rate tables. Each cost rate table has 125 possible entry lines, so you can assign dates on which a new cost rate takes effect. After you assign a resource to a task, you can specify which rate table should apply.

■ Applying Different Cost Rates to Assignments

↓ **THE BOTTOM LINE** Microsoft Project enables you to enter as many as five different pay rates for a resource. These pay rates may be applied to different assignments as necessary.

⊖ **APPLY A DIFFERENT COST RATE TO AN ASSIGNMENT**

USE the project schedule you created in the previous exercise.

1. On the Resource tab, click the **downward arrow** under the Team Planner button, then click **Task Usage**.

 **Tables ▼**

2. Press the **F5** key. Key **6** in the ID box, then click **OK**.

3. Click the **View** tab. In the Data group, click the **Tables** button and then select **Cost**.

4. Under task 6, click the **row heading** directly to the left of Yan Li so that Yan Li's entire assignment is selected.

5. Scroll the table portion (on the left) of the Task Usage view to the right until the Total Cost column is visible. You can see that the total cost of Yan's assignment to this task is $3,700. You can also see other assignment cost values, such as variance and actual cost, by dragging the vertical divider bar or scrolling the table to the right. Your screen should look similar to Figure 6-5.

Figure 6-5

Task Usage view showing the cost for Yan Li's assignment using cost rate table A

Yan li's cost for task 6 is $3,700 based on cost rate table A.

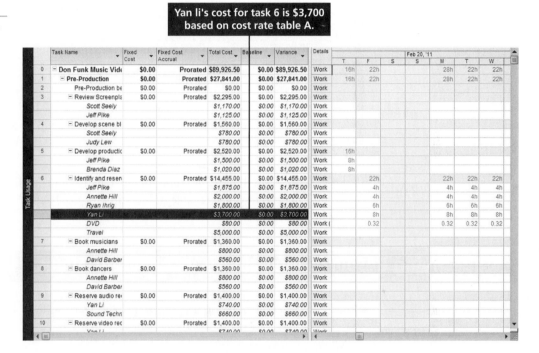

6. Double-click on **Yan Li's name**. The Assignment Information dialog box appears.

7. Click the **General** tab, if it is not already selected.

8. In the Cost rate table box, key or select **B**, then click **OK**. Microsoft Project applies Yan Li's cost rate table B to the assignment. The new cost of the assignment, $3,000, is reflected in the total cost column. Your screen should look similar to Figure 6-6.

ANOTHER WAY

If you find that you are frequently changing cost rate tables, it is faster to display the Cost Rate Table field directly in the Resource Usage or Task Usage view. To add the Cost Rate Table field, right-click a column heading, then select Insert Column. Next, select Cost Rate Table from the drop-down list.

9. **SAVE** the project schedule.

PAUSE. LEAVE Project open to use in the next exercise.

In this exercise, you applied an alternate rate table for a resource to reflect a different pay rate for different work. Remember, you can set up as many as five pay rates per resource. This

Figure 6-6

Task Usage view showing the
cost for Yan Li's assignment
using cost rate table B

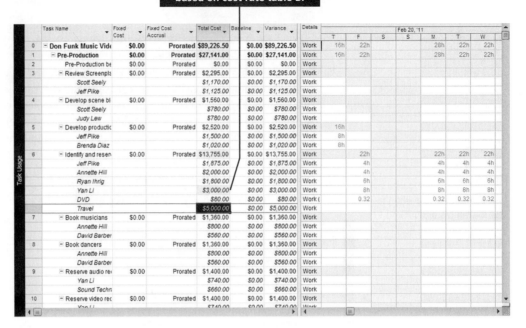

Yan Li's cost for task 6 is $3,000
based on cost rate table B.

	Task Name	Fixed Cost	Fixed Cost Accrual	Total Cost	Baseline	Variance	Details	T	F	S	S	M	T	W
0	Don Funk Music Vide	$0.00	Prorated	$89,226.50	$0.00	$89,226.50	Work	16h	22h			28h	22h	22h
1	Pre-Production	$0.00	Prorated	$27,141.00	$0.00	$27,141.00	Work	16h	22h			28h	22h	22h
2	Pre-Production be	$0.00	Prorated	$0.00	$0.00	$0.00	Work							
3	Review Screenpla	$0.00	Prorated	$2,295.00	$0.00	$2,295.00	Work							
	Scott Seely			$1,170.00	$0.00	$1,170.00	Work							
	Jeff Pike			$1,125.00	$0.00	$1,125.00	Work							
4	Develop scene bl	$0.00	Prorated	$1,560.00	$0.00	$1,560.00	Work							
	Scott Seely			$780.00	$0.00	$780.00	Work							
	Judy Lew			$780.00	$0.00	$780.00	Work							
5	Develop productic	$0.00	Prorated	$2,520.00	$0.00	$2,520.00	Work	16h						
	Jeff Pike			$1,500.00	$0.00	$1,500.00	Work	8h						
	Brenda Diaz			$1,020.00	$0.00	$1,020.00	Work	8h						
6	Identify and resen	$0.00	Prorated	$13,755.00	$0.00	$13,755.00	Work		22h			22h	22h	22h
	Jeff Pike			$1,875.00	$0.00	$1,875.00	Work		4h			4h	4h	4h
	Annette Hill			$2,000.00	$0.00	$2,000.00	Work		4h			4h	4h	4h
	Ryan Ihrig			$1,800.00	$0.00	$1,800.00	Work		6h			6h	6h	6h
	Yan Li			$3,000.00	$0.00	$3,000.00	Work		8h			8h	8h	8h
	DVD			$80.00	$0.00	$80.00	Work (		0.32			0.32	0.32	0.32
	Travel			$5,000.00	$0.00	$5,000.00	Work							
7	Book musicians	$0.00	Prorated	$1,360.00	$0.00	$1,360.00	Work							
	Annette Hill			$800.00	$0.00	$800.00	Work							
	David Barber			$560.00	$0.00	$560.00	Work							
8	Book dancers	$0.00	Prorated	$1,360.00	$0.00	$1,360.00	Work							
	Annette Hill			$800.00	$0.00	$800.00	Work							
	David Barber			$560.00	$0.00	$560.00	Work							
9	Reserve audio re	$0.00	Prorated	$1,400.00	$0.00	$1,400.00	Work							
	Yan Li			$740.00	$0.00	$740.00	Work							
	Sound Techn			$660.00	$0.00	$660.00	Work							
10	Reserve video rec	$0.00	Prorated	$1,400.00	$0.00	$1,400.00	Work							
	Yan Li			$740.00	$0.00	$740.00	Work							

enables you to assign different pay rates to different assignments for a resource. By default, Microsoft Project uses cost rate table A, but you can specify any time another rate table should be used.

■ Specifying Resource Availability at Different Times

THE BOTTOM LINE Sometimes, when working on a project schedule, you will find that a resource has varying availability. To control this availability, Microsoft Project uses Max. Units, or the maximum capacity of a resource to accomplish tasks.

⊖ SPECIFY A RESOURCE'S AVAILABILITY OVER TIME

USE the project schedule you created in the previous exercise.

  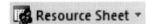

1. On the Ribbon, click the **Resource Sheet** button.
2. In the Resource Name column, double-click click the name of resource 38, **electrician**. The Resource Information dialog box appears.
3. Click the **General** tab, if it is not already selected.

   You originally planned that there would be three electricians available for the entire video production period, but you have just determined that there will only be two electricians available from May 1–May 20, 2011.

4. Under Resource Availability, in the first row of the Available From column, leave NA (Microsoft Project's term for a null field, or a field that is blank).
5. In the Available To cell in the first row, key or select **4/30/11**.
6. In the Available From cell in the second row, key or select **5/1/11**.
7. In the Available To cell in the second row, key or select **5/20/11**.
8. In the Units cell in the second row, key or select **200%**.
9. In the Available From cell in the third row, key or select **5/21/11**.

10. Leave the Available To cell in the third row blank. Microsoft Project will fill this with NA.

11. In the Units cell in the third row, key or select **300%**, then press **Enter**. Your screen should look similar to Figure 6-7.

Figure 6-7

Resource Information dialog box with resource availability dates

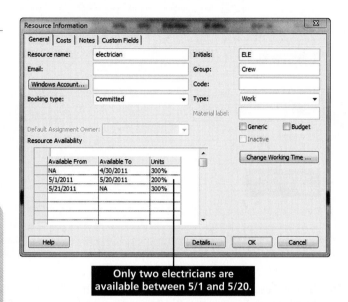

Only two electricians are available between 5/1 and 5/20.

TAKE NOTE*

Microsoft Project will display 200% in the Max. Units field only when the current date (based on your computer's system clock) is within the May 1–May 20 range. At other times, it will display 300%.

12. Click **OK** to close the Resource Information dialog box.

13. SAVE the project schedule.

  PAUSE. LEAVE Project open to use in the next exercise.

In this exercise, you set resource availability over time using the Resource Availability grid on the General tab of the Resource Information dialog box. Recall from Lessons 3 and 4 that a resource's capacity to work is measured in units. The Max. Units value stored in Microsoft Project is the maximum capacity of a resource to accomplish tasks. A resource's calendar determines when that resource is available to work. However, the resource's capacity to work (measured in units and limited by the Max. Units value) determines how much that resource can work within those hours without becoming overallocated.

You can set different Max. Units values to be applied over different time periods for any resource. Setting a resource's availability over time enables you to control exactly what a resource's Max. Units value is at any time.

■ Resolving Resource Overallocations Manually

THE BOTTOM LINE

A resource is overallocated when it is scheduled for work that exceeds its maximum capacity to work. You can resolve such situations manually within the project schedule.

➔ MANUALLY RESOLVE A RESOURCE OVERALLOCATION

USE the project schedule you created in the previous exercise.

1. On the View tab, click the **downward arrow** to the right of the Resource Sheet button, click **More Views**, select **Resource Allocation**, and click the **Apply** button. Microsoft Project switches to the Resource Allocation view. This is a split view that displays the Resource Usage view in the top pane and the Leveling Gantt view in the bottom pane. Your screen should look similar to Figure 6-8.

Figure 6-8

Resource Allocation view

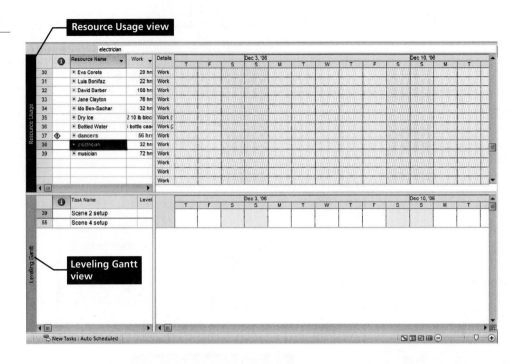

 Outline ▾

2. In the Resource Usage view (top pane), click the **Resource Name column heading**, then click the **Outline** button in the Ribbon. Select **Hide Subtasks**. (The column appears to go blank, but actually, the resources have just shifted up in the list because the tasks under the resource names have been hidden.)

3. In the Resource Usage view, scroll up vertically through the Resource Name column so that you can see the names. The names that you see formatted in red are overallocated resources.

4. In the Resource Name column, select the name of resource 27, **Greg Guzik**.

5. Click the **plus sign (+)** next to Greg Guzik's name to display his assignments. Scroll down to see the assignments, if necessary.

6. Press the **F5** key. Key **7/6/11** in the Date box, then click **OK**. The Leveling Gantt pane shows the task bars for two of Greg Guzik's assignments. Your screen should look similar to Figure 6-9.

Figure 6-9

Resource Allocation view showing Greg Guzik's overallocated assignments

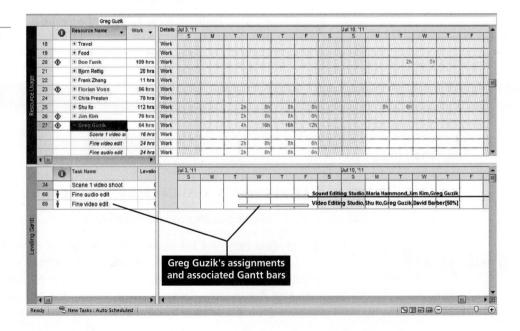

In the upper pane, notice that Greg is assigned full-time to two tasks that both start on Tuesday, July 5. He is therefore overallocated for the duration of both tasks. In the lower pane, you can see the Gantt bars for the two tasks that have caused Greg to be overallocated during this period. For tasks 68 and 69, Greg is assigned eight hours of work on both Wednesday and Thursday, and six hours of work on Friday. This results in 16 hours of work on two days, and 12 hours of work on another—which is beyond Greg's capacity to work. In addition, Greg is assigned four hours of work on Tuesday, performing two tasks at the same time. However, this assignment is *not* shown in red. This is because the default overallocation setting is set to look for overallocations on a "day-by-day" basis. Because Greg has eight hours of availability that day, Project does not view this situation as an overallocation.

7. In the Resource Name column, double-click Greg's second assignment, **Fine video edit**. The Assignment Information dialog box appears.

8. Click the **General** tab, if it is not already selected.

9. In the Units box, key or select **50%**, then click **OK** to close the Assignment Information dialog box.

Note that Greg's daily work assignments on this task are reduced, but the task duration is increased. You want to reduce the work but not increase the duration of the task. Also note the SmartTag indicator that has been activated next to the name of the assignment.

10. Click the **SmartTag Actions** button. Review the options in the list that appears. Your screen should look similar to Figure 6-10.

Figure 6-10

Resource Allocation view with SmartTag action list displayed

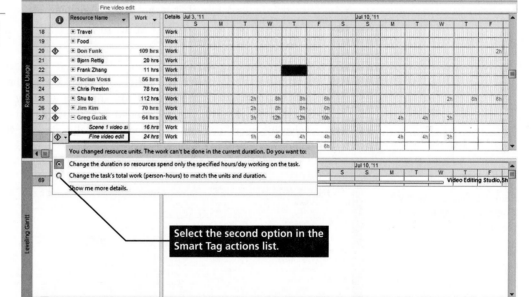

11. Click **Change the task's total work (person-hours) to match the units and duration** in the SmartTag Actions list. Microsoft Project reduces Greg's work assignments on the task and restores the task to its original duration. Your screen should look similar to Figure 6-11.

Figure 6-11

Resource Allocation view with
corrected work values

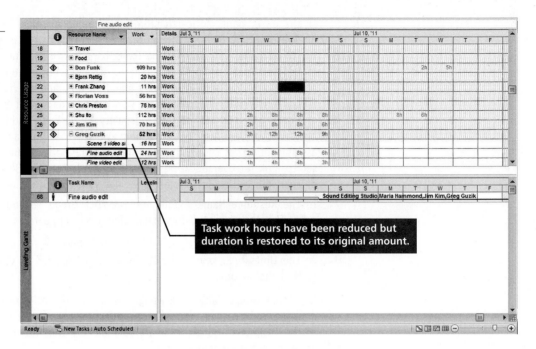

Task work hours have been reduced but
duration is restored to its original amount.

Notice that Greg is still overallocated. To remedy this situation, you will now
reduce the assignment units on his second task.

12. In the Resource Name column, double-click Greg's second assignment, **Fine audio
edit**. The Assignment Information dialog box appears.

13. Click the **General** tab, if it is not already visible.

14. In the Units box, key or select **50%**, then click **OK** to close the Assignment
Information dialog box.

15. Click the **SmartTag Actions** button. Click **Change the task's total work
(person-hours) to match the units and duration** in the SmartTag Actions list.
Greg's assignments on Wednesday and Thursday are now reduced to eight hours
each day. You have manually changed Greg's assignments to reduce his work and
resolve his overallocation. He is now fully allocated on these days. Your screen
should look similar to Figure 6-12.

Figure 6-12

Resource Allocation view with
Greg Guzik's overallocation
resolved

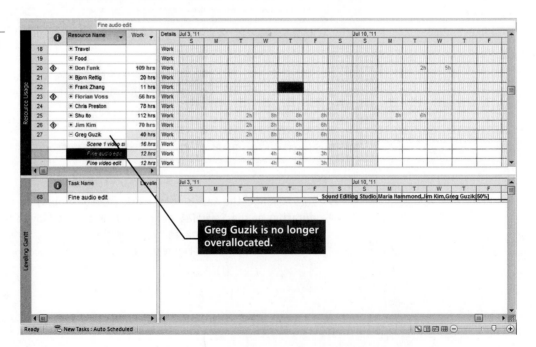

Greg Guzik is no longer
overallocated.

16. **SAVE** the project schedule.

   PAUSE. LEAVE Project open to use in the next exercise.

In this exercise, you manually resolved a resource overallocation. Recall from Lesson 4 that a resource's capacity to work is called allocation, and a resource is said to be in one of three states:

- **Underallocated:** The state in which the work assigned to the resource is less than the resource's maximum capacity.
- **Fully allocated:** The state in which the total work of a resource's task assignments is exactly equal to the resource's work capacity.
- **Overallocated:** The state in which the resource is assigned to do more work than can be done within its normal work capacity.

Manually editing an assignment is one way to resolve a resource overallocation, but there are several other methods as well:

- You can replace the overallocated resource with another resource using the Replace button in the Assign Resources dialog box.
- You can reduce the value in the Units field in the Assignment Information or Assign Resources dialog box.
- If the overallocation is not extreme (for instance, nine hours of work assigned in a normal eight-hour workday), you can just allow the overallocation to remain in the schedule.

In Microsoft Project 2010, overallocations are also noted when you assign a work resource to working times outside its normal working hours. Recall that in Lesson 4 you assigned a Task Calendar for overnight beach filming. This resulted in an overallocation of the work resources assigned to that task. However, these resources are not truly overallocated by definition. Rather, this is simply the software's way of notifying you that you have resources assigned to work outside their normal working hours.

■ SOFTWARE ORIENTATION

Microsoft Project's Resource Leveling Dialog Box

The Resource Leveling dialog box allows you to specify the rules and options that control how Microsoft Project performs resource leveling.

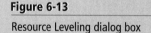

Figure 6-13

Resource Leveling dialog box

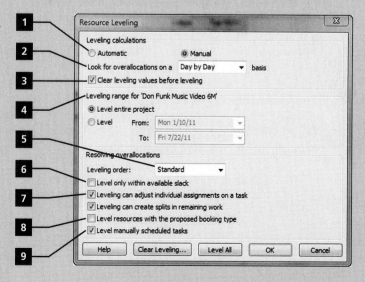

The options in the Resource Leveling Dialog box are as follows:

- **Leveling calculations:** These selections determine whether Microsoft Project levels resources constantly (Automatic) or only when you tell it to do so (Manual). Automatic leveling occurs as soon as a resource becomes overallocated.

- **Look for overallocations on a ...basis:** This selection determines the timeframe in which Microsoft Project looks for overallocations. If a resource is overallocated at the level you choose here, its name will be formatted in red. If a resource is not overallocated at the level you choose, there will be no indication of any overallocation.

- **Clear leveling values before leveling:** There may be times when you have to level resources repeatedly to get the results you want. (You might first try to level day by day, and then switch to hour by hour, for example.) If the Clear leveling values before leveling check box is selected, Microsoft Project removes any existing delays from all tasks before leveling.

- **Leveling range for...:** This selection determines whether you level the entire project or only those assignments that fall within a date range you specify. Leveling within a date range is advantageous when you have started tracking actual work and you want to level only the remaining assignments in a project.

- **Leveling order:** This setting allows you to control the priority Microsoft Project uses to determine which tasks it should delay to resolve a resource conflict. There are three options: ID Only, Standard, and Priority, Standard. The ID Only option delays tasks according to their ID numbers only. Use this option when your project schedule has no task relationships or constraints. The Standard option delays tasks according to their predecessor relationships, start dates, task constraints, slack, priority, and IDs. The Priority, Standard option looks at the task's priority value before other standard criteria.

- **Level only within available slack:** Clearing this setting allows Microsoft Project to extend the project's finish date, if necessary, to resolve resource overallocations. Selecting this setting would prevent Microsoft Project from extending the project's finish date in order to resolve resource overallocations. Instead, Project would use only the free slack of tasks, which may or may not be adequate to fully resolve resource overallocations.

- **Leveling can adjust individual assignments to work on a task:** This setting allows Microsoft Project to add leveling delay (or, if Leveling can create splits in remaining work is selected, to split work on assignments) independently of any other resources assigned to the same task. This could cause resources to start and finish work on a task at different times.

- **Leveling can create splits in remaining work:** This setting allows Microsoft Project to split work on a task in order to resolve an overallocation.

- **Level resources with the proposed booking type:** Use this option only when Microsoft Project 2010 is being employed in an enterprise environment, such as Project Server 2010. Selecting this option allows Microsoft Project to level resources in projects connected to Project Server 2010 that have a proposed booking type. Deselecting this option will cause the software to ignore all resources that have a proposed booking type.

- **Level manually scheduled tasks:** If your project contains manually scheduled tasks that have overallocated resources, selecting this option allows the software to split or delay these tasks. Leave this option selected if you want to maintain control and manually resolve overallocations on manually scheduled tasks.

■ Leveling Overallocated Resources

THE BOTTOM LINE   To avoid an overallocation situation, you can cause a resource's work on a specific task to be delayed through a process known as resource leveling.

→ **USE RESOURCE LEVELING TO RESOLVE AN OVERALLOCATION**

USE the project schedule you created in the previous exercise.

1. Click the **View** tab. In the Split View group, deselect the **Details** checkbox.
2. On the Ribbon, click **Resource Sheet**, located in the Resource Views group. The Resource Sheet view appears. Take note of the resource names that appear in red and have the Overallocated icon in the Indicators column.
3. Click on the **Resource** tab. In the Level group, select **Leveling Options**. The Resource Leveling dialog box appears.

TAKE NOTE *   Depending on previous uses of the Resource Leveling dialog box in Microsoft Project, the options you are selecting in steps 4 through 13 may already be chosen for you.

4. In the Resource Leveling dialog box, under Leveling calculations, select **Manual**, if it is not already selected.

TAKE NOTE *   All the settings in the Resource Leveling dialog box apply to all project schedules with which you work in Microsoft Project—*not* just the active project schedule. It might seem easier to use automatic leveling, but doing so will make frequent adjustments to project schedules whether or not you want these changes to occur. Because of this, it is recommended that you always have Manual Leveling calculations selected.

5. In the Look for overallocations on a ...basis box, select **Day by Day**.

TROUBLESHOOTING   In most projects, leveling in detail more precise than Day by Day can result in unrealistically precise adjustments to assignments.

6. Select the **Clear leveling values before leveling** box.
7. Under Leveling range for, select **Level entire project**.
8. Under Resolving overallocations, in the Leveling order box, select **Standard**.
9. Clear the **Level only within available slack** check box.
10. Select the **Leveling can adjust individual assignments on a task** check box.
11. Select the **Leveling can create splits in remaining work** check box.
12. Clear the **Level resources with the proposed booking type** check box.
13. Clear the **Level manually scheduled tasks** check box. Your screen should look similar to Figure 6-14.

Figure 6-14

Resource Leveling options dialog box

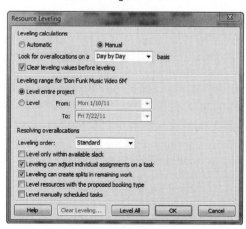

14. Click the **Level All** button.

If you click OK after setting the options, Microsoft Project will not perform leveling unless you have selected automatic leveling.

15. Microsoft Project levels the overallocated resources. Notice that resource 26, Jim Kim, is no longer overallocated. Some resources may still be formatted in red, meaning that these resources are overallocated because they have been assigned work during their normal nonworking times. Your screen should look similar to Figure 6-15.

Figure 6-15

Resource Sheet view after resource leveling

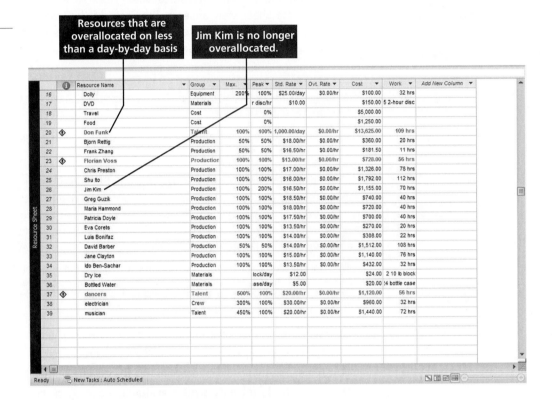

16. On the Ribbon, click the **downward arrow** under the Team Planner button. Select **More Views**, then select **Leveling Gantt**. Microsoft Project displays the Leveling Gantt view.

17. Press the **F5** key. Key **66** in the ID box. Your screen should look similar to Figure 6-16.

Notice that each task now has two bars. The tan bar on the top represents the preleveled task. The light blue bar on the bottom represents the leveled task. For this particular project, the effect leveling had on the project finish date was to extend it by about three days. You can see all of the preleveled start, duration, and finish values for any task by pointing to the desired green bar. The solid teal line to the right of any light blue bar represents the float (slack) for that task.

18. **SAVE** the project schedule, then **CLOSE** the file.

PAUSE. If you are continuing to the next lesson, keep Project open. If you are not continuing to additional lessons, **CLOSE** Project.

In this exercise, you used resource leveling to resolve overallocations. Recall that resource leveling is the process of delaying or splitting a resource's work on a task to resolve an overallocation.

Figure 6-16

Leveling Gantt view showing the effects of resource leveling

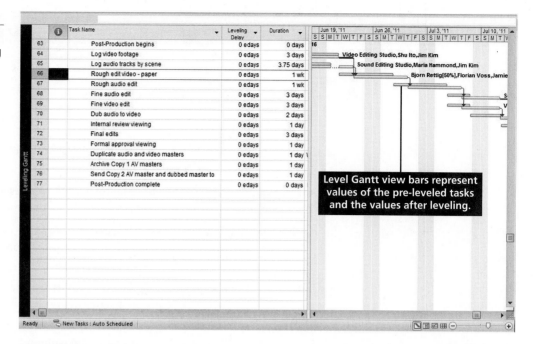

Level Gantt view bars represent values of the pre-leveled tasks and the values after leveling.

The options in the Resource Leveling dialog box enable you to set parameters for how you want Microsoft Project to resolve resource overallocations. Depending on the options you choose, Microsoft Project might try to level resources by delaying the start date of an assignment or task, or by splitting the work on the task.

TAKE NOTE ✱ Even though the effects of resource leveling might sometimes be significant, resource leveling never changes who is assigned to tasks, nor does it change the total work or assignment unit values of those assignments.

Resource leveling is a powerful tool, but it has limits. It can only do a few things: It adds delays to tasks, it splits tasks, and it adjusts resource assignments. It does this by following a complex set of rules and options that you specify in the Resource Leveling dialog box. Although resource leveling is very useful for fine-tuning, *it can't replace the judgment of a good project manager about task durations, relationships, and constraints, or about resource availability.* Resource leveling will work with all of this information as it exists in your project schedule, but it still might not be possible to completely resolve all resource overallocations within the timeframe you want without changing more basic task and resource information.

SUMMARY SKILL MATRIX

IN THIS LESSON, YOU LEARNED:	TASK
To enter material resource consumption rates.	Enter a variable consumption rate for a material resource.
To enter costs per use for resources.	Enter a cost per use for a resource.
To assign multiple pay rates for a resource.	Assign multiple pay rates for a resource.
To apply different cost rates to assignments.	Apply a different cost rate to an assignment.
To specify resource availability at different times.	Specify a resource's availability over time.
To resolve resource overallocations manually.	Manually resolve a resource overallocation.
To level overallocated resources.	Use resource leveling to resolve an overallocation.

■ Knowledge Assessment

Matching

Match the term in column 1 to its description in column 2.

Column 1	Column 2
1. Cost rate table	**a.** An absolute quantity of material resources will be used, no matter the duration of the task.
2. Underallocated	**b.** The total work of a resource's task assignments is exactly equal to that resource's work capacity.
3. Variable consumption rate	**c.** A resource is assigned to do more work than can be done within the normal capacity of the resource.
4. Units	**d.** The amount of the material resource consumed is dependent upon the duration of the task.
5. Allocation	**e.** The work assigned to a resource is less than the resource's maximum capacity.
6. Fixed consumption rate	**f.** The process of delaying or splitting a resource's work on a task to resolve an overallocation.
7. Overallocated	**g.** The maximum capacity of a resource to accomplish tasks.
8. Resource leveling	**h.** Resource pay rates that are stored on the Costs tab of the Resource Information dialog box.
9. Fully allocated	**i.** The portion of a resource's capacity devoted to work on a specific task.
10. Max. Units	**j.** The measurement of a resource's capacity to work.

True/False

Circle T if the statement is true or F if the statement is false.

T | F 1. Resource leveling cannot always resolve all resource overallocations.

T | F 2. A resource cannot have both a cost per use and a cost derived from its pay rate.

T | F 3. Resource leveling never changes who is assigned to tasks, nor does it change the total work value of those assignments.

T | F 4. You can resolve a resource overallocation by replacing the overallocated resource with another resource.

T | F 5. You can assign two types of consumption rates in Microsoft Project.

T | F 6. The settings in the Resource Leveling dialog box apply to all of the project schedules you work with in Microsoft Project.

T | F 7. You can have up to six cost rate tables for a resource.

T | F 8. It is not acceptable to allow a minor overallocation to remain in a schedule.

T | F 9. The default rate table in Microsoft Project is rate table 1.

T | F 10. When a variable consumption rate is assigned to a material resource and the duration of the task to which it is assigned changes, so do the calculated amount and cost of the material resource.

■ Competency Assessment

Project 6-1: Variable Consumption Rate for Water

As you review your Don Funk Music Video project schedule, you realize you need to make some adjustments to the bottled water material resource. Specifically, you want to use a variable rate of 0.5 cases of water per hour.

GET READY. Launch Microsoft Project if it is not already running. **OPEN** *Don Funk Music Video 6-1* from the data files for this lesson.

The *Don Funk Music Video 6-1* file for this lesson is available on the book companion website.

1. Scroll down in the task list to task 34, Scene 1 Video Shoot.
2. Click the **Resources** tab, then click the **Assign Resources** button.
3. In the Assign Resources dialog box, click the **Units** field for Bottled Water. Key **0.5/h** and press **Enter**.
4. Click the **Close** button in the Assign Resource dialog box.
5. **SAVE** the project schedule as *Don Funk Bottled Water* and **CLOSE** the file.
   PAUSE. LEAVE Project open to use in the next exercise.

Project 6-2: Office Remodel and Multiple Pay Rates

In the office remodel project you are currently managing, you need to set up different pay rates for one of the resources, Run Lui. He has different pay scales depending upon whether he is moving furniture and appliances or doing painting and material installation work.

OPEN *Office Remodel 6-2* from the data files for this lesson.

1. Click the **View** tab, then click **Resource Sheet** in the Resource Views group.
2. In the Resource Sheet view, double-click the name of resource 3, **Run Lui**. The Resource Information dialog box appears.
3. Click the **Costs** tab, if it is not already selected.
4. Under Cost rate tables, click the **B** tab.
5. Select the default entry of $0.00/h in the field directly below the Standard Rate column heading, key **12/h**, and press **Enter**.
6. In the Overtime Rate field, key **18.00/h**, then press **Enter**.
7. Click OK to close the Resource Information dialog box.

The *Office Remodel 6-2* file for this lesson is available on the book companion website.

8. **SAVE** the project schedule as *Office Remodel Multiple Rates* and **CLOSE** the file.
   PAUSE. LEAVE Project open to use in the next exercise.

■ Proficiency Assessment

Project 6-3: Hiring New Employee Resource Leveling

Several employees on the Hiring New Employee project schedule are overallocated. You want to use resource leveling to resolve these overallocations.

OPEN *Hiring New Employee 6-3* from the data files for this lesson.

1. Activate the Resource Sheet view.
2. Activate the Resource Leveling dialog box.
3. In the Resource Leveling dialog box, make the selections that correspond to the following options:
   - Level manually

- Level day by day
- Clear leveling values before leveling
- Level the entire project
- Use Standard leveling order
- Do not level within available slack
- Allow leveling to adjust individual assignments
- Allow leveling to create splits
- Do not level resources with a proposed booking type
- Do not level manually scheduled tasks

The *Hiring New Employee 6-3* file for this lesson is available on the book companion website.

4. Click the **Level All** button.
5. Change the view to Leveling Gantt.
6. Scroll to task 4 to view more of the leveled Gantt chart.
7. **SAVE** the project schedule as *Hiring New Employee Leveled* and **CLOSE** the file.

   PAUSE. LEAVE Project open to use in the next exercise.

Project 6-4: Employee Orientation—Specifying Conference Room Availability

You have just been told that the large conference room is not available for use from 9/1/11 through 9/9/11 and from 9/19/11 through 9/21/11. Although this does not immediately interfere with your current orientation schedule, you want to update the resource availability information so you can avoid conflicts if your schedule changes.

OPEN *Employee Orientation 6-4* from the data files for this lesson.

The *Employee Orientation 6-4* file for this lesson is available on the book companion website.

1. Activate the Resource Sheet view.
2. Select the **Large Conference Room** resource.
3. Activate the Resource Information dialog box. Activate the General tab, if it is not already selected.
4. Fill in the Resource Availability table to reflect that the conference room is available until 8/31/11, from 9/12 through 9/18/11, and after 9/21/09, but that it is not available on the dates noted in the instructions above. Close the Resource Information box when you are finished.
5. **SAVE** the project schedule as *Employee Orientation Conf Room Availability* and **CLOSE** the file.

   PAUSE. LEAVE Project open to use in the next exercise.

■ Mastery Assessment

Project 6-5: Applying a Different Cost Rate

In the office remodel project you are currently managing, you have set up different pay rates for one of the resources, Run Lui. Now you need to apply these pay rates to the appropriate assignments.

OPEN *Office Remodel 6-5* from the data files for this lesson.

The *Office Remodel 6-5* file for this lesson is available on the book companion website.

1. For Run Lui's assignment to tasks 2 and 18, change the cost rate table to B.
2. **SAVE** the project schedule as *Office Remodel Run Lui B*, then **CLOSE** the file.

   PAUSE. LEAVE Project open to use in the next exercise.

Project 6-6: Don Funk Music Video–Costs Per Use

You need to update the Don Funk Music Video project schedule to reflect several resources that have a cost associated with each use.

OPEN *Don Funk Music Video 6-6* from the data files for this lesson.

1. Enter the following cost per use information for the specified resources:
   - The musicians have a $100 travel and setup/breakdown fee each time they are used, payable at the beginning of the session.
   - The sound editing studio has a $50 cleaning fee per use, payable at the end of the session.
   - The video editing studio has a $50 cleaning fee per use, payable at the end of the session.
2. **SAVE** the project schedule as *Don Funk Cost Per Use* and **CLOSE** the file.
   CLOSE Project.

The *Don Funk Music Video 6-6* file for this lesson is available on the book companion website.

INTERNET READY

In this lesson, you learned about resources that have a cost associated with each use, and also about resources that have multiple cost rates depending upon their particular activity in a project. Both of these situations are common occurrences in project management.

Search the Internet for a project that has resources that fall into either or both categories. You can look for an actual Microsoft Project file, a template, a story about a current event, a press release from a company, or even a project run by a local business that is of interest to you. Write a brief description of the project (enough to familiarize your instructor with it), or save a copy of the Project file. Then make a list of the resources and describe how per-use costs or multiple cost rates might apply to these resources. For example:

- **Resource: Concert Hall:** Cost per use fee for cleaning and/or setup/cleanup; may have different rates for day and night use
- **Resource: Limousine:** Cost per use fee for gas or cleaning; may have different rates for weekdays and weekends

You can put your list into a Word file or an Excel file.

7 LESSON

Project Information: Sorting, Grouping, and Filtering

LESSON SKILL MATRIX

SKILL	TASK
Sorting Data	Sort data in a resource view.
Grouping Data	Group data in a resource view.
Filtering Data	Create and apply a filter in a view.
	Create a custom filter.

As a production manager for Southridge Video and the project manager for the new Don Funk music video, you have invested much time and effort into assembling your project schedule. You have entered and linked tasks, created work and material resources, and assigned these resources to the project tasks. Now that the key elements of the project schedule have been established, you need to view and analyze the project schedule information in different ways. After all, the best project schedule is only as good as the data you are able to get out of it. In this lesson, you will learn to use various tools in Microsoft Project 2010, such as views, tables, and reports, to modify the way your data is organized. You will also learn about several features that enable you to make custom changes to your data to suit your specific needs.

KEY TERMS
AutoFilter
filter
group
sort

■ SOFTWARE ORIENTATION

Microsoft Project's Sort Dialog Box

In Microsoft Project, you can use the Sort dialog box to sort task or resource information in the current view by a specified field or fields.

Figure 7-1

Sort dialog box

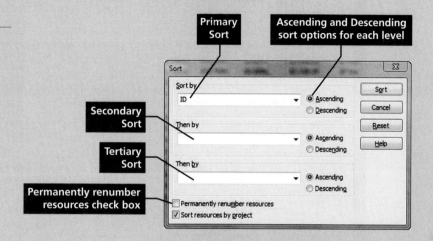

The Sort dialog box enables you to select up to three fields for three levels of sorts within sorts, to choose whether the view should be sorted in ascending or descending order, and to indicate whether items should be permanently renumbered according to the sort.

■ Sorting Data

↓
THE BOTTOM LINE
It is easiest to review and utilize data in Microsoft Project when you have organized the data so it fits your needs. The simplest way to reorganize task and resource data in Project is by sorting.

→ **SORT DATA IN A RESOURCE VIEW**

GET READY. Before you begin these steps, launch Microsoft Project. **OPEN** *Don Funk Music Video 7M* from the data files for this lesson. **SAVE** the file as *Don Funk Music Video 7* in the solutions folder for this lesson as directed by your instructor.

1. Click the **View** tab, then click **Resource Sheet**. The Resource Sheet view appears. The default view in the Resource Sheet is the Entry table. However, you want to look at the cost per resource, which is not displayed in the Entry table.

2. On the Ribbon, click the **Tables** button in the Data group, then select **Summary**. The Summary table appears in the Resource Sheet view. Your screen should look similar to Figure 7-2.

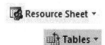

Figure 7-2

Resource Sheet with summary table applied

Cost per resource in the summary table

	Resource Name	Group	Max.	Pe	Std. Rate	Ovt. Rate	Cost	Work	Add New Column
		Production							
1	Jamie Reding	Production	100%	100%	$1,000.00/wk	$0.00/hr	$2,025.00	81 hrs	
2	Scott Seely	Production	100%	100%	$19.50/hr	$0.00/hr	$2,554.50	131 hrs	
3	Jeff Pike	Production	100%	100%	$750.00/wk	$0.00/hr	$5,156.25	275 hrs	
4	Judy Lew	Production	100%	159%	$19.50/hr	$0.00/hr	$1,306.50	67 hrs	
5	Brenda Diaz	Production	100%	100%	$12.75/hr	$0.00/hr	$1,109.25	87 hrs	
6	Brad Sutton	Production	100%	100%	$16.50/hr	$0.00/hr	$1,831.50	111 hrs	
7	Annette Hill	Production	50%	50%	$20.00/hr	$0.00/hr	$3,930.00	196.5 hrs	
8	Ryan Ihrig	Production	100%	100%	$12.00/hr	$0.00/hr	$1,884.00	157 hrs	
9	Yan Li	Production	100%	100%	$18.50/hr	$0.00/hr	$5,624.00	304 hrs	
10	Sound Technician	Crew	300%	100%	$16.50/hr	$0.00/hr	$2,508.00	152 hrs	
11	Digital Truck-Mounted	Equipment	200%	100%	$1,000.00/wk	$0.00/hr	$400.00	16 hrs	
12	Sound Editing Studio	Lab	100%	100%	$250.00/day	$0.00/hr	$1,500.00	48 hrs	
13	Light Banks	Equipment	400%	100%	$0.00/hr	$0.00/hr	$0.00	16 hrs	
14	Video Editing Studio	Lab	100%	100%	$250.00/hr	$0.00/hr	$24,500.00	98 hrs	
15	Microphone Bundles	Equipment	500%	100%	$0.00/hr	$0.00/hr	$0.00	16 hrs	
16	Dolly	Equipment	200%	100%	$25.00/day	$0.00/hr	$100.00	32 hrs	
17	DVD	Materials		c/day	$10.00		$120.00	2 2-hour disc	
18	Travel	Cost		0%			$5,000.00		
19	Food	Cost		0%			$1,250.00		
20	Don Funk	Talent	100%	100%	1,000.00/day	$0.00/hr	$13,625.00	109 hrs	
21	Bjorn Rettig	Production	50%	50%	$18.00/hr	$0.00/hr	$360.00	20 hrs	
22	Frank Zhang	Production	50%	50%	$16.50/hr	$0.00/hr	$181.50	11 hrs	
23	Florian Voss	Production	100%	100%	$13.00/hr	$0.00/hr	$728.00	56 hrs	
24	Chris Preston	Production	100%	100%	$17.00/hr	$0.00/hr	$1,326.00	78 hrs	
25	Shu Ito	Production	100%	100%	$16.00/hr	$0.00/hr	$1,792.00	112 hrs	
26	Jim Kim	Production	100%	100%	$16.50/hr	$0.00/hr	$759.00	46 hrs	
27	Greg Guzik	Production	100%	100%	$18.50/hr	$0.00/hr	$740.00	40 hrs	
28	Maria Hammond	Production	100%	100%	$18.00/hr	$0.00/hr	$720.00	40 hrs	
29	Patricia Doyle	Production	100%	100%	$17.50/hr	$0.00/hr	$700.00	40 hrs	

3. On the Ribbon, click the **Sort** button in the Data group, then click **Sort by**. The Sort dialog box appears (as displayed in Figure 7-1).

TAKE NOTE ★ Notice that in the Sort box, you can utilize up to three nested levels of sort criteria. Also, you can sort by any field, not just the fields that are visible in the active view.

4. In the **Sort by** section, select **Cost** from the drop-down menu. Next to that, click **Descending**. Make sure that the Permanently renumber resources check box at the bottom of the Sort dialog box is *not* checked.

TROUBLESHOOTING The Permanently renumber resources check box (or, when in a task view, Permanently renumber tasks) is a Project-level setting. If you check this box, Project will permanently renumber resources or tasks in *any* Microsoft Project file in which you sort. Because you may not want to permanently renumber tasks or resources every time you sort, it is a good idea to have this option turned off.

5. Click the **Sort** button. The Summary table is sorted from highest to lowest value in the Cost column. Your screen should look similar to Figure 7-3. This sort enables you to look at resource costs across the entire project.

TAKE NOTE ★ When you sort data in your project, the sort applies to the active view, no matter which table is currently displayed in the view. For example, if you sort the Task Usage view by finish date while the Entry table is visible and you then switch to the Cost table, you will see that the tasks are still sorted by finish date in the Cost column.

6. On the Ribbon, click **Sort**, then click **Sort by**. The Sort dialog box appears.

7. In the **Sort by** section, select **Group** from the drop-down menu. Next to that, click **Ascending**.

Figure 7-3

Resource Sheet sorted with highest-cost resource at the top

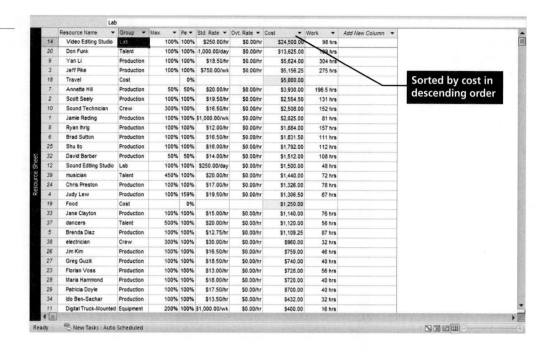

Sorted by cost in descending order

	Resource Name	Group	Max.	Pe	Std. Rate	Ovt. Rate	Cost	Work	Add New Column
14	Video Editing Studio	Lab	100%	100%	$250.00/hr	$0.00/hr	$24,500.00	98 hrs	
20	Don Funk	Talent	100%	100%	1,000.00/day	$0.00/hr	$13,625.00	199 hrs	
9	Yan Li	Production	100%	100%	$18.50/hr	$0.00/hr	$5,624.00	304 hrs	
3	Jeff Pike	Production	100%	100%	$750.00/wk	$0.00/hr	$5,156.25	275 hrs	
18	Travel	Cost		0%			$5,000.00		
7	Annette Hill	Production	50%	50%	$20.00/hr	$0.00/hr	$3,930.00	196.5 hrs	
2	Scott Seely	Production	100%	100%	$19.50/hr	$0.00/hr	$2,554.50	131 hrs	
10	Sound Technician	Crew	300%	100%	$16.50/hr	$0.00/hr	$2,508.00	152 hrs	
1	Jamie Reding	Production	100%	100%	$1,000.00/wk	$0.00/hr	$2,025.00	81 hrs	
8	Ryan Ihrig	Production	100%	100%	$12.00/hr	$0.00/hr	$1,884.00	157 hrs	
6	Brad Sutton	Production	100%	100%	$16.50/hr	$0.00/hr	$1,831.50	111 hrs	
25	Shu Ito	Production	100%	100%	$16.00/hr	$0.00/hr	$1,792.00	112 hrs	
32	David Barber	Production	50%	50%	$14.00/hr	$0.00/hr	$1,512.00	108 hrs	
12	Sound Editing Studio	Lab	100%	100%	$250.00/day	$0.00/hr	$1,500.00	48 hrs	
39	musician	Talent	450%	100%	$20.00/hr	$0.00/hr	$1,440.00	72 hrs	
24	Chris Preston	Production	100%	100%	$17.00/hr	$0.00/hr	$1,326.00	78 hrs	
4	Judy Lew	Production	100%	159%	$19.50/hr	$0.00/hr	$1,306.50	67 hrs	
19	Food	Cost		0%			$1,250.00		
33	Jane Clayton	Production	100%	100%	$15.00/hr	$0.00/hr	$1,140.00	76 hrs	
37	dancers	Talent	500%	100%	$20.00/hr	$0.00/hr	$1,120.00	56 hrs	
5	Brenda Diaz	Production	100%	100%	$12.75/hr	$0.00/hr	$1,109.25	87 hrs	
38	electrician	Crew	300%	100%	$30.00/hr	$0.00/hr	$960.00	32 hrs	
26	Jim Kim	Production	100%	100%	$16.50/hr	$0.00/hr	$759.00	46 hrs	
27	Greg Guzik	Production	100%	100%	$18.50/hr	$0.00/hr	$740.00	40 hrs	
23	Florian Voss	Production	100%	100%	$13.00/hr	$0.00/hr	$728.00	56 hrs	
28	Maria Hammond	Production	100%	100%	$18.00/hr	$0.00/hr	$720.00	40 hrs	
29	Patricia Doyle	Production	100%	100%	$17.50/hr	$0.00/hr	$700.00	40 hrs	
34	Ido Ben-Sachar	Production	100%	100%	$13.50/hr	$0.00/hr	$432.00	32 hrs	
11	Digital Truck-Mounted	Equipment	200%	100%	$1,000.00/wk	$0.00/hr	$400.00	16 hrs	

Ready   New Tasks : Auto Scheduled

8. In the Then by section, select **Cost** from the drop-down menu. Then click the radio button next to **Descending**. Make sure the Permanently renumber resources box is *not* checked. Your screen should look similar to Figure 7-4.

Figure 7-4

Sort dialog box with multiple sort criteria

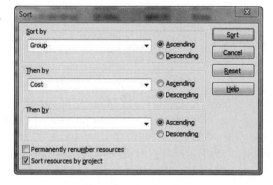

9. Click the **Sort** button. The Resource Sheet view is sorted to display resources sorted first by Group (Equipment, Talent, etc.) and then by Cost within each group. Your screen should look similar to Figure 7-5.

When you sort data in this way, it is easy to identify the most and least expensive resources in each group on your project. You can sort your data in any way that is beneficial to the analysis of your project. The sort order you most recently specified will remain in effect until you re-sort the view. Now you will restore the data to its original order.

10. On the Quick Access Toolbar, click the **Undo** button one time. The Undo button reverses the last sort you performed, restoring the data to the original sort order (by Cost only).

11. Now click the **Undo** button again. The data is restored to the original order in the Summary table of the Resource Sheet view (as displayed previously in Figure 7-2). The Multiple Level Undo enables you to undo actions or sets of actions while you are working on a project schedule.

Figure 7-5

Resource Sheet sorted by group, then by cost

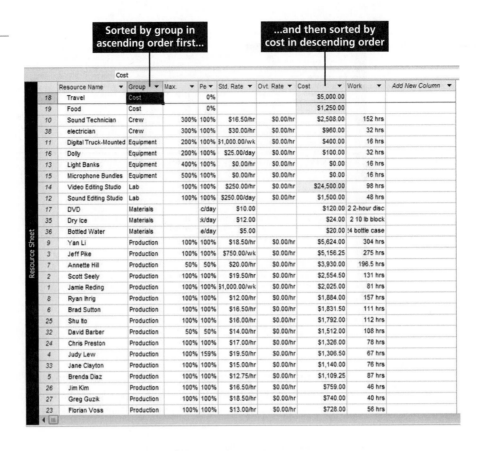

Sorted by group in ascending order first...

...and then sorted by cost in descending order

	Resource Name	Group	Max.	Pe	Std. Rate	Ovt. Rate	Cost	Work	Add New Column
18	Travel	Cost		0%			$5,000.00		
19	Food	Cost		0%			$1,250.00		
10	Sound Technician	Crew	300%	100%	$16.50/hr	$0.00/hr	$2,508.00	152 hrs	
38	electrician	Crew	300%	100%	$30.00/hr	$0.00/hr	$960.00	32 hrs	
11	Digital Truck-Mounted	Equipment	200%	100%	$1,000.00/wk	$0.00/hr	$400.00	16 hrs	
16	Dolly	Equipment	200%	100%	$25.00/day	$0.00/hr	$100.00	32 hrs	
13	Light Banks	Equipment	400%	100%	$0.00/hr	$0.00/hr	$0.00	16 hrs	
15	Microphone Bundles	Equipment	500%	100%	$0.00/hr	$0.00/hr	$0.00	16 hrs	
14	Video Editing Studio	Lab	100%	100%	$250.00/hr	$0.00/hr	$24,500.00	98 hrs	
12	Sound Editing Studio	Lab	100%	100%	$250.00/day	$0.00/hr	$1,500.00	48 hrs	
17	DVD	Materials		c/day	$10.00		$120.00	2 2-hour disc	
35	Dry Ice	Materials		k/day	$12.00		$24.00	2 10 lb block	
36	Bottled Water	Materials		e/day	$5.00		$20.00	:4 bottle case	
9	Yan Li	Production	100%	100%	$18.50/hr	$0.00/hr	$5,624.00	304 hrs	
3	Jeff Pike	Production	100%	100%	$750.00/wk	$0.00/hr	$5,156.25	275 hrs	
7	Annette Hill	Production	50%	50%	$20.00/hr	$0.00/hr	$3,930.00	196.5 hrs	
2	Scott Seely	Production	100%	100%	$19.50/hr	$0.00/hr	$2,554.50	131 hrs	
1	Jamie Reding	Production	100%	100%	$1,000.00/wk	$0.00/hr	$2,025.00	81 hrs	
8	Ryan Ihrig	Production	100%	100%	$12.00/hr	$0.00/hr	$1,884.00	157 hrs	
6	Brad Sutton	Production	100%	100%	$16.50/hr	$0.00/hr	$1,831.50	111 hrs	
25	Shu Ito	Production	100%	100%	$16.00/hr	$0.00/hr	$1,792.00	112 hrs	
32	David Barber	Production	50%	50%	$14.00/hr	$0.00/hr	$1,512.00	108 hrs	
24	Chris Preston	Production	100%	100%	$17.00/hr	$0.00/hr	$1,326.00	78 hrs	
4	Judy Lew	Production	100%	159%	$19.50/hr	$0.00/hr	$1,306.50	67 hrs	
33	Jane Clayton	Production	100%	100%	$15.00/hr	$0.00/hr	$1,140.00	76 hrs	
5	Brenda Diaz	Production	100%	100%	$12.75/hr	$0.00/hr	$1,109.25	87 hrs	
26	Jim Kim	Production	100%	100%	$16.50/hr	$0.00/hr	$759.00	46 hrs	
27	Greg Guzik	Production	100%	100%	$18.50/hr	$0.00/hr	$740.00	40 hrs	
23	Florian Voss	Production	100%	100%	$13.00/hr	$0.00/hr	$728.00	56 hrs	

ANOTHER WAY

You can also "unsort" your data by clicking the Sort button on the View tab, then clicking By ID.

12. SAVE the project schedule.

PAUSE. LEAVE the project schedule open to use in the next exercise.

You have just performed several sorts on your project data so you could more closely examine certain aspects of the project. A *sort* is a way of ordering task or resource information in a view by the criteria you specify. You can sort tasks or resources using predefined criteria, or you can create your own sort order with up to three levels (a group within a group within a group). If you need to sort data in a view with more than three criteria, start by sorting your least important factors first, then sort by your three most important factors.

Except for one instance, sorting does not change the actual data of your project schedule; rather, it simply reorders your data. Sorting allows you to arrange data in an order that answers a question you may have, or in a way that makes more sense or is more user-friendly to the project team. Note that there is no visual indicator that a task or resource view has been sorted other than the order in which the rows of data appear. Furthermore, unlike grouping and filtering, which you will learn about later in this lesson, you cannot save any custom-sort settings you have specified.

The one instance in which the actual data of your project is changed by sorting involves Project's option to renumber resource or task IDs after sorting. Once resources or tasks are renumbered by sorting, you can't restore their original numeric order. Sometimes, however, you might want to permanently renumber tasks or resources. For instance, at the beginning of a project, you might enter resource names as they are needed on the project. Then, when you are finished entering resources, you might want to sort them alphabetically and permanently renumber them.

The Multiple Level Undo function you used in this exercise is a valuable new tool in Microsoft Project. As you saw, this feature allows you to easily undo sets of actions you have performed in Microsoft Project. You can undo changes that you made purposely (as in this exercise) or reverse "mistakes" that you made while working on your project schedule. However, the functionality of Multiple Level Undo doesn't stop there. This feature enables you to make, undo, and redo changes to views, data, and options—giving you the ability to experiment with different scenarios without causing permanent undesired effects. You can test several approaches to resolving a problem or optimizing a project schedule in order to fully understand the implications of each choice. (You can also use Visual Change Highlighting as you are making changes to better see the effects of your actions.)

■ Grouping Data

↓
THE BOTTOM LINE   Another way to organize, view, and analyze the data in your project schedule is through grouping. Grouping enables you to organize the task and resource criteria in your schedule according to various criteria that you select.

→ GROUP DATA IN A RESOURCE VIEW

USE the project schedule you created in the previous exercise.

1. On the View tab, click the **downward arrow** in the Group by box (currently it has *No Group*), then click **Resource Group**. Microsoft Project reorganizes the data into resource groups and presents it in an expanded outline form. It also adds summary costs by group. Your screen should look similar to Figure 7-6.

Figure 7-6

Resource Sheet with data summarized and grouped by resource group

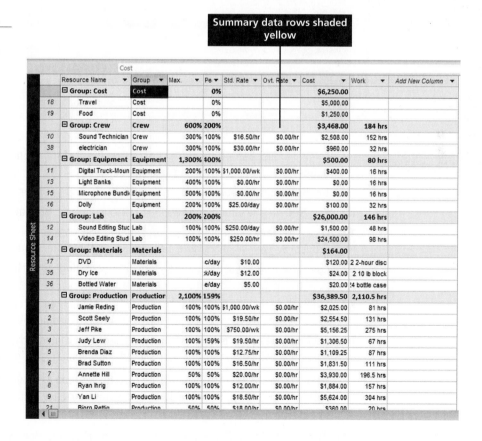

Note that the summary data rows are set off with a colored background (yellow in this case). Because the data in the summary rows is derived from subordinate data, it cannot be changed directly. To have more control over how your data is presented, you can create custom groups.

2. On the View tab, click the **downward arrow** in the Group by box (currently it has *Resource Group*), then click **More Groups**. The More Groups dialog box appears, displaying all of the predefined groups for tasks and resources available to you. You will create a new group that is similar to the Resource Group.

3. Select **Resource Group** (if it is not already selected), then click the **Copy** button. The Group Definition dialog box appears.

4. In the Names box, key **Resource Groups by Cost**.

5. In the Field Name column, click the **first empty cell** below Group.

6. Key or select **Cost**.

7. In the Order column for the Cost field, click **Ascending** to select it, then select **Descending** from the drop-down menu. The resources will be sorted within their groups by descending cost. The Group Definition dialog box should look similar to Figure 7-7.

Figure 7-7

Group Definition dialog box

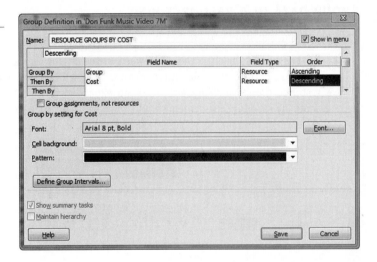

8. In the Group Definition dialog box, click the **Define Group Intervals** button. The Define Group Intervals dialog box appears.

9. In the Group on box, select **Interval** from the drop-down menu.

10. Key **500** in the Group interval box, then click the **OK** button.

11. Click the **Save** button in the Group Definition dialog box to close it. Resource Groups by Cost appears as a new group in the More Groups dialog box.

12. Click the **Apply** button in the More Groups dialog box. Microsoft Project applies the new group to the Resource Sheet view.

13. Right-click the Resource Name column heading, then select **Field Settings**. The Field Settings dialog box appears. You want to widen the Resource Name column.

14. Click the **Best Fit** button in the Field Settings dialog box. The Resource Name column is widened. Your screen should look similar to Figure 7-8.

Now, the resources are grouped by Resource Group (the yellow shaded cells), and within each group, they are further grouped by cost values at $500 increments (the blue shaded cells).

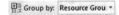

15. After reviewing the groupings you created, click the **downward arrow** next to Resource Groups by Cost in the Data group, then click **No Group**. Microsoft Project removes the groupings, restoring the original data. Displaying or removing a group has no effect on the data in the project.

Figure 7-8

Resource Sheet with
multiple-level grouping applied

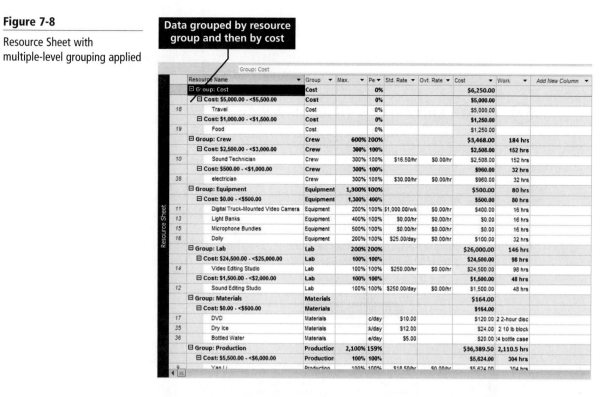

Data grouped by resource
group and then by cost

  ANOTHER WAY   You can also auto-fit any column by placing the cursor on the right-side dividing line
and double-clicking.

16. **SAVE** the project schedule.

PAUSE. LEAVE the project schedule open to use in the next exercise.

In this exercise, you reorganized your project data using grouping. A *group* is a way to reorder task or resource information in a table and to display summary values for each group according to various criteria you can choose. Grouping goes a step beyond sorting in that grouping your project data will add summary values, called "roll-ups," at customized intervals.

Grouping the data in a project schedule enables you to view your information from a variety of perspectives. It also allows for a more detailed level of data analysis and presentation. In your role as project manager, your project schedule helps you track the work and costs associated with your project. By using grouping, you also have the ability to look at more details—to understand not just what is happening on your project, but also why.

As with sorting, grouping does not change the fundamental structure of your project schedule but rather just reorganizes and summarizes it. Also like sorting, grouping applies to all tables you can display in a view. You can use any of the predefined groups, customize these predefined groups, or create your own.

■ Filtering Data

↓
THE BOTTOM LINE

The Microsoft Project feature known as filtering allows you to look only at specific task or resource data that meets specific criteria. Filtering hides task or resource data that does not meet the criteria you specify and displays only the data in which you are interested. You can use a predefined filter, use AutoFilters, or create a custom filter.

Creating and Applying a Filter

In this exercise, you create a filter that allows you to focus on tasks related to the video shoot.

 CREATE AND APPLY A FILTER IN A VIEW

USE the project schedule you created in the previous exercise.

1. On the View tab, click the **Gantt Chart** button in the Task Views group. The Gantt chart view appears.

2. In Microsoft Project 2010, AutoFilter is built into the task and resource views, and you will see arrows on the right side of each column heading. You can use these arrows to select the AutoFilter option you want to use. Adjust the width of the Gantt chart so that the Task Name, Duration, and Start columns are visible. Your screen should look similar to Figure 7-9.

Figure 7-9

Gantt chart view displaying AutoFilter buttons in each column

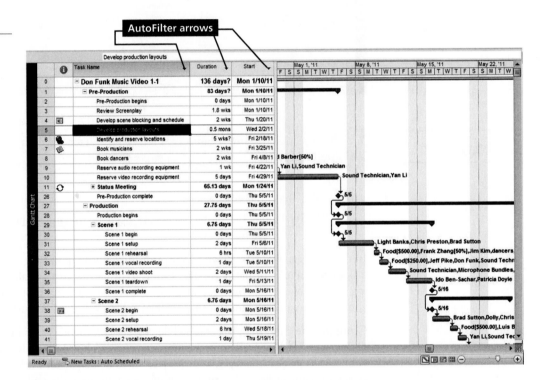

 To turn AutoFilter off or on, click the downward arrow in the (No Filter) box in the Data Group, then select Display AutoFilter.

3. Click the **downward arrow** in the Task Name column heading, point to Filters, then click **(Custom . . .)**. The Custom AutoFilter dialog box appears. You want to see just the tasks that contain the letter-string of *shoot*, so you need to set up the Custom AutoFilter to do this.

4. In the Name section, select **contains** from the drop-down list in the first box, if it is not already visible. In the adjacent box, key **shoot**. The Custom AutoFilter dialog box should look similar to Figure 7-10.

Figure 7-10

Custom AutoFilter dialog box with criteria entered

5. Click the **OK** button to apply the filter and close the Custom AutoFilter dialog box. Microsoft Project filters the task list to show only those tasks that contain the word *shoot*, as well as their summary tasks. Your screen should look similar to Figure 7-11.

Figure 7-11

Gantt chart view with custom AutoFilter applied

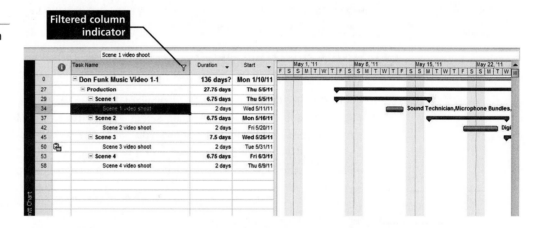

Note that on the right side of the Task Name column, a small "funnel" appears. This is a visual indicator that AutoFilter has been applied to this column in this view.

6. On the Ribbon, click the **downward arrow** in the Filter box in the Data group (currently has *No Filter*), then select **(No Filter)**. The AutoFilter is cleared, and all the tasks in the project schedule are displayed.

7. **SAVE** the project schedule.

   PAUSE. LEAVE the project schedule open to use in the next exercise.

⊕ ANOTHER WAY

You can also use the F3 key to remove any filter you apply.

In this exercise, you created and applied a filter to the project schedule to enable you to look at only the tasks dealing with scene shoots. A ***filter*** is a tool that enables you to see or highlight in a table only the task or resource information that meets the criteria you choose. Filtering doesn't change the data in your project schedule—it only changes the data's appearance.

There are two ways to apply filters to a view: by using predefined filters or by using AutoFilters.

- Predefined or custom filters allow you to see or highlight only the task or resource information that meets the criteria of the filter. For example, the Milestones filter displays only tasks that are milestones. Some predefined filters, such as the Date Range filter, require you to enter criteria (a date) to set up the filter.

 TAKE NOTE＊   If a task or a resource sheet view has a filter applied to it, the name of the filter will be displayed in the Filter box on the View tab.

- *AutoFilters* are used for more informal or impromptu filtering. An AutoFilter is a quick way to view only the task or resource information that meets the criteria you choose. When the AutoFilter feature is turned on, small downward arrows are visible adjacent to the column heading name. Clicking the arrow activates a list of criteria that can be used to filter the data. The criteria that are listed are appropriate for the type of data in the column.

You can also apply multiple column filters. Say you wanted to find all tasks that are more than one week in duration and start between 2/1/11 and 3/30/11. Here, you would apply an AutoFilter of "1 week or longer" to the duration column and then apply an AutoFilter of "Between" 2/1/11 and 3/30/11 to the start column.

■ Creating a Custom Filter

 THE BOTTOM LINE In the previous exercise, you used AutoFilter to apply a filter to the data of interest. Now, you will create a custom filter.

⊕ CREATE A CUSTOM FILTER

USE the project schedule you created in the previous exercise.

1. On the View tab, click the **downward arrow** in the Filter box in the Data group (currently has *No Filter*), then select **More Filters**. The More Filters dialog box appears. This dialog box shows you all of the predefined filters for tasks or resources that are available to you.
2. Click the **New** button. The Filter Definition dialog box appears.

 **ANOTHER WAY** You can also click the downward arrow in the (No Filter) box in the Data group, then select New Filter.

3. In the Name box, key **Unfinished Shoots**.
4. In the first row of the Field Name column, key or select **Name**.
5. In the first row of the Test column, key or select **contains**.
6. In the first row of the Value(s) column, key **shoot**. You have now finished entering the first criterion for the filter. Next you will enter the second criterion.
7. In the second row of the And/Or column, select **And**.
8. In the second row of the Field Name column, key or select **Actual Finish**.
9. In the second row of the Test column, key or select **equals**.
10. In the second row of the Value(s) column, key **NA**. NA is how Microsoft Project marks fields that do not yet have a value. In other words, any shooting task that does not yet have a value must be uncompleted. Your screen should look similar to Figure 7-12.

Figure 7-12

Filter Definition dialog box with custom criteria entered

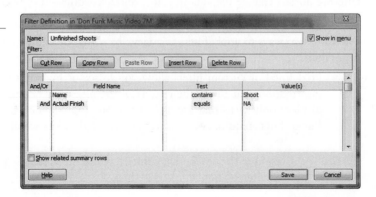

11. Click the **Save** button to close the Filter Definition dialog box. The new filter you just created, Unfinished Shoots, appears in the More Filters dialog box.

12. Locate and select the Unfinished Shoots filter in the list, if necessary. Click the **Apply** button. Microsoft Project applies the new filter to your project schedule in the Gantt chart view. Your screen should look similar to Figure 7-13.

Figure 7-13

Gantt chart view with
Unfinished Shoots filter applied

Take note of the gaps in the task IDs. This is one visual way you can tell that a filter has been applied. The tasks are filtered to show uncompleted tasks (and because you haven't started tracking actual work yet, all the shooting tasks are currently uncompleted).

13. On the View tab, click the **downward arrow** in the Filter box in the Data group (currently has *Unfinished Shoots*), then select **(No Filter)**. Microsoft Project removes the filter.

14. **SAVE** and **CLOSE** the project schedule.

PAUSE. If you are continuing to the next lesson, keep Project open. If you are not continuing to additional lessons, **CLOSE** Project.

In this exercise, you learned how to create and apply a custom filter. A custom filter works in the same way as a predefined filter, except that you (rather than Microsoft Project) have selected the filtering criterion. Remember that after filtering, you might see gaps in the task or resource ID numbers. The data has not been deleted—it is hidden only until you remove the filter. Also, as with sorting and grouping, filtering applies to all tables you can display in the active view. Some views that do not support tables, such as the Calendar view, do support filtering but not AutoFilters.

SKILL SUMMARY

IN THIS LESSON, YOU LEARNED:	TASK
To sort data.	Sort data in a resource view.
To group data.	Group data in a resource view.
To filter data.	Create and apply a filter in a view.
	Create a custom filter.

■ Knowledge Assessment

Fill in the Blank

Complete the following sentences by writing the correct word or words in the blanks provided.

1. _____ is a quick way to view only the task or resource information you choose.

2. In the Sort dialog box, you can utilize up to _____ nested levels of sort criteria.

3. When you use grouping, the _____ data rows are set off by a colored background.

4. When AutoFilter is turned on, small _____ are visible next to the column headings.

5. A way to reorder task or resource information in a table and to display summary values according to various criteria you can choose is called a(n) _____ .

6. The _____ dialog box shows you all of the predefined filters that are available to you for tasks or resources.

7. A(n) _____ is a way of ordering task or resource information in a view by the criteria you specify.

8. When you apply a filter, you may see gaps in the _____ .

9. When you sort data in your project, the sort applies to the active _____, no matter which table is displayed.

10. A tool that enables you to see or highlight in a table only the task or resource information that meets criteria you choose is a(n) _____ .

Multiple Choice

Select the best response for the following statements.

1. The simplest way to reorganize data in Microsoft Project is by:
   a. filtering.
   b. sorting.
   c. grouping.
   d. AutoFiltering.

2. The _____ function lets you reverse actions you have performed in Microsoft Project.
   a. Task Drivers
   b. Reverse Filtering
   c. Multiple Level Undo
   d. Ungrouping

3. The one instance in which the actual data of your project is changed by sorting is when:
   a. the Permanently renumber resources check box is selected.
   b. the Multiple Level Undo function is disabled.
   c. the project is saved before the sorting is reversed.
   d. All of the above

4. When you apply a group to your project schedule, the data in the summary rows cannot be changed directly because:

   a. it will cause the grouping to become permanent.

   b. it will alter the data in your project schedule.

   c. it is derived from subordinate data.

   d. it will cause an error in the grouping function.

5. When AutoFilter is on, clicking the downward arrow next to a column heading:

   a. sorts the data in the column in descending order.

   b. turns the AutoFilter off.

   c. automatically adjusts the column width.

   d. allows you to select criteria to apply to the filter.

6. Multiple Level Undo can be used:

   a. as many times as desired.

   b. up to 99 times, or until the original data is restored.

   c. up to 35 consecutive times.

   d. up to 50 consecutive times.

7. If a view has a filter applied to it, the name of the filter will be displayed in the Filter button on the _____ tab.

   a. Data

   b. Format

   c. View

   d. Resource Management

8. There is no visual indicator that a task or resource view has been sorted other than:

   a. the shaded summary rows.

   b. the small "s" at the top of each data column.

   c. the order in which the rows of data appear.

   d. There is no visual indicator to show a view has been sorted.

9. Grouping might be helpful if you are trying to see:

   a. only the tasks that contain the word "Weekly."

   b. the critical path tasks.

   c. the tasks ordered from highest to lowest cost.

   d. the total cost of each resource group.

10. You cannot save custom settings that you have specified for:

   a. sorting.

   b. grouping.

   c. filtering.

   d. All of the above

■ Competency Assessment

Project 7-1: Sorting by Standard Rate

You have some additional setup work that needs to be completed before the shooting of one of the Don Funk Music Video scenes can begin. Because you will need to pay overtime

(time and one-half) for this additional work, you would like to use an employee who has a low standard rate. Sort your resources according to Standard Rate and Max Units so that you can make your request from the lowest-cost group of employees.

GET READY. Launch Microsoft Project if it is not already running. **OPEN** *Don Funk Music Video 7-1* from the data files for this lesson.

1. Click the View tab, then in the **Resource Views** group, click **Resource Sheet**.
2. On the Ribbon, click **Sort**, then click **Sort by**.
3. In the Sort by section, select **Standard Rate** from the drop-down menu. Next to that, click **Descending**.
4. In the first Then by section, select **Max. Units** from the drop-down menu. Next to that, click **Descending**. Make sure the Permanently renumber resources box is not checked.
5. Click the **Sort** button.
6. **SAVE** the project schedule as *Don Funk Standard Rate Sort* and **CLOSE** the file. **LEAVE** Project open for the next exercise.

The *Don Funk Music Video 7-1* file for this lesson is available on the book companion website.

Project 7-2: Applying HR Filter

You are reviewing your project schedule for hiring a new employee. You want to specifically review the staff members from the Human Resources (HR) department who are involved with this project. Thus, you need to apply a filter that will screen out any staff except HR.

OPEN *Hiring New Employee 7-2* from the data files for this lesson.

1. Click the View tab, then click **Resource Sheet**.
2. Click the **downward arrow** in the Group column heading, point to **Filters**, then click **(Custom . . .)**.
3. In the Group section, select **contains** from the drop-down list in the first box, if it is not already visible. In the adjacent box, key **HR**.
4. Click the **OK** button.
5. **SAVE** the project schedule as *Hiring New Employee HR Filter* and **CLOSE** the file. **PAUSE. LEAVE** Project open to use in the next exercise.

The *Hiring New Employee 7-2* file for this lesson is available on the book companion website.

■ Proficiency Assessment

Project 7-3: Sorting Resource Groups by Standard Rate for Don Funk Music Video

You are working on employee reviews and pay increases for your staff for the upcoming year. You have decided it would be beneficial to be able to look at the standard rate variation within the resource groups working on this project. You need to set up a custom group that will enable you to do this.

OPEN *Don Funk Music Video 7-3* from the data files for this lesson.

1. Change the view to Resource Sheet view.
2. On the Ribbon, select **Group by: More Groups**.
3. Select **Resource Group**, then make a copy of this group.
4. In the Group Definition box, name the new group **Resource Groups by Standard Rate**.

The ***Don Funk Music Video 7-3*** file for this lesson is available on the book companion website.

5. On the first Then By line, set up the grouping by Standard Rate in descending order.
6. Click **Define Group Intervals**, then set up the resulting dialog box so that grouping is done on intervals of five.
7. Select the group you have created and apply it to your project schedule.
8. Widen the Resource Name field so that you can see the Standard Rate groupings.
9. **SAVE** the project schedule as ***Don Funk Resource Groupings*** and **CLOSE** the file.
   PAUSE. LEAVE Project open to use in the next exercise.

Project 7-4: Duration Sorting for Office Remodel

You are responsible for the kitchen and lunchroom remodel for your office. Your manager has asked you which tasks on the project are scheduled to take the longest. You need to do a quick sort on the tasks to respond to this question.

OPEN *Office Remodel 7-4* from the data files for this lesson.

The ***Office Remodel 7-4*** file for this lesson is available on the book companion website.

1. Change the view to Gantt chart view.
2. Change the table view to Summary.
3. From the View tab, select **Sort**, then **Sort by**.
4. Set up the dialog box to sort by duration in descending order. Make sure that the tasks are not permanently renumbered.
5. Perform the sort.
6. **SAVE** the project schedule as ***Office Remodel Duration Sort*** and **CLOSE** the file.
   PAUSE. LEAVE Project open to use in the next exercise.

■ Mastery Assessment

Project 7-5: Don Funk Filter for Don Funk Music Video

You are the project manager for the Don Funk Music Video. You need to review all of the production tasks to which Don Funk, the video's star, is assigned so that you can make sure his dressing room is prepared properly on those days. (Hint: Note that all of the production tasks contain the word "Scene.") You need to apply a filter to show only the production tasks with Don Funk assigned to them.

OPEN *Don Funk Music Video 7-5* from the data files for this lesson.

The ***Don Funk Music Video 7-5*** file for this lesson is available on the book companion website.

1. Open the More Filters dialog box.
2. Begin to build a new filter based on the Using Resource task filter.
3. Name the new filter **Don Funk Production Tasks**.
4. Build the first level of the filter based on Name, which contains **Scene**.
5. Using **And** to link the levels, add a second level of the filter based on Resource Names, which contains **Don Funk**.
6. Run the filter.
7. **SAVE** the project schedule as ***Don Funk Filter*** and **CLOSE** the file.
   PAUSE. LEAVE Project open to use in the next exercise.

Project 7-6: Costs and Durations for Hiring a New Employee

You want to compare the cost of tasks that have the same duration in your project schedule to hire a new employee. You therefore need to set up a custom group in order to group the data by duration and then by cost.

OPEN *Hiring New Employee 7-6* from the data files for this lesson.

The *Hiring New Employee 7-6* file for this lesson is available on the book companion website.

1. Switch to the Task Usage view.
2. Use the Duration group to set up a new custom group called **Duration-Cost**.
3. Set up the new group so that it groups by descending duration and then descending cost.
4. Apply the Duration-Cost group.
5. **SAVE** the project schedule as *Hiring Duration Cost Group* and **CLOSE** the file. **CLOSE** Project.

INTERNET READY

Over the last seven lessons, you have become familiar with the basics of Microsoft Project: tasks, resources, assignments, constraints, and resource allocation. You have learned that even the best project schedule is only as good as the information you can get out of it.

Search the Internet for current events in your city or state, and locate a story about a project that has not gone according to schedule (construction of a road or building, production of a new product, opening of a restaurant, etc.). Review the article; then, using what you have learned about Microsoft Project so far, write a short paragraph on what you believe went "wrong" with the project you selected. Make suggestions on how these problems could be avoided in the future. If necessary, perform additional Internet research on your selected current event.

WORKPLACE READY

Using Microsoft Project Templates

Suppose you are the conversion project manager at a company that processes electronic payments. You manage the "conversion" of new clients onto your data processing systems. Your manager has been impressed with your hard work and attention to detail, so he gives you a new project responsibility that is not in your range of experience–developing the project schedule for your company's upcoming move to a new office location. Although you are glad that your manager has confidence in you, you are a bit nervous because you are unfamiliar with the tasks involved in the process. You know that an office move involves more than just relocating furniture, phones, and computers, but where do you go from there?

Microsoft Project 2010 provides access to a number of templates at www.office.microsoft.com that are ready for you to download and customize for your specific project needs. Upon opening Microsoft Project, a new blank project schedule is automatically opened. If you click the File tab and then click New, the Available Templates screen opens. Microsoft Project 2010 no longer provides templates built into the software. The templates at Microsoft Office.com are always being updated, and going directly to the source will ensure you get the latest template. Microsoft Office.com provides several different options for starting a new project, as shown in Figure 7-14.

Figure 7-14

New project with the Available Templates screen

Using the Search Office.com box, you can search for a template online. You can also review the list of recently used templates. If you search online, you can browse templates by category. When you find a sample that you think will meet your needs, you can preview it in your web browser. If you like what you see, you can download the template, open it, and begin to make updates that reflect your project's specific requirements.

The project sample shown in Figure 7-15 is part of the Office Move template downloaded from Microsoft Office.com. You can add or delete tasks, change task durations, or rearrange summary tasks. You can add, delete, or rename resources, and then fill in resource details such as cost and assignment units. You can change dependencies, constraints, and calendars, all based on your actual project requirements.

Figure 7-15

Office Move template downloaded from Office.com

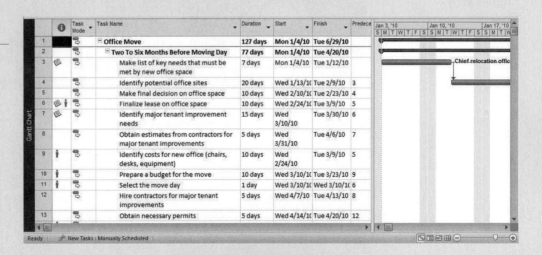

You can see that by starting with a Project template, you can create a project schedule that fits all of your needs in much less time than it would take to create the project from scratch.

8 LESSON

Project Schedule Formatting Fundamentals

LESSON SKILL MATRIX

SKILL	TASK
Gantt Chart Formatting	Modify the Gantt chart using the Bar Styles dialog box.
	Modify the Gantt chart using Gantt Chart Styles.
Drawing in a Gantt Chart	Add a text box to the Gantt chart.
Changing Text Appearance in a View	Change the appearance of text in a view.
Creating and Editing Tables	Create a custom table.
Creating Custom Views	Create a custom view.

As a production manager for Southridge Video and the project manager for the new Don Funk music video, you have the foundation of your project schedule in place. However, a project manager doesn't usually look at all of the data in a project schedule at once. In this lesson, you will learn to use various tools in Microsoft Project 2010, such as views and reports, to look at the elements or aspects of a project schedule in which you are currently interested. With these tools, you can significantly affect how your information appears by changing the data format to meet your needs.

KEY TERMS
charts
diagram view
field
forms
sheets
table
usage view
view

SOFTWARE ORIENTATION

Microsoft Project's Bar Styles Dialog Box

In Microsoft Project, you can use the Bar Styles dialog box (Figure 8-1) to customize the appearance of items on the Gantt chart. This dialog box enables you to change the appearance of items such as task bars, milestones, summary bars, and text. You can change characteristics such as bar types, patterns, colors, splits, and shapes.

Figure 8-1

Bar Styles dialog box

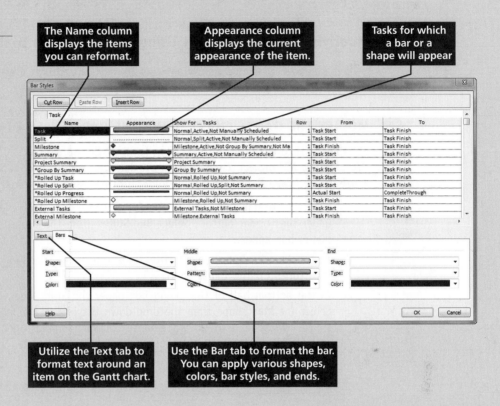

The Name column displays the items you can reformat.

Appearance column displays the current appearance of the item.

Tasks for which a bar or a shape will appear

Utilize the Text tab to format text around an item on the Gantt chart.

Use the Bar tab to format the bar. You can apply various shapes, colors, bar styles, and ends.

When customizing a Gantt chart, you may find it helpful to use one of the new features of the Project 2010 interface: the Format tab. In previous lessons, you may have noticed this tab at the top of your screen, just above the Ribbon. The Format tab provides you with quick access to the formatting options available in your current view. Figure 8-2 shows the Format tab for the Gantt chart view.

Figure 8-2

Format tab for the Gantt chart view

■ Gantt Chart Formatting

THE BOTTOM LINE

In Project 2010, the Gantt chart view consists of two parts: a table on the left, and a bar chart on the right. The default formatting of the Gantt chart view is useful for onscreen project schedule viewing and printing. However, you can change the formatting of almost any element on the Gantt chart to suit your needs. In this exercise, you will learn to format Gantt chart task bars. You can format whole categories of Gantt chart task bars via the Bar Styles dialog box, or you can format individual Gantt chart task bars directly.

Modifying the Gantt Chart Using the Bar Styles Dialog Box

In this exercise, you modify several items on the Gantt chart using the Bar Styles dialog box.

→ MODIFY THE GANTT CHART USING THE BAR STYLES DIALOG BOX

GET READY. Before you begin these steps, launch Microsoft Project. **OPEN** the *Don Funk Music Video 8M* project schedule from the data files for this lesson. **SAVE** the file as *Don Funk Music Video 8* in the solutions folder for this lesson as directed by your instructor.

1. Click the **Format** tab, then in the Bar Styles group, click the **downward arrow** under the Format button. Select **Bar Styles** from the drop-down list. The Bar Styles dialog box appears.
2. In the Name column, select **Milestone**. You want to change the shape of the milestones on the Gantt chart.
3. In the bottom half of the dialog box under the Start label, locate the Shape box. Select the **star** shape from the drop-down list in the Shape box. Note that the star shape now appears in the Appearance column for Milestone. Your screen should look similar to Figure 8-3.

Figure 8-3

Bar Styles dialog box displaying the star as the shape for milestones

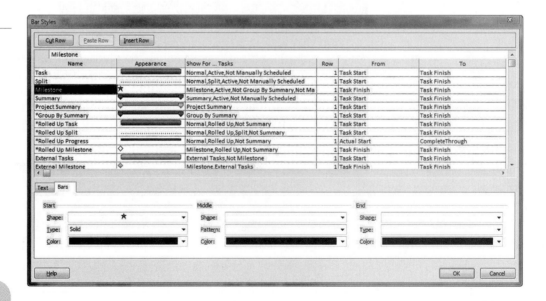

The *Don Funk Music Video 8M* file for this lesson is available on the book companion website.

4. In the bottom half of the dialog box, click the **Text** tab. You want to make a change to display resource initials rather than full names next to the task bars.
5. In the Name column at the top of the dialog box, select **Task**.

6. In the Text tab, in the *Right* box, select **Resource Names**, click the **downward arrow**, and then select **Resource Initials**. Your screen should look similar to Figure 8-4.

Figure 8-4

Bar Styles dialog box showing resource initials to be listed at the right of all task bars

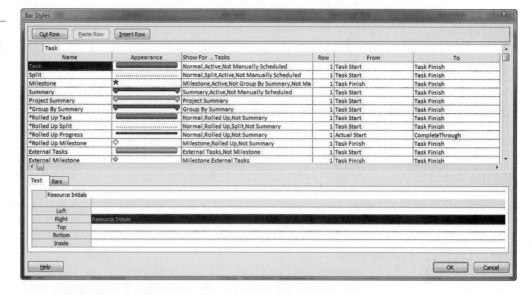

7. Click **OK** to close the Bar Styles dialog box. Microsoft Project applies the formatting changes you made to the Gantt chart.

8. Select the **name** of task 26, **Pre-production complete**. Press **Ctrl + Shift + F5**. This is the keyboard shortcut for Scroll to Task. Microsoft Project scrolls the Gantt chart bar view to task 26, where you can see the reformatted milestone and resource initials. Your screen should look similar to Figure 8-5.

Figure 8-5

Gantt chart view showing resource initials and the new shape for milestones

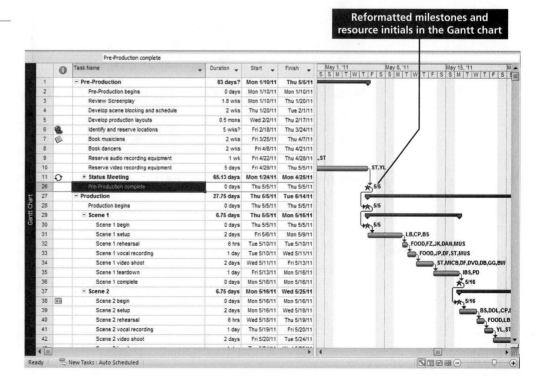

9. **SAVE** the project schedule.

PAUSE. LEAVE the project schedule open to use in the next exercise.

TAKE NOTE*

With the Bar Styles dialog box, the formatting changes you make to a type of item (e.g., a milestone) apply to all such items in the Gantt chart.

You just used the Bar Styles dialog box to make formatting changes to several items in the Gantt chart view. The Gantt chart is the primary way of viewing the data in a project schedule. It became the standard for visualizing project schedules in the early twentieth century, when American engineer and management consultant Henry L. Gantt developed a bar chart with two main principles: 1) to measure activities by the amount of time needed to complete them; and 2) to use space on the chart to represent the amount of an activity that should be done in a given period of time.

In Microsoft Project, the Gantt chart view is the default view. A *view* is a window through which you can see various elements of your project schedule. The two main view categories are named single view, which you will see later in this lesson, and combination view. Views are made up of one or more view formats. The five different view formats and their common uses are listed in Table 8-1.

Table 8-1

View formats

FORMAT	PURPOSE OR USE
Charts	Present information graphically, such as the Gantt chart.
Sheets	Present information in rows and columns, such as the Task Sheet or the Resource Sheet.
Forms	Present detailed information in a structured format about one task or resource at a time, such as the Task Form.
Diagram	Present information in diagram format, such as the Network Diagram.
Usage	Present task or resource information on the left side and time-phased information on the right, such as the Resource Usage or Task Usage views.

Modifying the Gantt Chart Using Gantt Chart Styles

In this exercise, you create a custom Gantt chart, format it using predefined Gantt Chart Styles, and save your custom view.

⊙ MODIFY THE GANTT CHART USING GANTT CHART STYLES

USE the project schedule you created in the previous exercise.

1. Click the **Format** tab under Gantt Chart Tools, if necessary.

 2. In the Show/Hide group, click the **Project Summary Task** box.

3. Press the **F5** key. In the ID box, key **0**, then click **OK**. Microsoft Project displays the project summary task (task ID 0) at the top of the Gantt chart view. Now you will make a few adjustments to your screen so that all of the summary task information is visible.

4. Drag the vertical divider bar between the table and chart to the right until at least the Duration and Start columns are visible, if necessary.

ANOTHER WAY You can also double-click the divider bar to snap the divider to the nearest column edge.

5. Double-click the right edge of the **Start** column, in the column heading, to expand the column so that you can see the entire value. Readjust the vertical divider bar as necessary. Your screen should look similar to Figure 8-6.

Figure 8-6

Gantt chart showing widened Start column and project summary task

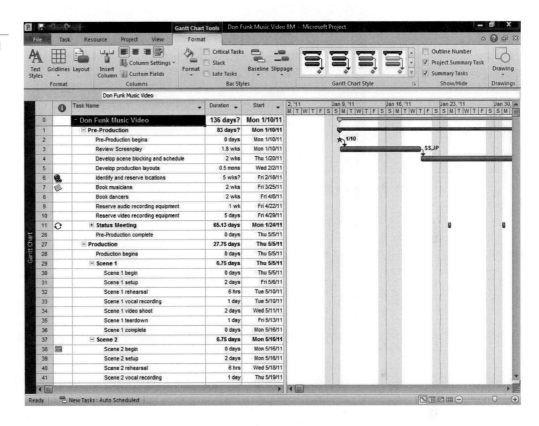

Before you make further formatting changes, you will make a copy of the Gantt chart view so that you will not affect the original Gantt chart view.

ANOTHER WAY Right-clicking anywhere in a column heading will activate the submenu for the column. Selecting Field Settings will display the Field Settings dialog box. In the dialog box, click the Best Fit button to automatically adjust the column width.

6. Click the **View** tab. In the Task Views group, click the **downward arrow** under the Gantt Chart button, then select **Save View**. The Save View dialog box appears with View 1 as the default name, as in Figure 8-7.

Figure 8-7

Save View dialog box

7. In the Name Field, key **My Custom Gantt Chart**, then click **OK.** The Save View dialog box closes. Note that the name of the new view is listed on the left edge of your screen. Your screen should look similar to Figure 8-8.

Figure 8-8

My Custom Gantt Chart view

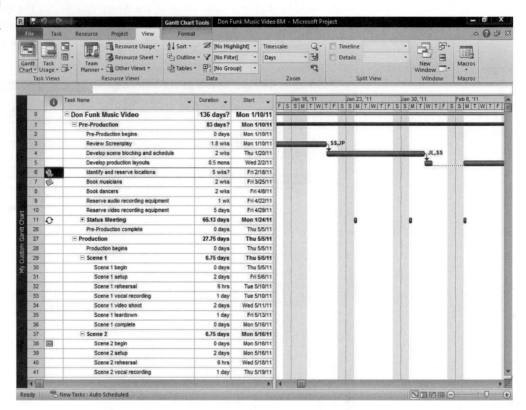

8. Click the **Format** tab. In the Gantt Chart Styles group, click the **More** button located at the lower right of the bar graphics; see Figure 8-9.

Figure 8-9

The More button displays pre-defined Gantt chart styles

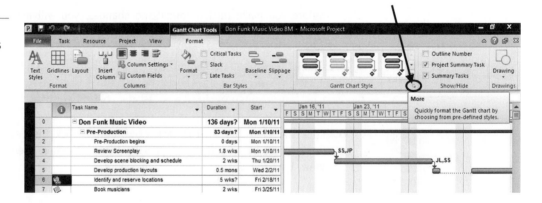

9. The predefined Gantt Chart Style options appear as in Figure 8-10. They are divided into two style categories, one for scheduling and one for presentations. Select the first option in the third row of the scheduling category.

Figure 8-10

Predefined Gantt chart styles

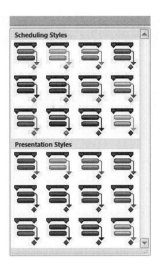

10. On the Format tab, in the Bar Styles group, click the **check box** for **Critical Tasks**.

11. Press the **F5** key. In the ID box, key **70** and press **Enter**. Notice that Tasks 73 through 77 are formatted to display in red. Your screen should look similar to Figure 8-11.

Figure 8-11

My Custom Gantt Chart view with new scheduling style applied and critical tasks

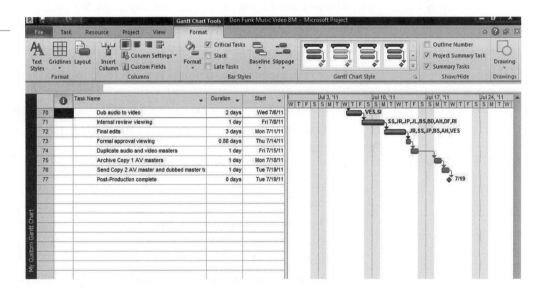

TAKE NOTE ★ Notice that the Resource Initials are still displayed to the right of the Gantt bars, but the Milestones have been changed back to the default diamond shape.

12. SAVE the project schedule.

PAUSE. LEAVE the project schedule open to use in the next exercise.

In this exercise, you made formatting changes to your project schedule using predefined Gantt Chart Styles. This is similar to making changes using the Bar Styles command; however, the predefined Gantt Chart Styles offers fewer choices than the Bar Styles command. As you review the formatting changes in the My Custom Gantt Chart view, remember that none of the data in the project schedule has changed—only the way it is formatted has changed. These formatting adjustments affect only the My Custom Gantt Chart view; all other views in Microsoft Project are unaffected.

■ Drawing in a Gantt Chart

THE BOTTOM LINE

Included in Microsoft Project is a Drawing toolbar that enables you to draw objects or text directly onto a Gantt chart. This feature allows you to call attention to a specific event or item. You can draw text boxes, arrows, and other items. In this exercise, you add a text box to the Gantt chart.

→ **ADD A TEXT BOX TO THE GANTT CHART**

USE the project schedule you created in the previous exercise.

1. Click the **Task** tab, then click the **downward arrow** under the Gantt Chart button and select **More Views**. The More Views dialog box appears.
2. In the More Views box, select **Detail Gantt**, then click **Apply**. The Detail Gantt view appears.

ANOTHER WAY

You can also right-click the view name bar at the left edge of the screen and select More Views from the drop-down menu.

3. Press the **F5** key. In the ID box, key **1**; in the Date box, key **5/8/11**; then press **Enter**. This brings you to a point in the Gantt chart where you want to place a text box. Click the **Format** tab, under Gantt Chart Tools. In the Drawings group, click the **Drawing** button. The Drawing drop-down menu appears.
4. On the Drawing drop-down menu, click the **Text Box** button, and then drag a small square somewhere around May 15th on the chart portion of the Detail Gantt view.
5. In the box you just drew, key **CMT Music Awards May 20–22**.
6. Right-click the **Text Box**, then click **Properties**. The Format Drawing dialog box appears.
7. Click the **Line and Fill** tab, if it is not already selected.
8. Select **lime** from the Color box under the Fill label (the fourth selection from the top).
9. Click the **Size and Position** tab.
10. Make sure that **Attach to Timescale** is selected. In the Date box, select or key **May 20, 2011**.
11. In the Vertical box, key **1**, then click **OK** to close the Format Drawing dialog box. Microsoft Project formats the text box with lime fill and positions it below the timescale on the date you specified.
12. If the text box is not visible on your screen, press the **F5** key.
13. In the Date box, select **May 15, 2011** and click **OK**. Microsoft Project scrolls the view to display the date you specified. Your screen should look similar to Figure 8-12.

Figure 8-12

Detail Gantt Chart view with text box attached to a specific date

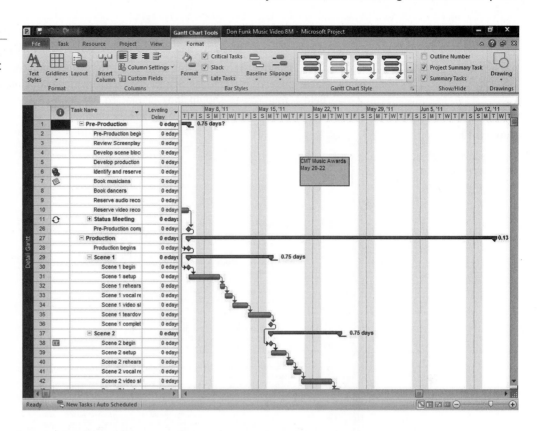

14. SAVE the project schedule.

PAUSE. LEAVE the project schedule open to use in the next exercise.

In this exercise, you used the Drawing toolbar to add a text box to the Gantt chart on your project schedule. You also linked your text box to a date. When you are adding drawing objects and linking them to your project schedule, there are two key considerations to remember:

- If the object you are adding is specific to a task, link the object to the Gantt bar. The object will move with the Gantt bar if it is rescheduled.
- If the object you are adding has information that is date specific, link the object to a date. The object will remain in the same position relative to the timescale, no matter what part of the timescale is in view.

■ Changing Text Appearance in a View

THE BOTTOM LINE

Because viewing the project schedule is key to understanding the status of a project, changing the formatting of the text in the schedule can help you view schedule information more quickly and easily. In this exercise, you use text styles and direct formatting to change the appearance of text in a view.

↪ **CHANGE APPEARANCE OF TEXT IN A VIEW**

USE the project schedule you created in the previous exercise.

1. Click the **Task** tab, click the **downward arrow** under the Gantt Chart button, and select **More Views**. The More Views dialog box appears.

2. Click **Task Sheet** in the Views box, then click the **Apply** button. The Task Sheet view appears. This view has only a single table; there is no chart component.

3. Click the **View** tab, click the **Tables** button, and then click **Summary**. The Summary table appears in the Task Sheet view. (You will be looking closely at the Cost field.) Your screen should look similar to Figure 8-13.

Figure 8-13

Task Sheet view with summary table applied

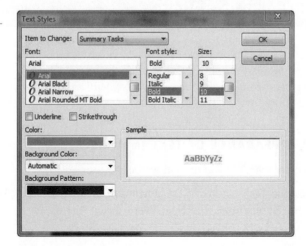

	Task	Task Name	Duration	Start	Finish	%	Cost	Work	Add New Column
0		Don Funk Music Vide	136 days?	Mon 1/10/1	Tue 7/19/11	0%	$88,956.50	,757.5 hrs	
1		Pre-Production	83 days?	Mon 1/10/11	Thu 5/5/11	0%	$27,841.00	1,314 hrs	
2		Pre-Production begi	0 days	Mon 1/10/11	Mon 1/10/11	0%	$0.00	0 hrs	
3		Review Screenplay	1.8 wks	Mon 1/10/11	Thu 1/20/11	0%	$2,295.00	120 hrs	
4		Develop scene bloc	2 wks	Thu 1/20/11	Tue 2/1/11	0%	$1,560.00	80 hrs	
5		Develop production	0.5 mons	Wed 2/2/11	Thu 2/17/11	0%	$2,520.00	160 hrs	
6		Identify and reserve	5 wks?	Fri 2/18/11	Thu 3/24/11	0%	$14,455.00	550 hrs	
7		Book musicians	2 wks	Fri 3/25/11	Thu 4/7/11	0%	$1,360.00	80 hrs	
8		Book dancers	2 wks	Fri 4/8/11	Thu 4/21/11	0%	$1,360.00	80 hrs	
9		Reserve audio reco	1 wk	Fri 4/22/11	Thu 4/28/11	0%	$1,400.00	80 hrs	
10		Reserve video reco	5 days	Fri 4/29/11		0%	$1,400.00	80 hrs	
11		Status Meeting	65.13 days	Mon 1/24/11	Mon 4/25/11	0%	$1,491.00	84 hrs	
26		Pre-Production com	0 days	Thu 5/5/11	Thu 5/5/11	0%	$0.00	0 hrs	
27		Production	27.75 days	Thu 5/5/11	Tue 6/14/11	0%	$23,369.50	709 hrs	
28		Production begins	0 days	Thu 5/5/11	Thu 5/5/11	0%	$0.00	0 hrs	
29		Scene 1	6.75 days	Thu 5/5/11	Mon 5/16/11	0%	$6,051.50	189 hrs	
30		Scene 1 begin	0 days	Thu 5/5/11	Thu 5/5/11	0%	$0.00	0 hrs	
31		Scene 1 setup	2 days	Fri 5/6/11	Mon 5/9/11	0%	$536.00	48 hrs	
32		Scene 1 rehears	6 hrs	Tue 5/10/11	Tue 5/10/11	0%	$888.50	21 hrs	
33		Scene 1 vocal re	1 day	Tue 5/10/11	Wed 5/11/11	0%	$1,692.00	32 hrs	
34		Scene 1 video sl	2 days	Wed 5/11/11	Fri 5/13/11	0%	$2,687.00	72 hrs	
35		Scene 1 teardov	1 day	Fri 5/13/11	Mon 5/16/11	0%	$248.00	16 hrs	
36		Scene 1 complet	0 days	Mon 5/16/11	Mon 5/16/11	0%	$0.00	0 hrs	
37		Scene 2	6.75 days	Mon 5/16/11	Wed 5/25/11	0%	$6,923.00	226 hrs	
38		Scene 2 begin	0 days	Mon 5/16/11	Mon 5/16/11	0%	$0.00	0 hrs	
39		Scene 2 setup	2 days	Mon 5/16/11	Wed 5/18/11	0%	$1,066.00	64 hrs	
40		Scene 2 rehears	6 hrs	Wed 5/18/11	Thu 5/19/11	0%	$824.00	18 hrs	
41		Scene 2 vocal re	1 day	Thu 5/19/11	Fri 5/20/11	0%	$1,440.00	32 hrs	
42		Scene 2 video sl	2 days	Fri 5/20/11	Tue 5/24/11	0%	$3,345.00	96 hrs	

Ready   New Tasks : Auto Scheduled

4. On the Ribbon, click **Format** under Task Sheet Tools, then click the **Text Styles** button in the Format group. The Text Styles dialog box appears.

Text Styles

TAKE NOTE*

The text styles in Microsoft Project are similar to styles in Microsoft Word. The Item to Change list in the Text Styles dialog box displays all the types of information in a project schedule you can consistently format.

5. In the Item to Change list, click **Summary Tasks**.
6. In the Size box, click **10**.
7. In the Color box, click **green**. Your screen should look similar to Figure 8-14.

Figure 8-14

Text Styles dialog box

8. Click **OK**. Microsoft Project applies the new format settings to all summary tasks in the project. Note that the project summary task was listed separately in the Item to Change list, so it is not affected by the changes you just made. Also, any new summary tasks added to the project will appear with the new formatting.

9. If any columns display pound signs (###), double-click between the text in the column labels to widen the columns as necessary. Your screen should look similar to Figure 8-15.

Figure 8-15

Task Sheet view with reformatted summary tasks

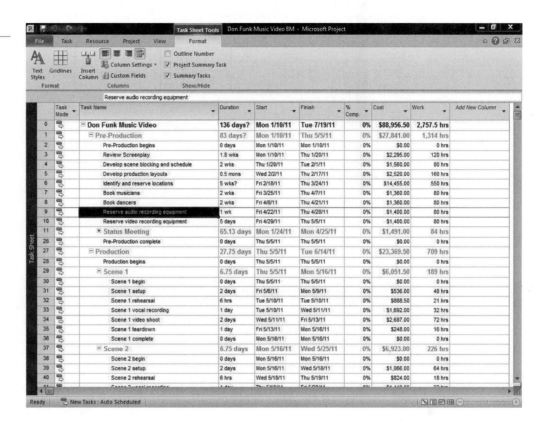

10. In the Summary table, click the **Cost** field for task 27, the Production summary task. You will now apply some direct formatting to only this field.

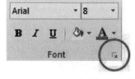

11. Click the **Task** tab, then click the arrow in the lower-right corner of the **Font** group. The Font dialog box appears. Although similar to the Text Styles dialog box, the options you choose here apply *only* to the selected text or cell.

12. In the Font Style box, click **Bold Italic**.

TROUBLESHOOTING You cannot use the Font dialog box on the Task tab to affect the formatting of empty rows in a table (changes made here only applies to selections of text). To set the default formatting of rows, use the Text Styles command on the Format tab.

13. Click **OK**. Microsoft Project applies bold italic formatting to the Cost field for task 27. Your screen should look similar to Figure 8-16.

Figure 8-16

Task Sheet view with cost cell for task 27 reformatted to bold italic

Task 27 Cost cell reformatted to bold italic

	Task Mode	Task Name	Duration	Start	Finish	% Comp.	Cost	Work	Add New Column
				$1,052.00					
3		Review Screenplay	1.8 wks	Mon 1/10/11	Thu 1/20/11	0%	$2,295.00	120 hrs	
4		Develop scene blocking and schedule	2 wks	Thu 1/20/11	Tue 2/1/11	0%	$1,560.00	80 hrs	
5		Develop production layouts	0.5 mons	Wed 2/2/11	Thu 2/17/11	0%	$2,520.00	160 hrs	
6		Identify and reserve locations	5 wks?	Fri 2/18/11	Thu 3/24/11	0%	$14,455.00	550 hrs	
7		Book musicians	2 wks	Fri 3/25/11	Thu 4/7/11	0%	$1,360.00	80 hrs	
8		Book dancers	2 wks	Fri 4/8/11	Thu 4/21/11	0%	$1,360.00	80 hrs	
9		Reserve audio recording equipment	1 wk	Fri 4/22/11	Thu 4/28/11	0%	$1,400.00	80 hrs	
10		Reserve video recording equipment	5 days	Fri 4/29/11	Thu 5/5/11	0%	$1,400.00	80 hrs	
11		⊞ Status Meeting	65.13 days	Mon 1/24/11	Mon 4/25/11	0%	$1,491.00	84 hrs	
26		Pre-Production complete	0 days	Thu 5/5/11	Thu 5/5/11	0%	$0.00	0 hrs	
27		⊟ Production	27.75 days	Thu 5/5/11	Tue 6/14/11	0%	*$23,369.50*	709 hrs	
28		Production begins	0 days	Thu 5/5/11	Thu 5/5/11	0%	$0.00	0 hrs	
29		⊟ Scene 1	6.75 days	Thu 5/5/11	Mon 5/16/11	0%	$6,051.50	189 hrs	
30		Scene 1 begin	0 days	Thu 5/5/11	Thu 5/5/11	0%	$0.00	0 hrs	
31		Scene 1 setup	2 days	Fri 5/6/11	Mon 5/9/11	0%	$536.00	48 hrs	
32		Scene 1 rehearsal	6 hrs	Tue 5/10/11	Tue 5/10/11	0%	$888.50	21 hrs	
33		Scene 1 vocal recording	1 day	Tue 5/10/11	Wed 5/11/11	0%	$1,692.00	32 hrs	
34		Scene 1 video shoot	2 days	Wed 5/11/11	Fri 5/13/11	0%	$2,687.00	72 hrs	
35		Scene 1 teardown	1 day	Fri 5/13/11	Mon 5/16/11	0%	$248.00	16 hrs	
36		Scene 1 complete	0 days	Mon 5/16/11	Mon 5/16/11	0%	$0.00	0 hrs	
37		⊟ Scene 2	6.75 days	Mon 5/16/11	Wed 5/25/11	0%	$6,923.00	226 hrs	
38		Scene 2 begin	0 days	Mon 5/16/11	Mon 5/16/11	0%	$0.00	0 hrs	
39		Scene 2 setup	2 days	Mon 5/16/11	Wed 5/18/11	0%	$1,068.00	64 hrs	
40		Scene 2 rehearsal	6 hrs	Wed 5/18/11	Thu 5/19/11	0%	$824.00	18 hrs	
41		Scene 2 vocal recording	1 day	Thu 5/19/11	Fri 5/20/11	0%	$1,440.00	32 hrs	
42		Scene 2 video shoot	2 days	Fri 5/20/11	Tue 5/24/11	0%	$3,345.00	96 hrs	
43		Scene 2 teardown	1 day	Tue 5/24/11	Wed 5/25/11	0%	$248.00	16 hrs	
44		Scene 2 complete	0 days	Wed 5/25/11	Wed 5/25/11	0%	$0.00	0 hrs	

Ready   New Tasks : Auto Scheduled

TAKE NOTE*

To remove direct formatting that has been applied to text and restore the formatting defined by the Text Style dialog box, first select the cell containing the formatted text you wish to restore. Then, in the Editing group on the Task tab, click the eraser icon, then click Clear Formatting.

> **14. SAVE** the project schedule.
>
> **PAUSE. LEAVE** the project schedule open to use in the next exercise.

In this exercise, you used text styles and direct formatting to customize the appearance of text in a view. Within a view, a table is a spreadsheet-like presentation of project data, organized in vertical columns and horizontal rows. Each column represents a *field name* in Microsoft Project, and each row represents a single resource or task. The intersection of a row and a column is called a cell or a *field*, and it holds the lowest-level information about a task, resource, or assignment.

When you format a category of text using the Text Styles dialog box, as you did when you formatted the summary tasks in this exercise, the formatting changes you make apply to all cases of that category (summary tasks, in this instance) in all the tables you can display in the active view. If you change the view, the format changes you made do not appear in the new view.

When you apply formatting to individual selections of text (such as the Cost field for task 27), the changes you make have no effect on other text in the view.

■ Creating and Editing Tables

THE BOTTOM LINE

Within Microsoft Project are a number of different tables that can be used in various views. These tables contain most of the commonly used data fields. However, you can create new tables that contain exactly the data you want, or you can modify any predefined table to meet your needs.

⊕ **CREATE A CUSTOM TABLE**

USE the project schedule you created in the previous exercise. Make sure that you are still in the Task Sheet view from the previous exercise.

1. Click the **View** tab. Then click **Tables** followed by **More Tables**. The More Tables dialog box appears and displays all of the predefined tables available to you, depending on the type of view currently displayed (task or resource).

2. Confirm that the **Task** button is selected as the Tables option. Select **Entry**, then click the **Copy** button. The Table Definition dialog box appears.

3. In the Name box, key **Music Video Schedule Table**. Now you will customize the table.

4. In the Field Name column, select the following field names and click **Delete Row** after selecting each name:

Indicators

Duration

Finish

Predecessors

Resource Names

After you have deleted these fields, your screen should look similar to Figure 8-17.

Figure 8-17

Table Definition dialog box

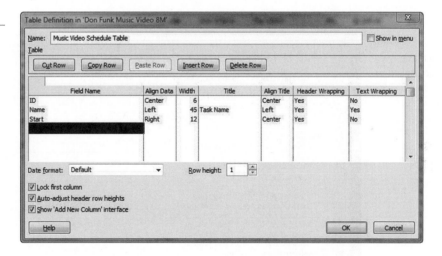

5. In the Field Name column, click the **downward arrow** in the next empty cell below Start, then select **Cast (Text1)** from the drop-down list.

6. In the Align Data column in the same row, select **Left**. In the Width column, key or select **30**.

7. In the Field Name column in the next empty row below Cast, select **Location(Text 2)** from the drop-down list.

8. In the Align Data column in the same row, select **Left**, then press **Enter**.

9. In the Field Name column, select **Start**, then click the **Cut Row** button.

10. In the Field Name column, select **Name**, then click the **Paste Row** button.

11. In the Date Format box, select **Mon 1/28/09 12:33 pm**. Your screen should look similar to Figure 8-18.

Figure 8-18

Table Definition dialog box
with Cast and Location fields
added

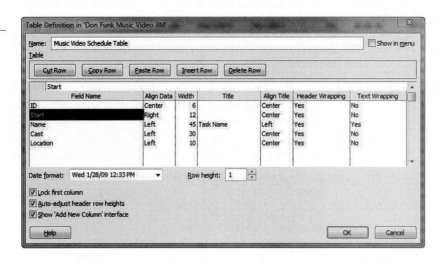

12. Click **OK** to close the Table Definition dialog box. The new table is highlighted in the More Tables dialog box.

13. Click **Apply**. Microsoft Project applies the new table to the Task Sheet view.

14. If the Start column does not display complete information, double-click the column heading's right edge to widen it. Your screen should look similar to Figure 8-19.

Figure 8-19

Task Sheet with the Music
Video Schedule table applied

	Start ▼	Task Name ▼	Cast ▼	Location ▼	Add New Column ▼
3	Mon 1/10/11 8:00 AM	Review Screenplay			
4	Thu 1/20/11 1:00 PM	Develop scene blocking and schedule			
5	Wed 2/2/11 8:00 AM	Develop production layouts			
6	Fri 2/18/11 8:00 AM	Identify and reserve locations			
7	Fri 3/25/11 8:00 AM	Book musicians			
8	Fri 4/8/11 8:00 AM	Book dancers			
9	Fri 4/22/11 8:00 AM	Reserve audio recording equipment			
10	Fri 4/29/11 8:00 AM	Reserve video recording equipment			
11	Mon 1/24/11 8:00 AM	⊞ Status Meeting			
26	Thu 5/5/11 5:00 PM	Pre-Production complete			
27	Thu 5/5/11 5:00 PM	⊟ Production			
28	Thu 5/5/11 5:00 PM	Production begins			
29	Thu 5/5/11 5:00 PM	⊟ Scene 1			
30	Thu 5/5/11 5:00 PM	Scene 1 begin			
31	Fri 5/6/11 8:00 AM	Scene 1 setup			
32	Tue 5/10/11 8:00 AM	Scene 1 rehearsal			
33	Tue 5/10/11 3:00 PM	Scene 1 vocal recording			
34	Wed 5/11/11 3:00 PM	Scene 1 video shoot	Don Funk, ski extras, Kim, Mike	Alpine Ski H	
35	Fri 5/13/11 3:00 PM	Scene 1 teardown			
36	Mon 5/16/11 3:00 PM	Scene 1 complete			
37	Mon 5/16/11 3:00 PM	⊟ Scene 2			
38	Mon 5/16/11 3:00 PM	Scene 2 begin			
39	Mon 5/16/11 3:00 PM	Scene 2 setup			
40	Wed 5/18/11 3:00 PM	Scene 2 rehearsal			
41	Thu 5/19/11 1:00 PM	Scene 2 vocal recording			
42	Fri 5/20/11 1:00 PM	Scene 2 video shoot	Don Funk, party crowd, Kim, Lisa, Os	Don Funk's I	
43	Tue 5/24/11 1:00 PM	Scene 2 teardown			
44	Wed 5/25/11 12:00 PM	Scene 2 complete			
45	Wed 5/25/11 12:00 PM	⊟ Scene 3			

Ready   New Tasks : Auto Scheduled

15. **SAVE** the project schedule.

PAUSE. LEAVE the project schedule open to use in the next exercise.

In this exercise, you created a custom table to display the information typically found on a video shooting schedule. Specifically, you modified an existing table to include additional data that was important to your project schedule. As you create future project schedules, keep in mind that you that you have three options when setting up tables: you can create a new table, redefine an existing table, or copy an existing table and modify it as needed. Also note that as you modify any table, you are changing the definition of that table.

■ Creating Custom Views

↓
THE BOTTOM LINE

Almost all of the work you perform in Microsoft Project is done in a view, which allows you to see your project schedule in a useful way. Microsoft Project includes numerous predefined views. You can use these views, edit an existing view, or create your own view. In this exercise, you create a custom view using the custom filter and custom table you created in earlier lessons.

 CREATE A CUSTOM VIEW

USE the project schedule you created in the previous exercise.

1. On the View tab, click the **downward arrow** under the Gantt Chart button in the **View** group, then click **More Views**. The More Views dialog box appears, displaying all of the predefined views available to you.
2. Click the **New** button. The Define New View dialog box appears. Most views use only a single pane, but a view can consist of two separate panes.
3. Make sure **Single View** is selected, then click **OK**. The View Definition dialog box appears.
4. In the Name box, key **Music Video Schedule View**.
5. In the Screen box, select **Task Sheet** from the drop-down list.
6. In the Table box, select **Music Video Schedule Table** from the drop-down list. The specific groups in the drop-down list depend on the type of view you selected in step 5 (task or resource).
7. In the Group box, select **No Group** from the drop-down list. The specific groups in the drop-down list again depend on the type of view you selected in step 5.
8. In the Filter box, select **Unfinished Shoots** from the drop-down list. Yet again, the specific groups in the drop-down list depend on the type of view you selected in step 5. The View Definition dialog box shows all the elements that can make up a view. Your screen should look similar to Figure 8-20.

Figure 8-20

View Definition dialog box

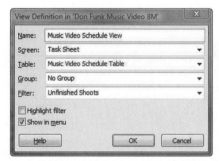

9. Select the **Show in Menu** check box, then click **OK** to close the View Definition dialog box. The new view appears and should be selected in the More Views dialog box.

TAKE NOTE*

When you select the Show in Menu check box, Microsoft Project adds the new view to the View bar. This custom view will be saved with this Microsoft Project data file, and you can use it whenever you need it.

10. Click **Apply**. Microsoft Project applies the new view. Your screen should look similar to Figure 8-21.

Figure 8-21

Custom view with Music Video Schedule Table and Unfinished Shoots filter

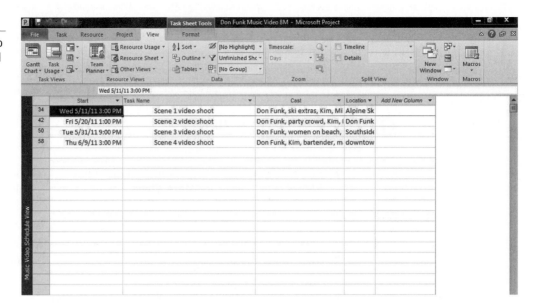

11. **SAVE** the project schedule. **CLOSE** the project schedule.

PAUSE. If you are continuing to the next lesson, keep Project open. If you are not continuing to additional lessons, **CLOSE** Project.

In this exercise, you created a custom view that enabled you to look specifically at information that was of interest to you. Recall that a view is a window through which you can see the various elements of a project schedule in a way that is helpful to the viewing audience. As you saw in this exercise, a view may contain elements such as tables, groups, or filters. You can combine these with other elements to create almost limitless custom views to suit any purpose.

SKILL SUMMARY

IN THIS LESSON, YOU LEARNED:	TASK
To format a Gantt chart.	Modify the Gantt chart using the Bar Styles dialog box.
	Modify the Gantt chart using Gantt Chart Styles.
To draw in a Gantt chart.	Add a text box to the Gantt chart.
To change text appearance in a view.	Change appearance of text in a view.
To create and edit tables.	Create a custom table.
To create custom views.	Create a custom view.

■ Knowledge Assessment

Matching

Match the term in column 1 to its description in column 2.

Column 1	Column 2
1. Field	**a.** A spreadsheet-like presentation of project data, organized in vertical columns and horizontal rows
2. Drawing	**b.** The default view in Microsoft Project
3. Table	**c.** The right side of the Gantt chart view
4. Format	**d.** The intersection of a row and a column in a table
5. Bar Styles	**e.** A view that presents information in rows and columns
6. View	**f.** A tab that allows you to add or change the appearance of a view
7. Gantt chart	**g.** Another name for field
8. Cell	**h.** The tool that enables you to add lines or text directly onto a Gantt chart
9. Bar chart	**i.** A window through which you can see the various elements of a project schedule
10. Sheet	**j.** The dialog box that can be used to format the graphical components of the Gantt chart view

True/False

Circle T if the statement is true or F if the statement is false.

T | F 1. When you make a change to a milestone using the Bar Styles dialog box, the change applies to all milestones in the Gantt chart.

T | F 2. The Drawing tool allows you to add text directly to a Gantt chart.

T | F 3. In Microsoft Project, you can edit predefined tables, but you cannot create new custom tables to suit your needs.

T | F 4. The Gantt chart view can include only the task data without the bar chart.

T | F 5. When you make formatting changes to your project schedule, the data does not change—only its appearance changes.

T | F 6. When you add, remove, or rearrange columns or change column widths, you are changing a table's definition.

T | F 7. If you add an object to a Gantt chart that is date specific, you should link it to the Gantt bar.

T | F 8. If you format data using the Font dialog box, the changes apply to only the data you have specifically selected.

T | F 9. Gantt Chart Styles offers more formatting choices than the Bar Styles dialog box.

T | F 10. Changing the appearance of data in a view can make it easier to read and understand project data.

■ Competency Assessment

Project 8-1: Modifying a Gantt Chart

You are reviewing your project schedule with your team. Several team members suggest that it would be nice to have the summary tasks stand out a bit more on the project schedule. You decide to format the summary tasks in purple with the task name listed on the right of the bar.

GET READY. Launch Microsoft Project if it is not already running.
OPEN *Don Funk Music Video 8-1* from the data files for this lesson.

1. Click the **Format** tab, then click the **Format** button in the Bar Styles group. Select **Bar Styles** from the drop-down list.
2. In the Name column, select **Summary**.
3. In the bottom half of the dialog box, make sure the **Bars** tab is selected. Under the Start, Middle, and End labels, select **purple** from the drop-down list in the Color boxes.
4. Click the **Text** tab.
5. Click the **Right** box. Click the **downward arrow**, then select **Name** from the drop-down list.
6. Click **OK**.
7. Select the name of task 26, **Pre-production complete**.
8. Click the **Task** tab, then click the **Scroll to Task** button.
9. SAVE the project schedule as *Don Funk Music Video Purple Summary*, then **CLOSE** the file.

    LEAVE Project open to use in the next exercise.

The *Don Funk Music Video 8-1* file for this lesson is available on the book companion website.

Project 8-2: Creating a Table

You have created a project schedule for interviewing and hiring a new employee. Now you would like to create a table to display the information found on an internal interview schedule.

OPEN *HR Interview and Hire Schedule 8-2* from the data files for this lesson.

1. Click the **View** tab. In the Task Views group, click the **downward arrow** under the Gantt Chart button, then click **More Views**.
2. Select **Task Sheet** from the More Views box and click **Apply**.
3. On the Ribbon, in the Data group, click **Tables**, then click **More Tables**.
4. Confirm that the **Task** button is selected as the Tables option. Select **Entry**, then click the **Copy** button.
5. In the Name box, key **Interview Schedule**. Select the **Show in Menu** checkbox.
6. In the Field Name column, select each of the following names and click **Delete Row** after selecting each:

    Indicators

    Finish

    Predecessors

    Resource Name
7. In the Date format box, select **1/28/09 12:33 pm**.
8. Click **OK**.
9. Make sure that **Interview Schedule** is selected in the More Tables dialog box, then click **Apply**.
10. SAVE the project schedule as *HR Interview Schedule* and **CLOSE** the file.

    LEAVE Project open to use in the next exercise.

The *HR Interview and Hire Schedule 8-2* file for this lesson is available on the book companion website.

■ Proficiency Assessment

Project 8-3: Calling Attention to Tasks

You have developed a project schedule for a kitchen/lunchroom remodel at your business. You are preparing to distribute the schedule to some of the contractors who will work on the project. You would like to call attention to the summary tasks and the specific tasks that these contractors will be undertaking.

OPEN *Office Remodel 8-3* from the data files for this lesson.

1. Change the view to Task Sheet.
2. Select **Text Styles** from the Format tab.
3. Select **Summary Tasks** as the item to change.
4. Select font size **10** and color **blue**. Click **OK**.
5. Select tasks **9 through 14**.
6. Activate the Font dialog box from the Task tab.
7. Select a Background color of **yellow** and click **OK**.
8. **SAVE** the project schedule as *Office Remodel Contractor Tasks* and **CLOSE** the file.
   LEAVE Project open to use in the next exercise.

The *Office Remodel 8-3* file for this lesson is available on the book companion website.

Project 8-4: Creating a Custom View

You have created an interviewing schedule for hiring a new employee at your company. You want to create a custom view for this project schedule that looks at only the summary tasks in the Interview Schedule format (which you created in Project 8-2).

OPEN *HR Interview Schedule 8-4* from the data files for this lesson.

1. From the More Views dialog box, click **New** to create a new view.
2. Select **Single View**.
3. Name the new view **Summary Interview Schedule**.
4. Select **Task Sheet** from the Screen box.
5. Select **Interview Schedule** from the Table box.
6. Select **No Group** from the Group box.
7. Select **Summary Tasks** from the Filter box.
8. Select the **Show in Menu** check box.
9. Apply the new view.
10. **SAVE** the project schedule as *HR Summary Interview Schedule*, then **CLOSE** the file.
    LEAVE Project open to use in the next exercise.

The *HR Interview Schedule 8-4* file for this lesson is available on the book companion website.

■ Mastery Assessment

Project 8-5: Emphasizing a Project's Critical Path

You need to make some additional formatting changes to the Don Funk Music Video so that the critical path is more visible for a presentation. You decide to make these changes using the Gantt Chart tool.

The *Don Funk Music Video 8-5* file for this lesson is available on the book companion website.

OPEN *Don Funk Music Video 8-5* from the data files for this lesson.

1. Make a copy of the Gantt chart view.
2. Name the new view **Custom Gantt 8-5**.
3. Apply the custom view you have just created.
4. Activate the Format ribbon from the Gantt Chart Tools.
5. Select a dark blue Gantt bar style for your presentation.
6. Select **Critical Path** as the type of information you want to display.
7. **SAVE** the project schedule as ***Don Funk Critical Path*** and **CLOSE** the file.
   LEAVE Project open to use in the next exercise.

Project 8-6: Attaching Task Information

You need to add some information about a new phone company billing to your Home Office project schedule. You need to use the Drawing function in Project to attach your information to some specific dates.

OPEN *Home Office Setup 8-6* from the data files for this lesson.

1. Apply the Detail Gantt view.
2. Shift the view so that the bar chart for task 1 is visible.
3. Activate the Drawing tool.
4. Insert a small text box on the Gantt bar chart.
5. In the text box, key **Billing starts when phone line installed**.
6. Activate the Format Drawing dialog box.
7. Fill the text box using yellow, and attach it to task 10.
8. Next to the ID box, select the attachment point on the left side of the task bar.
9. Apply your changes.
10. Scroll to task 10 so that the text box is visible. Adjust the size of the box as necessary to read the text.
11. **SAVE** the project schedule as ***Home Office Task Info***, then **CLOSE** the file.
    CLOSE Project.

The *Home Office Setup 8-6* file for this lesson is available on the book companion website.

INTERNET READY

In this lesson, you learned several ways to customize the format of your project schedule. By changing the appearance of the data in your schedule, you can make it easy for yourself and others to view and interpret your data.

Search the Internet for a detailed, complex project schedule that is of some interest to you (a good place to start is the Templates page of www.office.microsoft.com). Download the project schedule or template to your computer. Using the skills you learned in this lesson, modify the appearance of the schedule so that it is easier to follow. Apply new bar styles and colors, milestone markers, critical path indicators, text formatting, and drawing objects as appropriate. You can also apply custom tables and views to draw attention to a specific part of the project schedule. Save your modified project schedule so that you can compare the old and new versions of the schedule.

Customizing and Printing Project Information

LESSON SKILL MATRIX

SKILL	TASK
Customizing and Printing a View	Customize and print a Gantt chart view.
Customizing and Printing Reports	Customize and print a report.

You are a production manager for Southridge Video and the project manager for the new Don Funk music video. Your project schedule has been assembled, and now you need to prepare it for the acceptance presentation. You know that one of the most important responsibilities of any project manager is communicating project information. In this lesson, you learn how to work with some of the many views and reports in Microsoft Project 2010 in order to print your project schedule.

KEY TERMS
report
stakeholder
timescale

■ SOFTWARE ORIENTATION

Page Setup Dialog Box

The Page Setup dialog box (Figure 9-1) provides options for customizing the appearance of views and reports when they are displayed via the Print Preview function or printed on paper.

Figure 9-1

Page Setup (Gantt chart) dialog box with Legend tab activated

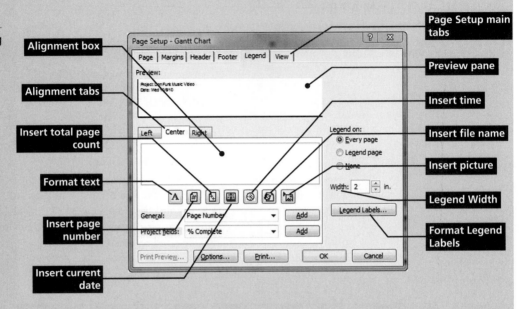

The Page Setup dialog box enables you to specify page options, such as margins and paper orientation and size. You can also customize the information in and presentation of headers, footers, legends, and view formatting.

■ Customizing and Printing a View

THE BOTTOM LINE

Using a view, you can see your project schedule information on screen. You can change what you see by customizing the view. You can also apply customized views when printing information on paper.

⊕ CUSTOMIZE AND PRINT A GANTT CHART VIEW

GET READY. Before you begin these steps, launch Microsoft Project 2010.

The *Don Funk Music Video 9M* file for this lesson is available on the book companion website.

1. **OPEN** the *Don Funk Music Video 9M* project schedule from the data files for this lesson.

2. **SAVE** the file as *Don Funk Music Video 9* in the solutions folder for this lesson, as directed by your instructor.

3. On the Ribbon, click the **File** tab, then click **Print**. Microsoft Project displays print options on the left side of the screen and the Gantt chart view on the right side, which is the Print Preview window. Your screen should look like Figure 9-2.

Figure 9-2

Print section of the File tab

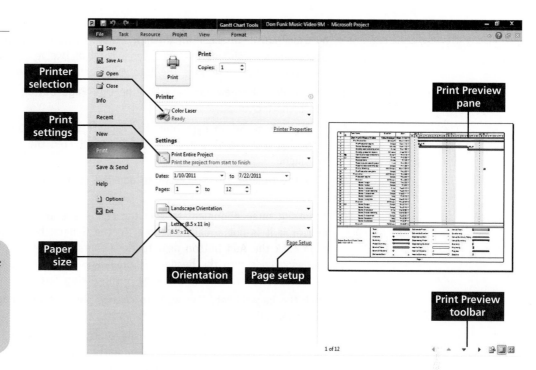

4. On the Print Preview toolbar, click the **Page Right** button three times to display different pages.

5. On the Print Preview toolbar, click the **Page Down** button once.

6. On the Print Preview toolbar, click the **Multiple Pages** button. Most of the pages of the Gantt chart appear in the Print Preview window. Note that when Multiple Pages Print Preview is active, the printed output is displayed on separate sheets. Navigate using the scroll control at the bottom of the Print Preview pane, as the Page Right, Page Left, Page Up, and Page Down buttons are all inactive. The paper size that is displayed is determined by your printer settings. Your screen should look similar to Figure 9-3.

Figure 9-3

Print Preview with Multiple Pages activated

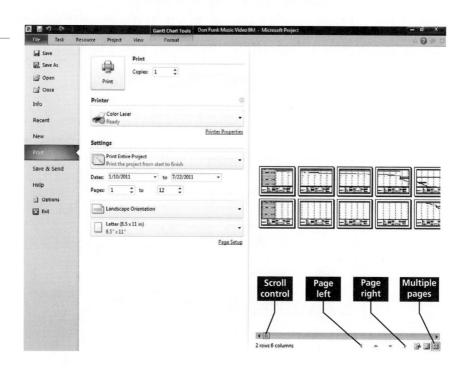

Note also that the left side of the Print Preview toolbar status bar reads "2 rows by 6 columns." In the Print Preview window, this means there are two rows of pages and six columns of pages, for a total of twelve pages. The status bar can help you quickly determine the total number of pages your printed view will be.

7. On the Print Preview toolbar, click the **One Page** button. The first page of the Gantt chart is displayed.

8. Click the **Page Setup** hyperlink. The Page Setup dialog box appears. This is the same dialog box that would appear if you selected the Page Setup option on the File menu.

9. Click the **Header** tab. You want to add the company name to the header that prints on each page.

10. There are three Alignment tabs in the center section of the Header tab box. Select **Center** if it is not already selected. In the General box, click **Company Name**, and then click the **Add** button next to the General box. Microsoft Project places the following code into the header: &[Company]. The software also displays a preview in the Preview window of the Page Setup dialog box.

11. Click the **Legend** tab. You want to change some of the content of the Gantt chart view's legend.

12. There are three Alignment tabs in the center of the Legend tab box. Click the **Left** tab. Currently, Microsoft Project is formatted to print the project title and current date on the left side of the legend. You also want to print the start date and duration on the right side of the legend.

13. Click the **Right** Alignment tab. Click in the Right Alignment box, then key **Start:** followed by a space.

14. In the General box, select **Project Start Date** from the drop-down list. Click the **Add** button next to the General box. Microsoft Project adds the label and code for the project start date to the legend.

15. Press **Enter** to add a second line to the legend, then key **Duration:** followed by a space.

16. In the Project Fields box, select **Scheduled Duration** from the drop-down list. Click the **Add** button next to the Project Fields box. Microsoft Project adds the label and code for project duration to the legend.

17. In the Width box, key or click **3**. This increases the width of the box that appears on the left side of the legend. Your screen should look similar to Figure 9-4.

Figure 9-4

Page Setup dialog box with custom selections for legend

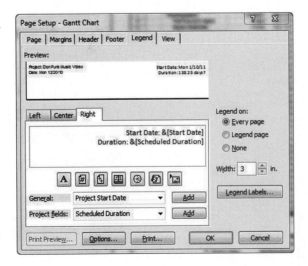

18. Click **OK** to close the Page Setup dialog box. Microsoft Project applies the custom changes to the legend.

19. Move your mouse cursor to the lower-left corner of the page preview (your cursor appears as a magnifying glass). Click the lower-left corner of the page. Microsoft Project zooms in to show the legend. Your screen should look similar to Figure 9-5.

Figure 9-5

Close-up view of wider legend area

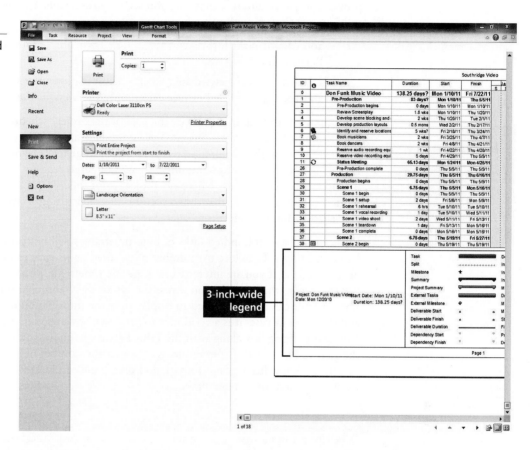

At this point, you can print the project schedule by clicking the Print button (the print preview is adequate for purposes of this lesson). Note that when printing in Microsoft Project 2010, there are additional options in the Print dialog box (the Print command is accessed from the File tab). For example, you can opt to print specific date or page ranges.

TAKE NOTE*

The data you added to the legend will print on every page of the printed output.

20. Click the **Task** tab to return to the Gantt chart view. Although you did not print, your changes to the header and the legend will be saved when you save the project file.

21. **SAVE** the project schedule.

PAUSE. LEAVE Project open to use in the next exercise.

In this exercise, you customized a view to add information that you wanted to include when printing your project schedule. Printing information from a project schedule to share with stakeholders is a common activity for project managers. *Stakeholders* are all people or organizations that might be affected by project activities, from resources working on the project to customers receiving the end result of the project.

In a view, you can enter, read, edit, and print information. Printing a view allows you to provide, on paper, almost everything you see on your screen. You can print any view you see in Microsoft Project, with just a few exceptions:

- You cannot print form views (e.g., Task Form) or certain diagrams, such as the Relationship Diagram.
- If you have two views displayed in a combination view (one view in the top pane and the other in the bottom pane), only the view in the active pane will print.

For a review of the types of views, including form views, refer back to Lesson 8.

It is important to keep in mind that the part of the project schedule you see on your screen is only a small part of the total project. For example, printing a six-month project with 75 tasks may require more than a dozen letter-sized pages. In general, Gantt charts and Network Diagrams can use significant amounts of paper on large projects. Some experienced project managers who regularly use Microsoft Project print their projects on poster-sized paper using plotters (a type of printer that draws pictures or graphs using attached pens) or other specialized printing equipment.

Projects with several hundred tasks or long timeframes will not print legibly on letter- or legal-sized paper. To reduce the number of required pages, you can print just summary tasks or filtered data. If you are interested in a specific timeframe, you can print just that portion of the *timescale*, which is the band across the top of the Gantt chart grid that denotes units of time. A filter can also be applied to display only the information of interest to a specific audience. In any case, it is a good idea to preview the views you want to print. By using the Page Setup dialog box along with the Print Preview window, you can control many features of the view to be printed. For example, you can set the number of pages on which the view will be printed, apply headers and footers, and determine content that appears in the legend of the Gantt chart and some other views.

When printing in views that contain a timescale, such as the Gantt chart view, you can change the number of pages required by adjusting the timescale before printing. To adjust the timescale so that it shows the largest time span in the smallest number of pages, click the View tab, then in the Zoom group, click Entire Project.

■ Customizing and Printing Reports

THE BOTTOM LINE

In Microsoft Project 2010, a *report* is a predefined format that is used to view or print project data. Microsoft Project includes several task, resource, and assignment reports you can edit to fit your needs.

⊕ CUSTOMIZE AND PRINT A REPORT

USE the project schedule you created in the previous exercise.

Reports

1. On the Ribbon, click the **Project** tab. In the Reports group, click the **Reports** button.
2. Click **Assignments**, then click the **Select** button. The Assignment Reports dialog box appears with a list of predefined reports.

3. In the Assignment Reports dialog box, select **Who Does What When**, then click the **Select** button. The Task report is displayed in the Print Preview window. Your screen should look similar to Figure 9-6.

Figure 9-6

Print preview of Who Does What When report

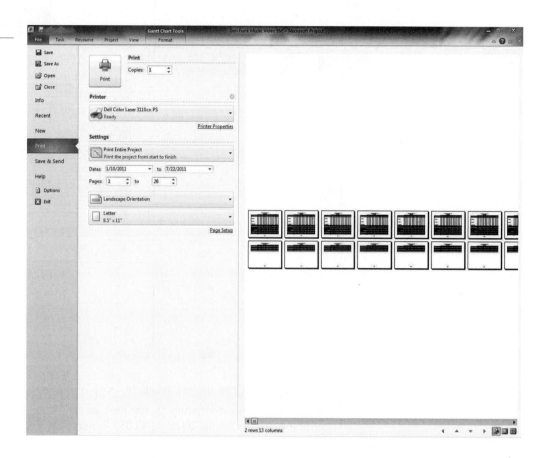

This report is a complete list of project resources and their project activity assignments. This type of report is known as a crosstab report. Notice that this report is set to print on 26 pages (2 rows by 13 columns), because the detail level is set to report work for each resource on a daily basis. You want to present this data in a different way, so you will edit this report.

4. On the Ribbon, click the **Project** tab. In the Reports group, click the **Reports** button. Click **Assignments**, then click the **Select** button.

5. In the Assignment Reports dialog box, select **Who Does What When**, then select the **Edit** button. The Crosstab Report dialog box appears.

6. In the Column box, ensure that **1** is in the count box, then select **Months** from the drop-down list. Selecting Months will group the work assignment totals, per resource, by the month in which they occur.

7. Clear the check box next to **And task assignments**. Clearing this check box will provide a list of resources and their respective work totals by month, with no assignments listed.

8. Click the **Details** tab. Select the check boxes for **Column** and **Row** totals.

9. Click **OK** to close the Crosstab Report dialog box.

10. Click **Select** to display customized the report. Your screen should look similar to Figure 9-7.

Figure 9-7

Modified report showing monthly totals for each resource's work assignments

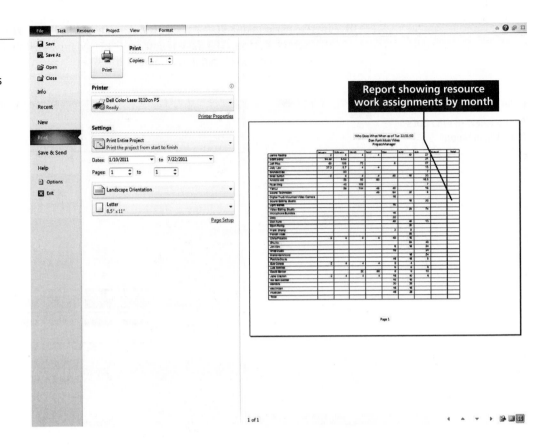

11. SAVE and **CLOSE** the project schedule.

PAUSE. If you are continuing to the next lesson, keep Project open. If you are not continuing to additional lessons, **CLOSE** Project.

In this exercise, you learned to customize and print a report. A report is a predefined format intended for printing Microsoft Project data. Reports are intended only for printing or viewing in the Print Preview window. You cannot enter data or work within reports. Microsoft Project provides a variety of assignment, task, and resource reports that you can edit to fit your needs.

Keep in mind that, although reports are different from views, some of the settings you specify for a view can affect certain reports:

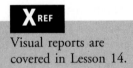

X REF

Visual reports are covered in Lesson 14.

- If subtasks are hidden under summary tasks in a view, reports that contain task lists will include only the summary tasks.
- If assignments are hidden under tasks or resources in a usage view, the usage reports will also hide the assignment details.

SKILL SUMMARY

IN THIS LESSON, YOU LEARNED:	TASK
To customize and print a view.	Customize and print a Gantt chart view.
To customize and print reports.	Customize and print a report.

■ Knowledge Assessment

Fill in the Blank

Complete the following sentences by writing the correct word or words in the blanks provided.

1. _____ _____ enables you to see on your screen what will print on paper before you print it.

2. People or organizations that might be affected by project activities are called _____.

3. If you have two views displayed in a combination view and want to print the view, only the view in the _____ pane will print.

4. When printing a Gantt chart view, you can change the number of pages required by adjusting the _____ before printing.

5. A common activity for project managers is to _____ information from the project schedule to share with stakeholders.

6. To add your company name so that it prints at the top of every page, use the _____ _____ dialog box to add the company name to the header.

7. A(n) _____ is a predefined format intended for printing Microsoft Project data.

8. To adapt a report to present the exact information you need, use the _____ _____ dialog box to select and edit the desired report.

9. If subtasks are hidden in a view, reports that contain task lists will include only _____ tasks.

10. In a report, you can only _____ information.

Multiple Choice

Select the best response for the following statements.

1. In a view, you can _____ information.
   a. enter
   b. edit
   c. print
   d. All of the above are correct.

2. If assignments are hidden under tasks or resources in a usage view, what will the usage report show?
   a. Tasks or resources with corresponding assignment details
   b. Only the tasks or resources
   c. Only overallocated assignment details
   d. It depends on how you set up the report.

3. In the Print Preview window, the status bar shows "4 rows by 3 columns." How many pages will be printed?
   a. 7
   b. 4
   c. 12
   d. 3

4. To see all of the pages of a view while using Print Preview, you can click which of the following buttons?

   a. Multiple Pages

   b. Page Right

   c. One Page

   d. Page Setup

5. For large projects with several hundred tasks, you can condense the information that will print by:

   a. printing just summary data.

   b. printing only the part of the timescale that is of interest.

   c. applying a filter to show only the information of interest.

   d. All of the above are correct.

6. If you want to print a list of tasks showing start dates, finish dates, and assigned resources, which view might you use?

   a. Tracking Gantt

   b. Task Sheet

   c. Resource Sheet

   d. Calendar

7. Which one of the following views cannot be printed in Microsoft Project?

   a. Tracking Gantt

   b. Calendar

   c. Task Form

   d. Resource Sheet

8. When printing a view with a timescale, you can adjust the timescale before printing to:

   a. force the end date of the project.

   b. adjust the number of pages required for printing.

   c. filter out unnecessary data.

   d. None of the above are correct.

9. In the legend section of a Gantt chart, you can add which of the following pieces information?

   a. Project Start Date

   b. Company Name

   c. Project Duration

   d. All of the above

10. The Custom Reports dialog box contains:

   a. all predefined reports plus any custom reports that have been added to Microsoft Project.

   b. all predefined reports in Microsoft Project.

   c. any custom reports that have been added to Microsoft Project.

   d. complex reports that have been specifically designed for certain businesses and industries.

■ Competency Assessment

Project 9-1: Printing a Gantt Chart View

You are preparing to print and distribute a copy of your project schedule to your team. You need to make several format changes to the printed version of the Gantt chart view before you distribute it.

GET READY. Launch Microsoft Project 2010 if it is not already running.
OPEN *Don Funk Music Video 9-1* from the data files for this lesson.

The *Don Funk Music Video 9-1* file for this lesson is available on the book companion website.

1. On the Ribbon, click the **File** tab. Select **Print** to view the print preview.
2. Under Settings, click the **Page Setup** hyperlink.
3. Click the **Header** tab, then click the **Center** tab in the alignment area.
4. In the alignment area, click to position your cursor at the end of &[Company]. Press **Enter**.
5. Key **2345 Main Street** and press **Enter**. Then key **New York, NY 11223**.
6. Click the **Footer** tab.
7. In the alignment box, click to position your cursor at the end of &[Page].
8. Key **of** (note that there is a space before and after the word "of"). Click the **Insert Total Page Count** button.
9. Click the **Legend** tab. Then, in the alignment area, click the **Left** tab.
10. In the alignment box, click to position your cursor at the end of &[Date]. Press **Enter**.
11. Click the **Insert Current Time** button.
12. Click **OK**.
13. Click **Close** on the Print Preview toolbar.
14. **SAVE** the project schedule as *Don Funk Printing Gantt View* and **CLOSE** the file.
    LEAVE Project open to use in the next exercise.

Project 9-2: HR Interview Schedule

For your HR Interview project schedule, you want to print a report that displays the resources' workload for each two-week period. You will customize an existing report to meet your requirements.

OPEN *HR Interview Schedule 9-2* from the data files for this lesson.

The *HR Interview Schedule 9-2* file for this lesson is available on the book companion website.

1. Click the **Project** tab, then click the **Reports** button in the Reports group.
2. Click the **Workload** button, then click the **Select** button.
3. Click the **Resource Usage** button, then click the **Edit** button.
4. On the Definition tab, change the column to reflect **every 2 weeks**.
5. Click the **Details** tab. In the date format, select the option that shows the project information in the following format: Week1, Week2 ...(From Start).
6. Click **OK**, then click **Select**.
7. **SAVE** the project schedule as *HR Interview Custom Critical Task Report*, then **CLOSE** the file.
   LEAVE Project open to use in the next exercise.

■ Proficiency Assessment

Project 9-3: Reducing Insurance Claim Project Schedule Printed Pages

You have a project schedule for processing an insurance claim that you want to print. This schedule has many tasks. Because you are distributing the schedule to a large number of people, you want to reduce the number of pages that will print by changing the timescale on the project.

OPEN *Insurance Claim 9-3* from the data files for this lesson.

The *Insurance Claim 9-3* file for this lesson is available on the book companion website.

1. On the View tab, select **Entire Project** in the Zoom group.
2. In the Data group, click the **down arrow** under the Outline button, then select **Outline Level 1**.
3. Use Print Preview to view the report.
4. Click **Page Setup**, then select the **Header** tab.
5. Key **Insurance Claim Processing** in the Center Alignment section.
6. Add the **Time** so that it will print under the date in the Left Alignment section of the Legend tab.
7. Close Print Preview.
8. SAVE the file as *Insurance Claim Condensed* and CLOSE the file.

   LEAVE Project open to use in the next exercise.

Project 9-4: Office Remodel Modified Resource View

You have developed a project schedule for the kitchen and lunchroom remodel at your office. You want to distribute a list of tasks by resource so that everyone can see at a glance the tasks for which they are responsible. You also want to customize this view to make it easier to read.

OPEN *Office Remodel 9-4* from the data files for this lesson.

The *Office Remodel 9-4* file for this lesson is available on the book companion website.

1. Switch the view to the Resource Usage view. Use the Auto-fit feature to show the entire width of the Resource Name column.
2. Click **Print Preview**.
3. Open the Page Setup dialog box.
4. On the View tab, set up the view so that the first three columns print on all pages.
5. On the Footer tab, within the Left Alignment tab, insert the date. Under the date, insert the time.
6. On the Right Alignment tab, key **Start** and insert the Start field.
7. Preview your modified view.
8. Close Print Preview.
9. SAVE the file as *Office Remodel Resource Usage*, then CLOSE the file.

   LEAVE Project open to use in the next exercise.

■ Mastery Assessment

Project 9-5: Don Funk Music Video Calendars

You would like to print a report to show the different calendars that are being used in the production of the Don Funk Music Video.

OPEN *Don Funk Music Video 9-5* from the data files for this lesson.

The *Don Funk Music Video 9-5* file for this lesson is available on the book companion website.

1. Using the Reports dialog box, review the predefined reports that are available for this project. You would like to print a report that shows the different calendars that have been defined for this project so that you can quickly refer to them when needed. Identify the report that meets this need.

2. In a separate Word document, write a short paragraph detailing the steps you took to be able to preview this report.

3. Save the Word document as *Don Funk Music Video Calendars*. Save the Project file as *Don Funk Music Video Calendars*. **CLOSE** both files.

   LEAVE Project open to use in the next exercise.

Project 9-6: HR Interview Custom Network Diagram

You want to view and print your HR Interview Schedule as a Network Diagram, as well as customize some of the fields for printing.

OPEN *HR Interview Schedule 9-6* from the data files for this lesson.

The *HR Interview Schedule 9-6* file for this lesson is available on the book companion website.

1. Change the view to the Network Diagram view.
2. Hide the summary tasks.
3. Activate the Page Setup dialog box.
4. In the Page Setup dialog box, make the following custom changes:

   • Increase the width of the Legend to 3 inches
   • Add the time to the left side of the Legend, under the date
   • Key **Start:** and insert the Start field on the right side of the Legend
   • Add the title "HR Interview Network Diagram" to the center of the header
   • Change the font of the title to Arial Bold 10pt. with color blue
   • Add your name to the second line of the header, under the project title
   • Have the legend print only on one page

5. Check your changes to make sure they appear correctly.
6. **SAVE** the file as *HR Interview Network Diagram* and **CLOSE** the file.

   CLOSE Project.

10 LESSON

Project Schedule Tracking Fundamentals

LESSON SKILL MATRIX

SKILL	TASK
Establishing a Project Baseline	Establish a project baseline.
Tracking a Project as Scheduled	Track a project as scheduled.
Entering the Completion Percentage for a Task	Enter the completion percentage for a task.
Identifying Overbudget Tasks and Resources	Identify overbudget tasks and resources.
Identifying Time and Schedule Problems	Reschedule uncompleted work.

You are a production manager for Southridge Video and the project manager for the new Don Funk music video. Prior to beginning work on the project, you focused on developing and communicating the project details. Now that work is starting, you are entering the next phase of project management: tracking progress. In order to manage your project properly, you need to know details such as who did what work, when the work was done, and the cost of the work. In this lesson, you use some of Microsoft Project's basic project tracking tools to save baselines, track actual work, enter completion percentages, and troubleshoot budget, time, and scheduling problems.

KEY TERMS
actual cost
actuals
baseline
baseline cost
current cost
planning
progress bar
remaining cost
sponsor
status date
timephased fields
tracking
variance

■ SOFTWARE ORIENTATION

Tracking Table

The Tracking Table (Figure 10-1) can be used to enter actual progress information for both tasks and resources.

Figure 10-1

The Tracking Table in the Gantt chart view

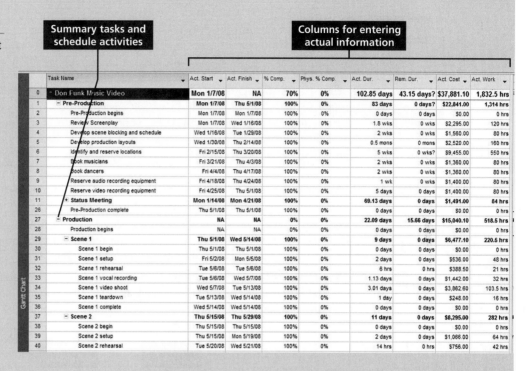

	Task Name	Act. Start	Act. Finish	% Comp.	Phys. % Comp.	Act. Dur.	Rem. Dur.	Act. Cost	Act. Work
0	Don Funk Music Video	Mon 1/7/08	NA	70%	0%	102.85 days	43.15 days?	$37,881.10	1,832.5 hrs
1	Pre-Production	Mon 1/7/08	Thu 5/1/08	100%	0%	83 days	0 days?	$22,841.00	1,314 hrs
2	Pre-Production begins	Mon 1/7/08	Mon 1/7/08	100%	0%	0 days	0 days	$0.00	0 hrs
3	Review Screenplay	Mon 1/7/08	Wed 1/16/08	100%	0%	1.8 wks	0 wks	$2,295.00	120 hrs
4	Develop scene blocking and schedule	Wed 1/16/08	Tue 1/29/08	100%	0%	2 wks	0 wks	$1,560.00	80 hrs
5	Develop production layouts	Wed 1/30/08	Thu 2/14/08	100%	0%	0.5 mons	0 mons	$2,520.00	160 hrs
6	Identify and reserve locations	Fri 2/15/08	Thu 3/20/08	100%	0%	5 wks	0 wks?	$9,455.00	550 hrs
7	Book musicians	Fri 3/21/08	Thu 4/3/08	100%	0%	2 wks	0 wks	$1,360.00	80 hrs
8	Book dancers	Fri 4/4/08	Thu 4/17/08	100%	0%	2 wks	0 wks	$1,360.00	80 hrs
9	Reserve audio recording equipment	Fri 4/18/08	Thu 4/24/08	100%	0%	1 wk	0 wks	$1,400.00	80 hrs
10	Reserve video recording equipment	Fri 4/25/08	Thu 5/1/08	100%	0%	5 days	0 days	$1,400.00	80 hrs
11	Status Meeting	Mon 1/14/08	Mon 4/21/08	100%	0%	69.13 days	0 days	$1,491.00	84 hrs
26	Pre-Production complete	Thu 5/1/08	Thu 5/1/08	100%	0%	0 days	0 days	$0.00	0 hrs
27	Production	NA	NA	0%	0%	22.09 days	15.66 days	$15,040.10	518.5 hrs
28	Production begins	NA	NA	0%	0%	0 days	0 days	$0.00	0 hrs
29	Scene 1	Thu 5/1/08	Wed 5/14/08	100%	0%	9 days	0 days	$6,477.10	220.5 hrs
30	Scene 1 begin	Thu 5/1/08	Thu 5/1/08	100%	0%	0 days	0 days	$0.00	0 hrs
31	Scene 1 setup	Fri 5/2/08	Mon 5/5/08	100%	0%	2 days	0 days	$536.00	48 hrs
32	Scene 1 rehearsal	Tue 5/6/08	Tue 5/6/08	100%	0%	6 hrs	0 hrs	$388.50	21 hrs
33	Scene 1 vocal recording	Tue 5/6/08	Wed 5/7/08	100%	0%	1.13 days	0 days	$1,442.00	32 hrs
34	Scene 1 video shoot	Wed 5/7/08	Tue 5/13/08	100%	0%	3.01 days	0 days	$3,862.60	103.5 hrs
35	Scene 1 teardown	Tue 5/13/08	Wed 5/14/08	100%	0%	1 day	0 days	$248.00	16 hrs
36	Scene 1 complete	Wed 5/14/08	Wed 5/14/08	100%	0%	0 days	0 days	$0.00	0 hrs
37	Scene 2	Thu 5/15/08	Thu 5/29/08	100%	0%	11 days	0 days	$8,295.00	282 hrs
38	Scene 2 begin	Thu 5/15/08	Thu 5/15/08	100%	0%	0 days	0 days	$0.00	0 hrs
39	Scene 2 setup	Thu 5/15/08	Mon 5/19/08	100%	0%	2 days	0 days	$1,066.00	64 hrs
40	Scene 2 rehearsal	Tue 5/20/08	Wed 5/21/08	100%	0%	14 hrs	0 hrs	$756.00	42 hrs

On the Tracking Table, you can enter values for actual start and finish dates, percentage complete, actual duration, remaining duration, and actual work.

■ Establishing a Project Baseline

↓ THE BOTTOM LINE

In order to evaluate how well a project is progressing, you need to review how well the project was originally planned. The schedule baseline is the project schedule that was approved by the project sponsor. This baseline can be saved and referred to at a later date to track project progress.

⊖ ESTABLISH A PROJECT BASELINE

GET READY. Before you begin these steps, launch Microsoft Project.

1. **OPEN** the *Don Funk Music Video 10M* project schedule from the data files for this lesson.

2. **SAVE** the file as *Don Funk Music Video 10* in the solutions folder for this lesson, as directed by your instructor.

Set
Baseline ▾

3. Click the **Project** tab. In the Schedule group, click the **Set Baseline** button, then select **Set Baseline**.

The ***Don Funk Music Video 10M*** file for this lesson is available on the book companion website.

You will go deeper into the Set Baseline dialog box in Lesson 11.

4. The Set Baseline dialog box appears. Accept all of the default settings in this dialog box by clicking **OK**.

   Microsoft Project saves the baseline, although there is no indication in the Gantt chart view that anything has changed. In the next few steps, you will explore some of the changes caused by saving the baseline.

 TAKE NOTE You can save up to 11 baselines in a single project schedule. The baselines are named Baseline (the first baseline you would normally save), Baseline 1, Baseline 2, and onward through Baseline 10. Saving multiple baselines is helpful if your project duration is especially long or if you have approved scope changes. You can save multiple baselines to record different sets of baseline values, then later compare these against one another and against actual values.

5. On the Ribbon, click the **View** tab, then click the downward arrow under Gantt Chart. Select **More Views**, and the More Views dialog box appears.

6. In the More Views box, select **Task Sheet** and click **Apply**. There is more room to see the fields in the table because the Gantt chart is not shown. Now you will switch to a different table in the Task Sheet view.

7. On the Ribbon, click **Tables**, then click **Variance**. The Variance table appears. This table includes both the Scheduled and Baseline columns so that you can compare them easily. Your screen should look similar to Figure 10-2.

Figure 10-2

Variance Table displaying scheduled and baseline information

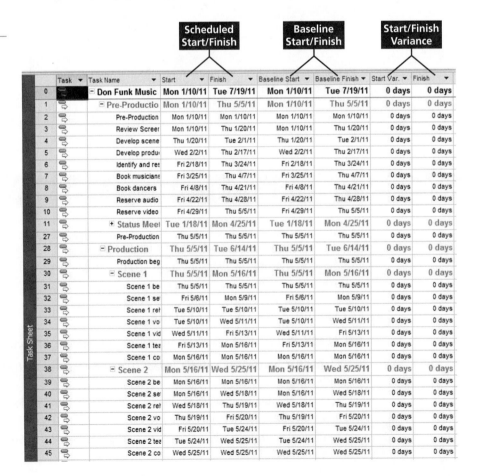

Note that at this point, the values in the Start and Baseline Start, as well as the values in the Finish and Baseline Finish, are identical. This is because no actual work has occurred and no changes to the scheduled work have been made. Once actual work has been recorded or schedule adjustments have been made, the scheduled values may differ from the baseline values. Any differences would be displayed in the Variance column.

8. SAVE the project schedule.

PAUSE. LEAVE Project open to use in the next exercise.

In this exercise, you learned how to save a baseline for your project schedule. A *baseline* is a collection of key values in the project schedule, such as the planned start dates, finish dates, and costs of the various tasks and assignments. A baseline allows you to begin the tracking phase of project management. Table 10-1 lists the specific types of fields saved in the baseline, which include the task, resource, and assignment fields, as well as the *timephased fields*—task, resource, and assignment values distributed over time.

Table 10-1

Baseline field types saved

Task fields	Start field
	Finish field
	Duration field
	Work and timephased Work fields
	Cost and timephased Cost fields
Resource fields	Work and timephased Work fields
	Cost and timephased Cost fields
Assignment fields	Start field
	Finish field
	Work and timephased Work fields
	Cost and timephased Cost fields

You should save a baseline when:

* You have developed the project schedule as much as possible. (You can still add tasks, resources, or assignments after work has begun. This is usually not avoidable.)
* Your project has been approved and accepted by the project sponsor.
* You have not started to enter actual values, such as a percentage of completion for the task.

The first phase of a project focuses on project *planning*—developing and communicating the details of the project before actual work begins. When work begins, so does the next phase of project management: tracking project progress. *Tracking* refers to collecting, entering, and analyzing actual project performance data, such as work on tasks, resource costs, and actual durations. These details are often called *actuals*, or project work completed and recorded in a Microsoft Project file. Accurately tracking project performance and comparing it against the original schedule helps you answer such questions as:

* Are tasks starting and finishing as planned? If not, what is the effect on the finish date?
* Are resources completing the proper amount of the scope? Are they doing unapproved work (scope creep)?

- Are resources requiring more or less than the scheduled amount of time to complete tasks?
- Are tasks being completed above or below scheduled cost?

There are several ways to track progress in Microsoft Project, depending on the level of detail or control required by you, the stakeholders, and the project *sponsor*—the individual or organization that provides financial support and supports the project team within the larger organization. Because tracking requires more work from you and possibly from the resources working on the project, you must determine the level of detail you need. In this lesson, we examine different levels of tracking:

- **Record project work as scheduled:** This works best if everything in the project occurs exactly as it was scheduled.
- **Record each task's percentage of completion:** You can do this at precise values or in increments, such as 25%, 50%, 75%, and 100%.
- **Record the actuals:** Here, the actual start, actual finish, actual work, and actual and remaining duration for each task or assignment are recorded.
- **Track assignment-level work by time period:** With this method, you record actual work values by day, week, or another time interval that you select. This is the most detailed level of tracking. It is rarely used as a method of tracking project progress because it is too costly.

You can also apply a combination of these approaches within a single project, because different parts of a project may have different tracking needs.

■ Tracking a Project as Scheduled

THE BOTTOM LINE

Once a baseline has been saved for a project schedule, the work that is done on the project can be tracked against the baseline values. The simplest approach to tracking is to report that the actual work is proceeding as planned. You record project actuals by updating work to the current date.

⊙ TRACK A PROJECT AS SCHEDULED

USE the project schedule you created in the previous exercise.

1. On the Ribbon, click **Gantt chart**. The Gantt chart view appears. Click the **Tables** button and select the **Entry** table.
2. Move the vertical divider bar to a point just to the right of the Start column.
3. Click the **Project** tab, then click **Update Project** in the Status group. The Update Project dialog box appears.

Update Project

4. Make sure the **Update work as complete through** option is selected. In the adjacent date box, key or select **February 7, 2011**, then click **OK**. Microsoft Project records the actual work for the projects that were scheduled to start before February 7. It also draws progress bars in the Gantt bars for those tasks to show this progress visually.

Scroll to Task

5. Select the name of task 5, **Develop production layouts**. Click the **Task** tab, then click **Scroll to Task** in the Editing group. Your screen should look similar to Figure 10-3.

Figure 10-3

Progress bars for completed
and in-progress tasks in the
Gantt chart view

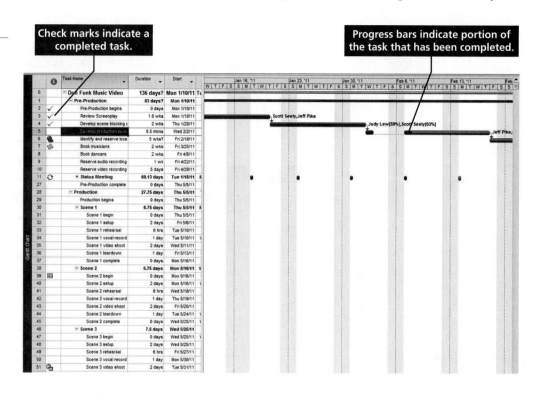

6. **SAVE** the project schedule.

PAUSE. LEAVE the project schedule open to use in the next exercise.

In this exercise, you updated the project to show that work had occurred as scheduled through a certain date. This date is sometimes called the data date or *status date*—the date up to or through which all progress information is collected and entered for a project. The *progress bar* in the Gantt chart view shows how much of each task has been completed. A check mark appears in the Indicators column for tasks 2, 3, and 4 to indicate these tasks have been completed. In addition, a progress bar is drawn through the entire length of these tasks' Gantt bars. Because only a portion of task 5 has been completed by February 7, the progress bar for this task extends only to February 7 and no check mark appears in the Indicators column.

Also notice that because some of the recurring status meetings have been completed by February 11, progress bars appear in the summary Gantt bars for those tasks.

■ Entering the Completion Percentage for a Task

THE BOTTOM LINE

As you continue to make progress on your project, it is important to record the work that has been done on each task. There are many ways to record this work. One of the quickest ways is to record the completion percentage of the task.

→ **ENTER THE COMPLETION PERCENTAGE FOR A TASK**

USE the project schedule you created in the previous exercise.

Tables ▾

1. Click the **View** tab, click the **Tables** button, and then select the **Work Table**.
2. Slide the vertical divider bar between the table and the Gantt bar chart so that more of the table columns are visible (notice the Work and % Work Complete columns). You will enter task completion percentages in the % Work Complete column.

Selected
Tasks

3. In the % Work Complete column for task 5, key or select **100**, then press **Enter**. Microsoft Project extends the progress bar through the length of the Gantt bar for task 5 and records the actual work for the task as scheduled.

4. On the Ribbon, click **Selected Tasks** in the Zoom group. Your screen should look similar to Figure 10-4.

Figure 10-4

Gantt chart view showing task 5 is 100% complete

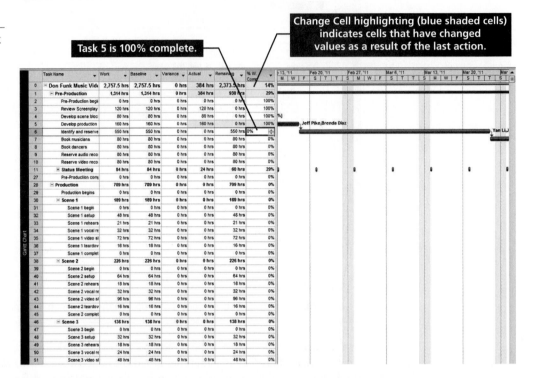

You can also use the schedule percent complete buttons to quickly update tasks that are 0%, 25%, 50%, 75%, and 100% complete. On the Ribbon, click the Task tab; these buttons are located in the Schedule group. Select the task you want to update, then click the appropriate percentage button.

TAKE NOTE*

5. In the % Work Complete field for task 6, key or select **50**, then press **Enter**. Microsoft Project records the actual work for the task as scheduled, calculates the remaining work, and updates the progress line through 50 percent of the Gantt bar.

6. **SAVE** and **CLOSE** the project schedule. In the next exercise, you will use an updated version of the Don Funk Music Video 10 project schedule to simulate the passage of time.

PAUSE. LEAVE Microsoft Project open to use in the next exercise.

TAKE NOTE*

You can view a task's completion percentage and other tracking information by pointing to a progress bar in a task's Gantt bar. A ScreenTip will appear.

In this exercise, you manually entered the completion percentage for a task. There are several ways you can quickly record task progress as a percentage:

- Use one of the % complete fields in either the Work Table or the Tracking Table.
- Use the preset buttons for recording 0%, 25%, 50%, 75%, and 100% completion on a task.
- Use the Update Tasks dialog box (on the Task tab, click the downward arrow to the right of the Mark on Track button, then click Update Tasks).

• Use the General tab of the Task Information dialog box (by double-clicking on the task you want to update) to update the Percent Complete field.

With the last two methods, you can enter any completion percentage you desire.

When you use any of these methods to enter a percentage other than 0% complete, Microsoft Project changes the task's actual start date to match its scheduled start date. It also calculates actual duration, remaining duration, actual costs, and other values based on the percentage you enter.

■ Identifying Overbudget Tasks and Resources

↓
THE BOTTOM LINE   So far, you have focused on a project's schedule as a key part of the overall success of the project. However, another critical piece of information is cost variance, or how the project's actual costs compare to the projected costs.

⊕ IDENTIFY OVERBUDGET TASKS AND RESOURCES

GET READY. To identify overbudget tasks and resources, perform the following steps:

1. **OPEN** the ***Don Funk Music Video 10MA*** project schedule from the data files for this lesson.

2. **SAVE** the file as ***Don Funk Music Video 10A*** in the solutions folder for this lesson, as directed by your instructor.

The ***Don Funk Music Video 10MA*** file for this lesson is available on the book companion website.

3. On the Ribbon, click the **Project** tab, then click **Project Information** in the Properties group. The Project Information dialog box appears.

4. Click the **Statistics** button. The Project Statistics dialog box appears. Your screen should look similar to Figure 10-5. Note that the Cost column displays the current, baseline, actual, and remaining cost values for the entire project:

• The *current cost* is the sum of the actual and remaining cost values.

• The *baseline cost* is the total planned cost of the project when the baseline was saved.

• The *actual cost* is the cost that has been incurred so far (after the indicated total work has been completed).

• The *remaining cost* is the difference between the current cost and the actual cost.

Figure 10-5

Project Statistics dialog box

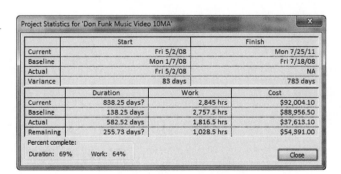

Project Statistics for 'Don Funk Music Video 10MA'				
	Start		Finish	
Current		Fri 5/2/08		Mon 7/25/11
Baseline		Mon 1/7/08		Fri 7/18/08
Actual		Fri 5/2/08		NA
Variance		83 days		783 days

	Duration	Work	Cost
Current	838.25 days?	2,845 hrs	$92,004.10
Baseline	138.25 days	2,757.5 hrs	$88,956.50
Actual	582.52 days	1,816.5 hrs	$37,613.10
Remaining	255.73 days?	1,028.5 hrs	$54,391.00

Percent complete:
Duration: 69%   Work: 64%   [Close]

In this case, it is obvious that some cost variance has occurred, but it is not possible to tell from the Project Statistics dialog box when or where the variance occurred.

5. Click the **Close** button. The Project Statistics dialog box closes.

6. On the Ribbon, click **View**. Click the **Tables** button, then click **Cost**. The Cost table appears in the Task Sheet view. Take a moment to review the columns in the Cost table. Note that although costs are not scheduled in the same sense that work is scheduled, costs (except fixed costs) are derived from the scheduled work.

ANOTHER WAY To change the table, you can also right-click the upper-left corner of the active table, then click Cost in the shortcut menu that appears.

7. Click the **Task Name** column heading. Next click the **Outline** button in the Data group, then select the **Hide Subtasks** button. Microsoft Project collapses the task list to display only the top summary tasks (which in this case correspond to the major phases of the project).

8. Click the **plus sign** next to task 28, Production. Microsoft Project expands the Production summary task to show the summary tasks for the individual scenes. Your screen should look similar to Figure 10-6.

Although Scenes 1 and 2 both had some variance, Scene 2 had the greater variance, so you will focus on that scene.

Figure 10-6

Task Sheet view with subtasks hidden

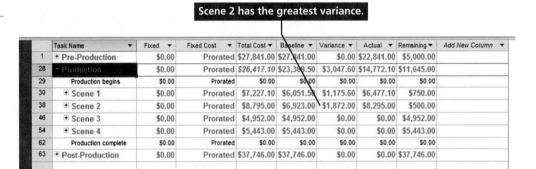

9. Click the **plus sign** next to summary task 38, Scene 2. Microsoft Project expands the Scene 2 summary task to show all of the subtasks. Your screen should look similar to Figure 10-7.

Figure 10-7

Scene 2 individual tasks in the Task Sheet view with the Cost table

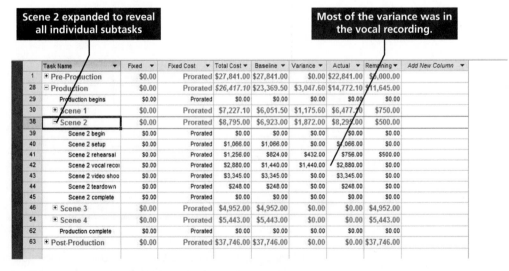

Take note of the variance column. It shows that most of the Scene 2 variance can be tracked to the Scene 2 vocal recording.

10. Click the **Task Name** column heading.

11. Click the **Outline** button, then click the **Show Subtasks** button. Microsoft Project expands all of the summary tasks to show all of the tasks in the project.

12. On the View tab, in the Data group, click the down arrow next to the Filter: selection box. Select **More Filters** from the list. The More Filters dialog box appears.

13. Select the **Cost Overbudget** filter and click **Apply**. Microsoft Project applies the filter to the task list to show only those tasks that had actual and scheduled costs greater than their baseline costs. Your screen should look similar to Figure 10-8.

Figure 10-8

Task Sheet view with the Cost Overbudget filter applied

	Task Name	Fixed Cost	Fixed Cost Accrual	Total Cost	Baseline	Variance	Actual	Remaining	Add New Column
28	– Production	$0.00	Prorated	$26,417.10	$23,369.50	$3,047.60	$14,772.10	$11,645.00	
30	⊟ Scene 1	$0.00	Prorated	$7,227.10	$6,051.50	$1,175.60	$6,477.10	$750.00	
35	Scene 1 video shoo	$0.00	Prorated	$3,862.60	$2,687.00	$1,175.60	$3,862.60	$0.00	
38	⊟ Scene 2	$0.00	Prorated	$8,795.00	$6,923.00	$1,872.00	$8,295.00	$500.00	
41	Scene 2 rehearsal	$0.00	Prorated	$1,256.00	$824.00	$432.00	$756.00	$500.00	
42	Scene 2 vocal reco	$0.00	Prorated	$2,880.00	$1,440.00	$1,440.00	$2,880.00	$0.00	

14. **SAVE** and **CLOSE** the project schedule. In the next exercise, you will use an updated version of the Don Funk Music Video 10 project schedule to simulate the passage of time.

PAUSE. LEAVE Microsoft Project open to use in the next exercise.

In this exercise, you used several different views and tables to identify tasks and resources that were over budget. Project managers and stakeholders often focus on the project schedule (did tasks start and finish on time?). For projects such as this one that include cost information, cost variance is another critical indicator of overall project health. A *variance* is any deviation from the baseline values. In Microsoft Project, evaluating cost variance enables you to make incremental budget adjustments for individual tasks so you can avoid exceeding your project's overall budget.

■ Identifying Time and Schedule Problems

THE BOTTOM LINE

In complex projects, it is highly likely that there will be some schedule variance. When this happens, the project manager must control the project by identifying, understanding, and correcting the problem.

⊕ RESCHEDULE UNCOMPLETED WORK

GET READY. To reschedule uncompleted work, perform the following tasks:

1. **OPEN** the *Don Funk Music Video 10MB* project schedule from the data files for this lesson.

2. **SAVE** the file as *Don Funk Music Video 10B* in the solutions folder for this lesson, as directed by your instructor.

3. Press the **F5** key, key **48** in the ID box, and click **OK**. The Gantt chart view scrolls to display the Gantt bar for task 48, Scene 3 setup. At this point in the project, the first two scheduled scenes have been completed. This task has one day of actual work completed and one day of scheduled work remaining.

4. Scroll the Gantt chart view so that the Scene 3 summary task appears near the top of the view. Your screen should look similar to Figure 10-9.

The *Don Funk Music Video 10MB* file for this lesson is available on the book companion website.

Figure 10-9

Gantt chart view showing task 48 prior to rescheduling the work

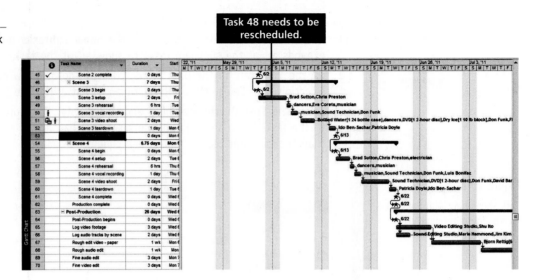

You have just been informed that on the afternoon of June 5, a lightning strike caused a nearby electrical transformer to short-circuit, and that repairs will not be completed until Thursday, June 9. You will not be able to resume work in the studio until Friday, June 10.

5. On the Ribbon, click the **Project** tab, then click **Update Project**. The Update Project dialog box appears.

Update Project

6. Select the **Reschedule uncompleted work to start after** option, and in the date box, key or select **06/09/11**.

7. Click **OK** to close the Update Project dialog box. Microsoft Project splits task 48 so that the incomplete portion is delayed until Friday, June 6. Your screen should look similar to Figure 10-10.

Figure 10-10

Gantt chart view after rescheduling uncompleted work on task 48

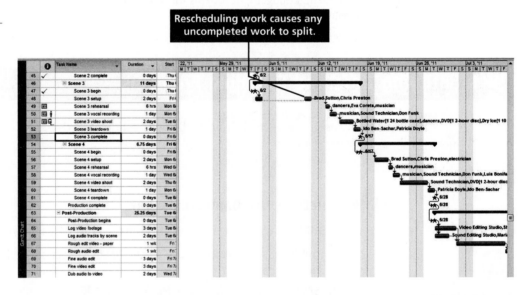

Note that although the duration of task 47 remains at two days, its finish and subsequent start dates for successor tasks have been pushed out. Remember that duration is the number of work periods required to complete a task, not elapsed time.

8. **SAVE** and **CLOSE** the project schedule.

PAUSE. If you are continuing to the next lesson, keep Project open. If you are not continuing to additional lessons, **CLOSE** Project.

In this exercise, you rescheduled an incomplete task due to an uncontrollable delay. Depending upon the length and complexity of your project, as a project manager, you may see one or many of these types of interruptions. When you reschedule incomplete work, you specify the date after which work can resume. Microsoft Project handles tasks in relation to the scheduled restart date in the following ways:

- If the task does not have any actual work recorded for it prior to the rescheduled date, and there is no constraint in place, the entire task is rescheduled to begin after that date.
- If the task has some actual work recorded prior to but not after the rescheduled date, the task is split so that all remaining work starts after the rescheduled date. The actual work is not affected.
- If the task has some actual work recorded for it both prior to and after the rescheduled date, the task is not affected.

Keep in mind that when you address a given problem by rescheduling a task, you may create other issues or problems in the remainder of the project. This is why project management is an iterative process: a change in one part of the schedule—be it a time, cost, or scope change—can and usually does affect the schedule elsewhere.

SKILL SUMMARY

In This Lesson, You Learned:	Task
To establish a project baseline.	Establish a project baseline.
To track a project as scheduled.	Track a project as scheduled.
To enter the completion percentage for a task.	Enter the completion percentage for a task.
To identify overbudget tasks and resources.	Identify overbudget tasks and resources.
To identify time and schedule problems.	Reschedule uncompleted work.

■ Knowledge Assessment

Matching

Match the term in column 1 to its description in column 2.

Column 1	Column 2
1. Actual cost	a. The collecting, entering, and analyzing of actual project performance data
2. Baseline	b. The individual or organization that provides financial support and supports the project team
3. Sponsor	c. The cost that has been incurred so far
4. Variance	d. In the Gantt chart view, shows how much of the task has been completed
5. % work complete	e. The total planned cost of the project when the baseline was saved
6. Current cost	f. Project work completed and recorded in a Microsoft Project file
7. Actuals	g. A collection of key values in the project schedule

8. Progress bar	**h.** The amount of work that has been completed in relation to the planned work value
9. Tracking	**i.** The sum of the actual and remaining cost values
10. Baseline cost	**j.** A deviation from the established schedule or budget

True/False

Circle T if the statement is true or F if the statement is false.

T | F **1.** You can save up to 11 different baselines for a single project schedule.

T | F **2.** You have to provide Microsoft Project a remaining duration value for it to calculate a percentage complete.

T | F **3.** A check mark in the Indicators column for a task means that the task is on schedule.

T | F **4.** You should save a project baseline when you have developed the project schedule as fully as possible.

T | F **5.** Planning refers to the collecting, entering, and analyzing of actual project performance data.

T | F **6.** If you reschedule an in-progress task, the delay is shown as a split on the Gantt chart.

T | F **7.** The only true indicator of project health is whether or not the project is on schedule.

T | F **8.** The Project Statistics dialog box pinpoints the point of cost variance in a project schedule.

T | F **9.** You can only enter completion percentages for a task in multiples of 10.

T | F **10.** The remaining cost is the difference between the current cost and the actual cost.

■ Competency Assessment

Project 10-1: Insurance Claim Processing Baseline

You are ready to begin entering actuals on your Insurance Claim Processing schedule. Before you do this, you need to save a baseline for your schedule.

GET READY. Launch Microsoft Project if it is not already running.

The *Insurance Claim Processing 10-1* file for this lesson is available on the book companion website.

OPEN *Insurance Claim Processing 10-1* from the data files for this lesson.

1. On the Project tab, click the **Set Baseline** button, then select **Set Baseline**.
2. In the Set Baseline dialog box, click **OK**.
3. **SAVE** the project schedule as *Insurance Schedule Processing Baseline*, then **CLOSE** the file.

   LEAVE Project open to use in the next exercise.

Project 10-2: Tracking a Project as Scheduled

Now that you have saved a baseline, you are now to enter actuals on your Insurance Claim Processing schedule.

OPEN *Insurance Schedule Processing Baseline* from the previous exercise.

1. On the Project tab, click the **Project Information button**.
2. In the Status Date box, enter **6/15/11**, then click **OK**.

3. Select tasks 1 through 53.

4. Click the **Task** tab, then select the **Mark on Track** button in the schedule group.

5. **SAVE** the project schedule as *Insurance Schedule Processing Tracked*.

   LEAVE Project open to use in the next exercise.

■ Proficiency Assessment

Project 10-3: Recording Completion Percentages for HR Interview Schedule

Now that portions of your HR Interview project have been completed, you need to record the completion percentages of several tasks.

OPEN *HR Interview Schedule 10-3* from the data files for this lesson.

The *HR Interview Schedule 10-3* file for this lesson is available on the book companion website.

1. Switch to the Work Table, then adjust the Gantt chart so that the Work and % Work Complete columns are visible.

2. Enter percentages to show that the project is 100% complete through task 10, and that task 11 is 25% complete. (Hint: Remember to make entries for the subtasks, not the summary tasks.)

3. **SAVE** the project schedule as *HR Interview Schedule Percentages*, then **CLOSE** the file.

   LEAVE Project open to use in the next exercise.

Project 10-4: Don Funk Music Video Overbudget Tasks

Even more progress has been made on the Don Funk Music Video, with tasks now complete through the Production phase. You need to analyze the project to determine the overbudget tasks.

OPEN *Don Funk Music Video 10-4* from the data files for this lesson.

The *Don Funk Music Video 10-4* file for this lesson is available on the book companion website.

1. Activate the Project Statistics box to view the costs for the project.

2. Display the Cost table.

3. Filter the tasks to show only those tasks that are overbudget.

4. Collapse all summary tasks (i.e., hide the subtasks) except for the summary task with the greatest cost variance.

5. **SAVE** the project schedule as *Don Funk Over Budget*, then **CLOSE** the file.

   LEAVE Project open to use in the next exercise.

■ Mastery Assessment

Project 10-5: Office Remodel Task Delay

You have just been informed that while the plumber was re-running the pipes for the office lunchroom remodel, a pipe burst and the floor was flooded with several inches of water. It will take a week to clean and dry the water damage. You need to reschedule the remaining work on incomplete tasks to restart when the cleanup is complete.

The *Office Remodel 10-5* file for this lesson is available on the book companion website.

OPEN the *Office Remodel 10-5* project schedule from the data files for this lesson.

1. Go to task 11.

2. Activate the Update Project dialog box.

3. Reschedule uncompleted work to start after Thursday, November 11, 2011.

4. **SAVE** the project schedule as *Office Remodel Reschedule*, then **CLOSE** the file.
LEAVE Project open to use in the next exercise.

Project 10-6: Tracking the Don Funk Music Video as Scheduled

The last phase of the Don Funk Music Video, Post-Production, is going well. Tasks are being completed on schedule. You want to update the project to show that tasks are complete through a specified current date.

OPEN the *Don Funk Music Video 10-6* project schedule from the data files for this lesson.

The *Don Funk Music Video 10-6* file for this lesson is available on the book companion website.

1. Activate the Update Project dialog box.

2. Update the project as complete through July 19, 2011.

3. Scroll the Gantt chart bars so that the task and progress bars on July 14, 2011, are visible.

4. **SAVE** the project schedule as *Don Funk On Schedule*, then **CLOSE** the file.
CLOSE Project.

■ Circling Back 2

Mete Goktepe is a project management specialist at Woodgrove Bank. He has put together the initial components of a project plan for a Request for Proposal (RFP) process to evaluate and select new commercial lending software. This process entails determining needs, identifying vendors, requesting proposals, reviewing proposals, and selecting the software.

Now that Mete has established the foundation of the project plan, he begins to put the plan into action.

→ Project 1: Setting Deadlines and Establishing Multiple Pay Rates

Acting as Mete, you need to set a deadline for one of the tasks in the project. You then need to establish and apply multiple pay rates for a resource.

GET READY. Launch Microsoft Project if it is not already running.

OPEN *RFP Bank Software Schedule* from the data files for this lesson.

The *RFP Bank Software Schedule* file for this lesson is available on the book companion website.

1. In the Task Name column, click the name of task 11, **RFP ready to release.**
2. On the Task tab, click the **Information** button in the Properties group.
3. On the Advanced tab, in the drop-down date box next to Deadline, key or select **5/27/11.**
4. Close the Task Information dialog box.
5. Scroll the Gantt bar chart to the right of task 11 to view the deadline marker.
6. On the Ribbon, click the **View** tab, then click **Resource Sheet.**
7. In the Resource Name column, double-click the name of resource 9, **Marc J. Ingle.** Because Marc J. Ingle's rate differs depending on whether he is doing document preparation or meeting facilitation, you need to enter a second rate for him.
8. In the Resource Information dialog box, click the **Costs** tab, if it is not already selected.
9. Under Cost rate tables, click the **B** tab.
10. Select the default entry of **$0.00/h** in the field directly below the Standard Rate column heading, key **1200/w**, and press **Enter.** Click **OK.**
11. On the View tab, click the **Task Usage** button.
12. On the Ribbon, click the **Tables** button, then select the **Cost** table.
13. Under task 5, double-click **Marc J. Ingle** to activate the Assignment Information dialog box.
14. Click the **General** tab, if it is not already selected.
15. In the Cost rate table box, key or select **B**, then click **OK.**
16. **SAVE** the project plan as *RFP Bank Software Multiple Rates* in the solutions folder for this lesson, as directed by your instructor.

    PAUSE. LEAVE Project and the project plan open to use in the next exercise.

→ Project 2: Formatting and Printing the Project Plan

Acting as Mete, you need to change the appearance of some of your data before sharing it with stakeholders. You then need to prepare to print the project plan for distribution.

USE the project schedule from the previous exercise.

1. **SAVE** the schedule as *RFP Bank Software Formatted.*
2. Click the **View** tab, then click **Gantt chart.**
3. Click the **Format** tab, then click the check box next to Project Summary Task in the Show/Hide group.

4. Adjust your screen so that the Duration and Start columns are fully visible and expanded to show entire values.

5. Click the **View** tab, then click **Other Views**, and then select **More Views**.

6. Make sure that the Gantt chart option is highlighted, then click the **Copy** button.

7. In the Name field, key **Custom Gantt Chart**, then click **OK**.

8. Make sure the **Custom Gantt Chart** option is highlighted, then click the **Apply** button.

9. Click the **Format** tab, then select the check box next to Critical in the Bar Styles group.

10. Save the project schedule.

11. Click the **File** tab, then select **Print**.

12. On the Print Preview screen, click the **Page Setup** hyperlink.

13. Click the **Header** tab. Select the **Center alignment** tab.

14. In the General box, click **Company Name**, then click the **Add** button.

15. Click the **Legend** tab, then select the **Left alignment** tab.

16. In the Alignment box, position your cursor after &[Date] and press **Enter**.

17. Key **Start Date:** followed by a space. In the General box, select **Project Start Date** from the drop-down list, then click **Add**.

18. Click **OK** to close the Page Setup dialog box.

19. On the Print Preview toolbar, click **Close**.

20. **SAVE** the project schedule.

    PAUSE. LEAVE Project and the project plan open to use in the next exercise.

⊙→ Project 3: Tracking the Project Plan

Now that work is starting on your project, it is time to begin tracking progress. You need to save a baseline, track actual work, and enter completion percentages.

GET READY. SAVE the open project schedule as *RFP Bank Software Tracked*.

1. Click the **Project** tab.

2. In the Schedule group, click the **Set Baseline** button, then select **Set Baseline**.

3. Accept all the defaults by clicking the **OK** button.

4. Select tasks **5** and **6**.

5. On the Ribbon, click **Update Project**.

6. Make sure the **Update work as complete through** option and **0%–100% complete** are both selected. In the adjacent date box, key or select **5/25/11**. Next to For, click **Selected tasks**, then click **OK**.

7. Click the **View** tab, then click the **Tables** button, and then select the **Work** table.

8. Drag your center divider to the right to reveal the %Work Complete column.

9. In the % Work Complete column for task 7, key or select **100**, then press **Enter**.

10. Click the name of task 8, **Draft RFP**. Press **Ctrl + Shift + F5** to scroll the Gantt chart view to the Gantt bar.

11. In the Actual cell for task 8, key **88** and press **Enter**.

12. Click the name of task 9, **Review RFP with management and commercial lending representatives**.

13. In the Actual cell for task 9, key **52** and press the **Tab** key.

14. In the Remaining cell for task 9, key **0** and press **Enter**.

15. **SAVE** and then **CLOSE** the project schedule.

    CLOSE Microsoft Project.

Advanced Project Schedule Tracking

LESSON SKILL MATRIX

SKILL	TASK
Recording Actual Start, Finish, and Duration Values of Tasks	Enter actual start date and duration for a task.
Adjusting Remaining Work or Duration of Tasks	Adjust actual and remaining work for a task.
Rescheduling Uncompleted Work	Reschedule incomplete work.
Saving an Interim Plan	Save an interim project plan.
Comparing Baseline, Interim, and Actual Plans	Compare the baseline, interim, and actual project plans.
Reporting Project Status	Report project variance with a "Stoplight" view.
Evaluating Performance with Earned Value Analysis	Set project status date and display the Earned Value table.

You are a project manager for Southridge Video, and recently, one of your primary responsibilities has been to manage the new Don Funk Music Video project. In an earlier lesson, you learned about some of the basic project schedule tracking features in Microsoft Office Project. In this lesson, you become familiar with some of the more advanced tracking functions that enable you to record the progress details of your project.

KEY TERMS
actual cost of work performed (ACWP)
budgeted cost of work performed (BCWP)
budgeted cost of work scheduled (BCWS)
cost performance index (CPI)
cost variance (CV)
earned value (EV)
interim plan
planned value (PV)
schedule performance index (SPI)
schedule variance (SV)
triple constraint

SOFTWARE ORIENTATION

Microsoft Project's Earned Value Table

The Earned Value table (Figure 11-1) displays a number of schedule indicator and cost indicator values that are useful in measuring a project's progress and forecasting its outcome through earned value analysis.

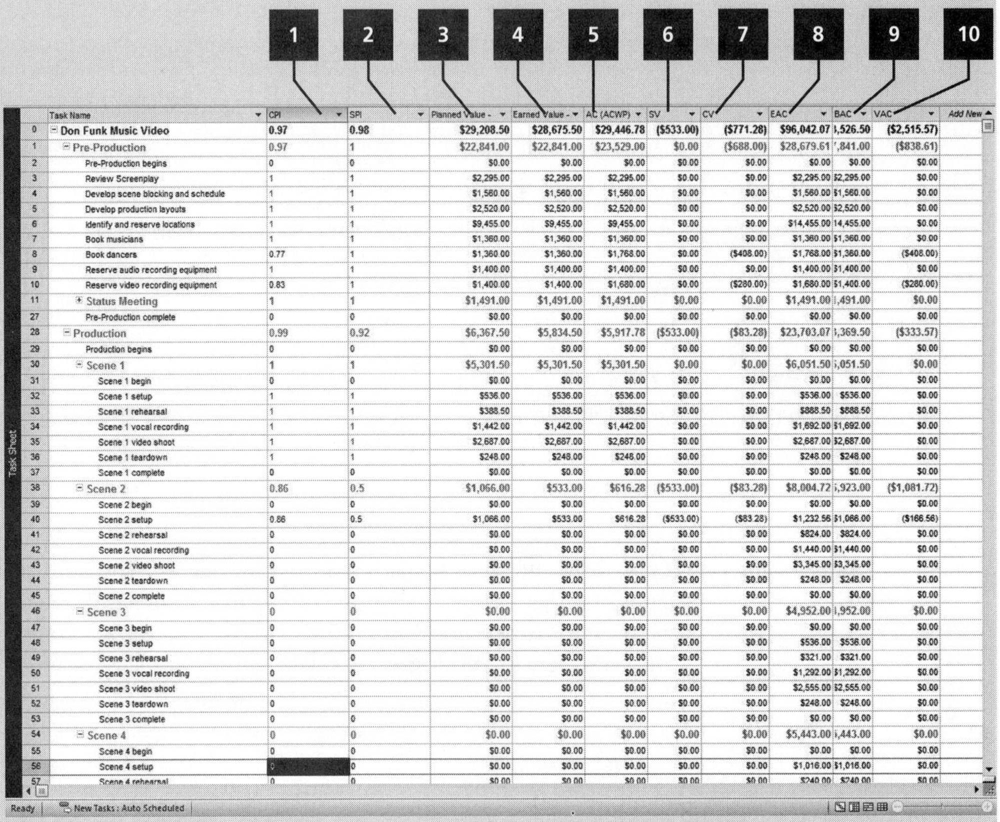

Figure 11-1

The Earned Value table in Task Sheet view

The columns in the Earned Value table are as follows:

1. **CPI:** Cost performance index, or the ratio of budgeted cost to actual cost, calculated as budgeted cost of work performed (BCWP) divided by actual cost of work performed (ACWP)

2. **SPI:** Schedule performance index, or the ratio of performed work to scheduled work, calculated as budgeted cost of work performed (BCWP) divided by budgeted cost of work scheduled (BCWS)

3. **PV:** Planned value (BCWS), or the value of the work scheduled to be complete as of the status date

4. **EV:** Earned value (BCWP), or the portion of the budgeted cost that should have been spent to complete each task's actual work performed up to the status date

5. **AC:** Actual cost (ACWP), or the actual cost incurred to complete each task's actual work up to the status date

6. **SV:** Schedule variance, or the difference between the budgeted cost of work performed (BCWP) and the budgeted cost of work scheduled (BCWS)

7. **CV:** Cost variance, or the difference between the budgeted cost of work performed (BCWP) and the actual cost of work performed (ACWP)

8. **EAC:** Estimate at completion, or the expected total cost of a task based on perform-ance up to the status date

9. **BAC:** Budget at completion, or the total planned cost

10. **VAC:** Variance at completion, or the difference between the BAC or baseline cost and the EAC

Most of these terms are discussed at the end of this lesson.

■ Recording Actual Start, Finish, and Duration Values of Tasks

↓
THE BOTTOM LINE

Once the details of a project schedule have been finalized and work has started, the project manager can begin to track progress on the project by recording actual start, finish, and duration values.

The **Don Funk Music Video 11MA** file for this lesson is available on the book companion website.

Scroll to Task

Mark on Track ▾

→ **ENTER ACTUAL START DATE AND DURATION FOR A TASK**

GET READY. Before you begin these steps, launch Microsoft Project.

1. **OPEN** the **Don Funk Music Video 11MA** project schedule from the data files for this lesson.

2. **SAVE** the file as **Don Funk Music Video 11A** in the solutions folder for this lesson, as directed by your instructor.

3. Navigate to and select task ID 7, **Book musicians**. On the Task tab, click the **Scroll to Task** button. This task started one day ahead of schedule, so you need to record this.

4. On the Ribbon, click the downward arrow next to the **Mark on Track** button, then select **Update Tasks**. The Update Tasks dialog box appears.

5. Under the Actual label, in the Start box, key or select **March 18, 2011**.

6. In the Actual dur box, key or select **2w**, then click **OK** to close the Update Tasks dialog box. Microsoft Project records the actual start date and work for task 7. Your screen should look similar to Figure 11-2.

Figure 11-2

Gantt chart showing actual start and work for task 7

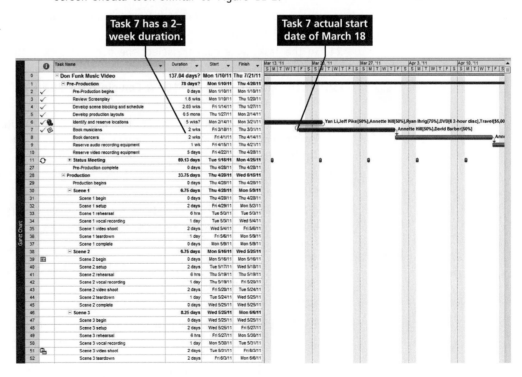

Task 7 has a 2–week duration.

Task 7 actual start date of March 18

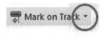

Scroll
to Task

7. In the Task Name column, select the name of task 8, **Book dancers.** You need to record that task 8 started on time but took three days longer than expected to complete.

8. On the Ribbon, click the downward arrow next to the **Mark on Track** button and select **Update Tasks.** The Update Tasks dialog box reappears.

9. In the Actual dur box, key **13d,** then click **OK.**

10. Click the **Scroll to Task** button so that the Gantt bar for task 8 is visible. Your screen should look similar to Figure 11-3.

Figure 11-3

Gantt chart showing updated progress for task 8

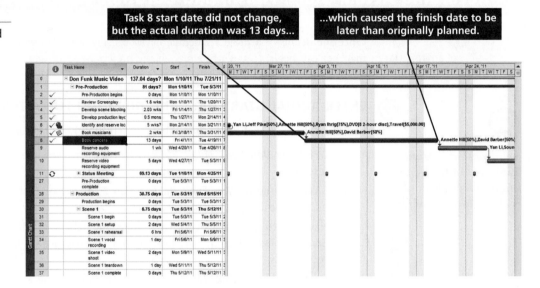

Microsoft Project records the actual duration of the task. The software assumes that the task started as scheduled because you did not specify an actual start date. However, the actual duration that you entered causes Project to calculate a finish date that is later than the originally scheduled finish date.

Next you will record that task 9 was completed as scheduled and that task 10 took longer than scheduled to complete.

11. In the Task Name column, select the name of task 9, **Reserve audio recording equipment.**

100%

12. On the Ribbon, click the **100% Complete** button in the Schedule group. Microsoft Project updates task 9 as 100% complete.

13. In the Task Name column, select the name of task 10, **Reserve video recording equipment.** Click the downward arrow next to the **Mark on Track** button and select **Update Tasks.** The Update Tasks dialog box reappears.

14. In the Actual dur box, key or select **6d,** then click **OK.** Microsoft Project records the actual duration of the task.

Scroll
to Task

15. On the Ribbon, click the **Scroll to Task** button. Microsoft Project scrolls the Gantt bar chart so that the bar for task 10 is visible. Your screen should look similar to Figure 11-4.

You can see that the Pre-Production phase of the Don Funk Music Video project has met its deadline of May 4, 2011.

16. **SAVE** the project schedule, then **CLOSE** the file.

PAUSE. LEAVE Project open to use in the next exercise.

Figure 11-4

Gantt chart showing completion information for tasks 9 and 10

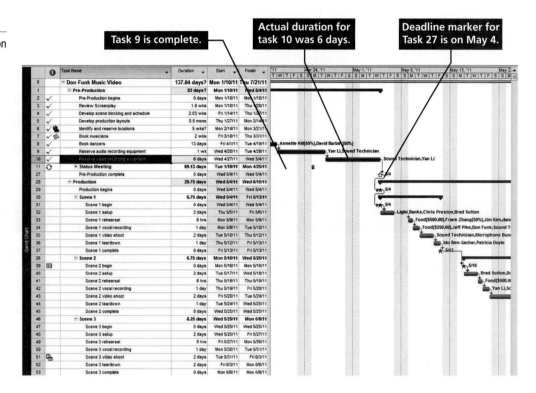

In this exercise, you entered actual start dates and durations for several tasks. Remember, as you learned in Lesson 10, that tracking actuals is essential to a well-managed project. As the project manager, you need to know how well the project team is performing and when to take corrective action. When you enter actual start, finish, or duration values, Microsoft Project updates the schedule and calculates the task's percentage of completion. When doing this, the software uses the following rules:

- When you enter a task's actual start date that is different from its planned start date, Microsoft Project recalculates the scheduled finish date.
- When you enter a task's actual finish date, Microsoft Project moves the scheduled finish date to match the actual finish date and assigns a completion percentage of 100%.
- When you enter an actual duration for a task that is less than the scheduled duration, Microsoft Project subtracts the actual duration from the scheduled duration to determine the remaining duration.
- When you enter a task's actual duration that is equal to the scheduled duration, Microsoft Project sets the task to 100% complete.
- When you enter an actual duration for a task that is longer than the scheduled duration, Microsoft Project adjusts the scheduled duration to match the actual duration and sets the task to 100%.

Evaluating the status of a project is not always easy or straightforward. When evaluating project status, keep the following issues in mind:

- For many tasks, it is difficult to evaluate a percentage of completion. For example, when is a design engineer 75% finished designing a new production process, or when is a computer engineer 50% finished coding a new software upgrade? Often, reporting work in progress is a best guess and therefore carries an inherent risk.
- The portion of a task's duration that has elapsed does not always equate to a percentage accomplished. For example, a front-loaded task might require a lot of effort initially, such that when 50% of its duration has elapsed, much more than 50% of its total work will be completed.

- The resources assigned to a task might have different criteria for what determines the task's completion than does the project manager or the resources assigned to successor tasks.

To avoid or minimize these and other problems that arise in project implementation, an effective project manager needs to carry out good project planning and communication. Determining how you will track project progress is a decision made during planning, and this information must be clearly communicated to all team members. No matter how much planning is done, large and complex projects almost always tend to have variance from the baseline.

■ Adjusting Remaining Work or Duration of Tasks

↓
THE BOTTOM LINE
While tracking actual values, it is also possible to adjust the work or duration remaining on a task.

➔ ADJUST ACTUAL AND REMAINING WORK FOR A TASK

The ***Don Funk Music Video 11MB*** file for this lesson is available on the book companion website.

GET READY. To continue with this lesson, you will use an updated version of the Don Funk Music Video project to simulate the passage of time since you completed the previous exercise.

1. **OPEN** the ***Don Funk Music Video 11MB*** project schedule from the data files for this lesson.
2. **SAVE** the file as ***Don Funk Music Video 11B*** in the solutions folder for this lesson, as directed by your instructor.
3. Click the **View** tab, then click **Task Usage**. The Task Usage view appears. Your screen should look similar to Figure 11-5.

Figure 11-5

Task Usage view

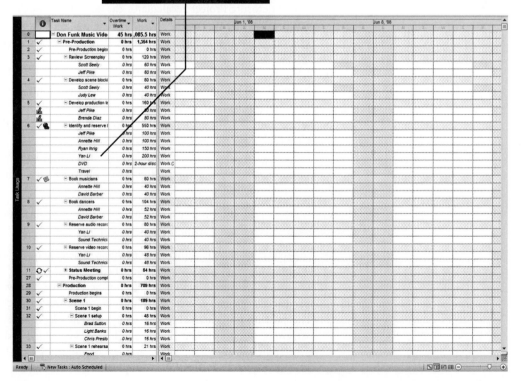

4. Press the **F5** key. In the ID box, key **40**, then click **OK**. Microsoft Project scrolls the timescaled portion of the view to display the scheduled work information for task 40.

5. On the Ribbon, click the **Tables** button and select the **Work** table. Microsoft Project displays the Work table in the Task Usage view.

6. Click the divider bar between the Task Usage table and the Work table, and drag the bar to the right until you can see all the columns in the Work table. Your screen should look similar to Figure 11-6.

Figure 11-6

Work table in the Task Usage view

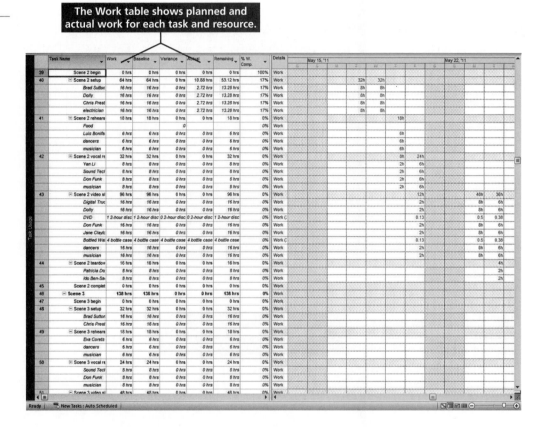

7. In the Actual column for task 40, key **20h**, then press **Tab**. Change highlighting (the light-blue shaded cells) shows that several things have occurred. First, because you entered the actual work at the task level, Microsoft Project distributed it among the assigned 54 resources. Second, Microsoft Project recalculated the remaining work value. Your screen should look similar to Figure 11-7.

TAKE NOTE * The mouse pointer changes to a two-headed arrow (pointing left and right) when it is in the correct position to drag the vertical divider bar.

8. In the Remaining column for task 40, key **54h** and press **Enter**. Notice that the new remaining work value was distributed among the assigned resources. Your screen should look similar to Figure 11-8.

9. **SAVE** the project schedule.

PAUSE. LEAVE Project open to use in the next exercise.

Figure 11-7

Work table showing the actual work completed for task 40

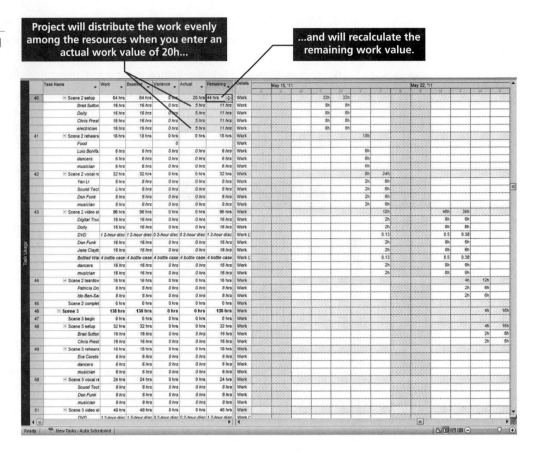

Figure 11-8

Work table showing remaining work for task 40

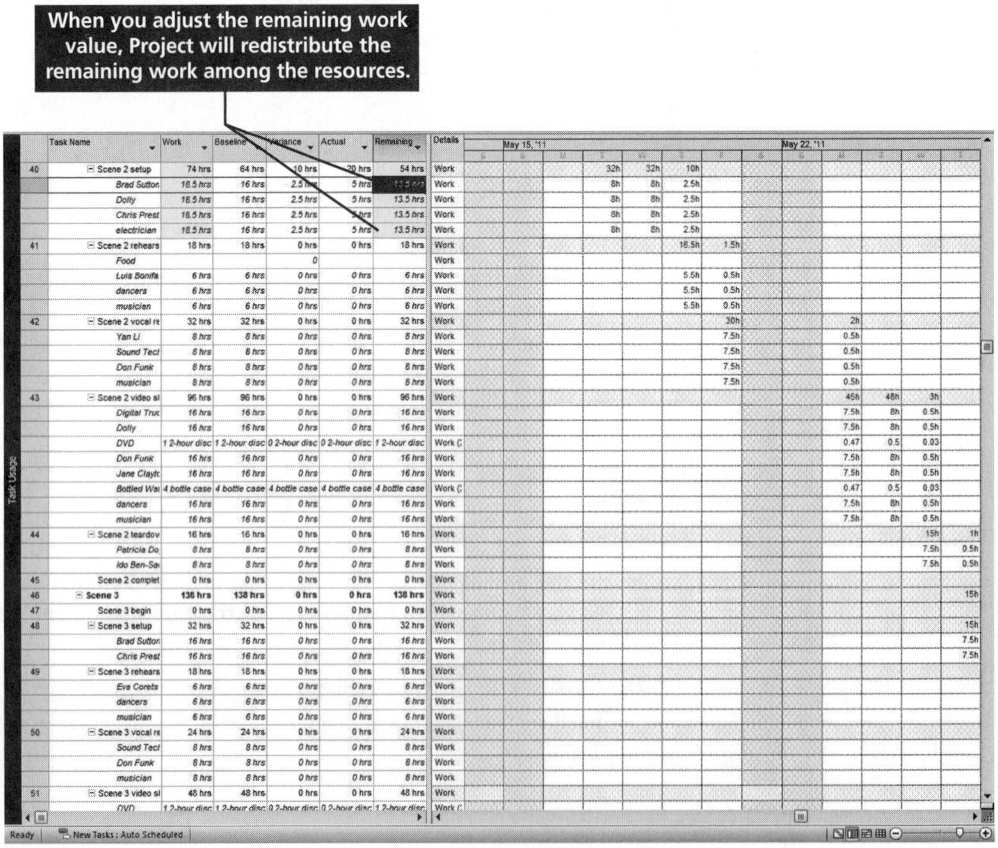

In this lesson, you adjusted actual and remaining work for a task in the project schedule. In addition to adjusting work, as you track actuals, you can also adjust duration and start and finish dates. Remember that only an incomplete task can have a remaining work or duration value. For example:

- A task that was scheduled for 40 hours is partially completed. The resources have performed 30 hours of work and expect to finish the entire task after working six more hours. As you learned in this lesson, you would enter 30 hours of actual work and six hours of remaining work using the Work table.

- A task that was scheduled for four days' duration is partially complete. Two days have elapsed, and the resources working on the task estimate they will need three additional days to complete the task. You can enter the actual and remaining duration via the Update Tasks dialog box (on the Task tab, select the downward arrow next to Mark on Track, then click Update Tasks).

It is important to remember that whenever you enter actual work values, Microsoft Project calculates actual cost values by default, and you cannot enter actual costs directly. If you want to enter actual cost values yourself, click the File tab, then select Options, then click the Schedule option. In the section under *Calculation*, set the option to Off. In the section for *Calculation options for this* project, deselect the option that reads *Actual costs are always calculated by Project.*

Once you turn off automatic calculation, you can enter or import task-level or assignment-level actual costs in the Actual Cost field. This field is available in several locations, such as the Cost table. You can also enter actual cost values on a daily or other interval in any usage view, such as the Task Usage view. Exercise caution, though, any time you enter costs manually, because entering actual costs for tasks or assignments prevents Microsoft Project from calculating costs based on resource rates and task progress.

■ Rescheduling Uncompleted Work

THE BOTTOM LINE

It is not uncommon for work delays to cause scheduling problems. As the project manager, you must understand the cause of the delays, as well as how rescheduling the work will ultimately affect the project schedule.

 RESCHEDULE INCOMPLETE WORK

USE the project schedule you created in the previous exercise.

1. Click the **Task** tab, then click the **Gantt chart** view button.
2. In the Task Name column, click the name of task 40, **Scene 2 setup**.
3. On the Ribbon, click the **Scroll to Task** button. Microsoft Project scrolls to task 40.
4. In the Task Name column, double-click the name of task 40. The Task Information dialog box appears.
5. Click the **General** tab, if it is not already selected.
6. In the Percent complete box, key or select **50%**, then click **OK**. Microsoft Project records progress for the task and updates the progress bar in the task's Gantt bar. Your screen should look similar to Figure 11-9.

   You have just been told that on the evening of May 17, the transformer that routes electricity to the studio for Scene 2 short-circuited, and it now needs to be replaced. As a result, you will not be able to resume work until Monday, May 23.

7. Click the **Project** tab, then click **Update Project**. The Update Project dialog box appears.

Figure 11-9

Gantt chart showing 50% completion for task 40

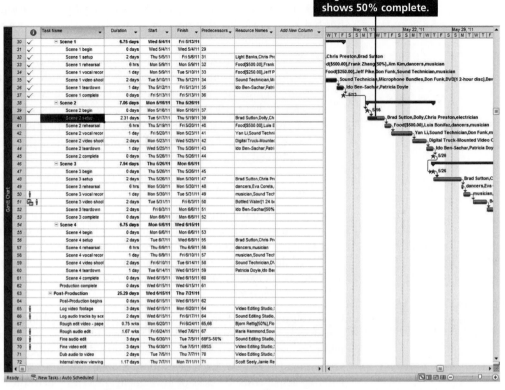

Progress bar for task 40 shows 50% complete.

8. Click **Reschedule uncompleted work to start after**, and in the date box, key or select **5/22/11**; then click **OK**. (If you get an informational message that Microsoft Project could not move some tasks due to constraints, click **OK**.) Microsoft Project splits task 40 so that the uncompleted portion of the task is delayed until Monday. Your screen should look similar to Figure 11-10.

Figure 11-10

Gantt chart view showing the split in task 40

Task is split to account for the delay.

You can see that although the duration of task 40 remained the same, its finish date and the subsequent start dates for successor tasks are now later. So, although you have resolved a specific problem, this has resulted in other potential problems in the remainder of the project.

It is possible to disable Microsoft Project's ability to reschedule uncompleted work on tasks that are showing any actual work. To do so, click the File tab, then select Options. In the Options dialog box, click the Schedule tab. Then, in the section that reads *Scheduling options for this project*, clear the *Split in-progress tasks* check box.

9. **SAVE** the project schedule.

PAUSE. LEAVE Project open to use in the next exercise.

In this exercise, you rescheduled some work that was delayed because of a problem in the studio. Schedule variance is usually the rule rather than the exception in any complex project. As the project manager, it is important that you know when and to what extent variance has occurred, and then take prompt corrective action to stay on track.

■ Saving an Interim Plan

THE BOTTOM LINE As you track actual values for a project schedule, it is often helpful to capture a snapshot of the current values at different times in the project's progress, and to save these values in an interim plan.

 SAVE AN INTERIM PROJECT PLAN

USE the project schedule you created in the previous exercise.

Set Baseline ▾

1. Click the **Project** tab, then click the **Set Baseline** button. Next, select **Set Baseline**. The Set Baseline dialog box appears.
2. Click **Set interim plan**. The Copy and Into boxes become active. Your screen should look similar to Figure 11-11.

Figure 11-11

Set Baseline dialog box with Set interim plan selected

The Copy and Into boxes enable you to select scheduled start and finish values for tasks that you want to save in the specific interim start and finish fields. These fields are numbered Start1 through Start10 and Finish1 through Finish10. Because this is the first interim project plan you have saved, use the default fields that appear in the Into box.

3. Click **OK** to save the interim project plan and close the Set Baseline dialog box. Microsoft Project saves each task's current scheduled start and finish values in the Start1 and Finish1 fields.

4. **SAVE** the project schedule.

PAUSE. LEAVE Project open to use in the next exercise.

In this exercise, you saved an interim baseline for your project schedule. Once you have saved the original baseline and then started tracking actuals, or any time you have adjusted the current schedule, it is helpful to take a snapshot of the current values—an *interim plan*. Similar to a baseline, an interim plan is a set of current values from the project schedule that Microsoft Project saves with the file. Unlike a baseline, however, an interim plan saves only the start and finish dates of tasks, not resource or assignment values. You can save up to 10 different interim plans during a project.

Depending on the scope and duration of the project, here are a few suggestions for times when you might want to save interim plans:

- At the end of a major phase of work
- At preset time intervals, such as weekly, biweekly, or monthly
- Just before or after entering a large number of actual values

■ Comparing Baseline, Interim, and Actual Plans

 THE BOTTOM LINE
Once you have saved a baseline and an interim project plan, it is useful to compare the baseline, interim, and actual plans to evaluate the progress of the project and any changes that have been made.

 COMPARE THE BASELINE, INTERIM, AND ACTUAL PROJECT SCHEDULES

USE the project schedule you created in the previous exercise. Because it can be helpful to compare actual progress with the initial schedule, you will display the current schedule along with the baseline and the interim project plan. You will begin by customizing a copy of the Tracking Gantt chart view.

 Other Views ▾

1. Click the **View** tab, click the **Other Views** button, and then click **More Views**. The More Views dialog box appears.

2. In the list, select **Tracking Gantt**, then click the **Copy** button. The View Definition dialog box appears.

3. In the Name box, key **Interim Tracking Gantt**, then click **OK**. The new view is listed in the More Views dialog box.

4. Make sure that **Interim Tracking Gantt** is selected in the More Views dialog box, then click **Apply**. Microsoft Project displays the new view (which is currently identical to the Tracking Gantt view), and the name of the new view is displayed in the vertical bar at the left of the screen.

 Format ▾

5. On the Ribbon, click the **Format** tab, then click the **Format** button and select **Bar Styles**. The Bar Styles dialog box appears.

6. Click the **Insert Row** button.

7. In the new cell directly below the Name column heading, key **Interim** and press **Tab**. In the same row, click the cell under the Show For...Tasks column heading, then select **Normal** from the drop-down list.

8. In the Row cell, select **2** from the drop-down list or key **2**.

9. Click the cell under the From column heading and select **Start1** from the drop-down list. Then click the cell under the To column heading and select **Finish1** from the drop-down list. You have now instructed Microsoft Project to display the first interim project plan start and finish dates as bars.

10. On the Bars tab, under the Middle label, in the Shape box, select the second shape (third option) down to make this bar the same shape as the other bars in the view.

11. In the Pattern box, select the sixth option—the first diagonally striped bar. In the Color box, select **orange** (the last color on the right, at the top of the theme colors.). Your screen should look similar to Figure 11-12.

Figure 11-12

Bar Styles dialog box with Interim plan Gantt bar formatting

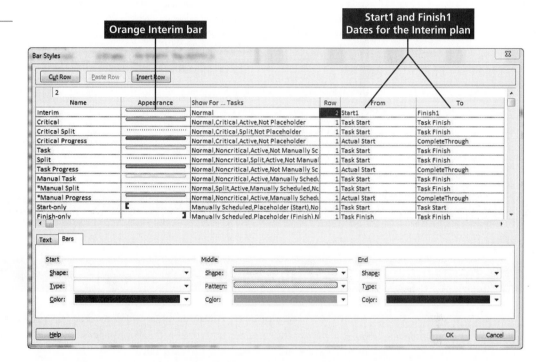

12. Click **OK** to close the Bar Styles dialog box.

13. Scroll the task list so that task 30 is the first task listed on your screen. Click the name of task 30, **Scene 1**, then click the **Task** tab. In the Editing group, click the **Scroll to Task** button. Your screen should look similar to Figure 11-13.

14. **SAVE** the project schedule.

    PAUSE. LEAVE Project open to use in the next exercise.

In this exercise, you compared baseline, interim, and actual plans in a single view. The custom view you created helps you evaluate the schedule adjustments you have made.

Look back to Figure 11-13 and examine task 40. Here you can see that the start of task 40 (the blue bar) corresponds exactly to the baseline (the black bar), but because this task was delayed, the remaining portion of the task bar and the interim task bar (the fuchsia bar) are scheduled later than the baseline. Any additional adjustments to the schedule (such as the entering of more actuals) might cause the scheduled and interim values to differ. You would see such differences in the positions of the baseline, scheduled, and interim Gantt bars.

Figure 11-13

Interim Tracking Gantt view showing the Baseline, Interim, and Scheduled task bars

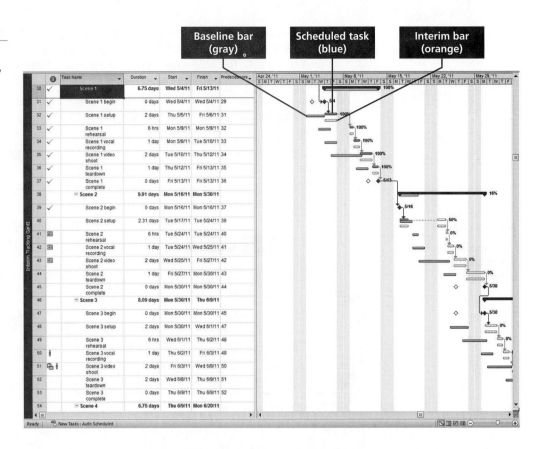

▪ Reporting Project Status

THE BOTTOM LINE

Microsoft Project provides many different ways to report a project's status in terms of budget or variance. A key part of a project manager's job is knowing which stakeholders need to see which details in which format.

→ REPORT PROJECT VARIANCE WITH A "STOPLIGHT" VIEW

USE the project schedule you created in the previous exercise.

Other Views ▾

1. Click the **View** tab, select **Other Views**, and then select **More Views**. In the drop-down list, select **Task Sheet**. Microsoft Project displays the Task Sheet view.

2. Click the **Tables** button, then select **Cost**.

Custom Fields

3. Click the **Project** tab, then click the **Custom Fields** button. The Customize Fields dialog box appears.

4. Under the Field label at the top of the dialog box, make sure that **Task** is selected. In the Type box, select **Number** from the drop-down list.

5. In the Field list, select **Overbudget (Number3)**.

6. Under the Custom attributes label, click the **Formula** button. The Formula dialog box is displayed. The formula shown in this dialog box has been pre-entered for accuracy and to save time. Your screen should look similar to Figure 11-14.

   The formula evaluates each task's cost variance. If the task falls within 30 percent above baseline, the formula assigns the number 30 to the task; if within 20 percent, a 20; and if within 10 percent, a 10.

7. Click **Cancel** to close the Formula dialog box.

Figure 11-14

Formula dialog box

8. In the Customize Fields dialog box, under the Values to display label, click the **Graphical Indicators** button. The Graphical Indicators dialog box appears. This dialog box enables you to specify a unique graphical indicator to display, depending on the value of a field for each task. To save time, the indicators have already been selected.

9. Click the first cell under the Image column heading, then click the drop-down arrow. Here you can see the many graphical indicators you can associate with the values of fields.

10. Click **Cancel** to close the Graphical Indicators dialog box, then click **Cancel** again to close the Customize Fields dialog box.

11. Right-click the **Fixed Cost** column heading. Select **Insert Column** from the list.

12. With your keyboard, start typing the word Over. Notice how Project narrows the list as you type. You can also navigate using the elevator boxes to **Overbudget (Number3)**. Microsoft Project displays the Overbudget column in the Cost table. Your screen should look similar to Figure 11-15.

Figure 11-15

Cost table with the Overbudget custom field displayed

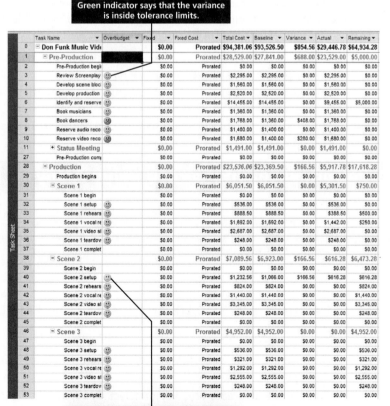

The custom field Overbudget (Number3) displays a graphical indicator that represents one of three different levels of cost variance. The graphical indicators change according to the ranges specified in the formula as each task's cost variance changes. This is a useful format for identifying tasks whose cost variance is higher than you would like (as indicated by the red and yellow indicators). This makes it easy for any stakeholder to quickly scan the task list and locate tasks that need further attention.

13. SAVE the project schedule.

PAUSE. LEAVE Project open to use in the next exercise.

In this lesson, you applied some custom formulas and graphical indicators to make it simple to review the status of tasks using the Task Sheet view. Communicating the project status to stakeholders is one of the most important functions of a project manager—and one that may occupy a significant portion of your working time. Thus, it is imperative that the project manager know who needs to know the project status and why, as well as in what format and level of detail these people require the information. The time to find the answers to these questions is in the initial planning stages of the project.

Once work on the project has commenced, your primary communication task will be reporting project status. This can take several forms:

- Status reports describing where the project is in terms of scope, cost, and schedule (These are often referred to as the *triple constraint*, which is a popular model of project management.)
- Progress reports that provide the specific accomplishments of the project team
- Forecasts that predict future project performance

Standard report formats may already exist if your organization is highly focused on projects and project management. If your organization does not have standard reports, you may be able to introduce project status formats that are based on clear communication and project management principles. For instance, you may be able to report project status in any of the following ways:

- By printing the Project Summary report
- By copying Microsoft Project data to other applications; for example, you could copy the Calendar view to Microsoft Word or Microsoft PowerPoint
- By saving Microsoft Project data in other formats, such as HTML or GIF

■ Evaluating Performance with Earned Value Analysis

 THE BOTTOM LINE
Earned value analysis is used to measure a project's progress in terms of both schedule and cost, as well as to help predict its outcome. Earned value can be used on any project in any industry to objectively track progress.

⊙ SET PROJECT STATUS DATE AND DISPLAY THE EARNED VALUE TABLE

USE the project schedule you created in the previous exercise.

Project Information

 Tables ▾

1. On the Ribbon, click **Project Information**. The Project Information dialog box appears.

2. In the Status date box, key or select **5/18/11**, then click **OK**.

3. Click the **View** tab. Click the **Tables** button, then select **More Tables**. The More Tables dialog box appears.

4. In the Tables list, select **Earned Value** and click **Apply**. Microsoft Project displays the Earned Value table in the Task Sheet view. If necessary, double-click between column headings to display all values. Your screen should look like Figure 11-16.

Figure 11-16

Earned Value table in the Task Sheet view

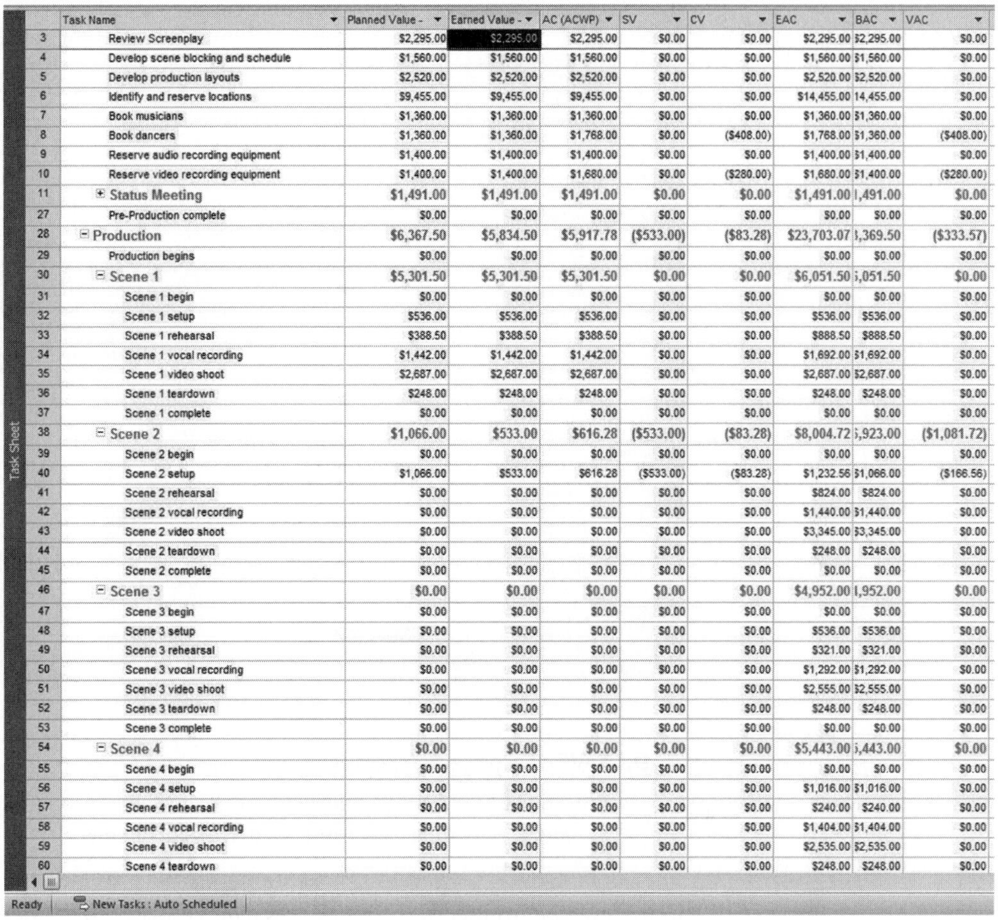

	Task Name	Planned Value -	Earned Value -	AC (ACWP)	SV	CV	EAC	BAC	VAC
3	Review Screenplay	$2,295.00	$2,295.00	$2,295.00	$0.00	$0.00	$2,295.00	$2,295.00	$0.00
4	Develop scene blocking and schedule	$1,560.00	$1,560.00	$1,560.00	$0.00	$0.00	$1,560.00	$1,560.00	$0.00
5	Develop production layouts	$2,520.00	$2,520.00	$2,520.00	$0.00	$0.00	$2,520.00	$2,520.00	$0.00
6	Identify and reserve locations	$9,455.00	$9,455.00	$9,455.00	$0.00	$0.00	$14,455.00	14,455.00	$0.00
7	Book musicians	$1,360.00	$1,360.00	$1,360.00	$0.00	$0.00	$1,360.00	$1,360.00	$0.00
8	Book dancers	$1,360.00	$1,360.00	$1,768.00	$0.00	($408.00)	$1,768.00	$1,360.00	($408.00)
9	Reserve audio recording equipment	$1,400.00	$1,400.00	$1,400.00	$0.00	$0.00	$1,400.00	$1,400.00	$0.00
10	Reserve video recording equipment	$1,400.00	$1,400.00	$1,680.00	$0.00	($280.00)	$1,680.00	$1,400.00	($280.00)
11	⊞ Status Meeting	$1,491.00	$1,491.00	$1,491.00	$0.00	$0.00	$1,491.00	1,491.00	$0.00
27	Pre-Production complete	$0.00	$0.00	$0.00	$0.00	$0.00	$0.00	$0.00	$0.00
28	⊟ Production	$6,367.50	$5,834.50	$5,917.78	($533.00)	($83.28)	$23,703.07	1,369.50	($333.57)
29	Production begins	$0.00	$0.00	$0.00	$0.00	$0.00	$0.00	$0.00	$0.00
30	⊟ Scene 1	$5,301.50	$5,301.50	$5,301.50	$0.00	$0.00	$6,051.50	5,051.50	$0.00
31	Scene 1 begin	$0.00	$0.00	$0.00	$0.00	$0.00	$0.00	$0.00	$0.00
32	Scene 1 setup	$536.00	$536.00	$536.00	$0.00	$0.00	$536.00	$536.00	$0.00
33	Scene 1 rehearsal	$388.50	$388.50	$388.50	$0.00	$0.00	$888.50	$888.50	$0.00
34	Scene 1 vocal recording	$1,442.00	$1,442.00	$1,442.00	$0.00	$0.00	$1,692.00	$1,692.00	$0.00
35	Scene 1 video shoot	$2,687.00	$2,687.00	$2,687.00	$0.00	$0.00	$2,687.00	$2,687.00	$0.00
36	Scene 1 teardown	$248.00	$248.00	$248.00	$0.00	$0.00	$248.00	$248.00	$0.00
37	Scene 1 complete	$0.00	$0.00	$0.00	$0.00	$0.00	$0.00	$0.00	$0.00
38	⊟ Scene 2	$1,066.00	$533.00	$616.28	($533.00)	($83.28)	$8,004.72	5,923.00	($1,081.72)
39	Scene 2 begin	$0.00	$0.00	$0.00	$0.00	$0.00	$0.00	$0.00	$0.00
40	Scene 2 setup	$1,066.00	$533.00	$616.28	($533.00)	($83.28)	$1,232.56	$1,066.00	($166.56)
41	Scene 2 rehearsal	$0.00	$0.00	$0.00	$0.00	$0.00	$824.00	$824.00	$0.00
42	Scene 2 vocal recording	$0.00	$0.00	$0.00	$0.00	$0.00	$1,440.00	$1,440.00	$0.00
43	Scene 2 video shoot	$0.00	$0.00	$0.00	$0.00	$0.00	$3,345.00	$3,345.00	$0.00
44	Scene 2 teardown	$0.00	$0.00	$0.00	$0.00	$0.00	$248.00	$248.00	$0.00
45	Scene 2 complete	$0.00	$0.00	$0.00	$0.00	$0.00	$0.00	$0.00	$0.00
46	⊟ Scene 3	$0.00	$0.00	$0.00	$0.00	$0.00	$4,952.00	1,952.00	$0.00
47	Scene 3 begin	$0.00	$0.00	$0.00	$0.00	$0.00	$0.00	$0.00	$0.00
48	Scene 3 setup	$0.00	$0.00	$0.00	$0.00	$0.00	$536.00	$536.00	$0.00
49	Scene 3 rehearsal	$0.00	$0.00	$0.00	$0.00	$0.00	$321.00	$321.00	$0.00
50	Scene 3 vocal recording	$0.00	$0.00	$0.00	$0.00	$0.00	$1,292.00	$1,292.00	$0.00
51	Scene 3 video shoot	$0.00	$0.00	$0.00	$0.00	$0.00	$2,555.00	$2,555.00	$0.00
52	Scene 3 teardown	$0.00	$0.00	$0.00	$0.00	$0.00	$248.00	$248.00	$0.00
53	Scene 3 complete	$0.00	$0.00	$0.00	$0.00	$0.00	$0.00	$0.00	$0.00
54	⊟ Scene 4	$0.00	$0.00	$0.00	$0.00	$0.00	$5,443.00	5,443.00	$0.00
55	Scene 4 begin	$0.00	$0.00	$0.00	$0.00	$0.00	$0.00	$0.00	$0.00
56	Scene 4 setup	$0.00	$0.00	$0.00	$0.00	$0.00	$1,016.00	$1,016.00	$0.00
57	Scene 4 rehearsal	$0.00	$0.00	$0.00	$0.00	$0.00	$240.00	$240.00	$0.00
58	Scene 4 vocal recording	$0.00	$0.00	$0.00	$0.00	$0.00	$1,404.00	$1,404.00	$0.00
59	Scene 4 video shoot	$0.00	$0.00	$0.00	$0.00	$0.00	$2,535.00	$2,535.00	$0.00
60	Scene 4 teardown	$0.00	$0.00	$0.00	$0.00	$0.00	$248.00	$248.00	$0.00

Ready   New Tasks : Auto Scheduled

Here you can see most of the earned value numbers detailed at the beginning of this lesson in the Software Orientation section.

TAKE NOTE ★   To see more information about any field, point to the column heading and read the screen tip that appears. Press the F1 key for additional information.

5. Right-click the name of the **Planned Value–PV** column and select **Insert Column**.
6. Key **SPI** and press **Enter**. Microsoft Project displays the SPI column in the Earned Value table.
7. Right-click the name of the **SPI** column and select **Insert Column**.

8. Key **CPI** and press **Enter**. Microsoft Project displays the CPI column in the Earned Value table. Your screen should look similar to Figure 11-17.

Figure 11-17

Earned Value table in the Task Sheet view with CPI and SPI columns added

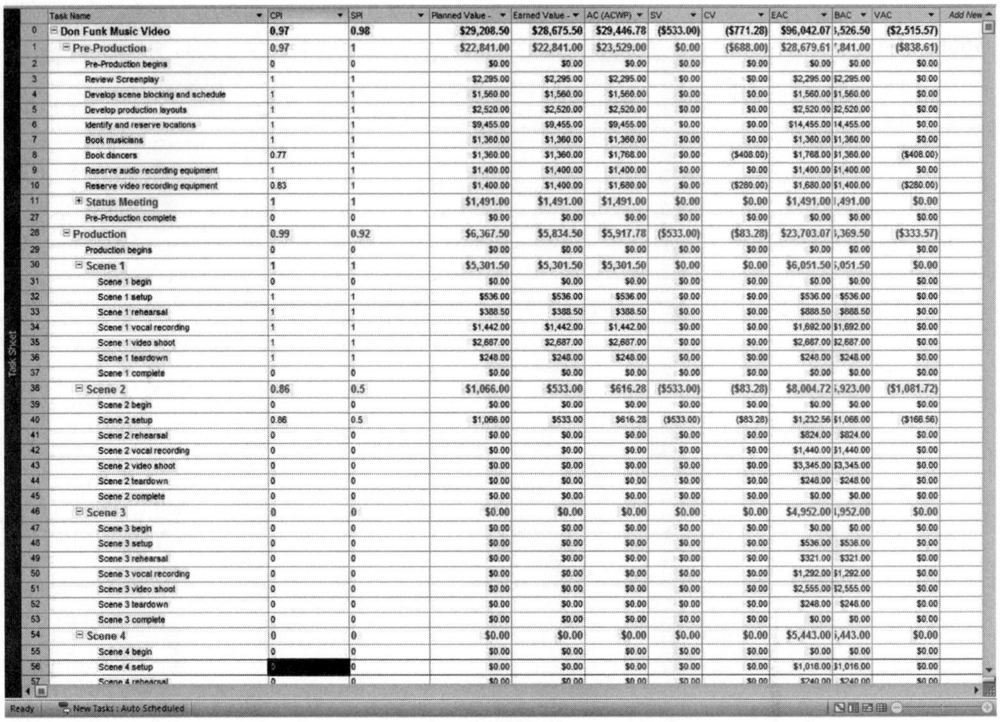

9. **SAVE** the project schedule.

PAUSE. LEAVE Project and your project schedule open so that you can refer to it as you are reading the exercise discussion below.

In this exercise, you set the project status date, displayed the Earned Value table, and added the Cost Performance Index (CPI) and Schedule Performance Index (SPI) columns. The status date is the date you want Microsoft Project to use when calculating the earned value numbers.

Looking at task and resource variance throughout a project's duration is a key project management activity. Unfortunately, it does not give you the true picture of a project's long-term health. For example, a task might be over budget and ahead of schedule (possibly not good) or over budget and behind schedule (definitely not good). Looking at schedule and budget variance by themselves does not tell you very much about performance trends that may continue throughout the project.

Instead, earned value analysis gives you a more complete picture of overall project performance in relation to both time and cost. Earned value analysis is used to measure the project's progress and help forecast its outcome. It focuses on schedule and budget performance in relation to baseline plans. The key difference between earned value analysis and simpler budget/schedule analysis can be thought of as follows:

- "What are the current performance results we are getting?" is the question answered by simple variance analysis.
- "Are we getting our money's worth for the current performance results we are getting?" is the question answered by earned value analysis.

Although the difference is subtle, it is important. Earned value analysis permits you look at project performance in a more detailed way. It allows you to identify two important things: the true cost of project results to date, and the performance trend that is likely to continue for the rest of the project.

Review the project schedule and steps you performed in this exercise. In order for Microsoft Project to calculate the earned value amounts for a project schedule, you must first do the following:

- Save a baseline so that Microsoft Project can calculate the budgeted cost of the work scheduled before you start tracking actual work. (The baseline was already saved when you opened the file for this lesson.)
- Record actual work on tasks or assignments. (You did this in previous exercises in this lesson.)
- Set the status date so that Microsoft Project can calculate actual project performance up to a certain point in time. If you do not specify a status date, Microsoft Project uses the current date.

Earned value analysis uses the following three key values to generate all other schedule indicator and cost indicator values:

- **The *planned value (PV)* or *budgeted cost of work scheduled (BCWS)*:** This is the value of the work scheduled to be completed as of the status date. Microsoft Project calculates this value by adding all the timephased baseline values for tasks up to the status date. The PV for the entire project is sometimes referred to as the BAC (budget at completion).
- **The *actual cost of work performed (ACWP)*:** This is the actual cost incurred to complete each task's actual work up to the status date.
- **The *earned value (EV)* or *budgeted cost of work performed (BCWP)*:** This is the portion of the budgeted cost that should have been spent to complete each task's actual work performed up to the status date. This value is called "earned value" because it is literally the value earned by the work performed.

The earned value schedule and the cost variances are directly related. The earned value cost indicator fields are in one table, and the earned value schedule indicators are in another table. A third table then combines the key fields of both schedule and cost indicators.

Using the above key values, Microsoft Project can also calculate some other important indicators of project performance:

- The project's **cost variance *(CV)*** is the difference between the budgeted and actual cost of work performed.
- The project's **schedule variance *(SV)*** is the difference between the budgeted cost of work performed and the budgeted cost of work scheduled.

It might seem strange to think of being ahead of or behind schedule in terms of dollars. However, keep in mind that dollars buy work, and work drives tasks to be completed. You will find that viewing both cost and schedule variance in the same unit of measure makes it easier to compare the two, as well as other earned value numbers that are also measured in dollars.

Finally, there are two other earned value numbers that serve as helpful indicators:

- The **cost performance index *(CPI)*** is the ratio of budgeted cost to actual cost, or EV (BCWP) divided by AC (ACWP).
- The **schedule performance index *(SPI)*** is the ratio of performed work to schedule work, or EV (BCWP) divided by PV (BCWS).

The CPI and SPI allow you to evaluate a project's performance and compare the performance of multiple projects in a consistent way. In the Don Funk Music Video, the CPI and SPI provide information about each task and phase in the project and about the project as a whole:

- The CPI for the Don Funk Music Video project (as of the status date) is 0.97. You can interpret this as meaning that for every dollar's worth of work that has been paid for, 97 cents' worth of work was actually accomplished.

• The SPI for the Don Funk Music Video project (as of the status date) is 0.98. This can be interpreted as meaning that for every dollar's worth of work that was planned to be accomplished, 98 cents' worth of work was accomplished.

Although both the SPI and CPI are slightly different for the Don Funk Music Video project, keep in mind that these ratios can change as work is completed and other factors change.

Earned value analysis is one of the more complicated things you can do in Microsoft Project, but it provides valuable project status information. Earned value analysis also again illustrates why it is a good idea to enter task and resource cost information into a project schedule any time you have it.

SKILL SUMMARY

IN THIS LESSON, YOU LEARNED:	TASK
To record actual start, finish, and duration values of tasks.	Enter actual start date and duration for a task.
To adjust remaining work or duration of tasks.	Adjust actual and remaining work for a task.
To reschedule uncompleted work.	Reschedule incomplete work.
To save an interim plan.	Save an interim project plan.
To compare baseline, interim, and actual plans.	Compare the baseline, interim, and actual project plans.
To report project status.	Report project variance with a "Stoplight" view.
To evaluate performance with earned value analysis.	Set project status date and display the Earned Value table.

■ Knowledge Assessment

Fill in the Blank

Complete the following sentences by writing the correct word or words in the blanks provided.

1. The _____ is a popular model of project management that uses time, cost, and scope.

2. A snapshot of current values from the project schedule that Microsoft Project saves with the file is called a(n) _____.

3. _____ is the difference between the budgeted cost of work performed and the budgeted cost of work scheduled.

4. The ratio of performed work to scheduled work is the _____.

5. _____ is used to measure a project's progress by giving a more complete picture of overall project performance in relation to both time and cost.

6. You specify the _____ that you want Microsoft Project to use when calculating earned value numbers.

7. The _____ is the actual cost incurred to complete each task's actual work up to the status date.

8. The difference between the budgeted and actual cost of work performed is the _____ .

9. The ratio of budgeted cost to actual cost is the _____ .

10. You can save up to _____ different interim plans during a project.

Multiple Choice

Select the best response for the following statements.

1. The term that means the same as earned value (EV) is:
   a. actual cost of work performed (ACWP).
   b. budgeted cost of work performed (BCWP).
   c. cost performance index (CPI).
   d. budgeted cost of work scheduled (BCWS).

2. Only a(n)_____ can have a remaining work or duration value.
   a. delayed task
   b. incomplete task
   c. complete task
   d. overbudget task

3. Which of the following would NOT be an optimum time to save an interim project plan?
   a. At the end of a major phase
   b. At preset time intervals
   c. At the end of the project
   d. Just before entering a large number of actuals

4. The value of the work scheduled to be completed as of the status date is the:
   a. SPI.
   b. EV.
   c. PV.
   d. CPI.

5. Which dialog box is used to record actual work done on a task?
   a. Update Task
   b. Project Information
   c. Task Drivers
   d. Task Information

6. By default, whenever you enter actual work values, Microsoft Project:
   a. calculates actual cost values.
   b. determines estimated cost values.
   c. predicts the final project end date.
   d. All of the above

7. The term that means the same as budgeted cost of work scheduled (BCWS) is:
   a. planned value (PV).
   b. cost variance (CV).
   c. schedule variance (SV).
   d. earned value (EV).

8. Which of the following is NOT a rule used by Microsoft Project when updating a project schedule based on the actual start, finish, or duration values you have entered?

   a. When you enter a task's actual start date, Microsoft Project calculates the scheduled finish date to match the actual start date and the task's planned duration.

   b. When you enter a task's actual duration that is equal to the scheduled duration, Microsoft Project sets the task to 100% complete.

   c. When you enter a task's actual finish date, Microsoft Project moves the scheduled finish date to match the actual finish date and assigns a completion percentage of 100%.

   d. When you enter an actual duration for a task that is longer than the scheduled duration, Microsoft Project subtracts the actual duration from the scheduled duration to determine the remaining duration.

9. Which of the following is NOT something that must be done in order for Microsoft Project to calculate earned value amounts for a project schedule?

   a. Save a baseline plan

   b. Finish at least 50% of the project schedule

   c. Record actual work on tasks or assignments

   d. Set a status date (or allow the default of the current date)

10. The portion of the budgeted cost that should have been spent to complete each task's actual work performed up to the status date is the:

   a. CPI.

   b. PV.

   c. EV.

   d. SPI.

■ Competency Assessment

Project 11-1: Recording Actuals for Office Lunchroom Remodel

Work has finally started on the lunchroom remodel at your office. You need to update some of the task information to reflect actuals that have been provided to you. In particular, you need to note that task 6 started one day early but took the scheduled amount of time, and that task 7 started on time but took one day longer to complete.

GET READY. Launch Microsoft Project if it is not already running. **OPEN** *Office Remodel 11-1* from the data files for this lesson.

The *Office Remodel 11-1* file for this lesson is available on the book companion website.

1. Click the name of task 6, **Tear out inside dividing walls**.
2. Click the downward arrow next to the Mark On Track button, then select **Update Tasks**.
3. Under the Actual label, in the Start box, key or select **10/24/11**.
4. In the Actual dur box, key or select **2d**, then click **OK**.
5. Select the name of task 7, **Remove drywall from main walls**.
6. Click the downward arrow next to the Mark On Track button, then select **Update Tasks**.
7. In the Actual dur box, key or select **3d**, then click **OK**.
8. **SAVE** the project schedule as *Office Remodel Actuals*, then **CLOSE** the file.

   PAUSE. LEAVE Project open to use in the next exercise.

Project 11-2: Saving an Interim Plan for HR Interview Schedule

More than half of the tasks have been completed for the HR Interview project schedule. You would like to save an interim plan at this point.

OPEN *HR Interview Schedule 11-2* from the data files for this lesson.

The *HR Interview Schedule 11-2* file for this lesson is available on the book companion website.

1. Click the **Project** tab, then click the **Set Baseline button** and select **Set Baseline**.
2. Select **Set interim plan**.
3. Under Set interim plan, in the Into box, select **Start3/Finish3** from the drop-down list.
4. Click **OK**.
5. Click the name of task 18, then click the **Scroll to Task** button on the Standard toolbar.
6. **SAVE** the project schedule as *HR Interview Interim3*, then **CLOSE** the file.
   PAUSE. LEAVE Project open to use in the next exercise.

■ Proficiency Assessment

Project 11-3: Comparing Baseline, Interim, and Actual Plans for the Office Lunchroom Remodel

Now that work is in progress for your office lunchroom remodel, you'd like to evaluate the progress of the project. You know that one way to do this is to compare baseline, interim, and actual plans for the project.

OPEN *Office Remodel 11-3* from the data files for this lesson.

The *Office Remodel 11-3* file for this lesson is available on the book companion website.

1. Activate the Set Baseline dialog box, then set (save) an interim plan.
2. Make a copy of the Tracking Gantt view. Name the copy **Tracking Gantt–Interim**.
3. Activate the new Tracking Gantt–Interim view.
4. Activate the Bar Styles dialog box.
5. Insert a new row. Name the new row **Interim**, and in the Show For...Tasks column, select **Normal**. Set the row to **2**.
6. Select **Start1** in the From column heading and **Finish1** in the To column heading.
7. On the Bars tab, under the Middle label, in the Shape box, select the second bar option. In the Pattern box, select the third option. In the color box, select **orange**. Apply your selections.
8. Scroll to task 11.
9. **SAVE** the project schedule as *Office Remodel Interim*, then **CLOSE** the file.
   PAUSE. LEAVE Project open to use in the next exercise.

Project 11-4: Don Funk Music Video Earned Value Analysis

More time has passed since you performed your previous earned value analysis on the Don Funk Music Video project, and additional tasks have been completed. You need to set a new status date and display the Earned Value Table.

OPEN *Don Funk Music Video 11-4* from the data files for this lesson.

The *Don Funk Music Video 11-4* file for this lesson is available on the book companion website.

1. In the Project Information dialog box, set a status date of **6/29/11**.
2. Change the view to the Task Sheet view.
3. Apply the Earned Value table from the More Tables dialog box.

4. Insert the SPI and CPI columns to the left of the Planned Value-PV column.

5. Click the name of task 63 and scroll your task list so that task 63 is visible in the middle of your screen.

6. **SAVE** the project schedule as **Don Funk Earned Value** and **CLOSE** the file.

   PAUSE. LEAVE Project open to use in the next exercise.

■ Mastery Assessment

Project 11-5: Rescheduling Work on Insurance Claim Process

On your Insurance Claim Process project, you have just been informed that there will be a delay in making repairs. Work has started but cannot continue because a part is backordered and will not arrive at the body shop until June 20, 2011.

OPEN *Insurance Claim Process 11-5* from the data files for this lesson.

The *Insurance Claim Process 11-5* file for this lesson is available on the book companion website.

1. Update task 18 to show that work is 30% complete.

2. Reschedule the remaining work to start after 6/20/11.

3. **SAVE** the file as *Insurance Claim Process Reschedule*, then **CLOSE** the file.

   PAUSE. LEAVE Project open to use in the next exercise.

Project 11-6: Adjusting Remaining Work and Duration

You now have more actuals to enter into the Don Funk Music Video project schedule. Update the work (as provided below) in the Work table of the Task Usage view.

OPEN *Don Funk Music Video 11-6* from the data files for this lesson.

The *Don Funk Music Video 11-6* file for this lesson is available on the book companion website.

1. For task 48, Scene 3 setup, 34 hours of actual work have been completed and 0 hours of work are remaining.

2. For task 49, Scene 3 rehearsal, 12 hours of actual work have been completed and 8 hours of work are remaining.

3. **SAVE** the project schedule as *Don Funk Adjusted*, then **CLOSE** the file.

   CLOSE Project.

INTERNET READY

This lesson provided a brief introduction to earned value analysis. Search the Internet for more information on earned value analysis. Look for information on its history and development (i.e., who developed it and the original industry in which it was used) and its integration into modern project management, as well as more information on the various indicators discussed in this lesson. Write a brief (1–2 page) document summarizing your research. Comment on how you might be able to use earned value analysis even as a beginning project manager.

Integrating Microsoft Project with Other Programs

LESSON SKILL MATRIX

SKILL	TASK
Using a GIF Image to Display Project Information	Use a GIF image to display project information.
Using the Timeline View to Display Project Information	Use the Timeline view to display project information.
Saving Project Information in Other File Formats	Save information from Microsoft Project in a different file format.

As a project manager for Southridge Video, communicating project information is a critical part of your role. You know that even though printing project information is a common way to share details with stakeholders, it has some limitations. Sometimes, project details are out of date by the time you print them. In addition, you must spend the time and financial resources to copy and distribute your information. On the other hand, publishing information online allows you to provide updates in "real time" and more easily share details with a large audience of online viewers. In this lesson, you will learn various ways of getting information in and out of Microsoft Project by importing and exporting data between Project and other applications.

KEY TERMS
Copy Picture
data map
export map
Graphics Interchange
Format (GIF)
import map
OLE
Timeline view

■ SOFTWARE ORIENTATION

The Copy Picture Dialog Box

Microsoft Project's Copy Picture feature (see Figure 12-1) enables you to copy images and create snapshots of a view.

Figure 12-1

Copy Picture dialog box

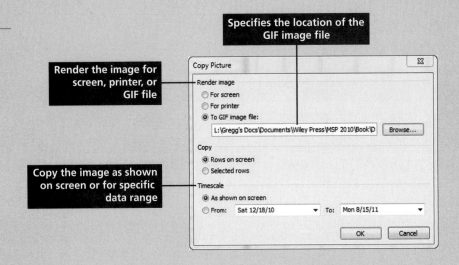

In the Copy Picture dialog box, you can render an image for the screen, for a printer, or to a GIF file. You can also copy the entire view visible on the screen or just selected rows of a table, as well as a specified range of time.

■ Using a GIF Image to Display Project Information

↓ THE BOTTOM LINE

It is often useful to copy information from Microsoft Project into other programs and formats in order to communicate project details to stakeholders.

The *Don Funk Music Video 12M* file for this lesson is available on the book companion website.

⊕ USE A GIF IMAGE TO DISPLAY PROJECT INFORMATION

GET READY. Before you begin these steps, launch Microsoft Project.

1. **OPEN** the *Don Funk Music Video 12M* project schedule from the data files for this lesson.
2. **SAVE** the file as *Don Funk Music Video 12* in the solutions folder for this lesson, as directed by your instructor.
3. On the Ribbon, click the **View** tab. Point to the **Filter:** selection box, click the downward arrow, and select **Summary Tasks.** Microsoft Project filters the Gantt chart to show only summary tasks.
4. On the Ribbon, in the Zoom group, click **Entire Project.** Your screen should look similar to Figure 12-2.

Figure 12-2

Gantt chart view filtered for summary tasks with entire project duration visible

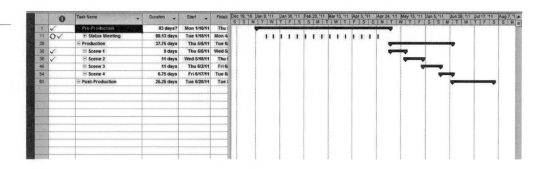

 Copy ▾

5. Click the **Task** tab, then click the downward arrow next to the Copy button. Select **Copy Picture**. The Copy Picture dialog box appears.

6. In the Copy Picture dialog box, under the Render image label, click **To GIF image file**. The Microsoft Project default suggests that you save the file in the same location as the practice file and with the same name, except with a .gif extension. Save your file as ***Don Funk Music Video 12*** in the location specified by your instructor. Your screen should look similar to Figure 12-3.

Figure 12-3

Copy Picture dialog box

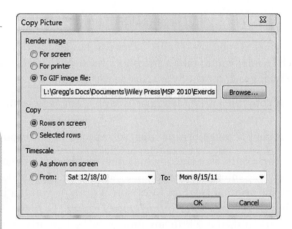

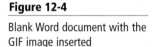 **TAKE NOTE***

When you take a snapshot of a view, the Copy Picture dialog box enables you to select how you want to render the image. The first two options, For screen and For printer, copy the image to the Windows clipboard. The To GIF image file option enables you to save the image as a GIF file.

7. Click **OK** to close the Copy Picture dialog box. The GIF image is saved.

8. Open Microsoft Word and begin with a blank document. Click the **Insert** tab, then select **Picture**.

9. Locate the GIF image named ***Don Funk Music Video 12*** in the location where your instructor directed you to save it. Select the GIF image, then click **Insert**. Your screen should look similar to Figure 12-4.

Figure 12-4

Blank Word document with the GIF image inserted

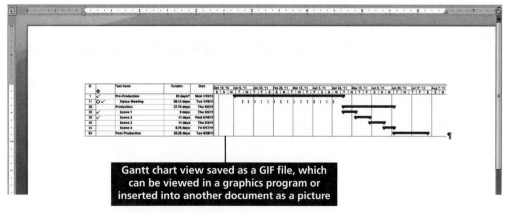

Gantt chart view saved as a GIF file, which can be viewed in a graphics program or inserted into another document as a picture

TROUBLESHOOTING The Copy Picture feature is unavailable when a form view, such as the Task Form or Relationship Diagram view, is displayed.

10. CLOSE the program you used to display the GIF file. If the view does not automatically return to Microsoft Project, select **Don Funk Music Video 12** from the Project button at the bottom of your screen.

TAKE NOTE * In addition to saving GIF images of views in Microsoft Project, you can save Microsoft Project data as an XML file for publishing to the Web or to an intranet site.

11. SAVE the project schedule.

PAUSE. LEAVE Project open to use in the next exercise.

In this exercise, you made a copy of a view in Microsoft Project to display in another program. As you learned in previous lessons, communicating project details to resources, managers, and other stakeholders is an important part of being a successful project manager. Making a copy of parts of your project to share with stakeholders is one way to effectively communicate your progress.

Microsoft Project supports the standard copy and paste functionality of most Microsoft Windows programs. As you saw in this exercise, it has an additional feature, called *Copy Picture*, which enables you to take a snapshot of a view. With Copy Picture, you have several options when taking snapshots of the active view:

- You can copy the entire view that is visible on the screen, or just selected rows of a table in a view.
- You can copy a range of time that you specify or show on the screen.

With either of these options, you copy onto the Windows Clipboard an image that is optimized for pasting into another program for onscreen viewing (such as Microsoft PowerPoint) or for printing (such as Microsoft Word). As you did in this exercise, you can also save the image to a *Graphics Interchange Format (GIF)* file. Once you save the image to a GIF file, you can then use it in any program that supports the GIF format. You can also use it with HTML content on a Web page.

■ Using the Timeline View to Display Project Information

 THE BOTTOM LINE There are times when you may need to present high-level information from a project schedule in order to communicate an overview to stakeholders. Although there are several methods and options available to transfer text and graphics, Microsoft Project's new feature called the *Timeline view* can be used to present high-level information clearly.

 USE THE TIMELINE VIEW TO DISPLAY PROJECT INFORMATION

USE the project schedule you created in the previous exercise.

1. Click the **View** tab. In the Split View group, select the **check box** next to **Timeline**. The new Timeline view appears above the Gantt chart view. Your screen should look like Figure 12-5.

Figure 12-5

Gantt chart view with Timeline view above

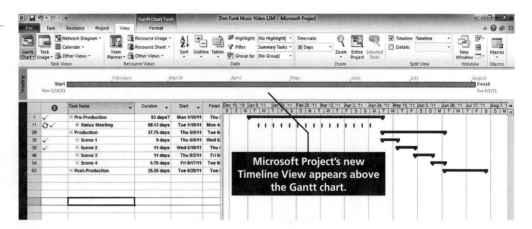

2. Select all visible summary tasks. Place your cursor on the selected cells and right-click. From the menu, select **Add to Timeline**. Note that the Status meetings were not added to the timeline.

3. You will be formatting the Timeline view area. Use your mouse to expand the Timeline area in a similar way as you move the vertical divider bar between the Gantt chart and the table area, meaning that you place your mouse cursor on the horizontal divider, then click and drag downward to expand the Timeline view area. Your screen should look like Figure 12-6.

Figure 12-6

Expanded Timeline view area

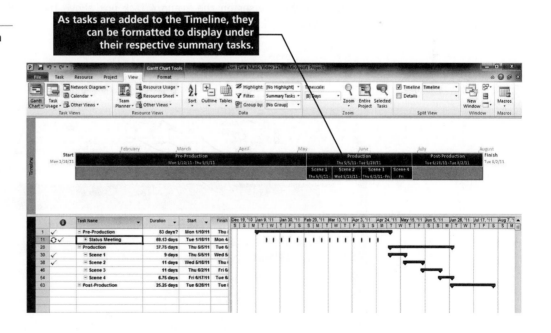

 You can use the Existing Tasks button to add or remove tasks from the Timeline.

4. Click within the Timeline view area to activate that window. Then click the **Format** tab under the Timeline Tools tab.

Text Lines: 1 ▾

Date Format ▾

5. Note that the dates listed for each of the Scene Summary tasks are not completely visible. On the Ribbon, in the Show/Hide group, click the downward arrow for the **Text Lines:** box and select 2.

6. On the Ribbon, select the **Date Format** button. From the list, select the option that displays dates in Month/Day format. Your screen should look like Figure 12-7.

Figure 12-7

Timeline view with reformatted dates

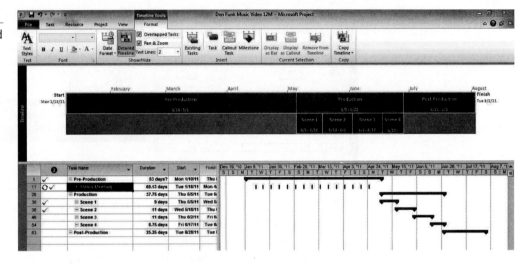

7. Note that Scene 4 still does not show the starting and ending dates. On the Timeline, click the **Scene 4** box; then, on the Ribbon, in the Current Selection group, click **Display as Callout.** By default, Microsoft Project displays the task above the Timeline. Notice that the dates are now visible.

Display as Callout

8. Place your cursor on the Scene 4 task box above the Timeline, then drag it to below the Timeline. Your screen should look similar to Figure 12-8.

Figure 12-8

Timeline view with summary task 54 displayed as a callout

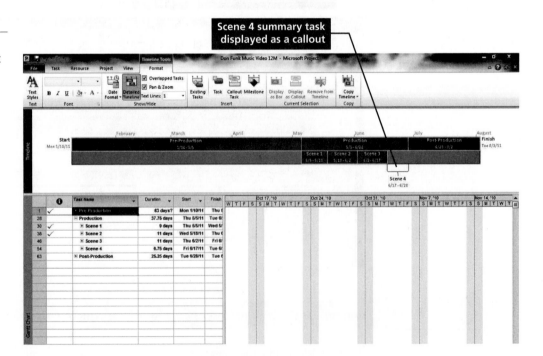

Copy Timeline ▾

9. Now that you have the Timeline formatted and displaying the information you want, you will copy it for presentation. On the Ribbon, click the **Copy Timeline** button. From the list, select **For Presentation**.

10. Open Microsoft PowerPoint. Start with a new blank presentation. Right-click the first slide and select **Layout**. From the list, select **Blank**.

11. Insert the Timeline view you just copied by pressing **Ctrl + V** or clicking the **Paste** button on the Home tab.

> **TAKE NOTE ✱** You can also paste the image into an email message or a variety of other types of documents.

12. Close the PowerPoint document without saving the changes.

13. In Microsoft Project, press the **F3** key to clear the Summary Tasks filter.

14. On the Ribbon, clear the check box for the Timeline view. Microsoft removes the split window with the Timeline area.

15. **SAVE** the project schedule.

    PAUSE. LEAVE Project open to use in the next exercise.

In this exercise, you made a snapshot of a Timeline view and pasted the image into a blank PowerPoint presentation you are preparing for Don Funk's agent. In general, you can copy and paste data to and from Microsoft Project using Project's various copy and paste commands (Copy, Copy Picture, Copy Cell, Paste, Paste Special, etc.). When you *copy data from* Microsoft Project, you can choose one of two options to achieve your desired results:

- You can copy text (such as task names or dates) from a table and paste it as text into the destination program. Using a Copy command enables you to edit data in the destination program.

- You can copy a graphic image of a view from Microsoft Project and paste it as a graphic image in the destination program (as you did in this exercise). You can create a graphic image of a view or part of a view using the Copy Picture command. Using the Copy Picture command results in an image that can be edited only with a graphics editing program (such as Microsoft Paint).

When you *paste data into* Microsoft Project from other programs, you also have two options to achieve your desired results:

- You can paste text (such as a task list) into a table in Microsoft Project. For example, you could paste a series of resource names that are organized in a vertical column from Microsoft Excel to the Resource Name column in Microsoft Project.

- You can paste a graphic image or an OLE object from another program into a graphical portion of a Gantt chart view; into a task, resource, or assignment note; into a form view, such as the Task form view; or even into the header, footer, or legend of a view or report.

> **TAKE NOTE ✱** *OLE* is a protocol that allows you to transfer information, such as a chart or text (as an OLE object), to documents in different programs.

Be careful when pasting text as multiple columns. First, make sure that the order of the information in the source program matches the order of columns in the Microsoft Project table. (You can rearrange the order of the columns in the source program to match the order of the columns in Microsoft Project, or vice versa.) Second, make sure that the columns in the source program support the same type of data as do the columns in Microsoft Project (text, currency, numbers, etc.).

For more information about printing views and reports, refer back to Lesson 9.

■ Saving Project Information in Other File Formats

THE BOTTOM LINE

You can import and/or export information between your project schedule to and from sources outside Microsoft Project. For example, you can import/export in XML format, as a Microsoft Database file, or directly to and from Excel. By using import/export maps to specify how the data will be used, Microsoft Project prepares the data for either importing or exporting.

⊕ SAVE PROJECT INFORMATION IN OTHER FILE FORMATS

USE the project schedule you created in the previous exercise. You have been asked to provide project cost information to the accounting department, which does not have or use Microsoft Project. You need to provide task-level details on planned costs and actual costs for your project.

1. On the View tab, click the **Other Views** button, then click **More Views**. The More Views dialog box appears.
2. In the dialog box, locate and select the **Task Sheet** view. Click the **Apply** button.
3. Click the **Tables** button and select the **Cost** table.
4. Click the **File** tab and select **Save as**. Save your file in the location specified by your instructor.
5. Click the downward arrow next to the Save as type: box and select **Excel Workbook**.
6. In the Filename: box, key **Music Video Task Costs**. Then click the **Save** button. The Export Wizard appears.
7. Click the **Next** button. The Export Wizard–Data page appears. Ensure **Selected Data** is selected.
8. Click the **Next** button. The Export Wizard–Map page appears. The Export Wizard uses maps to organize the way data is structured when exporting from Microsoft Project.
9. Make sure that **New Map** is selected, then click the **Next** button. The Export Wizard–Map Options page appears.
10. Select the **Tasks** check box. Make sure that the **Export includes headers** check box is also selected. ("Headers" means column headings in this case.)
11. Click the **Next** button. The Export Wizard–Task Mapping page appears. This is where you select the table that will be used for the export and specify how you want to map the data from the source worksheet to the fields in Microsoft Project.
12. In the dialog box, select the **Base on Table** button. Microsoft Project displays a list of tables in the project file. Select the **Cost** table and click **OK**. Microsoft Project uses the column (field) names from the cost table, then suggests the Microsoft Excel header row names in the preview area. Review the fields on this screen. Your screen should look similar to Figure 12-9.
13. Click the **Next** button. The Import Wizard–End of Map Definition page appears. On this screen, you have the opportunity to save the settings for the new import map, if you desire. This is useful when you anticipate importing similar data into Microsoft Project in the future. For now, you will skip this step. Click the **Finish** button.
14. Find the Excel Workbook file named **Music Video Task Costs** in the location where your instructor directed you to save it earlier, and open the file.

Figure 12-9

Export Wizard-Task Mapping dialog box showing a preview of Excel data

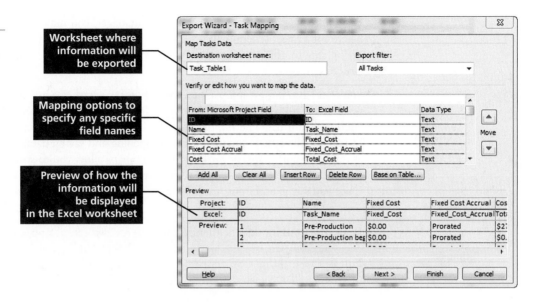

15. In Microsoft Excel, auto-fit the columns to display all the data. Note that the formatting is not in currency. Using the features of Excel, change the Total Costs, Baseline, Variance, Actual, and Remaining columns to the currency format. Format the column headers by centering and changing them to a bold font. Your screen should look similar to Figure 12-10.

Figure 12-10

Excel spreadsheet after formatting the cost-related columns

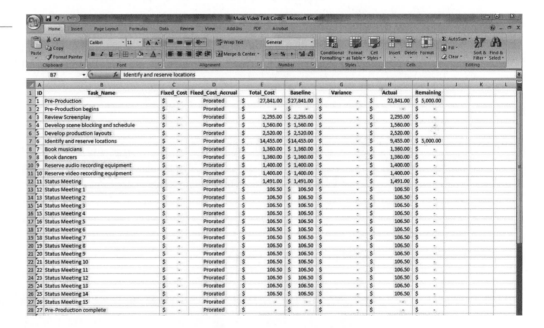

16. **SAVE** the Excel file in the solutions folder as directed by your instructor. **CLOSE** the Excel file.

17. **SAVE** the *Don Funk Music Video 12* project schedule, then **CLOSE** this file.

 PAUSE. If you are continuing to the next lesson, keep Project open. If you are not continuing to additional lessons, **CLOSE** Project.

In this exercise, you saved information from the cost table in Microsoft Project into an Excel workbook and then set up an export map to control how the data was exported to Microsoft

Excel. As you gain experience as a project manager, you may need to export data from a Microsoft Project schedule to a variety of sources. Microsoft Project uses export maps when saving data to other file formats. An *export map* specifies the exact data to export and how to structure it.

You could also import information into Project, such as resource costs from a database or a resource list from a document. Microsoft Project uses import maps when opening data from another file format. The *import map* specifies the exact data to import and how to structure it. In fact, the same maps are used for both opening and saving data, so they are often referred to as import/export maps, or *data maps*. Data maps allow you to specify how you want individual fields in the source program's file to correspond to individual fields in the destination program. Once you set up an import/export map, you can use it over and over again.

TROUBLESHOOTING

If you are working independently (outside of this lesson) and are trying to import an Excel file, but you are unable to view saved Microsoft Excel files from the Microsoft Project Open dialog box, you may need to save your files as Microsoft Excel 97–2003 files rather than Excel Workbook (2010 or 2007) files.

When importing information from other file formats, Microsoft Project has a security setting that may prevent you from opening legacy or non-default file formats. Depending on the default settings in your version of Microsoft Project, you may see a Microsoft Office Project dialog box with the following message when you try to open a file:

You are trying to open a file saved in an older file format. Your settings do not allow you to open files saved in older file formats. To change your settings, navigate to the 'Security' tab in the Options dialog box.

In order to change your settings, click the File tab, then select Options. In the Options dialog box, select the Trust Center option. In the Microsoft Project Trust Center section, click the Trust Center Settings button. Click the Legacy Formats option, then select *Prompt when loading files with legacy or non default file format* and click OK. Click OK again to close the Options dialog box.

TROUBLESHOOTING

To create a Microsoft Project file from a SharePoint list, your organization must use SharePoint 2010 or SharePoint Server 2010 to utilize this functionality. Also, the list must be a *Task List* rather than a simple *List*.

SKILL SUMMARY

IN THIS LESSON, YOU LEARNED:	TASK
To use a GIF image to display project information.	Use a GIF image to display project information.
To use the Timeline view to display project information.	Use the Timeline view to display project information.
To save project information in different file formats.	Save information from Microsoft Project in a different file format.

■ Knowledge Assessment

Matching

Match the term in column 1 to its description in column 2.

	Column 1		Column 2
1.	Copy Picture	**a.**	A set of specifications for moving specific data to Microsoft Project fields
2.	Import map	**b.**	A set of step-by-step prompts that walks you through opening a different file format in Microsoft Project
3.	OLE	**c.**	A set of specifications for moving specific data from Microsoft Project fields
4.	Export map	**d.**	A function used to copy portions of a table rather than copying a graphic image
5.	GIF	**e.**	A feature that allows you to copy images and create snapshots of a view
6.	Import Wizard	**f.**	A protocol that enables you to transfer information to documents in different programs
7.	Copy	**g.**	Also known as an import/export map
8.	Copy Cell	**h.**	A file type that enables you to publish Microsoft Project data to the Web or an intranet site
9.	Data map	**i.**	Graphics Interchange Format, a file format that enables you to save an image for use in other programs
10.	XML	**j.**	A function that allows you to copy data from Microsoft Project and edit it in the destination program

True/False

Circle T if the statement is true or F if the statement is false.

T | F 1. When saving a snapshot as a GIF file, the default location and name recommended by Microsoft Project are the same name and location as the file being copied, except with a .gif extension.

T | F 2. When moving data from another program into Microsoft Project, Microsoft Project is referred to as the source program.

T | F 3. It is possible to import data from many different sources for use in Microsoft Project.

T | F 4. The Timeline view can be printed directly to a printer.

T | F 5. Microsoft Project uses a GIF map to specify the exact data to export and how to structure it.

T | F 6. When you create a data map, it can only be used once.

T | F 7. When you copy the Timeline view, Microsoft Project allows the Timeline to be saved in its original size only.

T | F 8. When importing or exporting data, Microsoft Project is always the destination program.

T | F 9. You can use the Paste function in Microsoft Project to paste a graphic image from another program into the graphical portion of a Gantt chart view.

T | F 10. When you use the Copy Picture function in Microsoft Project, you can specify the range of time that you want to copy.

▪ Competency Assessment

Project 12-1: Displaying Project Information

Several stakeholders of the Don Funk Music Video have asked for an update on the status and schedule for Scenes 3 and 4 of the music video. You need to take a snapshot of the current state of the project for these scenes so that you can send it to them for review. You have decided that the best way to accomplish this is to build a filter, then copy a picture of the Gantt view.

GET READY. Launch Microsoft Project if it is not already running.

The ***Don Funk Music Video 12-1*** file for this lesson is available on the book companion website.

OPEN the ***Don Funk Music Video 12-1*** project schedule from the data files for this lesson.

1. Click the **View** tab, then select the downward arrow next to the Filter: box. Select **Display AutoFilter**.
2. Click the downward arrow in the **Task Name** column heading. Select **Filters**, then select **Custom**.
3. In the Custom AutoFilter dialog box, in the first row of boxes, select **contains**, then key **Scene 3**.
4. Select the radio button for **OR**.
5. In the second row, select **contains**, then key **Scene 4**. Click **OK**.
6. Click the **Task** tab, click **Copy**, and then click the **Copy Picture** button.
7. In the Copy Picture dialog box, under the Render image label, click **To GIF image file**. Name the file ***Don Funk GIF***, using the folder hierarchy as directed by your instructor. Click **OK**.
8. Locate the ***Don Funk GIF*** file in the location where you saved it. Select the image, then click **Open**.
9. View the image in your default program for viewing .gif files.
10. **CLOSE** the program you used to display the .gif file.
11. **SAVE** the project schedule as ***Don Funk GIF***, then **CLOSE** the file.

    PAUSE. LEAVE Project open to use in the next exercise.

Project 12-2: HR Interview Critical Task Letter

Your manager is traveling on business but has asked for an update on the critical tasks of the HR Interview Schedule. You need to copy an image from your Project schedule and paste it into a memo to send to your manager.

OPEN the ***HR Interview Schedule 12-2*** project schedule from the data files for this lesson. **START** Microsoft Word or WordPad, then locate and **OPEN** the document named ***Memo to Manager 12-2*** from the data files for this lesson.

The ***HR Interview Schedule 12-2*** and ***Memo to Manager 12-2*** files for this lesson are available on the book companion website.

1. Make sure Microsoft Project is in the active view. On the Ribbon, click the **Format** tab. In the Bar Styles group, select the check box for **Critical Tasks**.
2. On the Ribbon, click the **View** tab, then click the **Filter** box. Select **Critical**.
3. In the **Zoom** group, click **Entire Project**, then click **OK**.
4. Click the **Task** tab, then click **Copy**, then click the **Copy Picture** button.
5. Under the Render image label, select **For screen** and click **OK**.
6. Switch the view to Microsoft Word or WordPad.
7. In the ***Memo to Manager 12-2*** document, highlight the phrase "(Insert image here.)"

8. Paste the snapshot into the *Memo to Manager 12-2* document. If you are using WordPad, you may need resize the image (by dragging the handles on the image sides and/or corners) so that it will fit within the memo area.

9. **SAVE** the document as *Memo to Manager*. **CLOSE** the document.

10. **SAVE** the project schedule as *HR Interview Critical*, then **CLOSE** the file.

PAUSE. LEAVE Project open to use in the next exercise.

■ Proficiency Assessment

Project 12-3: Preparing an Actual Cost Report

You have been asked to prepare a schedule of costs for your project. You have worked with several co-workers in accounting to get a general idea of how detailed the information needs to be, and the accounting department has requested that this information be provided to them in Microsoft Excel. Now you need to export this information from Microsoft Project.

GET READY. Launch Microsoft Project if it is not already running.

OPEN the *Don Funk Music Video 12-3* project schedule from the data files for this lesson.

The *Don Funk Music Video 12-3* file for this lesson is available on the book companion website.

1. Activate the Task Sheet view and display the Cost table.

2. Hide the Fixed Cost column and display the Project Summary Task.

3. Save the file as an Excel workbook named, *Don Funk Video Costs to Date*. Save the file in the same location as the data files for this lesson.

4. Using the Export Wizard, select the following:

    Data: Selected Data

    Map: New map

    Map Options: Tasks, Export includes headers

    Task Mapping: Base the export on the Cost Table

5. Finish the Export Wizard. If you receive a Microsoft Office Project message regarding older file formats, click **Yes**.

6. Open Microsoft Excel and verify that the information was exported in the proper format. Format the Excel file as needed.

7. **SAVE** and **CLOSE** the Excel file.

8. **SAVE** the new project schedule as *Actual Cost Report* and leave the file **OPEN** for the next exercise.

PAUSE. LEAVE Project open to use in the next exercise.

Project 12-4: Internship Report Using the Copy Picture Feature

An intern who has been working with you on the Don Funk Music Video is writing a report to turn in to the Internship office at her university. She has asked if you could provide a snapshot of Scenes 1 and 2 of the project schedule to use as an illustration in her report.

USE the project schedule you created in the previous exercise.

1. Display the Gantt chart view.

2. Zoom the view to show the Scene 1 and Scene 2 tasks.

3. Click the name of task 30, **Scene 1**. Scroll the view so that task 29 is the first task below the Task Name column heading. Scroll the bar chart to this task.

4. Click and drag your cursor to select tasks 30 through 45.

5. Copy the picture using these options:
   - For screen
   - Selected rows
   - As shown on screen
6. Switch your view to Microsoft Word or WordPad.
7. **PASTE** the image into the open blank document.
8. **SAVE** the document as *Don Funk Scene 1-2*, then **CLOSE** Word or WordPad.
9. **CLOSE** the *Don Funk Music Video 12-3* project schedule without saving.

   PAUSE. LEAVE Project open to use in the next exercise.

■ Mastery Assessment

Project 12-5: Building a Resource List

You are assembling a resource list for several upcoming projects at Southridge Video. Because several people will use this resource list for different purposes, you want to build this list in an Excel file for ease of use by everyone.

GET READY. START Microsoft Excel and **OPEN** a new workbook, if necessary.

1. Enter the following data into the Microsoft Excel worksheet, using column names. You may use the column names provided, or substitute a column name that you think more closely corresponds with the column names in Microsoft Project.

Name	Initials	Rate
Mary Baker	MB	18.50/hr
Ryan Calafato	RC	20.00/hr
John Frum	JF	1000/wk
Arlene Huff	AH	25.00/hr
Linda Martin	LM	2000/wk
Merav Netz	MN	18.50/hr
John Peoples	JP	20.00/hr
Ivo Salmre	IS	1500/wk
Tony Wang	TW	19.00/hr

2. Name the worksheet **Resources** (on the tab at the lower-left corner of the workbook).
3. **SAVE** the file as *General Resources List*. If you are using Excel 2010, set the file type as Microsoft Excel 97-2003 Workbook.
4. **CLOSE** the file, then **CLOSE** Microsoft Excel.

   PAUSE. Continue to the next exercise.

Project 12-6: General Resource Project Schedule

Now that you have developed and distributed a general resource list, you would like to import it into Microsoft Project so that you can begin to use it on your own projects.

LAUNCH Microsoft Project if it is not already running.

1. Locate and open the *General Resources List* Microsoft Excel workbook you created in the previous exercise.

2. Using the Import Wizard, create a new map as a new project to map resource information.

3. Map the data using the sheet named Resources, then verify or edit the mapping that Microsoft Project suggests.

4. Finish the mapping without saving the map.

5. If you receive a Microsoft Office Project message regarding older file formats, click **Yes**.

6. In the new project schedule that is generated, change the view to Resource Sheet view.

7. **SAVE** the project schedule as **General Resources List**, then **CLOSE** the file. **CLOSE** Project.

INTERNET READY

As you learned in this lesson, it is possible to import data from a variety of sources for use in Microsoft Project. One of the most useful functions for beginning project managers is the ability to import a task or resource list from Microsoft Excel or Word, or a SharePoint list into Project.

Search the Internet for a Microsoft Word or Excel template or file that provides a list of data that could be tracked in greater detail using Microsoft Project. Some examples might be a marketing research schedule, a task list for planning a wedding or building a house, activities for searching for new employment, or possibly planning an office move. Review in detail the file that you select. (If possible, download the file or template.) Write several paragraphs explaining the layout of the file you have selected and the information it contains, then explain how the data could be better managed in Microsoft Project. Include ideas on tasks, resources, timelines, critical path, and costs.

Project Schedule Optimization

LESSON SKILL MATRIX

SKILL	TASK
Making Time and Date Adjustments	Adjust fiscal year settings within Microsoft Project.
Viewing the Project's Critical Path	View the project's critical path.
Delaying the Start of Assignments	Delay the start of a resource assignment.
Applying Contours to Assignments	Apply a contour to a resource assignment.
	Edit a task assignment manually.
Optimizing the Project Schedule	Identify the project finish date and total cost.
	Compress the project schedule to pull in the project finish date.

You are a project manager for Southridge Video, and one of your primary responsibilities is managing the new Don Funk Music Video project. Your project is underway and is slightly behind schedule. Recently, you have been focusing on using some of the advanced features of Microsoft Project to save a baseline and commence and track project work. In this lesson, you perform additional fine-tuning activities on your project schedule by focusing on assignment adjustments, critical paths, and the project's finish date.

KEY TERMS
contour
crashing
fast-tracking
optimizing
predefined contour

■ **SOFTWARE ORIENTATION**

The Calendar Tab of the Options Dialog Box

Microsoft Project's Calendar Options (see Figure 13-1) are used to provide basic time values, such as hours per day or week, fiscal year settings, and the first day of the week.

Figure 13-1

Calendar Options

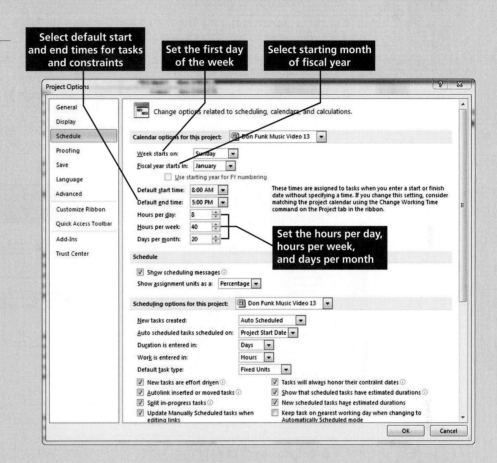

Keep in mind that the Calendar tab has nothing to do with Microsoft Project's base, project, resource, or task calendars. The settings on the Calendar tab affect only the time conversions for task durations that you enter into Microsoft Project, not when work can be scheduled.

■ **Making Time and Date Adjustments**

THE BOTTOM LINE

As part of its project management capabilities, Microsoft Project has a scheduling engine that works with time. Because time is always part of the "project equation," it is critical that the project manager understand the array of time and date settings used by Microsoft Project.

The *Don Funk Music Video 13M* file for this lesson is available on the book companion website.

 ADJUST FISCAL YEAR SETTINGS WITHIN MICROSOFT PROJECT

GET READY. Before you begin these steps, launch Microsoft Project.

1. **OPEN** the *Don Funk Music Video 13M* project schedule from the data files for this lesson.

2. **SAVE** the file as *Don Funk Music Video 13* in the solutions folder for this lesson, as directed by your instructor.

3. On the Gantt chart, drag the divider bar (between the table portion and the graph portion of the Gantt chart) to the right until the Start and Finish columns are visible.

4. On the Ribbon, click the **File** tab, then select **Options**. In the Project Options dialog box, select **Schedule**.

5. In the Calendar Options area, click the *Fiscal year starts in:* box, select **July**, and then click **OK** to close the Options dialog box.

6. Press the **F5** key. In the ID box, key **60**, then click **OK.** Your screen should look similar to Figure 13-2.

Figure 13-2

Gantt chart view showing the fiscal year timescale

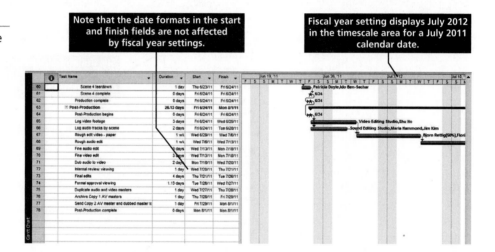

When you select the starting month of the fiscal year, Microsoft Project reformats the dates on the Gantt chart timescale to use the fiscal year, not the calendar year. The months of July–December 2011 now show a 2012 year to reflect that the 2012 fiscal year runs from July 1, 2011 through June 30, 2012.

7. Click the **Undo** button to restore the dates to the calendar year format.

8. Drag the divider back to the right edge of the Duration column.

9. **SAVE** the project schedule.

PAUSE. LEAVE Project open to use in the next exercise.

ANOTHER WAY

You can restore the calendar year format by returning to the Calendar tab of the Options dialog box and selecting January in the Fiscal year starts in: box.

In this exercise, you changed the timescale view to accommodate a fiscal year—any 12-consecutive-month period defined for accounting purposes—rather than a calendar year—a 12-month period from January to December. Using a fiscal year timescale is most appropriate if there are stakeholders who are accustomed to analyzing information in a fiscal year format. Otherwise, use the calendar year format.

There are many other options for controlling time in Microsoft Project through the Calendar tab of the Options dialog box. You use the Calendar tab to define basic time values, such as how many hours a day or a week should equal, or how many days should equal one month. You can also control other time settings, such as which day is the first day of the week (this varies from country to country).

The Calendar tab can be confusing, however, because it has nothing to do with Microsoft Project's base, project, resource, or task calendars. (You control these calendars through the Change Working time dialog box on the Tools menu.) The settings on the Calendar tab affect only the time conversions for task durations that you enter into Microsoft Project, such as how many hours equal one day—not when work can be scheduled. For example, if your project is planned for 10 hours a day, five days per week, you would set the Calendar tab's hours per day to 10 and hours per week to 50.

The Default Start Time and Default End Time settings on the Calendar tab can also be confusing. These settings are not related to working time values for calendars. Rather, the Default Start Time and Default End Time settings have a specific purpose. These settings supply the default start and end time for task constraints or for actual start and finish dates in which you enter a date but do not include a time. For example, if you enter a Must Start On constraint value of January 14, 2011, for a task but do not specify a start time, Microsoft Project will use the Default Start Time value that is set on the Calendar tab.

■ Viewing the Project's Critical Path

↓
THE BOTTOM LINE   One of the most important parts of a project schedule is the project's critical path. The critical path is the series of tasks that affect the project's end date.

⊙ **VIEW THE PROJECT'S CRITICAL PATH**

USE the project schedule you created in the previous exercise.

Other Views ▾

1. On the Ribbon, click the **View** tab, then click the **Other Views** button. From the list, select **More Views.** The More Views dialog box appears.

2. In the More Views dialog box, select **Detail Gantt,** then click **Apply.**

Tables ▾

3. On the Ribbon, click the **Tables** button, then select **Entry.**

4. Move the divider bar back to cover the Duration column.

5. Press the **F5** key. In the ID box, key **54,** then click **OK.** Microsoft Project displays the Scene 4 summary task at the top of your screen; this is a convenient location to view both noncritical and critical tasks.

Slippage
▾

6. On the Ribbon, click the **Format** tab. Click the **Slippage** button. Select any baseline that does not have a date. Microsoft Project removes the slippage lines in front of the tasks. Your screen should look similar to Figure 13-3.

Figure 13-3

Detail Gantt view showing critical tasks, noncritical tasks, and slack (float)

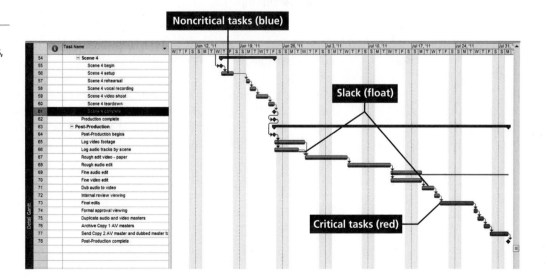

In the Detail Gantt view, noncritical tasks appear in blue and critical tasks are in red. In this view, you can also see some tasks that have free slack. A thin teal line represents the free slack for a given task. Note the slack for task 66. Why does the critical path start so much later in the project? The answer lies in the total slack.

 Tables ▾

7. On the Ribbon, click the **View** tab, click the **Tables** button, and then click **Schedule**. The Schedule table appears in the Detail Gantt view.

8. Drag the divider bar to the right until all columns in the Schedule table are visible. Press the **F5** key and in the ID box, key **68**. Click OK. Your screen should look similar to Figure 13-4.

Figure 13-4

Schedule table showing free float and total float for each task

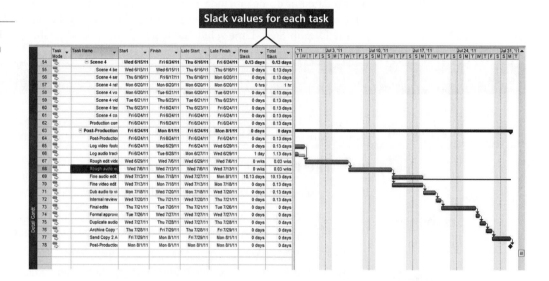

Review the free slack and total slack for each task. Recall from Lesson 4 that *free slack* is the amount of time the finish date of a task can be delayed before the start of any successor task is affected. *Total slack* is the amount of time the finish date on a task can be delayed before completion of the project will be delayed. A task may have total slack, free slack, or both. Slack can be a positive value, a negative value, or a value of zero.

9. Drag the divider bar back to the left to show just the Task Name column. Select tasks **54 through 78**.

Selected Tasks

10. On the Ribbon, in the Zoom group, click **Selected Tasks**.

11. On the Ribbon, click the **File** tab, then click **Options**. Select **Advanced**, then scroll to last section of the window, which is the Calculation options for this project section.

12. Select the **Calculate multiple critical paths** check box near the bottom of the dialog box, then click **OK**. Microsoft Project reformats the tasks in the remaining scenes and the Production phase to show the true critical path. Your screen should look similar to Figure 13-5.

Figure 13-5

Detail Gantt with multiple
critical paths option on

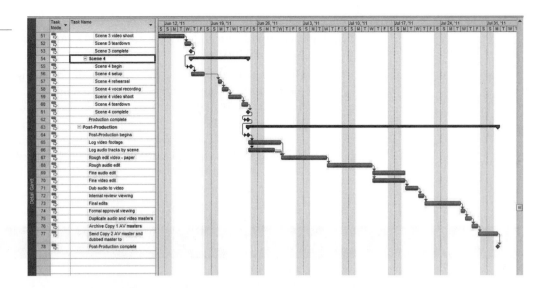

13. On the Quick Access Toolbar, click the **Undo** button. Microsoft Project reverts to
the single critical path for the project.

14. On the Ribbon, click the **View** tab, then click the **Tables** button, and then click
Entry.

15. Drag the vertical divider bar to the right of the Duration column.

16. **SAVE** the project schedule.

PAUSE. LEAVE Project open to use in the next exercise.

In this exercise, you reviewed the critical path of your project schedule and the free and total
slack for some of the tasks. As discussed in several previous lessons, one of the most important
factors that should be monitored in any project schedule is the project's critical path. Keep in
mind that "critical" does not refer to the importance of these tasks in relation to the overall
project, but rather to how the tasks' scheduling will affect the project's finish date. As a
project manager, it is important for you to understand how changes in schedule, resource
assignments, constraints, etc., will affect this key series of tasks. After a task on the critical
path is complete, it is no longer critical, because it can no longer affect the project's finish
date. During the life of a project, it is normal that the critical path will occasionally change.

In previous lessons, only a single critical path per project has been emphasized: the critical
path that determines the project's finish date. However, as you saw in this exercise, Microsoft
Project can identify a critical path within any chain of linked tasks. This is especially useful
when a project is divided into distinct phases. In this exercise, the Pre-Production critical path
was made up of only the status meeting tasks. Usually, the critical path within a phase will
contain a much more distinct line of tasks.

Most projects have a specific due date by which they need to be complete. If you want to
shorten the duration of a project to make the end date occur sooner, you must shorten the
critical path (in project management jargon, this is called "schedule compression"). In reality,
compressing a schedule can be accomplished in various ways, but these can be classified into
two categories:

- *Fast-tracking*: Performing two or more project tasks in parallel that would
  otherwise be done in series, or one right after the other. By overlapping the tasks,
  more work gets completed in a shorter amount of time.
- *Crashing*: Adding more resources to the critical path tasks. This could take the
  form of working extra shifts, working overtime, adding more work resources to a
  task, or outsourcing (paying to have some work done outside the organization).

Prior to starting actual work on the project, it is critical that the project manager closely manage both the critical path and the float (called "slack" in Microsoft Project). This involves the following responsibilities:

- Knowing the tasks that are on the critical path and being able to evaluate the risk to project success if any of the tasks are not completed as scheduled. Any delays in completing tasks on the critical path delay the completion date of the project.
- Knowing where the slack is in the project. On a complex project, the critical path may change frequently. Tasks with very little free slack might become critical as the project begins and the actuals start to vary from the schedule. In addition, tasks that initially had no free slack (and therefore were on the critical path) might get free slack as other tasks move onto the critical path.

■ Delaying the Start of Assignments

THE BOTTOM LINE

If more than one resource is assigned to a task, you may not want all the resources to start working on the task at the same time. Thus, you can delay the start of work for one or more resources assigned to a task.

➔ DELAY THE START OF A RESOURCE ASSIGNMENT

USE the project schedule you created in the previous exercise.

1. On the Ribbon, click the **View** tab, then click **Task Usage**. The Task Usage view appears.

2. Press the **F5** key. Key **75** in the ID box, then click **OK**. Microsoft Project displays the *Duplicate audio and video masters* task. Your screen should look similar to Figure 13-6.

Figure 13-6

Task Usage view at task 75

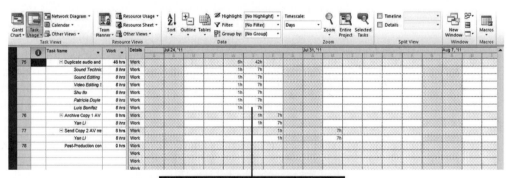

Luis Bonifaz will inspect the final copies of the masters, so you want to delay his work on this task until Thursday, July 29, 2011.

3. In the Task Name column, double-click the name of the resource **Luis Bonifaz**. The Assignment Information dialog box appears.

4. Click the **General** tab, if it is not already selected.

5. In the Start box, key or select **7/29/11**, then click **OK** to close the Assignment Information dialog box. Microsoft Project adjusts Luis Bonifaz's assignment on this task so that he works eight hours on Friday. The other resources assigned to this task are not affected. Your screen should look similar to Figure 13-7.

Figure 13-7

Task Usage view showing the delay in Luis Bonifaz's work

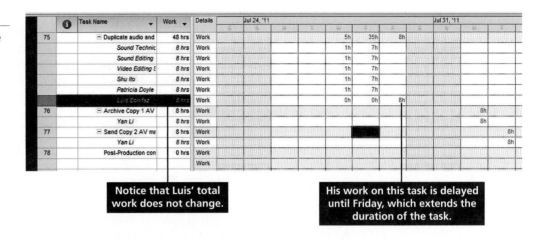

Notice that Luis' total work does not change.

His work on this task is delayed until Friday, which extends the duration of the task.

6. **SAVE** the project schedule.

PAUSE. LEAVE Project open to use in the next exercise.

In this exercise, you delayed the start of work for a resource assigned to a task. You can delay the start of work for any number of resources assigned to a task. However, if you need to delay the start of work for all resources on a particular task, it is better to just reschedule the start date of the task (rather than adjusting each resource's assignment).

■ Applying Contours to Assignments

THE BOTTOM LINE   You can control the amount of time a resource works on a task by applying a work contour. A contour describes the way the resource's work is distributed over time.

Applying a Contour to a Resource Assignment

To optimize your project schedule, you can apply a predefined contour to a task's assignments.

➔ APPLY A CONTOUR TO A RESOURCE ASSIGNMENT

USE the project schedule you created in the previous exercise.

1. Press the **F5** key. Key **70** in the ID box, then click **OK**. Microsoft Project scrolls to task 70. Your screen should look similar to Figure 13-8.

Figure 13-8

Timescaled data for task 70

These assignments have a flat contour.

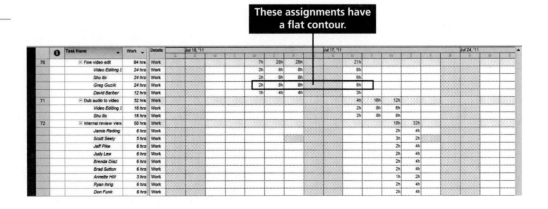

This task has four resources assigned to it. The timescaled data illustrates that three of the four resources are scheduled to work on this task for two hours the first day, eight hours the next two days, and six hours the last day. The last resource, David Barber, is only working on this project half-time. All these assignments have a flat contour—Microsoft Project schedules their work based on a regular rate of eight hours per day. (The resources work only a portion of the first day because they are scheduled on another task.) This is the default work contour type that Microsoft Project uses when scheduling work.

You want to change Greg Guzik's assignment on this task so that he starts with a brief daily assignment and increases his work time as the task progresses. He will still be working on the task after the other resources have finished their assignments.

2. In the Task Name column under task 70, double-click the name **Greg Guzik**. The Assignment Information dialog box appears.

3. Click the **General** tab, if it is not already selected.

4. In the Work contour box, select **Back Loaded**, then click **OK** to close the Assignment Information dialog box. Microsoft Project applies the contour to Greg Guzik's assignment and reschedules his work on the task. Scroll your screen so that you can see all of Greg's assignments on this task. Your screen should look similar to Figure 13-9.

Figure 13-9

Task Usage view with a back-loaded contour on Greg Guzik's assignment

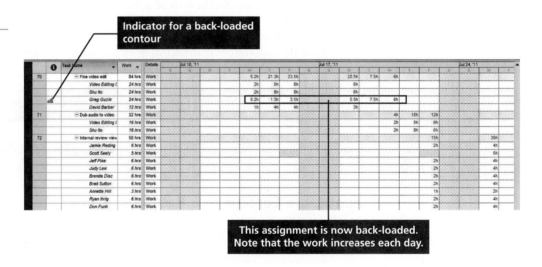

5. Point to the contour indicator in the Indicators column. Microsoft Project displays a screen tip describing the type of contour applied to this assignment.

TROUBLESHOOTING Note that applying a contour to this assignment caused the overall duration of the task to be extended. If you do not want a contour to extend a task's duration, you need to change the Task Type (on the Advanced tab of the Task Information dialog box) to Fixed Duration *before* you apply the contour. When you apply a contour *after* changing to a task type such as fixed duration, Microsoft Project will recalculate the resource's work value so that he or she works less in the same time period.

6. **SAVE** the project schedule.

PAUSE. LEAVE Project open to use in the next exercise.

In this exercise, you applied a predefined work contour to an assignment. A *contour* determines how a resource's work on a task is scheduled over time. In general, *predefined contours* describe how work is distributed over time in terms of graphical patterns. Some options are Bell, Front Loaded, Back Loaded, Double Peak, and Turtle. Predefined contours work best for assignments for which you can estimate a probable pattern of effort. For instance, if a task might require significant ramp-up time, a back-loaded contour might be beneficial, because the resource will be most productive toward the end of the assignment.

Keep in mind that because Greg Guzik's assignment to this task finishes later than the other resource assignments, Greg Guzik sets the finish date of the task. Therefore, it could be said that Greg Guzik is the "driving resource" of this task because his assignment determines, or drives, the finish date of the task.

Manually Editing a Task Assignment

It is also possible to manually edit the assignment values for a resource assigned to a task, rather than applying a contour. For example, because the reality is that a project manager does not plan Greg Guzik's work for 12 minutes (or 0.2h) on 7/13/11, manual editing of the assignment is necessary.

⊙ EDIT A TASK ASSIGNMENT MANUALLY

USE the project schedule you created in the previous exercise.

1. In the timescaled grid area, click the **cell** at the intersection of Greg Guzik and 7/13/11.

   After conferring with Greg, you decide to change this assignment to make it more realistic. Greg states that he can work for an hour on the first day, three hours on the second day, six hours on the third day, six hours on the fourth day, and eight hours on the last day. Note that Greg's total assigned work on this task is 24 hours.

2. Key the following hours in the corresponding cells:

   7/13/11: **1**

   7/14/11: **3**

   7/15/11: **6**

   7/18/11: **6**

   7/19/11: **8**

   7/20/11: **0**

3. Point to the contour indicator in the Indicators column. Microsoft Project displays a ScreenTip on this assignment. Notice that Greg's assignment is now a bit more realistic. Your screen should look similar to Figure 13-10.

Figure 13-10

Task Usage view with edited work assignments for Greg Guzik

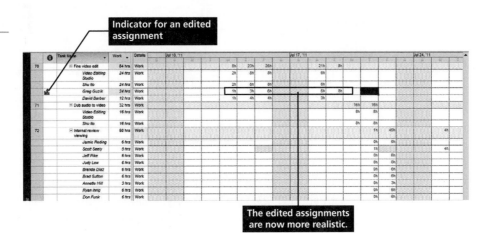

4. **SAVE** the project schedule.

PAUSE. LEAVE Project open to use in the next exercise.

In this exercise, you manually edited the assignment for a resource by directly changing the assignment values in the timescaled grid of the Task Usage view. You may have noticed that when you deleted the last contoured work day by entering zero work hours, the tasks after task 70 shifted back to reflect the shortened duration of task 51.

You can either use predefined contours or make manual edits to a resource's work assignments. How you contour or edit an assignment depends on what you need to accomplish.

■ Optimizing the Project Schedule

THE BOTTOM LINE

As work continues on your project, you will be tracking actuals and updating your project schedule. An important part of project management is verifying that the project has been optimized. This might mean reducing cost, duration, scope, or any combination of these aspects.

Identifying the Project Finish Date and Total Cost

In order to optimize a project schedule, you must first identify and understand the project's duration, finish date, and total cost.

 IDENTIFY THE PROJECT FINISH DATE AND TOTAL COST

USE the project schedule you created in the previous exercise.

1. On the Ribbon, click the **View** tab, click the **Other Views** button, and then click **More Views**. The More Views dialog box appears.

2. In the More Views dialog box, select **Detail Gantt**, then click **Apply**. The Detail Gantt view appears.

3. On the Ribbon, click the **Project** tab, then click the **Project Information** button. Click the **Statistics** button. The Project Statistics dialog box appears. Your screen should look similar to Figure 13-11.

Figure 13-11

Project Statistics dialog box

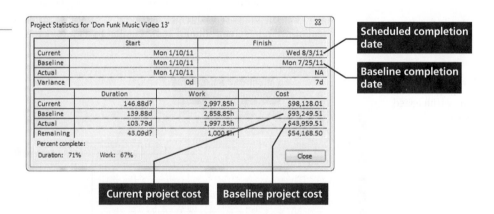

Notice that the Current Finish Date is 8/03/11. This is later than the Baseline Finish Date of 7/25/11. Therefore, you have a positive variance of seven days, which means you are scheduled to finish seven working days later than planned. This box also provides the current calculated cost: just over $98,000. This value is the sum of all actual costs to date and the remaining planned task and resource costs in the project. These include actual and planned fixed costs, per-use costs, and the costs of resource assignments.

ANOTHER WAY

You can also view the same details you see in the Project Statistics dialog box (and more) in the Project Summary Report. This report is helpful for communicating high-level project information to stakeholders. You can access the Project Summary Report on the Project tab in the Reports section. The Project Summary Report is located in the Overview category.

4. Click **Close** to close the Project Statistics dialog box.
5. **SAVE** the project schedule.
   PAUSE. LEAVE Project open to use in the next exercise.

In this exercise, you reviewed project details such as duration, finish date, and total cost. It is helpful to review this information so that you understand the nature of your project and how it can best be optimized. Optimizing is adjusting the aspects of the project schedule, such as cost, duration, and scope (or any combination of these), to achieve a desired project schedule result. A desired result may be a target finish date, duration, or overall cost.

Now, let's look forward to the next exercise. Assume that you have shared the project details from above with the project stakeholders. The stakeholders expected that the project would be slightly over budget, but they did not expect that it would be a week or more beyond the agreed-to finish date. The current projected budget overrun is acceptable and can even increase slightly—but only if the project manager can get the project to within two days of the baseline finish date.

Compressing the Project Schedule

Now that you have reviewed the project details, you can focus on pulling in the project finish date.

➔ COMPRESS THE PROJECT SCHEDULE TO PULL IN THE PROJECT FINISH DATE

USE the project schedule you created in the previous exercise.

1. Press the **F5** key. In the ID box key **46**, then click **OK**. Because you need to pull in the project finish date, your focus will be on the critical tasks.
2. Scroll through and review the task list. Note that tasks 49 through 51 are noncritical. Shortening the duration of noncritical tasks will have no effect on the project finish date. To shorten the project finish date, you must work with the critical tasks after task 51.
3. On the Ribbon, click the **View** tab. In the Filter: box, click the down-arrow, then select **Critical** from the list.

▼ [No Filter]

4. If necessary, scroll the Gantt chart view to the right so that you can see the entire Gantt bar for task 70. Your screen should look similar to Figure 13-12.

Figure 13-12

Gantt chart displaying critical task 70

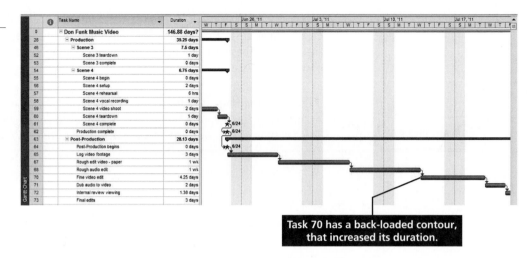

Task 70 has a back-loaded contour, that increased its duration.

Recall that in an earlier exercise, you applied a back-loaded contour to Greg Guzik's assignment to this task, lengthening its duration. To leave this assignment contour in place but start subsequent tasks earlier, you will add lead time to task 71, task 70's successor task.

5. In the Task Name column, double-click the name of task 71, **Dub audio to video**. The Task Information dialog box appears.

6. Click the **Predecessors** tab.

7. In the Lag field for the predecessor task 70, key **−25%**, then press **Enter**. Click **OK** to close the Task Information dialog box.

Applying a lead time to the task relationship between tasks 70 and 71 causes task 71 and all successor tasks to start earlier. Entering this particular lead causes the successor task 71 to begin when 75% of the predecessor task 70's duration has elapsed. Your screen should look similar to Figure 13-13.

Figure 13-13

Gantt chart view showing that a lead has been applied between task 70 and 71

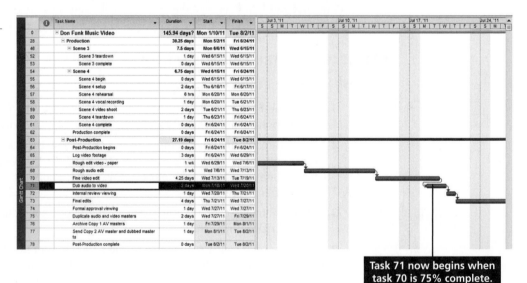

Task 71 now begins when task 70 is 75% complete.

8. Double-click task 68, **Rough audio edit**. You realize that you can gain some additional time by adjusting the relationship of tasks 67 and 68, because these can be performed at roughly the same time.

9. Click the **Predecessor** tab. In the Lag field, key **−2d**. Click **OK**. Your screen should look similar to Figure 13-14.

Figure 13-14

Gantt chart with two days' lead between tasks 67 and 68

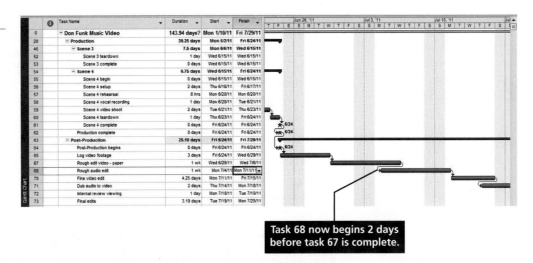

Task 68 now begins 2 days before task 67 is complete.

This process is called fast-tracking—doing tasks in parallel that were originally planned to be done in series. You can review the Detail Gantt view (or display the Project Information dialog box) to see that the final task of the project now ends on 7/29/11. This is still more than three days after your desired finish date. To compress the project duration further, you will apply overtime work to some assignments.

Task Usage ▾

10. On the View tab, click the **Task Usage** button. The Task Usage view appears.

11. Click the **Work** column heading. On the Ribbon, click the **Format** tab, then click the **Insert Column** button.

12. Key **Over**, then select **Overtime Work** from the list. Microsoft Project inserts the Overtime Work column between the Task Name and Work columns. Drag the divider bar between the table and bar portions of the Gantt chart to the right until the Duration column is visible. The specific task for which you wish to apply overtime is task 67.

13. Press the **F5** key. In the ID box, key **67**, then click **OK**. Microsoft Project scrolls the Task Usage view to display the assignments of task 67. Your screen should look similar to Figure 13-15.

Figure 13-15

Gantt chart showing critical path starts at task 51

Overtime Work column

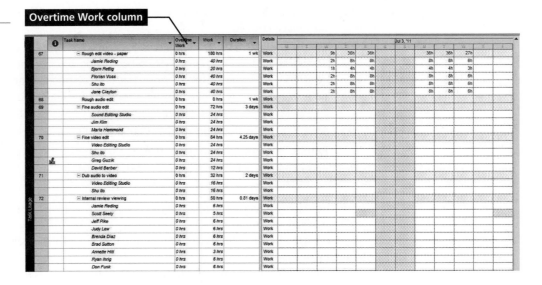

TAKE NOTE*

Entering overtime work for an assignment does not add work to the assignment. Rather, it indicates how much of the work assigned is overtime. Adding overtime work reduces the overall duration of the assignment.

Currently, four of the resources are assigned 40 hours of regular work to this task. Bjorn Rettig is assigned 20 hours of work because his Max. Units value is 50%. To shorten the task's duration without changing the total work in the task (for each assignment except Bjorn Rettig), you will record that 10 of the 40 hours of work is overtime work. You will record five hours of overtime work for Bjorn Rettig.

14. Click the **Overtime Work cell** for Jamie Reding, the first resource assigned to task 67.

15. Key **10** and press **Enter**.

16. Repeat steps 13 and 14 for Florian Voss, Shu Ito, and Jane Clayton.

17. Repeat steps 13 and 14 for Bjorn Rettig, except key **5** in the Overtime Work cell. Your screen should look similar to Figure 13-16.

Figure 13-16

Task Usage view showing the change in task duration with overtime work added

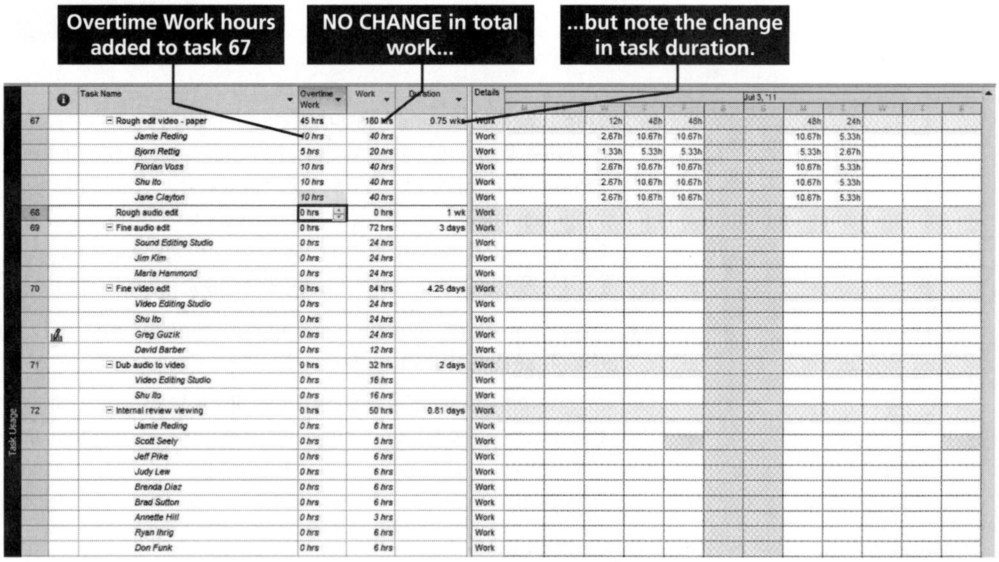

18. On the Ribbon, click the **Gantt Chart** button. Clear the critical task filter by selecting the **Filter** box and choosing (No Filter).

19. Press the **F5** key. Key **67** in the ID box, then click **OK**. Notice now that task 67 is no longer critical.

20. On the Ribbon, click the Project tab, then click **Project Information**. Click the **Statistics** button. The Project Statistics dialog box appears. Note that the new finish date is 7/27/11. Click **OK** to close the Project Information dialog box. The finish date is now only two days shy of your baseline finish date, which is acceptable to the stakeholders. You will stop your project optimization work here.

21. **SAVE** the project schedule, then **CLOSE** the file.

    PAUSE. If you are continuing to the next lesson, keep Project open. If you are not continuing to additional lessons, **CLOSE** Project.

In this exercise, you compressed a project schedule by applying lead time to some tasks and allowing overtime for another task. ***Optimizing*** a project schedule and responding to variance are issues that Microsoft Project cannot automate. As a project manager, you must know the nature of your projects and how they should be optimized. As you saw in this exercise, you might need to make trade-offs, such as cutting scope, adding resources, allowing overtime, or adding lead time.

In this exercise, although you stopped your optimization work when you achieved your desired finish date, keep in mind that once actual work starts, variance will almost certainly appear and the critical path and project finish date are likely to change. For this reason, properly identifying and responding to variance is a key project management skill.

SKILL SUMMARY

IN THIS LESSON, YOU LEARNED:	TASK
To make time and date adjustments.	Adjust fiscal year settings within Microsoft Project.
To view the project's critical path.	View the project's critical path.
To delay the start of assignments.	Delay the start of a resource assignment.
To apply a contour to a resource.	Apply a contour to a resource assignment.
	Edit a task assignment manually.
To optimize the project schedule.	Identify the project finish date and total cost. Compress the project schedule to pull in the project finish date.

■ Knowledge Assessment

Fill in the Blank

Complete the following sentences by writing the correct word or words in the blanks provided.

1. A(n) _____ determines how a resource's work on a task is scheduled over time.

2. The _____ section of the Options dialog box provides an option to change the view to fiscal year rather than calendar year.

3. The _____ _____ is the series of tasks that will extend the project's end date if they are delayed.

4. Adjusting aspects of a project schedule, such as cost, duration, and scope, to achieve a desired project schedule result is known as _____.

5. For a task on the critical path, "critical" refers to how the task's scheduling will affect the project's _____ _____.

6. _____ _____ is the amount of time that the finish date of a task can be delayed before the start of a successor task must be rescheduled.

7. A(n) _____ contour describes how work is distributed over time in terms of graphical patterns.

8. It is important to optimize your project schedule prior to saving a(n) _____.

9. Decreasing a project's duration is known as _____ _____.

10. The amount of time by which the finish date on a task can be delayed before completion of the project will be delayed is known as _____ _____.

Multiple Choice

Select the best response for the following statements.

1. Using a fiscal year view is most appropriate when:
   a. you want to view the costs for individual tasks.
   b. you need to pull in the project end date.
   c. there are stakeholders who are accustomed to analyzing data in this format.
   d. you need to combine projects with other project managers.

2. Predefined contours work best when you can estimate:
   a. the finish date of the task.
   b. a probable pattern of effort.
   c. the overallocation of a resource.
   d. None of the above

3. A task may have:
   a. total slack.
   b. free slack.
   c. partial slack.
   d. both total slack and free slack.

4. A task that has free slack before a project begins:
   a. might become critical as the project gets underway and actuals are entered.
   b. will always have free slack.
   c. can never affect the critical path.
   d. should be optimized as soon as possible.

5. You cannot use the Calendar options to:
   a. define how many hours are in a day.
   b. identify which is the first day of the week.
   c. set up the base calendar.
   d. define how many days should equal one month.

6. If a resource's assignment determines the finish date of a task, it is said that this resource is the:
   a. driving resource.
   b. critical resource.
   c. final resource.
   d. end resource.

7. Which of the following is not a predefined contour?
   a. Bell
   b. Half Pike
   c. Front Loaded
   d. Turtle

8. You can view the costs of a project in the:
   a. Project Information dialog box.
   b. Project Cost dialog box.
   c. Project Statistics dialog box.
   d. Detailed Gantt chart view.

9. Once work has commenced on a project:

    a. the critical path cannot change.

    b. variance can no longer appear.

    c. the finish date is likely to change.

    d. a task cannot move from noncritical to critical.

10. The Default Start Time and Default End Time settings on the Calendar options:

    a. are not related to the working time values for calendars.

    b. supply the default start and end time for task constraints.

    c. supply the default start and end time for actual start and finish dates in which you enter a date but do not include a time.

    d. All of the above

■ Competency Assessment

Project 13-1: Switching to Fiscal Year View for Office Remodel

The Facility Management department would like to see the project schedule for your lunchroom office remodel in a fiscal year view. For your company, the fiscal year begins on October 1.

GET READY. Launch Microsoft Project if it is not already running.

OPEN *Office Remodel 13-1* from the data files for this lesson.

The *Office Remodel 13-1* file for this lesson is available on the book companion website.

1. On the Gantt chart, drag the vertical divider bar to the right to expose the Start and Finish columns.
2. On the Ribbon, click the **File** tab, then select **Options**.
3. Click the **Schedule** section.
4. In the *Fiscal year starts in:* box, select **October**, then click **OK** to close the Options dialog box.
5. **SAVE** the project schedule as *Office Remodel Fiscal Year* and **CLOSE** the file.

PAUSE. LEAVE Project open to use in the next exercise.

Project 13-2: Compressing the HR Interview Project Schedule

After a team meeting regarding the HR Interview project schedule, it is decided that you need to wrap up your interviewing process before the beginning of December. November 28 is your target date. Make lead time and overtime adjustments to your project schedule to bring in the finish date.

OPEN *HR Interview Schedule 13-2* from the data files for this lesson.

The *HR Interview Schedule 13-2* file for this lesson is available on the book companion website.

1. On the Ribbon, click the **View tab**, then click the **Other Views** button. From the list, select **More Views**.
2. In the More Views dialog box, select **Detail Gantt**, then click **Apply**.
3. Click the name of task 1, **HR Interview Schedule**, then press **Ctrl + Shift + F5** to scroll to that task.
4. Double-click the name of task 6, **Assemble potential candidate applications and resumes**.
5. In the Task Information dialog box, click the **Predecessors** tab, if necessary.
6. In the Lag field for the predecessor task 5, key **−50%**, then press **Enter**. Click **OK**.
7. On the Ribbon, click the **Task Usage** button.

8. Right-click the **Work** column heading and select Insert Column from the drop-down menu.

9. Key **Overtime**, then select the **Overtime Work field name.**

10. Scroll down in the task list until you reach task 12.

11. Under task 12, click the **Overtime Work cell** for Keith Harris.

12. Key **8** and press **Enter.**

13. Repeat steps 11 and 12 for Mu Zheng and Megan Sherman.

14. On the Ribbon, click the **Other Views** button, then click **More Views.** In the More Views dialog box, select **Detail Gantt,** then click **Apply.**

15. Press the **F5** key. Key **30** in the ID box, then click **OK.** Point your cursor to the Interview Process Complete Milestone and note the new finish date.

16. **SAVE** the project schedule as *HR Interview Compressed* and **CLOSE** the file.

    PAUSE. LEAVE Project open to use in the next exercise.

■ Proficiency Assessment

Project 13-3: Office Remodel Cost and Finish Date

Before you begin to optimize your Office Remodel project schedule, you need to identify the project finish date and total cost.

OPEN *Office Remodel 13-3* from the data files for this lesson.

The *Office Remodel 13-3* file for this lesson is available on the book companion website.

1. Activate the More Views dialog box, then apply the Detail Gantt view.

2. Activate the Project Information dialog box.

3. In a separate Word document, document the Finish date of the project.

4. Activate the Project Statistics dialog box.

5. Continuing in the same Word document, document the current cost of the project.

6. Close the Project Statistics dialog box.

7. **SAVE** the project schedule as *Office Remodel Finish-Cost.* **SAVE** the Word document as *Office Remodel Finish-Cost.* **CLOSE** both files.

   PAUSE. LEAVE Project open to use in the next exercise.

Project 13-4: Don Funk Resource Assignment Contour

You are working on the Don Funk Music Video and want to apply a predefined contour for Annette Hill's assignment to task 7, Book musicians. Because of other commitments, she will work more hours on the front end of this task.

OPEN *Don Funk Music Video 13-4* from the data files for this lesson.

The *Don Funk Music Video 13-4* file for this lesson is available on the book companion website.

1. Activate the Task Usage view.

2. Scroll to task 7.

3. Select the name **Annette Hill.**

4. Activate the General tab of the Assignment Information dialog box.

5. Apply a front-loaded contour to this resource for this assignment.

6. Scroll the screen so that you can see Annette's later assignments on this task.

7. **SAVE** the project schedule as *Don Funk Contour* and **CLOSE** the file.

   PAUSE. LEAVE Project open to use in the next exercise.

■ Mastery Assessment

Project 13-5: Employee Orientation Assignment Delay

During your employee orientation, you will be presenting an overview of the profit-sharing plan at your company. Kevin McDowell will talk to the new hires after Sidney Higa has finished. You need to delay the start of Kevin's assignment until after Sidney Higa has completed her assignment.

OPEN *Employee Orientation 13-5* from the data files for this lesson.

1. Switch to the Task Usage view.
2. For task 19, *Overview of profit sharing plan,* delay Kevin McDowell's 0.5h assignment from 11:00 AM until 11:30 AM.
3. **SAVE** the project schedule as ***Employee Orientation Manual Edit***, then **CLOSE** the file.
   PAUSE. LEAVE Project open to use in the next exercise.

The *Employee Orientation 13-5* file for this lesson is available on the book companion website.

Project 13-6: Insurance Claim Process Delayed Start

On your Insurance Claim Process project schedule, you need to edit Chris Gray's assignment on task 18, Repair performed, so that he does not start work until after the other resource assigned to the task.

OPEN *Insurance Claim Process 13-6* from the data files for this lesson.

1. Activate the Task Usage view.
2. Using the Assignment Information dialog box, edit Chris Gray's assignment on task 18 so that the start of his work on this task is delayed until Wednesday, June 15, 2011.
3. **SAVE** the project schedule as ***Insurance Claim Delayed Start***, then **CLOSE** the file.
   CLOSE Project.

The *Insurance Claim Process 13-6* file for this lesson is available on the book companion website.

14 LESSON

Advanced Project Schedule Formatting

LESSON SKILL MATRIX

SKILL	TASK
Customizing the Calendar View	Format bar styles for tasks in the Calendar view.
Using Task IDs and WBS Codes	Work with Unique IDs and WBS codes.
Formatting the Network Diagram	Format items in the Network Diagram view.
Using Visual Reports	Create and print a Visual Report.

You are a project manager for Southridge Video, and recently one of your primary responsibilities has been to manage the new Don Funk Music Video project. In an earlier lesson, you learned about some of the basic formatting features in Microsoft Project 2010 that allow you to change the way your data appears. In this lesson, you learn about some of the more powerful formatting and reporting features that enable you to organize and analyze data using additional tools, such as a spreadsheet application.

KEY TERMS
mask
Network Diagram
node
outline number
Unique ID
visual report
work breakdown structure
 (WBS) code

▪ SOFTWARE ORIENTATION

WBS Codes and Unique IDs in the Task Sheet View

Unique IDs are unique identifiers for tasks and resources. Work breakdown structure (WBS) codes show the outline hierarchy of a project (see Figure 14-1).

Figure 14-1

WBS codes and Unique IDs in the Task Sheet view

Unique ID is the entry order of tasks and resources.

WBS column represents the hierarchical outline of the tasks.

	ⓘ	Unique ID ▾	WBS ▾	Task Name ▾	Duration ▾	Start ▾	Finish ▾	Predecessors ▾
0		0	0	⊟ Don Funk Music Video	139.5 days?	Mon 1/10/11	Mon 7/25/11	
1		12	1	⊟ Pre-Production	83 days?	Mon 1/10/11	Thu 5/5/11	
2		11	1.1	Pre-Production begins	0 days	Mon 1/10/11	Mon 1/10/11	
3		1	1.2	Review Screenplay	1.8 wks	Mon 1/10/11	Thu 1/20/11	2
4	📊	2	1.3	Develop scene blocking and schedule	2 wks	Thu 1/20/11	Tue 2/1/11	3
5		3	1.4	Develop production layouts	0.5 mons	Wed 2/2/11	Thu 2/17/11	4
6	✆	4	1.5	Identify and reserve locations	5 wks?	Fri 2/18/11	Thu 3/24/11	5
7	📝	5	1.6	Book musicians	2 wks	Fri 3/25/11	Thu 4/7/11	6
8		6	1.7	Book dancers	2 wks	Fri 4/8/11	Thu 4/21/11	7
9		7	1.8	Reserve audio recording equipment	1 wk	Fri 4/22/11	Thu 4/28/11	8
10		8	1.9	Reserve video recording equipment	5 days	Fri 4/29/11	Thu 5/5/11	9
11	🔄	71	1.10	⊞ Status Meeting	69.13 days	Tue 1/18/11	Mon 4/25/11	
27		10	1.11	Pre-Production complete	0 days	Thu 5/5/11	Thu 5/5/11	10
28		13	2	⊟ Production	30.75 days	Thu 5/5/11	Fri 6/17/11	
29		16	2.1	Production begins	0 days	Thu 5/5/11	Thu 5/5/11	27
30		27	2.2	⊟ Scene 1	6.75 days	Thu 5/5/11	Mon 5/16/11	
31		25	2.2.1	Scene 1 begin	0 days	Thu 5/5/11	Thu 5/5/11	29
32		19	2.2.2	Scene 1 setup	2 days	Fri 5/6/11	Mon 5/9/11	31
33		20	2.2.3	Scene 1 rehearsal	6 hrs	Tue 5/10/11	Tue 5/10/11	32
34		21	2.2.4	Scene 1 vocal recording	1 day	Tue 5/10/11	Wed 5/11/11	33
35		22	2.2.5	Scene 1 video shoot	2 days	Wed 5/11/11	Fri 5/13/11	34
36		23	2.2.6	Scene 1 teardown	1 day	Fri 5/13/11	Mon 5/16/11	35
37		26	2.2.7	Scene 1 complete	0 days	Mon 5/16/11	Mon 5/16/11	36
38		36	2.3	⊟ Scene 2	6.75 days	Thu 5/19/11	Fri 5/27/11	
39	🖼	37	2.3.1	Scene 2 begin	0 days	Thu 5/19/11	Thu 5/19/11	37
40		38	2.3.2	Scene 2 setup	2 days	Thu 5/19/11	Fri 5/20/11	39
41		39	2.3.3	Scene 2 rehearsal	6 hrs	Mon 5/23/11	Mon 5/23/11	40
42		40	2.3.4	Scene 2 vocal recording	1 day	Mon 5/23/11	Tue 5/24/11	41
43		41	2.3.5	Scene 2 video shoot	2 days	Tue 5/24/11	Thu 5/26/11	42

A Unique ID tracks the order in which you enter tasks and resources. WBS codes are numeric representations of the outline hierarchy of a project.

▪ Customizing the Calendar View

↓ **THE BOTTOM LINE**

The Calendar view is one of the simplest views available in Microsoft Project 2010. It can be customized in several different ways.

The **Don Funk Music Video 14M** file for this lesson is available on the book companion website.

➔ **FORMAT BAR STYLES FOR TASKS IN THE CALENDAR VIEW**

GET READY. Before you begin these steps, launch Microsoft Project.

1. **OPEN** the **Don Funk Music Video 14M** project schedule from the data files for this lesson.
2. **SAVE** the file as **Don Funk Music Video 14** in the solutions folder for this lesson, as directed by your instructor.

Calendar ▾

3. On the Ribbon, click the **View** tab, then click the **Calendar view** button. The Calendar view appears. Your screen should look similar to Figure 14-2.

Figure 14-2

Calendar view

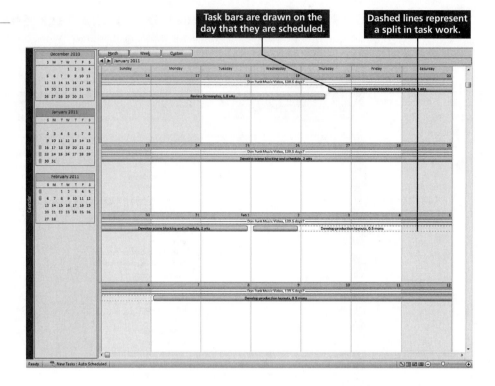

The Calendar view displays four weeks at a time and looks similar to a month-at-a-glance calendar. Task bars are drawn on the days for which tasks are scheduled.

Bar Styles

4. On the Ribbon, click the **Format** tab, then click **Bar Styles**. The Bar Styles dialog box appears.

5. In the Task type box, click **Summary**.

6. In the Bar type box, click **Line**. Summary tasks will be shown with a line.

7. In the Task type box, click **Critical**.

8. In the Pattern box, click the second option, the **solid bar**.

9. In the Color box, click **red**. Critical tasks will be shown with a solid red bar.

10. Make sure that the check boxes for Shadow, Bar rounding, and Wrap text in bars are selected. Your screen should look similar to Figure 14-3.

Figure 14-3

Bar Styles dialog box with selected formatting of critical tasks

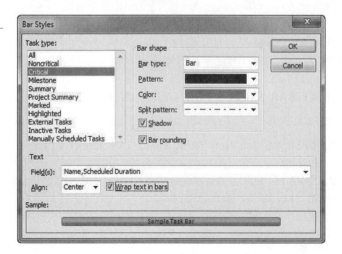

11. Click **OK** to close the Bar Styles dialog box.

12. You might see a message from the Planning Wizard notifying you that some Gantt bars may be different heights. Click **OK**.

13. Move your pointer to the divider bar between the weeks of the calendar. Your pointer will change to a bar with perpendicular arrows. Your screen should look like Figure 14-4.

Figure 14-4

Calendar view with pointer positioned on the horizontal dividing bar

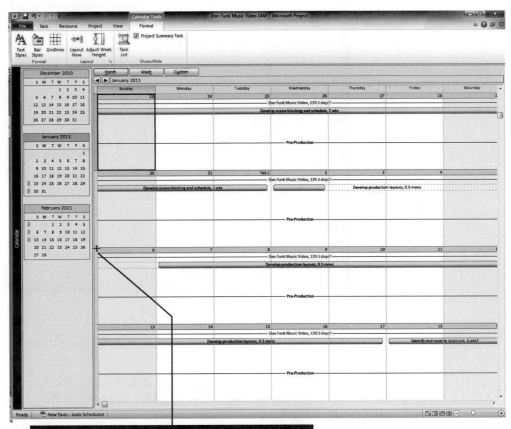

Position the pointer on the divider bar, then click and drag to expand the height of the calendar row.

14. Drag the line to the bottom of the screen to show only one week at a time.

15. Press the **F5** key. In the Date box (not the ID box), key or select **07/15/11**, then click **OK**. The Calendar view displays the first critical tasks using the revised formatting. Your screen should look similar to Figure 14-5.

Figure 14-5

Calendar view showing reformatting of critical tasks

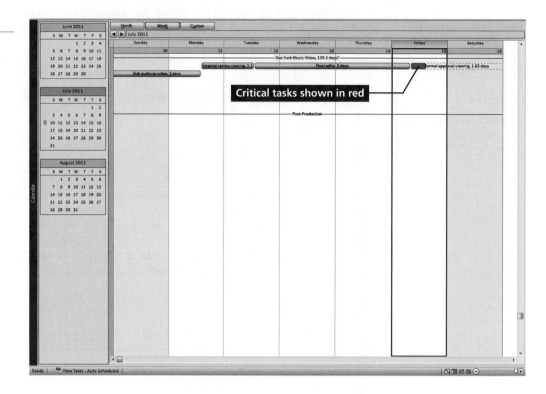

16. SAVE the project schedule.

PAUSE. LEAVE Project open to use in the next exercise.

In this exercise, you reformatted two of the bar styles in the Calendar view. The Calendar view is one of the simplest views available in Microsoft Project, and it offers several formatting options. This view is often used for sharing schedule information with resources or other stakeholders who prefer a more traditional monthly or weekly view, rather than a detailed view such as the Gantt chart.

■ Using Task IDs and WBS Codes

↓
THE BOTTOM LINE

Microsoft Project organizes and tracks the tasks entered into a project schedule using several unique identifiers: Task IDs, Unique IDs, and work breakdown structure (WBS) codes. You can structure the Task Sheet view so that columns for these identifiers are displayed.

⊕ WORK WITH UNIQUE IDS AND WBS CODES

USE the project schedule you created in the previous exercise.

1. On the Ribbon, click the **View** tab, then click the **Other Views** button. Next click **More Views**.

2. In the More Views dialog box, select **Task Sheet**, then click the **Apply** button. The project appears in the Task Sheet view.

3. On the Ribbon, click the **Tables** button, then select the **Entry** table.

4. Right-click the **Task Name** column heading. On the menu that appears, click **Insert Column.**

5. From your keyboard, key **UN**. Three fields appear at the top of the column. Your screen should look similar to Figure 14-6.

Figure 14-6

Column field list narrowed to all fields that start with the letters UN

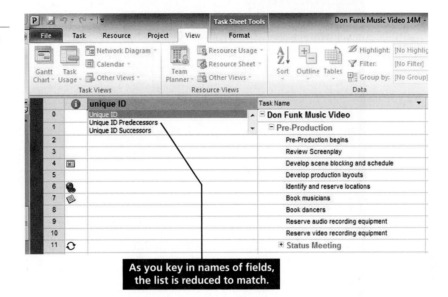

As you key in names of fields, the list is reduced to match.

6. In the list that remains, click **Unique ID**. Microsoft Project inserts the Unique ID column to the left of the Task Name column.

   The Unique ID column indicates the order in which the tasks were entered into the project. Cutting and pasting a task causes its Unique ID value to change. You can see that the tasks in this project were entered in a different order from that in which they are currently displayed.

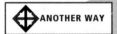ANOTHER WAY   You can also insert a column by clicking the Format tab, then clicking the Insert Column button.

7. Right-click the **Task Name** column heading. On the menu that appears, click **Insert Column.**

8. From your keyboard, key **WBS**. Three fields appear at the top of the column.

9. In the list that remains, click **WBS**. Microsoft Project inserts the WBS column to the left of the Task Name column. WBS codes represent the hierarchy of summary and subtasks in the project.

TAKE NOTE*   If you ever want to reorder tasks to reflect the order in which they were entered, you can sort the Task Sheet by Unique ID.

The WBS numbering system is standard in project management. You can see that in the WBS structure, the top-level summary tasks are sequentially numbered with a single digit, the second-level summary tasks or subtasks add a period and a second digit to the first digit, and so on.

10. Place your cursor on the right dividing line between the WBS column heading and the Task Name column heading, then double-click to auto-fit the column. Repeat the same procedure for the Unique ID column. Your screen should look similar to Figure 14-7.

Figure 14-7

Task Sheet view with the inserted WBS and Unique ID fields

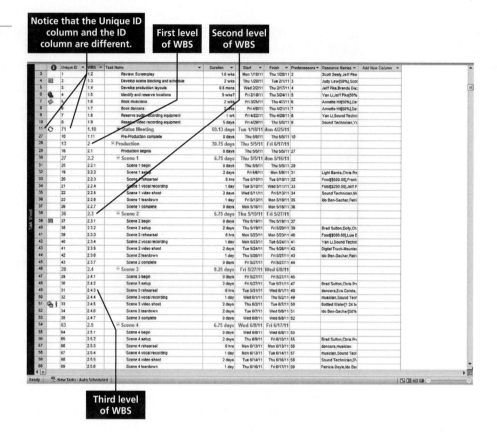

11. In the Task ID column (the leftmost column), select **7** and **8**. This selects the entire rows for the tasks "Book musicians" and "Book dancers."

12. On the Ribbon, click the **Task** tab. In the Schedule group, click the **Indent** button. Microsoft Project makes tasks 7 and 8 subtasks of task 6. Your screen should look similar to Figure 14-8.

Figure 14-8

Task Sheet view showing the reordering of tasks 7 and 8

Note that the Task and Unique ID values for these tasks are not affected, but the WBS codes were changed. The WBS codes for tasks 7 and 8 now list them at the third level of the project hierarchy. In addition, the other tasks in the 1.x branch of the WBS are renumbered. For example, "Reserve audio recording equipment" is renumbered from 1.8 to 1.6.

Cut

13. Click any cell in the table area to deselect tasks 7 and 8. Now select the entire row of task 7. On the Ribbon, click **Cut**. Microsoft Project cuts the selected task to the Windows Clipboard. Your screen should look similar to Figure 14-9.

Figure 14-9

Task Sheet view showing renumbering of tasks after task 7 is removed

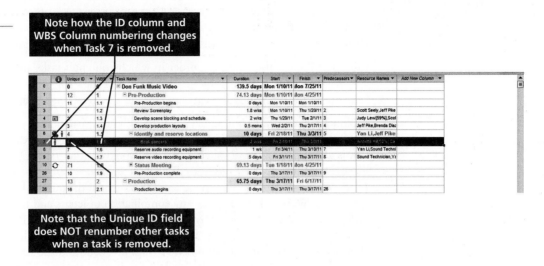

Note how the ID column and WBS Column numbering changes when Task 7 is removed.

Note that the Unique ID field does NOT renumber other tasks when a task is removed.

Note that the Task IDs are renumbered, the Unique IDs are unchanged, and only the WBS codes in the Pre-Production phase are renumbered. The WBS codes in the other phases of the project are unaffected because that part of the project hierarchy did not change.

Paste

14. Select task 4. On the Ribbon, click the **Paste** button. Click **OK** when the warning message is displayed. Microsoft Project pastes back into the task list the task you previously cut. Your screen should look similar to Figure 14-10.

Figure 14-10

Task Sheet view with the Book Musicians task inserted

Note the renumbering of WBS field on other tasks in the Pre-Production Phase.

Unique ID field brings up the next sequential number to show when it was added to the project file.

Note that, again, the Task IDs and the WBS codes in the Pre-Production phase are renumbered. The Unique ID for the pasted task is then updated with the next sequential number to specify when it was added to the project.

15. On the Quick Access Toolbar, click the **Undo** button three times. The task list is restored to its original order.

16. SAVE the project schedule.

PAUSE. LEAVE Project open to use in the next exercise.

In this lesson, you added Unique ID and WBS code columns to the Task Sheet view, then explored how these identifiers change when you move, delete, or add tasks. Each task in a Microsoft Project schedule has a unique identifier, called the Task ID, for each task that you enter. When you insert, move, or delete a task, Microsoft Project updates the Task ID numbers so that the numbers always reflect the current task order. The Task ID column appears (by default) on the left side of most task tables in Microsoft Project. Note that resources have Resource IDs assigned to them, and they behave like a Task ID.

Microsoft Project also tracks the order in which you enter tasks and resources. The *Unique ID* task and resource fields store this entry order. If tasks or resources are reorganized and you later need to see their original entry order, you can view this in the Unique ID field.

Although these identifiers uniquely identify each task, they do not give you any information about the task's place in the hierarchy of the project structure. For example, you can't tell if a task is a summary task or a subtask by simply looking at its Task ID. A better way to show the hierarchy of a project structure is to display the *outline numbers* or *work breakdown structure (WBS) codes* of tasks—the numeric representations of the outline hierarchy of a project. You can change WBS codes to include any combination of letters and numbers that you desire, but outline numbers are numeric only and are generated by Microsoft Project. When working with these codes, the *mask*, or appearance, defines the format of the code—the order and number of alphabetic, numeric, and alphanumeric strings in a code and the separators between them. Initially, outline numbers and WBS codes of tasks are identical. Microsoft Project also stores the Predecessor and Successor values for tasks' Unique IDs and WBS codes. Because the WBS codes indicate the place of every task in the project hierarchy, it is common to use WBS codes instead of Task IDs or names when referencing tasks between team members on a project.

If you are working on a complex project, the WBS or standard outline options available in Microsoft Project may not be sufficient for your report or analysis requirements. If this occurs, you can investigate Microsoft Project's capabilities to handle custom outline numbers to identify a hierarchy within a project schedule. For example, you can define a custom outline number that links different outline levels of a project's structure with different levels of the organization's structure. (The top level might be a regional division, the second level a business unit, and the third level a local team.) You could also use custom outline numbers to associate different outline levels of a project's WBS with internal cost centers or job tracking codes.

After you have applied a custom outline number to your project schedule, you can then group, sort, and filter tasks and resources by their outline numbers. You can apply up to ten levels of a custom outline number for tasks and ten for resources in a single Microsoft Project file.

■ Formatting the Network Diagram

 THE BOTTOM LINE

In traditional project management, a Network Diagram is a standard way for representing project activities and their relationships in a flowchart format.

⊙ FORMAT ITEMS IN THE NETWORK DIAGRAM VIEW

USE the project schedule you created in the previous exercise.

1. On the Ribbon, click the **View** tab, then click **Network Diagram**. The Network Diagram view appears. Your screen should look similar to Figure 14-11.

   The focus of the Network Diagram is task relationships and sequencing (rather than durations). Each task is represented as a box, or node, containing several pieces of information about the task. The relationships between tasks are represented as lines and arrows.

Figure 14-11

Network Diagram view

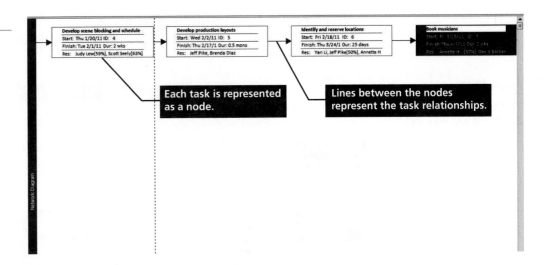

2. On the Ribbon, click the **Format** tab, then click **Box Styles**. The Box Styles dialog box appears. Your screen should look similar to Figure 14-12.

Box
Styles

Figure 14-12

Network Diagram's Box Styles dialog box

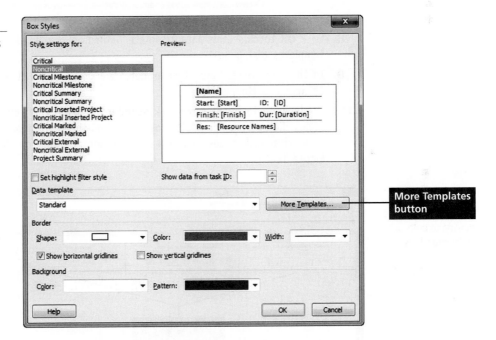

3. Click **More Templates**. The Data Templates dialog box appears.

4. In the *Templates in Network Diagram* list, make sure that Standard is selected, then click the **Copy** button. The Data Template Definition dialog box appears. You will add the WBS code value to the lower-right corner of the node.

5. In the Template name box, key **Standard + WBS**.

6. Below Choose cell(s), click the empty cell below Duration and to the right of Resource Names.

7. In the drop-down list that becomes active, key or select **WBS**. This will add the WBS code to the standard box style in the Network Diagram. Your screen should look similar to Figure 14-13.

Figure 14-13

Data Template Definition box customized with WBS field

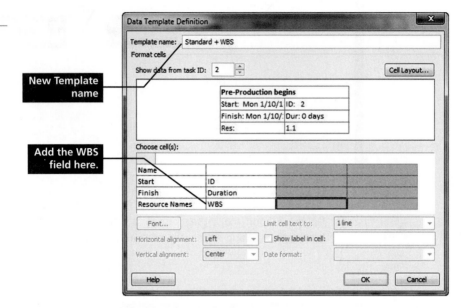

8. Click **OK** to close the Data Template Definition box. Click **Close** to close the Data Templates dialog box.

9. In the Box Styles dialog box, under *Style settings for*, click and drag to select **Critical** and **Noncritical**.

10. In the Data template box, click **Standard + WBS**, then click **OK** to close the Box Styles dialog box. Microsoft Project applies the revised box style to the critical and noncritical task nodes in the Network Diagram. Your screen should look similar to Figure 14-14.

Figure 14-14

Network Diagram with revised box style applied to both critical and noncritical tasks

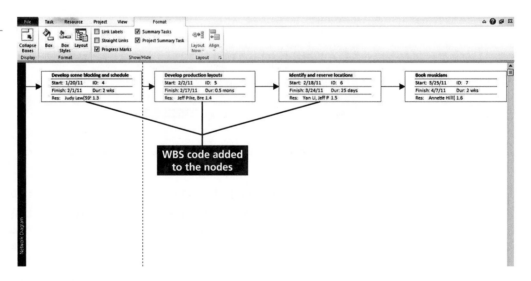

Microsoft Project adds the WBS code to the nodes for critical and noncritical tasks. Scroll left and right to review some of the other nodes in the Network Diagram. As you can see, the nodes representing other types of tasks, such as summary tasks, are not affected. If you want to apply the new template to other task types, you would do so in the Box Styles dialog box.

11. SAVE the project schedule.

PAUSE. LEAVE Project open to use in the next exercise.

In this lesson, you applied and formatted the Network Diagram. The ***Network Diagram*** is a standard way of representing the logical order of project activities and their relationships. Tasks are represented as boxes, or ***nodes***, and the relationships between tasks are drawn as lines connecting nodes. The Network Diagram is not a timescaled view like the Gantt chart. Rather, it shows project activities in a flowchart format so that you can focus on the relationships between activities rather than their durations.

■ Using Visual Reports

THE BOTTOM LINE

The Visual Reports feature of Microsoft Project 2010 combines the power of Microsoft Excel and Microsoft Visio with the data of your project. You can use a preformatted report, edit a report, or create a new report that includes a specific set of fields from Microsoft Project.

⊕ CREATE A VISUAL REPORT

Visual Reports

USE the project schedule you created in the previous exercise.

1. On the Ribbon, click the **Project** tab, then select the **Visual Reports** button. The Visual Reports dialog box appears. Your screen should look like Figure 14-15.

Figure 14-15

Visual Reports dialog box

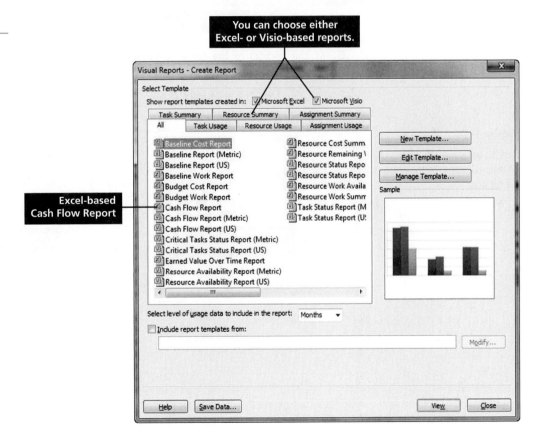

You can choose either Excel- or Visio-based reports.

Excel-based Cash Flow Report

2. Click the **Task Usage** tab, then click **Cash Flow Report.**

3. In the *Select level of usage data to include in the report:* box, select **Months**.

4. Click the **View** button. The Visual Report engine gathers data from your project file and builds an Online Analytical Processing (OLAP) cube. Microsoft Excel opens, and the report is presented in Chart form from a preformatted report template. Your screen should look similar to Figure 14-16.

Figure 14-16

Visual report named "Cash Flow Report" displayed in Microsoft Excel

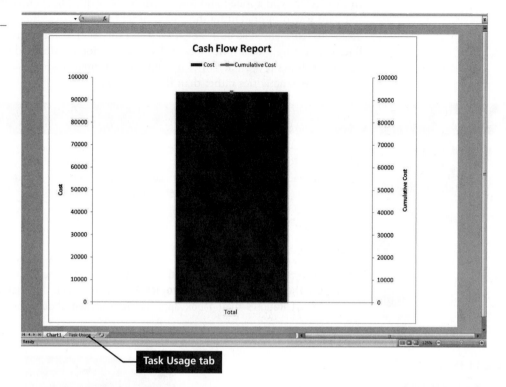

5. At the bottom of the Excel window, select the **Task Usage** sheet tab.

6. In the PivotTable Field List box, navigate to the **Time** field. Place your cursor on Monthly Calendar and drag it to the **Row Labels** box. Your screen should look similar to Figure 14-17.

Figure 14-17

Task Usage sheet tab with Monthly Calendar in the Row Labels area

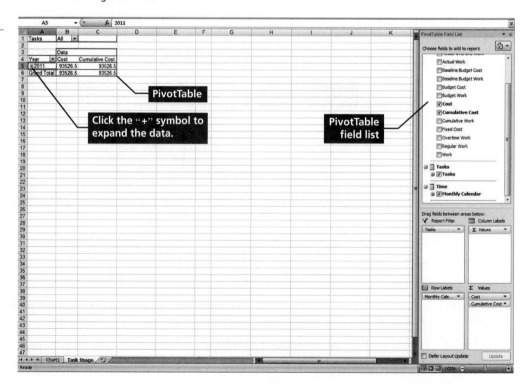

7. In the PivotTable area, click the expand button next to the year 2011 to reveal all the available time data. Your screen should look similar to Figure 14-18.

Figure 14-18

Cash Flow Report PivotTable with all time data showing

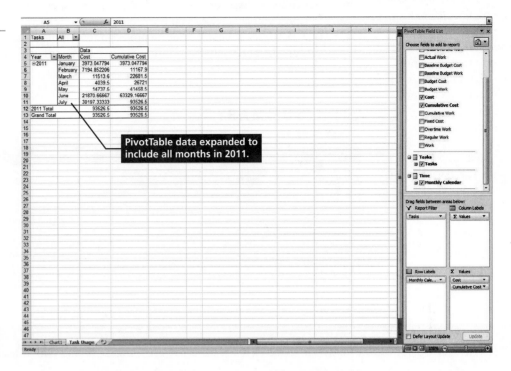

8. Click the **Chart1** sheet tab at the bottom of the screen. Your screen should look similar to Figure 14-19.

Figure 14-19

Cash Flow Report chart with the expanded time data

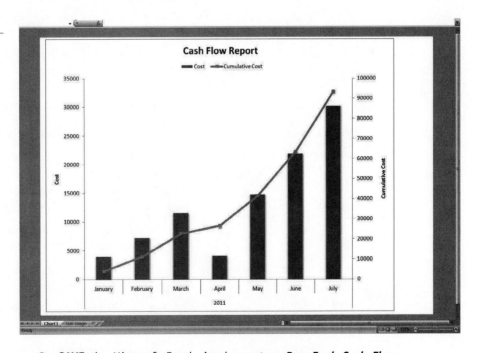

9. SAVE the Microsoft Excel visual report as *Don Funk Cash Flow*.

10. CLOSE Microsoft Excel.

11. SAVE the project schedule, then **CLOSE** the file.

PAUSE. If you are continuing to the next lesson, keep Project open. If you are not continuing to additional lessons, **CLOSE** Project.

X REF

For a review of formatting and printing basic reports, see Lesson 9.

In this exercise, you created a new, visual report that included a custom table and filter, then viewed the report in the Print Preview window. A *visual report* uses data from a Project file and creates either an Excel or Visio based file with an associated graphic, depending on which type/style report you choose. As you learned in previous lessons, reports are a primary way that project managers can communicate project information to stakeholders. Keep in mind that reports are designed only for printing or viewing, and they do not allow any data entry or manipulation.

SKILL SUMMARY

IN THIS LESSON, YOU LEARNED:	TASK
To customize the Calendar view.	Format bar styles for tasks in the Calendar view.
To use Task IDs and WBS codes.	Work with Unique IDs and WBS codes.
To format the Network Diagram.	Format items in the Network Diagram view.
To create and print visual reports.	Use visual reports.

■ Knowledge Assessment

Matching

Match the term in column 1 to its description in column 2.

Column 1	Column 2
1. Task ID	a. A numeric-only representation of the outline hierarchy of a project, generated by Microsoft Project
2. Nodes	b. Defines the format of the outline and WBS codes
3. Unique ID	c. The view that looks similar to a "month-at-a-glance"
4. Network Diagram	d. A representation of the outline hierarchy of a project, which you can change to include any combination of letters and numbers
5. Lines	e. A unique identifier that tracks the order in which you enter tasks and resources
6. Outline numbers	f. Represent the relationships between tasks on a Network Diagram
7. Mask	g. A standard way of representing project activities in a flowchart format
8. Reports	h. The boxes used to represent tasks in a Network Diagram
9. WBS codes	i. The primary way that project managers communicate project information to stakeholders
10. Calendar	j. The unique identifier that Microsoft Project assigns to each task sequentially as you enter it

True/False

Circle T if the statement is true or F if the statement is false.

T F **1.** The Visual Reports feature uses Microsoft Word and Excel to produce reports based on Project data.

T F **2.** You can apply up to ten levels of a custom outline number for tasks in a single Microsoft Project file.

T F **3.** Reports do not allow any data entry or manipulation.

T F **4.** WBS codes can include letters and numbers.

T F **5.** The Network Diagram view is one of the simplest views available in Microsoft Project.

T F **6.** If you want to reorder tasks by the order in which they were entered, you can sort them by Task ID.

T F **7.** In the WBS structure, top-level summary tasks are sequentially numbered with a single digit.

T F **8.** The Network Diagram focuses on task durations.

T F **9.** By default, the Calendar view displays three months at a time.

T F **10.** The Unique ID shows a task's place in the hierarchy of the project schedule.

■ Competency Assessment

Project 14-1: Using WBS Codes for New Employee Orientation

You and your team are reviewing the project schedule for your company's new employee orientation. You agree that it would be easier to refer to tasks by their WBS codes, so you need to change the view of your schedule to reflect this. You also need to make changes in hierarchy to a few of the tasks.

GET READY. Launch Microsoft Project if it is not already running.
OPEN *Employee Orientation Schedule 14-1* from the data files for this lesson.

The *Employee Orientation Schedule 14-1* file for this lesson is available on the book companion website.

1. On the Ribbon, click **View**, then click **Other Views**, and then click **More Views**.
2. In the More Views dialog box, select **Task Sheet**, then click **Apply**.
3. Right-click the **Task Name** column heading. On the menu that appears, click **Insert Column**.
4. From your keyboard, key **WBS**, then select **WBS** from the file list.
5. In the Task ID column, click and drag to select tasks **22** and **23**.
6. On the Ribbon, click the **Task** tab. In the Schedule group, click the **Indent** button.
7. **SAVE** the project schedule as *Employee Orientation WBS*, then **CLOSE** the file.
   PAUSE. LEAVE Project open to use in the next exercise.

Project 14-2: Don Funk Cash Flow Report

One of the finance managers on the Don Funk Music Video project has asked for a chart that summarizes the cash flow of the project by month. You need to produce and print (preview) this report for him.

OPEN *Don Funk Music Video 14-2* from the data files for this lesson.

The *Don Funk Music Video 14-2* file for this lesson is available on the book companion website.

1. On the Ribbon, click the **Project** tab, then click the **Visual Reports** button.
2. In the Visual Reports dialog box, click **Cash Flow Report**.

3. In the *Select level of usage data to include in the report:* box, select **Months**, then click the **View** button.

4. At the bottom of the Excel window, select the **Task Usage** sheet tab.

5. In the PivotTable Field List box, navigate to the **Time** field. Place your cursor on Monthly Calendar and drag it to the **Row Labels** box.

6. Click the **Chart** sheet tab at the bottom of the screen.

7. **SAVE** the Excel report as *Don Funk Monthly Cash Flow Report*. **CLOSE** the Excel file.

8. **CLOSE** Microsoft Excel.

9. **SAVE** the project schedule as *Don Funk Visual Cash Flow Report* and **CLOSE** the file.

PAUSE. LEAVE Project open to use in the next exercise.

■ Proficiency Assessment

Project 14-3: Customizing Calendar View for Insurance Claim Process

You would like to hand out a monthly view of the insurance claim process so that agents and adjustors can keep a quick reference for this process at their fingertips. You need to change the view of your project schedule to a calendar view, as well as change the bar style formatting for a couple of task types.

OPEN *Insurance Claim Processing 14-3* from the data files for this lesson.

The *Insurance Claim Processing 14-3* file for this lesson is available on the book companion website.

1. From the View tab, change to the Calendar view.

2. Activate the Bar Styles dialog box on the Format tab.

3. Select **Critical** in the Task type box. Change the pattern to the last bar (checkered) in the drop-down list, and change the color to red.

4. Select **Project Summary** in the Task type box. Change the bar type to None.

5. Close the Bar Styles dialog box.

6. Double-click the divider bar between the calendar rows (weeks) to expand the row height.

7. **SAVE** the project schedule as *Insurance Claim Calendar View* and **CLOSE** the file.

PAUSE. LEAVE Project open to use in the next exercise.

Project 14-4: New Employee Orientation Network Diagram

Because the timeline for your New Employee Orientation is so short, you would like to focus on the relationships between tasks rather than their durations. You want to change the view to the Network Diagram and reformat some of the elements of the Network Diagram.

OPEN *Employee Orientation Schedule 14-4* from the data files for this lesson.

The *Employee Orientation Schedule 14-4* file for this lesson is available on the book companion website.

1. From the View tab, activate the Network diagram.

2. Activate the Box Styles dialog box from the Format tab.

3. Select **Critical Summary** from the *Style settings for* box if it is not already selected. Set the Data template for these boxes to **WBS**.

4. Select **Noncritical Summary** from the *Style settings for* box. Set the Data template for these boxes to **WBS**.

5. Close the Box Styles dialog box.

6. **SAVE** the project schedule as *Employee Orientation Network Diagram* and **CLOSE** the file.

PAUSE. LEAVE Project open to use in the next exercise.

■ Mastery Assessment

Project 14-5: HR Interview Visual Critical Tasks

The HR Group Manager has requested a summary report for weekly resource work assignments on this project, but she would like to see it chart form. You need to create this report.

OPEN *HR Interview Project 14-5* from the data files for this lesson.

1. Activate the Visual Reports dialog box, then select the **Resource Work Summary Report.**
2. Produce the report data at the weekly level.
3. Filter out the Unassigned work assignments.
4. Preview the report to make sure your changes meet the needs of the HR Manager.
5. **SAVE** the report as *Weekly Work Summary Report.* **CLOSE** Microsoft Excel.
6. **SAVE** the project schedule as *HR Interview Weekly Work Summary Report* and **CLOSE** the file.

   PAUSE. LEAVE Project open to use in the next exercise.

@

The *HR Interview Project 14-5* file for this lesson is available on the book companion website.

Project 14-6: Insurance Claim Processing WBS Codes

You want to add the Unique ID and WBS columns to your Insurance Claim Processing project schedule. You would also like to explore how several changes to your project schedule will affect the Unique ID and WBS codes.

OPEN *Insurance Claim Processing 14-6* from the data files for this lesson.

1. Insert the Unique ID and WBS columns to the left of the Task Name column.
2. Save the project schedule as *Insurance Claim WBS.*
3. In a separate Word document, explain how the Unique ID and WBS codes are affected in each of the following independent situations (*Hint:* After documenting the changes for a given situation, close the file without saving. Reopen the solution file *Insurance Claim WBS* to explore and document each situation):

   • Tasks 7 and 8 are indented under task 3
   • Task 25 is indented under task 22
   • Task 11 is cut and then inserted below task 7 (*Hint:* Describe each part of this step separately.)

4. **SAVE** the Word document as *Insurance Claim WBS.*
5. **CLOSE** both files.
   CLOSE Project.

The *Insurance Claim Processing 14-6* file for this lesson is available on the book companion website.

INTERNET READY

Search the Internet for information on using WBS codes in a project schedule. Look for any documents explaining how to apply, use, format, or troubleshoot these codes. Review the information you find.

Now, locate a project schedule template on the Internet, or use a project schedule from your personal experience. Experiment with indenting and outdenting tasks, as well as with adding, moving, and deleting tasks. Study how WBS codes are affected with each change. Build on the knowledge you gained from this lesson, especially from Project 14-6.

15 LESSON

Managing Multiple Projects

LESSON SKILL MATRIX

SKILL	TASK
Managing Consolidated Projects	Create a consolidated project schedule.
Creating Dependencies Between Projects	Link tasks from two different project schedules.

As a project manager for Southridge video, you are responsible for managing several other projects in addition to the Don Funk Music Video. Now that progress is being made on some of your projects, you would like to find an easier way to work with multiple project files. In this lesson, you learn to use some of the features Microsoft Project provides that enable you to consolidate multiple project files and create cross-project links.

KEY TERMS
consolidated project
ghost task
inserted project
master project
subproject

■ SOFTWARE ORIENTATION

Consolidated Project Gantt Chart View

The Gantt chart view of a consolidated project (see Figure 15-1) allows you to see multiple projects collected in one project schedule so that you can filter, sort, and group the data, as well as see task relationships among projects.

Figure 15-1

Gantt Chart View of a consolidated project file

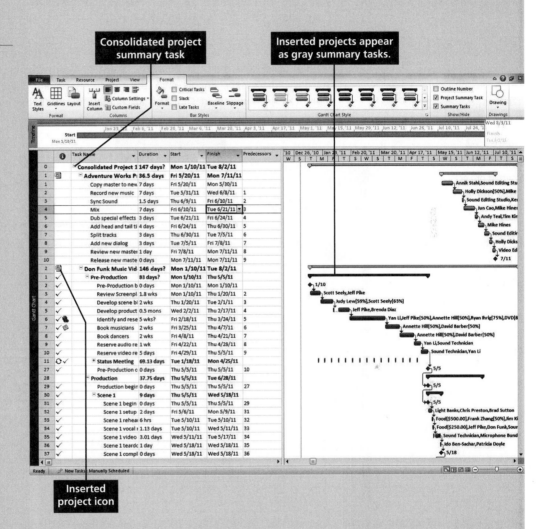

In the Gantt chart view of a consolidated project, the inserted projects appear as summary tasks with gray Gantt bars. Also, an inserted project icon appears in the Indicators column.

■ Managing Consolidated Projects

THE BOTTOM LINE

In Microsoft Project 2010, a consolidated project enables a project manager to link and manage multiple projects within one master project file.

 CREATE A CONSOLIDATED PROJECT SCHEDULE

GET READY. Before you begin these steps, launch Microsoft Project.

1. **OPEN** the *Don Funk Music Video 15M* and *Adventure Works Promo 15M* project schedules from the data files for this lesson.

The *Don Funk Music Video 15M* and *Adventure Works Promo 15M* files for this lesson are available on the book companion website.

New Window

2. **SAVE** the files as *Don Funk Music Video 15* and *Adventure Works Promo 15* in the solutions folder for this lesson, as directed by your instructor. Make sure the *Don Funk Music Video 15* project schedule is in the active window.

3. On the Ribbon, click the **View** tab, then click **New Window.** The New Window dialog box appears.

4. In the Projects list, select the names of both open projects either by holding down the **Ctrl** key while clicking or by clicking and dragging to select both names. After you have selected both project schedules, click the **OK** button. Microsoft Project opens both files in a new window with the Timeline view at the top.

5. On the Ribbon, click **Entire Project** in the Zoom group. Microsoft Project adjusts the timescale in the Gantt chart so that the full duration of both projects is visible. Make sure that the Duration, Start, and Finish columns are visible on your screen. If necessary, double-click the right edge of any columns that display pound signs (###). Your screen should look similar to Figure 15-2.

Figure 15-2

Gantt chart view with both inserted projects

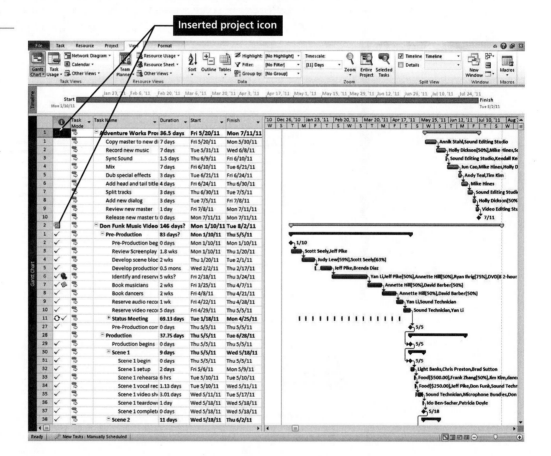

TAKE NOTE ★ When you point to the Inserted Project icon in the Indicators column, Microsoft Project displays the full path to the inserted project file.

6. Right-click the **Task Mode** column and select **Hide Column**.

7. **SAVE** the consolidated project schedule as *Consolidated Project 15*. If you are prompted to save changes to the inserted projects, click the **Yes to All** button.

Project Summary Task

8. On the Ribbon, click the **Format** tab. In the Show/Hide group, click the check box to activate the **Project Summary Task**. Microsoft Project displays the Consolidated Project 15 summary task. Your screen should look similar to Figure 15-3.

Figure 15-3

Gantt chart with consolidated project summary task

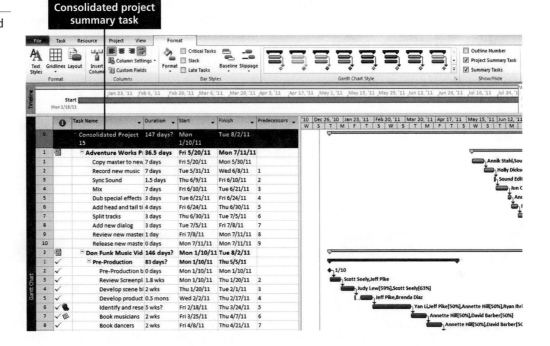

The values of the consolidated project summary task, such as duration and work, represent the rolled-up (or combined) values of both inserted projects. As Southridge Video acquires contracts for more projects, inserting them into the consolidated project schedule in this way provides a single location in which to view all the company's activities.

TAKE NOTE*   If you want to add more project schedules to a consolidated project, click Insert on the menu bar, then click Project.

9. SAVE the consolidated project schedule, as well as the individual project schedules.
PAUSE. LEAVE Project open to use in the next exercise.

In real life, it is rare that a project manager would manage only a single, small project from beginning to end. Usually, he or she is managing several complex projects that involve several people working on different tasks at different times and locations, and often for different supervisors.

As you saw in this exercise, Microsoft Project enables you to combine two (or more) projects to form a consolidated project. A ***consolidated project*** is a Microsoft Project file that contains other Microsoft Project files, called inserted projects. An ***inserted project*** is the Microsoft Project file that is inserted into another Microsoft Project file. Consolidated projects are also known as ***master projects***, and inserted projects are also known as ***subprojects***. The inserted projects do not really reside within the consolidated project. Rather, they are linked to it in such a way that they can be viewed and edited from the consolidated project. If an inserted project is edited outside the consolidated project, the updated information appears in the consolidated project the next time it is opened. When you save a consolidated project, any changes you have made to inserted projects are saved in the source file as well.

Using a consolidated project gives you the capacity to do such things as:

- See all of your organization's project schedules in a single view.
- "Roll up" project information to higher management levels. For example, one group's project may be an inserted project for the department's consolidated project, which then may be an inserted project for the company's consolidated project.
- Divide your project schedule into separate project schedules to match the nature of your project. For example, you could divide your project schedule into separate schedules by phase, component, or location. You could then group the information back together in a consolidated project schedule for a view of the complete project.
- See the information for all of your projects in one location so you can filter, sort, and group the data as needed.

Consolidated projects use the standard Microsoft Project outlining features. In a consolidated project, the Gantt bar for an inserted project is gray, and an inserted project icon appears in the Indicators column. Also, when you save a consolidated project, any changes you have made to an inserted project are saved in the source file as well. It is possible to add an unlimited number of project schedules to a consolidated project file (although in real life, you are limited by time and space constraints).

■ Creating Dependencies Among Projects

↓ **THE BOTTOM LINE**

Sometimes, tasks or phases in one project may depend on tasks or phases in other projects. Microsoft Project enables you to show these relationships by linking tasks between two or more projects. When tasks from different projects are linked, Project creates an external task in each project file to display the link. These external tasks are sometime called *ghost tasks*.

⊕ **LINK TASKS FROM TWO DIFFERENT PROJECT SCHEDULES**

USE the project schedules you created in the previous exercise.

1. On the Ribbon, click the **View** tab. In the Window group, click the **Switch Windows** button. Then click **Adventure Works Promo 15**. The Adventure Works Promo 15 project schedule is now visible in the active window.
2. In the Task Name column, click the name of task 9, **Review new master**.
3. Press **Ctrl + Shift + F5**. On the right of the task's Gantt bar, note that one of the resources assigned to this task is Video Editing Studio. You want to use this video studio for work on the Don Funk Music Video 15 project after this task is completed, so you need to link task 9 to a task in the Don Funk Music Video 15 project schedule.
4. On the Ribbon, click the **Switch Windows** button, then click **Don Funk Music Video 15**.
5. Press the **F5** key. In the ID box, key **70**, then click **OK**. Notice that the Video Editing Studio is a resource on this task.
6. On the Ribbon, click the **Switch Windows** button again, then click **Consolidated Project 15**.
7. In the task name column in the Adventure Works Promo 15 project, click the name of task 9, **Review new master**.
8. Scroll down in the task name column to the Don Funk Music Video 15 project and locate task 70, **Fine Video Edit**. Hold down the **Ctrl** key and select task 70.

9. On the Ribbon, click the **Task** tab. Then, in the Schedule group, click the **Link Tasks** button.

ANOTHER WAY
When viewing a consolidated project, you can quickly create cross-project links by pressing the F2 key.

TAKE NOTE✱
If you point to the Gantt bar for the ghost task, Microsoft Project will display a ScreenTip that contains details about the ghost task, including the full path to the external project where the ghost task (the external predecessor) resides.

10. On the Ribbon, click the **View** tab. In the Window group, click the **Switch Windows** button, then click **Adventure Works Promo 15**. The Adventure Works Promo 15 project schedule is now visible in the active window.

Microsoft Project inserted a ghost task named Fine video edit into the project. This ghost task represents task 70 from the ***Don Funk Music Video 15*** project. Because task 10 is a successor task with no other links to this project, it has no effect on other tasks here. Your screen should look similar to Figure 15-4.

Figure 15-4

Gantt chart view with ghost task from Don Funk Music Video project

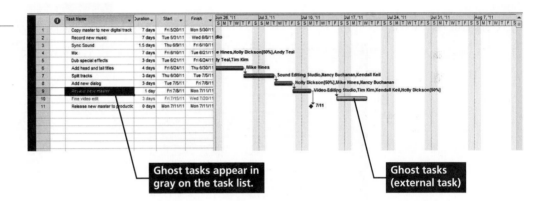

Ghost tasks appear in gray on the task list.

Ghost tasks (external task)

Now you will switch views to look at the ghost task in the ***Don Funk Music Video 15*** project schedule.

11. On the Ribbon, click the **Switch Windows** button, then click **Don Funk Music Video 15**. You can see that the ghost task 70, Review new master, is a predecessor for task 71, Fine video edit. The link between these two project schedules will remain until you break it. If this task is delayed, it could affect task 71. When you delete a task in the source schedule or the ghost task in the destination schedule, Microsoft Project also deletes the corresponding task or ghost task in the other schedule.

12. On the Ribbon, click the **Switch Windows** button, then click **Consolidated Project 15**. You can see the link between the task Review new master (task 9) in the first inserted project and the task Fine video edit (task 71) in the second inserted project. The cross-project link does not appear as a ghost task because you are looking at the consolidated project file. Your screen should look similar to Figure 15-5 and Figure 15-6 (note that you may need to scroll your screen to see the entire link).

ANOTHER WAY
You can also view the links between projects by selecting the Links Between Projects button, located on the Project tab.

TAKE NOTE✱
If you do not want to see cross-project links, click the File tab, then click Options. Next, under the Advanced options, in the Cross-project linking options section, clear the Show external successors or Show external predecessors check box.

Figure 15-5

Consolidated project files
displaying the link between
Adventure Works task 9...

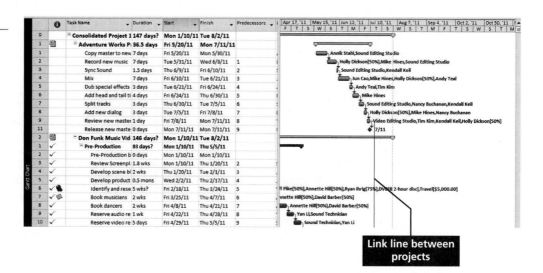

Link line between projects

Figure 15-6

...and Don Funk task 71.

Link line between projects

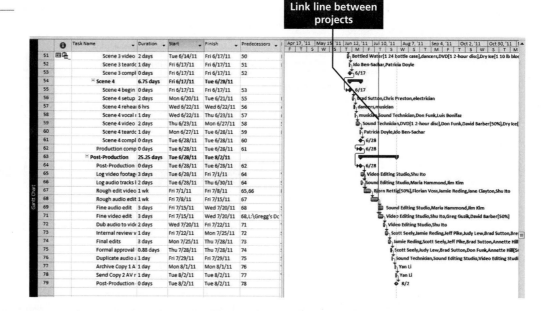

 NOTE* **TAKE NOTE*** Whenever you open a project schedule with cross-project links, Microsoft Project will prompt you to update these cross-project links. You can suppress this prompt if you prefer not to be reminded. You can also tell Microsoft Project to automatically accept updated data from the linked project file. To do so, click the File tab, then click Options. Next, under the Advanced options, in the Cross-project linking options section, select the options you want.

13. SAVE all of the project schedules, then **CLOSE** all files.

PAUSE. If you are continuing to the next lesson, keep Project open. If you are not continuing to additional lessons, **CLOSE** Project.

In this exercise, you linked a task in one project to a task in another project to show a dependency. Most projects are like this—they do not exist in a vacuum. There are various reasons you might need to create dependencies between projects. Some of the more common reasons are as follows:

- The completion of a task in one project might make possible the start of a task in another project. For example, one project manager may need to complete a geological study before a second project manager can begin to construct a building. These two tasks may be managed in separate project files (perhaps because they are being completed by different departments of the same company, or even by two different companies), but they still have a logical dependency on each other.
- A person or piece of equipment might be assigned to a task in one project, and you might need to delay the start of a task in another project until that resource completes the first task. Here, the only commonality between the two tasks is that the same resource is required for both.

Task relationships among project files are similar to the task links (relationships) between tasks within a project file, except that external predecessor and successor tasks have gray task names and Gantt bars. Sometimes these tasks are called ghost tasks because they are not linked to tasks within the project file, only to tasks in other project files.

SKILL SUMMARY

In This Lesson, You Learned:	Task
To manage consolidated projects.	Create a consolidated project schedule.
To create dependencies between projects.	Link tasks from two different project schedules.

■ Knowledge Assessment

Fill in the Blank

Complete the following sentences by writing the correct word or words in the blanks provided.

1. For a consolidated project, the Gantt bar is _____ in color, by default.

2. A(n) _____ _____ is the Microsoft Project file that is put into another Microsoft Project file.

3. If you point to the Gantt bar for a ghost task, Microsoft Project displays a(n) _____ _____ that contains the details about the ghost task.

4. Another name for an inserted project is a(n) _____.

5. To initially select the projects that you want to combine into a consolidated project, use the _____ dialog box.

6. A(n) _____ _____ is a Microsoft Project file that contains other Microsoft Project files.

7. The values of a consolidated project, such as duration and work, represent the rolled-up _____ _____ values of the inserted projects.

8. Another name for a consolidated project is a(n) _____ project file.

9. You can create a(n) _____ between projects if the completion of a task in one project will make possible the start of a task in another project.

10. A(n) _____ _____ is not linked to a task within the consolidated project file, only to tasks in another project file.

Multiple Choice

Select the best response for the following statements.

1. How many project schedules can you add to a consolidated project file?

   a. Two

   b. Three

   c. Ten

   d. An unlimited number

2. By default, when you save a consolidated project:

   a. only the consolidated project is saved.

   b. only changes to the inserted project source files are saved.

   c. changes to both the consolidated project and the inserted project source files are saved.

   d. the consolidated project is saved within the first inserted project.

3. When you insert a project in a consolidated project, an inserted project icon appears:

   a. in the Task Information dialog box.

   b. in the Indicators column.

   c. in the Task Name column.

   d. in the Project Information dialog box.

4. In a consolidated project, inserted projects:

   a. do not really reside within the consolidated project.

   b. can only be edited outside the consolidated project.

   c. reside within the consolidated project.

   d. None of the above

5. Which of the following is a valid reason to use a consolidated project schedule?

   a. To see all of your company's project schedules in a single view

   b. To see all of your projects' information in a single view so you can filter, group, and sort data

   c. To "roll up" project information to higher levels of management

   d. All of the above

6. A cross project link is called a(n):

   a. dependency.

   b. subproject.

   c. integrated project.

   d. co-dependency.

7. The external predecessor and successor tasks in the task relationships between project files are sometimes called:

   a. inserted tasks.

   b. phantom tasks.

   c. ghost tasks.

   d. subtasks.

8. To add schedules to a consolidated project:

   a. on the Project tab, click Move Project.

   b. on the View tab, click Add Project.

   c. on the File tab, click New.

   d. on the Project tab, click Subproject.

9. Another name for a consolidated project is a(n):

    a. inserted project.

    b. subproject.

    c. master project.

    d. summary project.

10. When you create a task dependency between projects, what format do you key in the ID column of the Predecessors tab of the Task Information dialog box?

    a. File Name\Task ID

    b. File Name, Task ID

    c. File Name/Task ID

    d. File Name—Task ID

■ Competency Assessment

Project 15-1: Southridge Video Consolidated Project Schedule

The director of Southridge Video would like to see a consolidated project schedule for all of the projects on which Southridge Video is currently working, both internal and external. You are beginning to assemble the consolidated schedule.

GET READY. Launch Microsoft Project if it is not already running.

OPEN the *Don Funk Music Video 15-1* and *Gregory Weber Biography 15-1* project schedules from the data files for this lesson. **SAVE** the files as *Don Funk Consolidated* and *Gregory Weber Consolidated*.

The *Don Funk Music Video 15-1* and *Gregory Weber Biography 15-1* files for this lesson are available on the book companion website.

1. On the Ribbon, click the **View** tab, then click **New Window**.

2. In the Projects list, select the names of both open projects. After you have selected both project schedules, click **OK**.

3. Right-click the **Task Mode** column and select **Hide Column**.

4. On the Ribbon, click **Entire Project** in the Zoom group.

5. **SAVE** the consolidated project schedule as *Southridge Video Consolidated*. If you are prompted to save changes to the inserted projects, click the **Yes to All** button.

6. On the Ribbon, click the **Format** tab. In the Show/Hide group, click the check box to activate the **Project Summary Task**.

7. **SAVE** the consolidated project schedule, as well as the individual project schedules. **DO NOT CLOSE** the files.

   LEAVE Project and the three files open to use in the next exercise.

Project 15-2: Don Funk–Gregory Weber Dependency

Now that you have created a consolidated file for the Don Funk and Gregory Weber projects, you need to link the inserted schedules to show a dependency between them. Due to resource constraints, one of the tasks (task 3) in the Gregory Weber project cannot begin until another task (task 62) in the Don Funk project is complete.

USE the project schedules you created in the previous exercise.

1. On the Ribbon, click **Switch Windows**, then click **Southridge Video Consolidated**.

2. In the task name column, click the name of task 62, **Production Complete**, in the Don Funk Consolidated schedule.

3. Scroll up in the file and locate task 3, Review Screenplay, in the Gregory Weber Consolidated schedule.

4. Press and hold the **Ctrl** key while selecting **task 3**.

5. On the Ribbon, click the **Task** tab. In the Schedule group, click the **Link Tasks** button.

6. **SAVE** the consolidated file as *Southridge Video Consolidated 2*. If you are prompted to save changes to the inserted projects, click the **Yes to All** button. **CLOSE** all files.

   LEAVE Project open to use in the next exercise.

■ Proficiency Assessment

Project 15-3: Gregory Weber Biography Inserted Project

The *Gregory Weber Biography 15-3* file for this lesson is available on the book companion website.

The *Gregory Weber Interview 15-3* file for this lesson is available on the book companion website.

You are the project manager on a new project for Southridge Video: a biography of Gregory Weber. An interview with Gregory Weber is a part of the production phase of the overall project. Make the Gregory Weber Interview an inserted project of the Gregory Weber Biography project schedule, inserted below the Production task.

OPEN *Gregory Weber Biography 15-3* from the data files for this lesson.

1. Click the name of task 11, **Post-Production**.

2. On the Ribbon, click the **Project** tab, then click **Subproject**.

3. Using the Insert Project dialog box, find and select the *Gregory Weber Interview 15-3* file, then click **Insert**.

4. On the Ribbon, click the **Task** tab, then click the **Indent** button (green arrow).

5. Click the **plus sign** (+) next to the Gregory Weber Interview task name. (If necessary, identify the location of the file.)

6. **SAVE** the project schedule as *Gregory Weber Biography Consolidated*. If you are prompted to save changes to the inserted project, click the **Yes to All** button. **CLOSE** the file.

   PAUSE. Leave Project open to use in the next exercise.

Project 15-4: Southridge Video Consolidated Dependencies

The *Don Funk Music Video 15-4* and *Gregory Weber Interview 15-4* files for this lesson are available on the book companion website.

You need to create a consolidated project schedule for Southridge Video, and then you need to create a dependency between the inserted projects.

OPEN *Don Funk Music Video 15-4* and *Gregory Weber Interview 15-4* from the data files for this lesson.

SAVE the files as *Don Funk Dependency* and *Gregory Weber Dependency*.

1. On the Ribbon, click the **View** tab, then click **New Window**.

2. In the Projects list, select the names of both open projects. After you have selected both project schedules, click **OK**.

3. **SAVE** the consolidated project schedule as *Southridge Video Dependency*. If you are prompted to save changes to the inserted projects, click the **Yes to All** button.

4. Make sure the consolidated project schedule is visible in the active window.

5. Click the name of Don Funk Music Video task 72.

6. Hold down the **Ctrl** key and click the name of task 5, **Set up for interview**.

7. Press the **F2** key to link the tasks.

8. Click the name of task 72 of the Don Funk Dependency inserted project, then scroll the Gantt chart so the Gantt bar for this task is visible.

9. **SAVE** all project schedules and **CLOSE** all files.

   PAUSE. LEAVE Project open to use in the next exercise.

■ Mastery Assessment

Project 15-5: Consolidating Three Projects

In addition to two Human Resource-based projects you manage, you have also been asked to oversee the remodel of the lunchroom at your office. You have decided to put all three projects into one consolidated project so that you can see all of your responsibilities in a single place.

OPEN *HR Interview Schedule 15-5, Office Remodel 15-5*, and *New Employee Orientation 15-5* from the data files for this lesson.

The *HR Interview Schedule 15-5, Office Remodel 15-5*, and *New Employee Orientation 15-5* files for this lesson are available on the book companion website.

SAVE the files as *HR Interview 3Consolidated, Office Remodel 3Consolidated*, and *New Employee 3Consolidated*.

1. Insert all three project schedules into a new project schedule.
2. **SAVE** the new project schedule as *Triple Consolidated*. If you are prompted to save changes to the inserted projects, click the **Yes to All** button.
3. Activate the summary task for this project schedule.
4. Zoom the Gantt chart to show the entire project.
5. **SAVE** all the project schedules.

   LEAVE Project and the project schedules open to use in the next exercise.

Project 15-6: Establishing Dependencies in a Triple-Consolidated Schedule

Now that you have created a consolidated schedule for the three projects for which you are responsible, you also need to establish some dependencies across the inserted projects.

USE the *Triple Consolidated, HR Interview 3Consolidated*, and *New Employee 3Consolidated* project schedules you created in the previous exercise.

1. Link task 31 of HR Interview 3Consolidated with task 3 of New Employee 3Consolidated by making task 31 a predecessor of task 3. (*Hint:* Make sure that New Employee 3Consolidated is in the active window, and use the Predecessors tab of the Task Information dialog box to make task 31 of HR Interview 3Consolidated a predecessor of New Employee3 Consolidated.)
2. Change the active window to Triple Consolidated, and review the link you just created.
3. **SAVE** the project schedule as *Triple Consolidated Dependency*. If you are prompted to save changes to the inserted projects, click the **Yes to All** button.
4. **CLOSE** all open files.

   CLOSE Project.

INTERNET READY

In this lesson, you learned how to create a consolidated project file, and how to link tasks between inserted project files. These skills are important because in real life, it is rare that anyone manages only a single project at a time. In fact, taking on new projects and multitasking seems to be the trend in today's business (and personal) world. By multitasking, you can accomplish more—but not everyone is born with the knack for managing multiple projects. It is a skill you need to practice and fine-tune.

Search the Internet for information on managing multiple projects. Look for information that will help you fine-tune your project management skills. You might find websites, white papers, user groups, or other sources that provide helpful information. Take note of what you find from these multiple sources. Develop a bulleted list or write a few paragraphs that highlight practical suggestions that will help you better manage multiple projects.

Working with Resource Pools

LESSON SKILL MATRIX

SKILL	TASK
Developing a Resource Pool	Develop a resource pool.
Viewing Assignment Details in a Resource Pool	View assignment details in the resource pool.
Revising Assignments in a Sharer File	Revise assignments in a sharer file.
Updating Resource Information in a Resource Pool	Update working time for a resource in a resource pool.
Updating Working Time for All Projects in a Resource Pool	Update working time for all sharer files via the resource pool.
Adding New Project Schedules to a Resource Pool	Add new files to the resource pool.
Revising a Sharer File and Updating a Resource Pool	Revise a sharer file and manually update the resource pool.

You are a project manager for Southridge Video, and recently one of your primary responsibilities has been to manage the new Don Funk Music Video project. However, you also have several other projects to manage. These projects often share resources and are worked on simultaneously. Microsoft Project has several features that facilitate working with multiple project schedules. In this lesson, you learn how to work with a resource pool, as well as how to review consolidated projects and their relation to resource pools.

KEY TERMS
line manager
program office
resource manager
resource pool
sharer files

■ SOFTWARE ORIENTATION

The Share Resources Dialog Box
In Microsoft Project, you can use the Share Resources dialog box (see Figure 16-1) to create a resource pool.

Figure 16-1

Share Resources dialog box

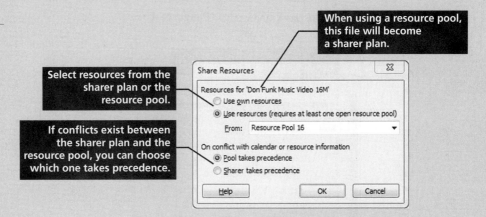

When using a resource pool, this file will become a sharer plan.

Select resources from the sharer plan or the resource pool.

If conflicts exist between the sharer plan and the resource pool, you can choose which one takes precedence.

The Share Resources dialog box enables you to select the options you want when creating a resource pool, including the project schedule or resource pool to which you want to add your file as a sharer file. You can also specify whether you want the resource pool or the sharer file to take precedence in case of conflict.

■ Developing a Resource Pool

↓ **THE BOTTOM LINE**   A resource pool can help a project manager see the extent to which resources are utilized across multiple and simultaneous projects.

 → **DEVELOP A RESOURCE POOL**

The ***Don Funk Music Video 16M*** file for this lesson is available on the book companion website.

The ***Adventure Works Promo 16M*** file for this lesson is available on the book companion website.

Create

GET READY. Before you begin these steps, launch Microsoft Project.

1. **OPEN** the ***Don Funk Music Video 16M*** project schedule from the data files for this lesson.
2. **SAVE** the file as ***Don Funk Music Video 16*** in the solutions folder for this lesson, as directed by your instructor.
3. **OPEN** the ***Adventure Works Promo 16M*** project schedule from the data files for this lesson.
4. **SAVE** the file as ***Adventure Works Promo 16*** in the solutions folder for this lesson, as directed by your instructor.
5. On the Ribbon, click the **File** tab, then click **New**. In the Available Templates section, click **Blank Project**, then click the **Create** button. A blank project opens.
6. On the Ribbon, click the **File** tab, then click **Save As**.
7. In the Save in box, locate your solution folder, as directed by your instructor. In the File name box, key ***Resource Pool 16***, then click **Save**.

Although you can choose any name you want for a resource pool, it is a good idea to indicate that it is a resource pool as part of the filename.

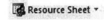

8. On the Ribbon, click the **View** tab; then, in the Window group, click **Arrange All**. Microsoft Project arranges the three project schedule windows within the Microsoft Project window. (It is not necessary to arrange the project windows this way to create a resource pool, but it is helpful for viewing purposes in this lesson.)

9. On the Ribbon, click **Resource Sheet**. Your screen should look similar to Figure 16-2.

Figure 16-2

Resource Sheet views of all three project files

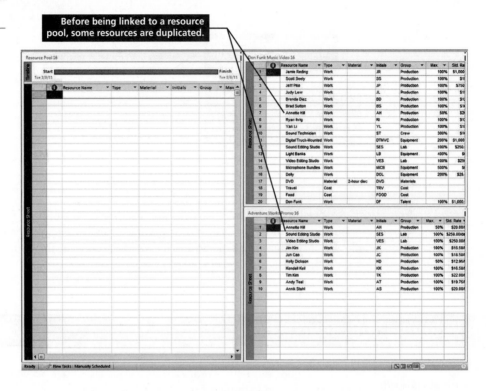

Notice that in the resource lists for the two project schedules, several resources appear in both lists. These include Annette Hill, Jane Clayton, Sound Technician, electrician, and microphone bundles, among others. None of these resources are overallocated in either project.

10. Click the **title bar** of the Don Funk Music Video 16 window.

11. On the Ribbon, click the **Resources** tab, then select the **Resource Pool** button. From the drop-down list, click **Share Resources**. The Share Resources dialog box appears.

12. Under *Resources for 'Don Funk Music Video 16'*, click **Use resources**. In the From: list, select **Resource Pool 16** from the drop-down list, if it is not already selected. Your screen should look similar to Figure 16-3.

Figure 16-3

Share Resources dialog box

13. Click **OK** to close the Share Resources dialog box. The resource information from the Don Funk Music Video 16 project schedule appears in the Resource Pool 16 file.

14. Click the **title bar** of the Adventure Works Promo 16 window.

15. On the Ribbon, click the **Resources** tab, then select the **Resource Pool** button. From the drop-down list, click **Share Resources**. The Share Resources dialog box appears.

16. Under Resources for 'Adventure Works Promo 16,' click **Use resources**. In the From: list, make sure that **Resource Pool 16** is selected.

17. Under the On conflict with calendar or resource information label, make sure that **Pool takes precedence** is selected. Selecting this option causes Microsoft Project to use resource information (such as cost rates) in the resource pool rather than in the sharer file should it find any differences between the two project schedules.

18. Click **OK** to close the Share Resources dialog box. The resource information from the Adventure Works Promo 16 project schedule appears in the resource pool. Your screen should look similar to Figure 16-4.

Figure 16-4

Resource Pool 16 with resources shared

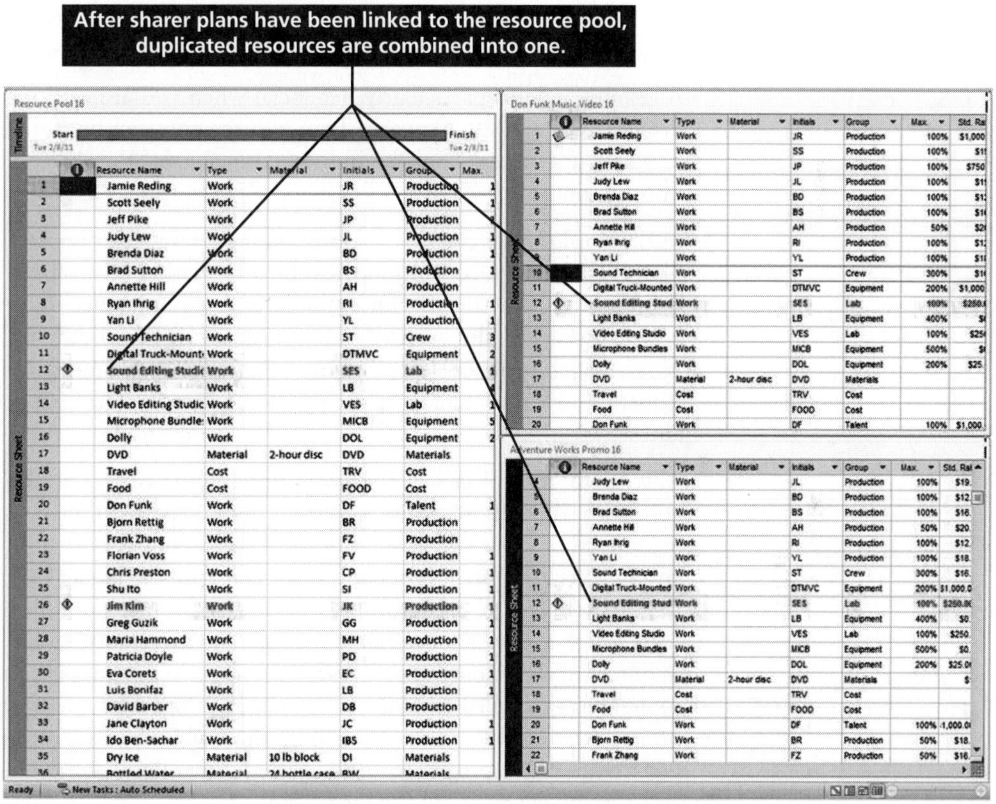

TAKE NOTE*

If you decide at some point in the future that you do not want to use a resource pool with a project schedule, you can break the link. On the Ribbon, click the Resources tab, then click the Resource Pool button. From the drop-down list, click Share Resources. Finally, in the Share Resources dialog box, under Resources for '<current project name>', click Use own resources.

After sharer plans have been linked to the resource pool, duplicated resources are combined into one.

19. **SAVE** each project schedule by clicking its title bar, then clicking the **File** tab, and then clicking **Save**.

PAUSE. LEAVE Project open to use in the next exercise.

In this exercise, you created a resource pool across two individual project schedules. A **_resource pool_** is a project file from which other project schedules gather their resource information, and it contains only resource information. As a project manager works to manage multiple projects, work resources are often assigned to more than one project at a time. It can be difficult to manage the resources' time among multiple projects, especially if different project managers are involved for each project. For example, a technical editor might have task assignments on three different productions. In each project, the editor might be fully allocated or even underallocated, but when you add together all of the tasks from the three projects, you might find that the editor is actually overallocated.

A resource pool can help you monitor how resources are utilized across multiple projects. It contains information about all resources' task assignments from all the project schedules linked to the resource pool. If you change resource information—such as cost rates, maximum units, and nonworking time—in the resource pool, all linked project schedules will use the updated information. The project schedules that are linked to the resource pool are called *sharer files*.

If you manage only one project and your resources are not used in other projects, then using a resource pool will provide no additional benefit. However, if your organization must manage multiple projects at the same time, setting up a resource pool allows you to do such things as:

- Enter resource information once, but use it in multiple project schedules
- View resources' assignment details from multiple projects in a single place
- View assignment costs per resource across multiple projects
- Identify resources that are overallocated across multiple projects, even if they are only fully allocated or underallocated in individual projects
- Enter resource information, such as nonworking time, in any of the individual schedules or in the resource pool so that it is available in the other sharer files

A resource pool is particularly beneficial when you are working with other Microsoft Project users across a network. The resource pool can be stored in a central location—such as a network server—and the individual owners of the sharer files can share the network resource pool.

In the previous exercise, the resource pool contains the resource information from both sharer files. Microsoft Project consolidates the information from sharer files based on the name of the resource. Annette Hill, for example, is listed only once in the resource pool, no matter how many sharer files list her as a resource. Keep in mind, however, that Microsoft Project *cannot* match variations of a resource's name—say, Annette Hill from one sharer file and Annette L. Hill from another. Thus, it's good to develop a convention for naming a resource and stick with it.

Any Microsoft Project schedule, with or without tasks, can serve as a resource pool. It is a good idea, though, to specify a file that does not contain tasks as the resource pool. This is because any project with tasks will come to an end at some point, and you might not want assignments for those tasks (along with their costs and other details) to be included indefinitely in the resource pool. In addition, a dedicated resource pool file without tasks allows people such as line managers or resource managers to maintain some information about their resources in the resource pool. A *line manager* is a manager of a group of resources and is sometimes also called a functional manager. A *resource manager* oversees resource usage in project activities specifically to manage the time and cost of resources. These people might not have a role in project management, and therefore, they would not need to deal with task-specific details in the resource pool.

■ Viewing Assignment Details in a Resource Pool

THE BOTTOM LINE By viewing project assignments in a resource pool, you can see, in a combined format, how all resources for the sharer projects are allocated.

 VIEW ASSIGNMENT DETAILS IN THE RESOURCE POOL

USE the project schedules you created in the previous exercise.

1. Double-click the **title bar** of the Resource Pool 16 window. The resource pool window maximizes to fill the active window. In the resource pool, you can view all resources from the two sharer files.

Resource
Pool ▾

2. On the Ribbon, click the **View** tab, then click **Resource Usage**. The Resource Usage view appears.

3. In the Resource Name column, scroll to select the name of resource 14, **Video Editing Studio**. Click the **plus sign (+)** next to Video Editing Studio's name to expand its assignment list. Your screen should look similar to Figure 16-5.

Figure 16-5

Resource Usage view with all of the Video Editing Studio assignments showing

Video Editing Studio resource has been expanded to show all tasks assigned.

X REF

For a review of resolving problems with resource allocation, see Lesson 6.

☐ Details   ▾

4. Press **Ctrl + Shift + F5**. The timescale details on the right side of the active window scroll horizontally to show the Video Editing Studio's earliest assignments.

5. Scroll the timescale details to the right until you can see the assignments for the Video Editing Studio during the weeks of July 3, 2011, and July 10, 2011.

6. On the Ribbon, click the **Details** check box. The Resource Usage/Resource Form combination view is activated. Your screen should look similar to Figure 16-6. Your projects may be listed in a different order in the Resource Form window depending on which one you opened first.

Figure 16-6

Combination view consisting of the Resource Usage view (top) and the Resource Form (bottom) for the Video Editing Studio

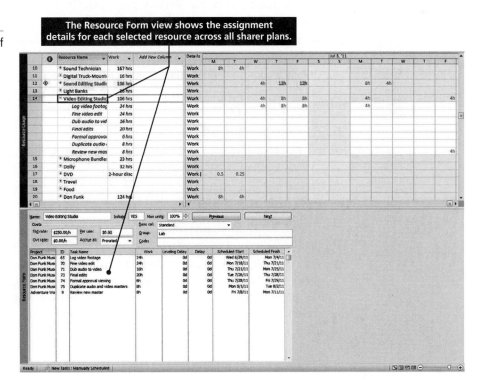

The Resource Form view shows the assignment details for each selected resource across all sharer plans.

In this view, you can see all of the resources in the resource pool and their assignments (in the upper pane), as well as the additional details for the resources (in the lower pane) for all sharer files. Note, for example, that the Fine video edit task to which the Video Editing Studio is assigned is from the Don Funk Music Video project, and the Review new master task is from the Adventure Works Promo project. Although the Video Editing Studio was not overallocated in either project, it is actually overallocated when you look at its assignments across projects in this way.

Take a minute to select different resource names in the Resource Usage view and review their assignment details in the Resource Form.

7. On the Ribbon, clear the **Details** check box.

8. **SAVE** the project schedule.

PAUSE. LEAVE Project open to use in the next exercise.

In this lesson, you changed the view of the resource pool to be better able to view and analyze the information it contains. One of the most important benefits of using a resource pool is that it enables you to see how resources are allocated across projects. You can pinpoint resources that are overallocated across the multiple projects to which they are assigned.

■ Revising Assignments in a Sharer File

 **THE BOTTOM LINE**
When you make changes to resource assignments in a sharer file, these changes will be reflected in the resource pool as well.

⊕ REVISE ASSIGNMENTS IN A SHARER FILE

USE the project schedules you used in the previous exercise. Make sure that ***Resource Pool 16*** is the project schedule in the active window.

1. In the Resource Usage view, scroll until you see resource 40, Arlene Huff, in the Resource Name column, then click her name.

2. On the Ribbon, click the **Details** check box. In the lower window, you can see that Arlene Huff has no task assignments in either sharer file.

3. On the Ribbon, click the **Switch Windows** button, then click **Don Funk Music Video 16**. The Don Funk Music Video 16 project is now in the active window.

4. On the Ribbon, click the **Gantt chart** button. The Gantt chart appears.

5. Press the **F5** key. In the ID box, key **68**, then click **OK**. The Gantt chart view scrolls to task 68.

6. Click the name of task 68, **Rough audio edit**.

7. On the Ribbon, click the **Resource** tab, then click the **Assign Resources** button. The Assign Resources dialog box appears.

8. In the Resource Name column in the Assign Resources dialog box, select **Arlene Huff**, then click **Assign**.

9. Click **Close** to close the Assign Resources dialog box.

10. On the Ribbon, click the **View** tab, then click the **Switch Windows** button.

11. From the list, click **Resource Pool 16** to switch back to the resource pool. Arlene Huff's new task assignment appears in the resource pool. You may need to scroll the upper window (the Resource Usage view) to see Arlene Huff's name. Your screen should look similar to Figure 16-7.

Figure 16-7

Resource Pool 16 with Arlene Huff assigned to task 68 in the Don Funk project

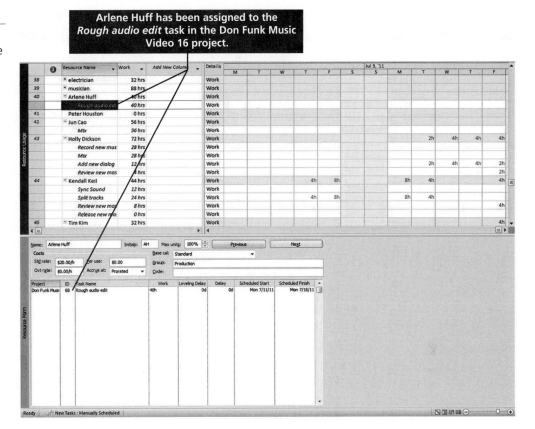

12. **SAVE** each project schedule. (You can either use the task bar at the bottom of your screen to bring each schedule to the active window to save it, or you can click **Window** on the Ribbon and then select each schedule.)

13. After saving the project schedules, make sure that **Resource Pool 16** is in the active window.

PAUSE. LEAVE Project open to use in the next exercise.

 **ANOTHER WAY**   You can also use the Go To dialog box (the F5 key) and enter Arlene's resource ID number to move the view to Arlene Huff's name.

In this exercise, you made a resource assignment from the resource pool into a sharer file, then viewed the change posted to the resource pool. Recall that an assignment is the matching of a resource to a task. The resource's assignment details originate in a sharer file, and Microsoft Project updates the resource pool with assignment details as you make them in the sharer file.

■ Updating Resource Information in a Resource Pool

THE BOTTOM LINE When a resource's information is updated in a resource pool, it is also updated in all sharer files linked to that resource pool.

→ UPDATE WORKING TIME FOR A RESOURCE IN A RESOURCE POOL

USE the project schedules you used in the previous exercise.

You have just been told that Jim Kim is not available to work on July 7–8, 2011, because he will be attending a training program.

1. In the Resource Name column, scroll to select resource name 26, **Jim Kim**.

2. Click the **plus sign** (+) next to Jim Kim's name to display all of his assignments below his name. If necessary, scroll the Resource Usage view vertically so that all of Jim Kim's assignments are visible. Note that Jim is assigned 24 hours of work on the task of Add new dialog for the Adventure Works Promo 16 project during the week of July 3.

3. Double-click **Jim Kim's** name. The Resource Information dialog box appears. Click the **General** tab, if necessary.

4. Click the **Change Working Time** button. The Change Working Time dialog box appears.

5. Drag the vertical scroll bar or click the arrows next to the calendar until July 2011 appears.

6. Select the dates July 7 and July 8.

7. On the Exceptions tab below the calendar, under the Name column heading, click the first empty cell. Key **Training Class** and press **Enter**. Microsoft Project fills the Start and Finish cells with 7/7/2011 and 7/8/2011 respectively, and it sets these dates to nonworking time. Your screen should look like Figure 16-8.

Figure 16-8

Change Working Time dialog box for Jim Kim

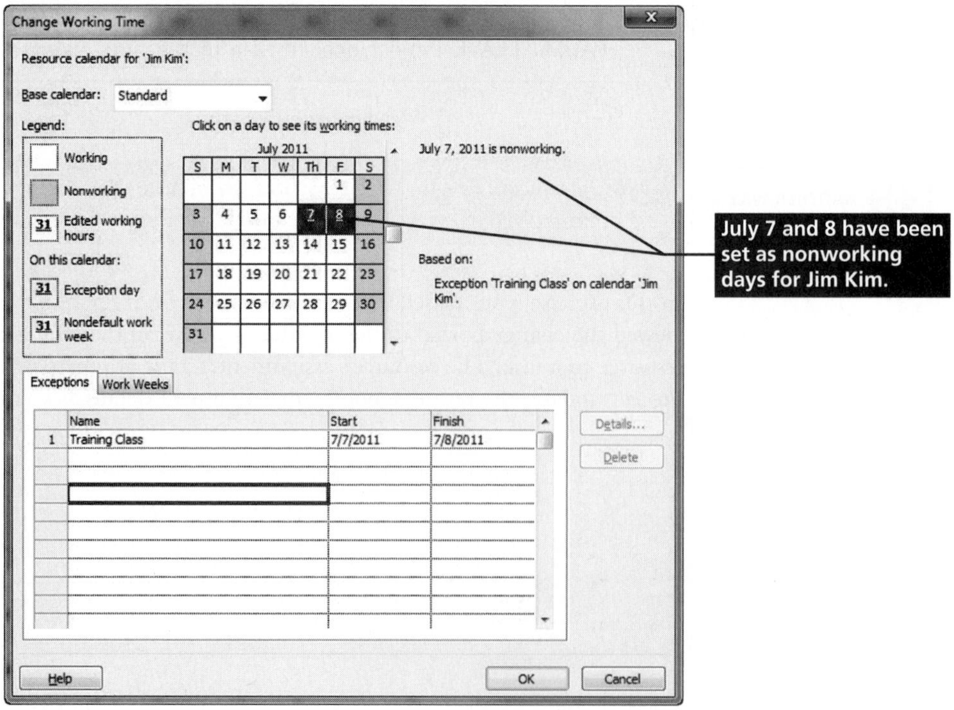

8. Click **OK** to close the Change Working Time dialog box. Click **OK** again to close the Resource Information dialog box. Scroll the screen so that July 7 and July 8 are visible. Notice that Jim Kim now has no work scheduled for July 7 and July 8, 2011 (previously he did). Your screen should look similar to Figure 16-9.

Figure 16-9

Resource Usage view showing nonworking days for Jim Kim

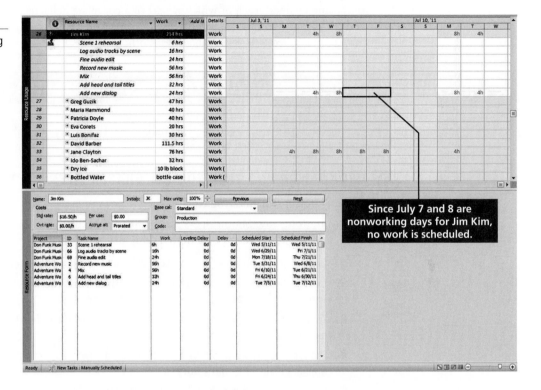

Since July 7 and 8 are nonworking days for Jim Kim, no work is scheduled.

9. On the Ribbon, click the **Switch Windows** button, then click **Adventure Works Promo 16**.

10. In the Resource Name column, select the resource name of **Jim Kim** (resource 26).

11. Double-click **Jim Kim's** name. In the Resource Information dialog box that appears, click the **Change Working Time** button. The Change Working Time dialog box appears.

12. Drag the vertical scroll bar or click the arrows next to the calendar until July 2011 appears. Click the date **July 7**, then click **July 8**. The notes next to the calendar indicate that both of these days are nonworking days.

13. Click **Cancel** to close the Change Working Time dialog box. Click **Cancel** again to close the Resource Information dialog box.

14. **SAVE** all of the project schedules.

PAUSE. LEAVE Project open to use in the next exercise.

In this exercise, you updated a resource's calendar in the resource pool, then verified that this change was reflected in the sharer file. This is another key benefit of using resource pools—you have a central location to enter resource details, such as working time and cost rates, and any updates you make to the resource pool are made available in all of the sharer files. This is particularly useful in organizations with large numbers of resources working on multiple projects. In larger organizations, employees such as line managers, resource managers, or even staff in a program office may be responsible for keeping general resource information updates. A *program office* is a group that oversees a collection of projects (such as producing doors and producing engines), each of which is part of a complete deliverable (such as an automobile) and the organization's strategic objectives. Depending on the organization, a program office may also be called a project management office, or PMO.

■ Updating Working Time for All Projects in a Resource Pool

↓
THE BOTTOM LINE

Any working time change that you make in a resource pool will update to all sharer files.

→ UPDATE WORKING TIME FOR ALL SHARER FILES VIA THE RESOURCE POOL

USE the project schedules you used in the previous exercise.

The entire company (Southridge Video) will be attending a company picnic on July 15, 2011, and you want this to be a nonworking day for all sharer projects.

Change Working Time

1. On the Ribbon, click the **Switch Windows** button, then click **Resource Pool 16.**
2. On the Ribbon, click the **Project** tab, then click the **Change Working Time** button. The Change Working Time dialog box appears.
3. In the *For calendar* box, select **Standard (Project Calendar)** from the drop-down menu.
4. Drag the vertical scroll bar or click the arrows next to the calendar until July 2011 appears. Click the date **July 15.**
5. On the Exceptions tab below the calendar, under the Name column heading, click the first empty cell. Key **Company Picnic** and press **Enter.** Microsoft Project fills the Start and Finish cells with 7/15/2011 and sets the time to nonworking. Your screen should look similar to Figure 16-10.

Figure 16-10

Change Working Time dialog box for the Project Calendar

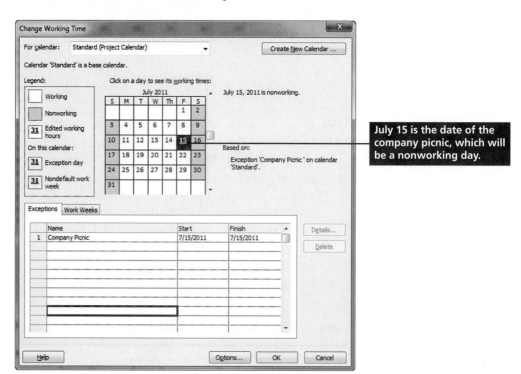

6. Click **OK** to close the Change Working Time dialog box.

7. On the Ribbon, click the **View** tab, then click the **Switch Windows** button, and next click **Don Funk Music Video 16**.

8. On the Ribbon, click the **Project** tab, then click the **Change Working Time** button. The Change Working Time dialog box appears.

9. Make sure that **Standard (Project Calendar)** is selected in the *For calendar* box, then drag the vertical scroll bar or click the arrows next to the calendar until July 2011 appears. Notice that July 15, 2011, is flagged as a nonworking day and the details are shown on the Exceptions tab below the calendar.

10. Click **Cancel** to close the Change Working Time dialog box.

If you desire, you can switch the view to the Adventure Works Promo 16 project and use the same steps to verify that July 15, 2011, is also a nonworking day for that project.

11. **SAVE** all the project schedules, then **CLOSE** all the files.

PAUSE. LEAVE Project open to use in the next exercise.

In this exercise, you made a change to the base calendar for the resource pool, then verified this change in one of the sharer files. This is another key advantage of using a resource pool. By changing the base calendar for the resource pool, the change is updated for *all* sharer files that use that calendar.

TROUBLESHOOTING

By default, all sharer files share the same base calendars, and any changes you make in a base calendar in one sharer file are reflected in all other sharer files using that base calendar through the resource pool. If you have a certain sharer file for which you want to use different base calendar working times, you must change the base calendar that sharer file uses. This different base calendar will still be available for use in all other sharer files through the resource pool, but it will apply only to those sharer files in which you select it as the base calendar.

■ Adding New Project Schedules to a Resource Pool

↓
THE BOTTOM LINE

Project schedules can be made into sharer files for a resource pool at any time. For this reason, it is a good idea to make all project schedules into sharer files (once you have set up a resource pool).

The *Resource Pool 16MA* file for this lesson is available on the book companion website.

Resource Sheet ▾

→ **ADD NEW FILES TO THE RESOURCE POOL**

GET READY. To add new files to the resource pool, do the following:

1. **OPEN** *Resource Pool 16MA* from the data files for this lesson. When prompted, click the **second option** to open the file as read-write, then click **OK**.

2. **SAVE** the file as *Resource Pool 16A* in the solutions folder for this lesson, as directed by your instructor.

3. On the Ribbon, click the **View** tab, then click **Resource Sheet**. The Resource Sheet View appears.

> **TAKE NOTE★** The default option is for Microsoft Project to open resource pools as read-only. You might want to choose this option if you and other Microsoft Project users are sharing a resource pool across a network. However, if you store the resource pool locally, you should open it as read-write.

4. On the Ribbon, clear the check box for **Details** in the Split View group.

5. On the Ribbon, click the **File** tab, then select **New**. Click **Blank Project**, then click the **Create** button.

6. On the Ribbon, click the **File** tab, then click **Save As**. The Save As dialog box appears.

7. In the *Save in* box, locate your solution folder as directed by your instructor. In the *File name* box, key **Coho Winery Project 16**, then click **Save**.

8. On the Ribbon, click the **Resource** tab, then click the **Assign Resources** button. The Assign Resources dialog box appears.

The Assign Resources box is currently empty because you have not yet entered any resource information into this project schedule.

9. On the Ribbon, click the **Resource Pool** button, then click **Share Resources**. The Share Resources dialog box appears.

10. Under *Resources for 'Coho Winery Project 16,'* select **Use Resources**.

11. In the *From* list, make sure that **Resource Pool 16A** is selected in the drop-down list. Your screen should look similar to Figure 16-11.

Figure 16-11

Share Resources dialog box

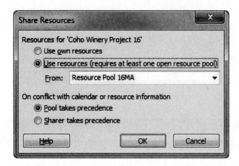

12. Click **OK** to close the Share Resources dialog box. In the Assign Resources dialog box, you can now see all of the resources from the resource pool. These resources are now ready for assignment to tasks in this project. Your screen should look similar to Figure 16-12.

Figure 16-12

Assign Resources dialog box for Coho Winery Project 16

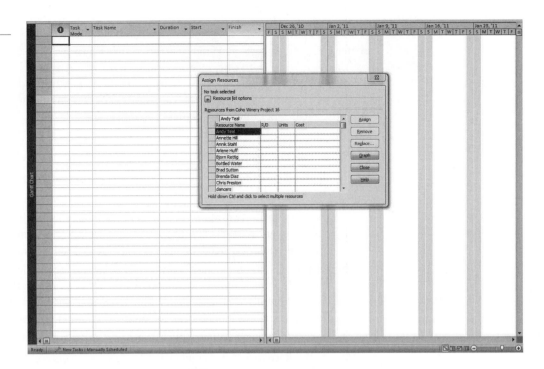

13. Click **Close** to close the Assign Resources dialog box.

14. **SAVE** the project schedules, then **CLOSE** the files.

PAUSE. LEAVE Project open to use in the next exercise.

In this exercise, you created a project schedule and made it a sharer file for the resource pool. You can do this at any time: when initially entering the project schedule's tasks, after you have assigned resources to tasks, or even after work has begun. Once you have set up a resource pool, you might find it helpful to make sharer files of projects in progress and of all new projects. This is a good way to become accustomed to relying on the resource pool for resource information.

■ Revising a Sharer File and Updating a Resource Pool

↓
THE BOTTOM LINE

Sometimes, you may have a resource pool open as read-only. In this case, you must manually update resource information to the resource pool.

⊙ **REVISE A SHARER FILE AND MANUALLY UPDATE THE RESOURCE POOL**

GET READY. To revise a sharer file and manually update the resource pool, do the following:

1. **OPEN** *Adventure Works Promo 16* from your solution files for this lesson (this is a project schedule you used in a previous exercise, but we want to open it now as read-only). Select the **Open resource pool to see assignments across all sharer files** option, then click **OK**.

2. On the Ribbon, click the **View** tab, then click **Gantt chart**.

3. In the Task Name column, click the name of task 6, **Add head and tail titles**. Press **Ctrl + Shift + F5** to bring the data into view.

4. On the Ribbon, click the **Resource** tab, then click the **Assign Resources** button. The Assign Resources dialog box appears.

5. In the Resource Name column in the Assign Resources dialog box, select **Frank Zhang**, then click the **Assign** button.

> **TAKE NOTE***
>
> Keep in mind that only assignment information is saved to the resource pool from the sharer file. Any changes you make in the sharer file to resource details, such as cost rates or Max. units, are not saved in the resource pool when you update. If you want to change resource details, you must open the resource pool as read-write. Once it is open as read-write, you can change resource details in either the resource pool or the sharer file, and Microsoft Project will update the other file.

6. In the Task Name column, click the name of task 9, **Review new master**.

7. In the Resource Name column in the Assign Resources dialog box, select **Holly Dickson**, then click the **Remove** button.

   You have made two assignment changes in the sharer file. Because the resource pool is open as read-only, these changes were not automatically saved in the resource pool. You need to update the resource pool manually.

8. On the Ribbon, click the **Resource Pool** button, then click **Update Resource Pool**. Microsoft Project updates the assignment information in the resource pool file with the new details from the sharer file. If anyone opens or refreshes the resource pool from now on, the updated assignment information will be available.

9. In the Task Name column, click the name of task 3, **Sync Sound**.

10. In the Resource Name column in the Assign Resources dialog box, select **Arlene Huff**, then click the **Assign** button.

11. Click the **Close** button to close the Assign Resources dialog box. Your screen should look similar to Figure 16-13.

Figure 16-13

Adventure Works Promo schedule with revised resources

12. On the Ribbon, click the **File** tab, then click **Close**. When prompted to save changes, click **Yes**. Microsoft Project determines that because the resource pool was opened as read-only, the assignment changes you just made in the sharer file have not been updated in the resource pool file. A dialog box appears, and you are offered a choice as to whether you want to update the resource pool. Your screen should look similar to Figure 16-14.

Figure 16-14

Dialog box asking to save the resource pool information

13. After you review the options in the dialog box, click **OK**. Microsoft Project updates the assignment information with the new details from the sharer file. The resource pool remains open as read-only.

14. On the Ribbon, click the **File** tab, then click **Close**. Because the resource pool was opened as read-only, Microsoft Project closes it without prompting you to save changes.

PAUSE. If you are continuing to the next lesson, keep Project open. If you are not continuing to additional lessons, **CLOSE** Project.

In this exercise, you made changes to a sharer file and updated a resource pool that had been opened as read-only (as if you were on a network, rather than working with local files). This is an important concept because if you are sharing a resource pool with other Microsoft Project users across a network, whoever has the resource pool open as read-write prevents others from updating resource information. For this reason, it is a good idea to open the resource pool as read-only and to use the Update Resource Pool command only when you need to update the resource pool with assignment information. Once this is done, anyone else who opens the resource pool will see the latest assignment information.

SKILL SUMMARY

IN THIS LESSON, YOU LEARNED:	TASK
To develop a resource pool.	Develop a resource pool.
To view assignment details in a resource pool.	View assignment details in the resource pool.
To revise assignments in a sharer file.	Revise assignments in a sharer file.
To update resource information in a resource pool.	Update working time for a resource in a resource pool.
To update working time for all projects in a resource pool.	Update working time for all sharer files via the resource pool.
To add new project schedules to a resource pool.	Add new files to the resource pool.
To revise a sharer file and update a resource pool.	Revise a sharer file and manually update the resource pool.

■ Knowledge Assessment

Matching

Match the term in column 1 to its description in column 2.

Column 1

1. Line manager

2. Resource pool

3. Assignment

Column 2

a. Project schedules that are linked to the resource pool

b. A group that oversees a collection of projects, each of which may be part of a complete deliverable

c. Situation in which the work assigned to a resource is more than can be done within the normal work capacity of the resource

4. Program office   d. A manager of a group of resources

5. Underallocated   e. Dialog box that enables you to specify how resources will be used across project schedules

6. Resource manager   f. A project file from which other project schedules gather their resource information

7. Split view   g. The matching of a resource to a task

8. Share Resources   h. An active view that is composed of two views that divide the screen horizontally

9. Overallocated   i. The work assigned to a resource is less than the resource's maximum capacity

10. Sharer file   j. A manager who oversees resource usage in project activities to manage the time and cost of resources

True/False

Circle T if the statement is true or F if the statement is false.

T | F 1. You can link a maximum of three sharer files to a resource pool.

T | F 2. Any Microsoft Project schedule can serve as a resource pool.

T | F 3. If you decide that you do not want to use a resource pool with a project schedule, it is possible to break the link between the resource pool and sharer file.

T | F 4. If you have a resource pool open as read-only and make changes to a sharer file, only assignment information is saved to the resource pool from the sharer file.

T | F 5. Microsoft Project does not update the resource pool with assignment details as you make them in the sharer file.

T | F 6. When you save a resource pool, you must use "resource pool" as part of the filename.

T | F 7. A project schedule can be made into a sharer file for a resource pool only before work has started.

T | F 8. For a resource pool on a network, multiple users can simultaneously have the resource pool open as read-write.

T | F 9. If you change resource information, such as cost rates, in a resource pool, all linked projects will use the updated information.

T | F 10. By default, all sharer files use the same base calendar.

■ Competency Assessment

Project 16-1: Adding a Sharer File to the Southridge Video Resource Pool

You have created a resource pool for two of the Southridge Video projects on which you are working. You have been assigned to work on another project, and you want to add this sharer file to the resource pool as well.

GET READY. Launch Microsoft Project if it is not already running.

OPEN *Southridge Video Resource Pool 16-1* from the data files for this lesson. When prompted, click the second option to open the file as read-write, then click **OK**. Next, **OPEN** *Gregory Weber Biography 16-1* from the data files for this lesson.

The *Southridge Video Resource Pool 16-1* and *Gregory Weber Biography 16-1* files for this lesson are available on the book companion website.

SAVE the files as *Southridge Video Resource Pool* and *Gregory Weber Biography*.

1. On the Ribbon, click **Switch Windows**, then click *Gregory Weber Biography*.
2. On the Ribbon, click the **View** tab, then click **Resource Sheet**.

3. On the Ribbon, click the **Resource** tab, then click the **Resource Pool** button, and then click **Share Resources**.

4. Under *Resources for 'Gregory Weber Biography,'* select the **Use resources** option.

5. In the *From* list, make sure that **Southridge Video Resource Pool** is selected from the drop-down list, then click **OK**.

6. **SAVE** the project schedules.

7. **CLOSE** the *Gregory Weber Biography* project schedule. **LEAVE** the *Southridge Video Resource Pool* project schedule open.

   PAUSE. LEAVE Project open to use in the next exercise.

Project 16-2: Updating Working Time in the Southridge Video Resource Pool

Arlene Huff has just informed you that she is unable to work on June 14, 2011, due to a personal commitment. You need to update her resource information to reflect this date as nonworking time.

SAVE the open *Southridge Video Resource Pool* as *Southridge Video Resource Pool 2*.

1. On the Ribbon, click the **View** tab, then click **Resource Usage**.

2. In the Resource Name column, double-click **Arlene Huff**.

3. In the Resource Information dialog box, click the **Change Working Time** button.

4. Drag the vertical scroll bar or click the arrows next to the calendar until June 2011 appears.

5. Select the date **June 14**.

6. On the Exceptions tab below the calendar, under the Name column heading, click the first empty cell. Key **Vacation Day** and press **Enter**.

7. Click **OK** in the Change Working Time dialog box.

8. Click **OK** in the Resource Information Dialog box.

9. **SAVE** the project schedule, then **CLOSE** the file.

   PAUSE. LEAVE Project open to use in the next exercise.

■ Proficiency Assessment

Project 16-3: Revising the Employee Orientation Sharer File and Updating the HR Resource Pool

You need to make several changes to the Employee Orientation Schedule, but you want to open the HR Resource Pool as read-only so that others can still read the file while you are using it. You will then need to update the resource pool with your changes.

(To set up this exercise, you first need to build a resource pool from the Employee Orientation Schedule and HR Interview Schedule projects. After creating and saving the resource pool and sharer files, you will reopen the necessary files for this exercise.)

The *Employee Orientation Schedule 16-3* and *HR Interview Schedule 16-3* files for this lesson are available on the book companion website.

OPEN *Employee Orientation Schedule 16-3* and *HR Interview Schedule 16-3* from the data files for this lesson.

SAVE the project schedules as *Employee Orientation Schedule 3* and *HR Interview Schedule 3*.

1. **OPEN** a new, blank project schedule.

2. **SAVE** the new file as *HR Resource Pool 3*.

3. Change the view to the Resource Sheet view.

4. Arrange all three open files in the active window.

5. Use the Share Resources dialog box to add the resources from *HR Interview Schedule 3* to *HR Resource Pool 3*.

6. Use the Share Resources dialog box to add the resources from *Employee Orientation Schedule 3* to *HR Resource Pool 3*.

7. SAVE all three open files, then CLOSE the files.

8. OPEN *Employee Orientation Schedule 3* from your solution file location. When prompted, select the option to open the resource pool.

9. Make sure that the *Employee Orientation Schedule* project fills the active window. Change the view to the Gantt chart view.

10. Select the name of task 11, **Tour Customer Service Center**.

11. Activate the Assign Resources dialog box.

12. Assign Jason Watters to this task.

13. Select the name of task 10, **Measuring for uniforms**.

14. Assign Britta Simon to this task.

15. Close the Assign Resources dialog box.

16. Activate the Resource Sharing options on the Tools menu, then update the resource pool.

17. CLOSE *Employee Orientation Schedule 3*. When you are prompted to save, click **Yes**. In the dialog box that appears, click **OK**.

18. CLOSE *HR Resource Pool 3*.

PAUSE. LEAVE Project open to use in the next exercise.

Project 16-4: Updating Working Time for All Projects in Southridge Video Resource Pool

You need to make a change to working time for all employees of Southridge Video to reflect two days that everyone will be spending at the National Videographers' Conference. You need to reflect this as nonworking time in all sharer files.

OPEN *Southridge Video Resource Pool 16-4* from the data files for this lesson. When prompted, click the second option to open the file as read-write, then click **OK**. Next, OPEN *Don Funk Music Video 16-4* and *Adventure Works Promo 16-4* from the data files for this lesson.

The *Southridge Video Resource Pool 16-4*, *Don Funk Music Video 16-4*, and *Adventure Works Promo 16-4* files for this lesson are available on the book companion website.

SAVE the files as *Don Funk Music Video 4*, *Adventure Works Promo 4*, and *Southridge Video Resource Pool 4*.

1. Expand *Southridge Video Resource Pool 4* to fill the active window, if it is not already expanded.

2. Activate the Change Working Time dialog box from the Tools menu.

3. Select the **Standard (Project Calendar)** as the calendar to which you want to apply your change.

4. Select the dates of March 17-18, 2011.

5. Add the National Videographers' Conference to the Exceptions tab.

6. Close the Change Working Time dialog box.

7. Verify the working time change in the two sharer files.

8. SAVE all open project schedules, then CLOSE the files.

PAUSE. LEAVE Project open to use in the next exercise.

■ Mastery Assessment

Project 16-5: Creating a Human Resources Schedule Resource Pool

You have several human resources project schedules that are active in your department. You need to create a resource pool and link these schedules to it.

OPEN *Employee Orientation Schedule 16-5* and *HR Interview Schedule 16-5* from the data files for this lesson.

SAVE the files as *Employee Orientation Schedule* and *HR Interview Schedule*.

The *Employee Orientation Schedule 16-5* and *HR Interview Schedule 16-5* files for this lesson are available on the book companion website.

1. **OPEN** a new file and save it as *HR Resource Pool*.
2. Link the *Employee Orientation Schedule* project to the resource pool using the Share Resources dialog box.
3. Link the HR Interview Schedule project to the resource pool using the Share Resources dialog box. Make sure that the pool takes precedence.
4. **SAVE** all three project schedules.

    PAUSE. LEAVE Project and all three schedules open to use in the next exercise.

Project 16-6: Updating Assignments in a Sharer File to the HR Resource Pool

You now need to make several updates to the sharer schedules linked to the HR Resource Pool.

SAVE the open schedules from the previous exercise as *HR Resource Pool 6, HR Interview Schedule 6*, and *Employee Orientation Schedule 6*.

1. In the HR Interview Schedule 6 project schedule, for task 6, replace Keith Harris with **Garth Fort** using the Assign Resources dialog box.
2. In the HR Interview Schedule 6 project schedule, for task 19, remove Keith Harris' assignment to this task using the Assign Resources dialog box.
3. In the Employee Orientation Schedule 6 project schedule, for task 12, assign Karen Berg to this task using the Assign Resources dialog box.
4. **SAVE** all of the project schedules, then **CLOSE** the files.

    CLOSE Project.

17 LESSON

Customizing Microsoft Project

LESSON SKILL MATRIX

SKILL	TASK
Defining General Preferences	Specify the default path for use in the Open and Save As dialog boxes.
Working with Templates	Create a new template based on a current project schedule.
Working with the Organizer	Copy a custom view from one project schedule to another using the Organizer.

Now that you have worked with project schedules extensively, it is time to learn about some of the ways you can customize Microsoft Project to fit your own preferences. Some of the customization options you see in Project are similar to those you see in other Microsoft Office programs, such as Word or Excel. In this lesson, you learn how to customize some general settings, create your own templates, and use the Organizer.

KEY TERMS
global template
Organizer
template

■ **SOFTWARE ORIENTATION**

The Organizer Dialog Box

In Microsoft Project, the Organizer (see Figure 17-1) is the feature that enables you to share elements between Microsoft Project files.

Figure 17-1

Organizer dialog box

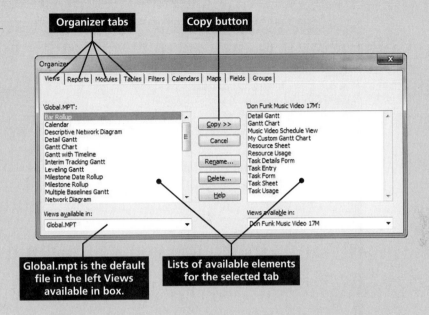

The Organizer dialog box enables you to copy views, tables, filters, and other items between the Global.mpt template and other Microsoft Project files, or between two different Microsoft Project files.

■ Defining General Preferences

 THE BOTTOM LINE   You are able to make choices that customize Microsoft Project. These choices enable you to specify personal preferences regarding how Project operates.

⊖ **SPECIFY THE DEFAULT PATH FOR USE IN THE OPEN AND SAVE AS DIALOG BOXES**

GET READY. Before you begin these steps, launch Microsoft Project.

The *Don Funk Music Video 17M* file for this lesson is available on the book companion website.

1. **OPEN** the *Don Funk Music Video 17M* project schedule from the data files for this lesson.

2. **SAVE** the file as *Don Funk Music Video 17* in the solutions folder for this lesson, as directed by your instructor.

3. On the Ribbon, click the **File** tab, then click **Options**. The Project Options dialog box appears.

4. In the Project Options dialog box, click the **Save** tab. Your screen should look similar to Figure 17-2.

Figure 17-2

Save tab of the Project Options dialog box

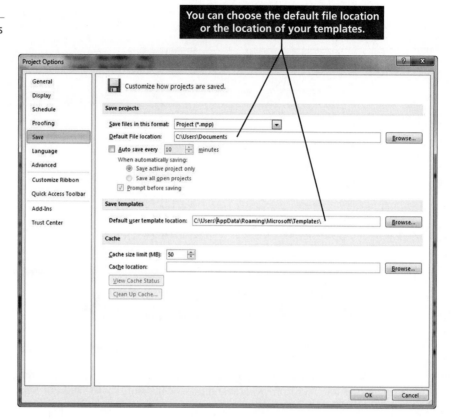

You can choose the default file location or the location of your templates.

5. In the Save Projects section, ensure **Project** is selected in the *Save Files in this format* box.

6. To the right of the Default File Locations box, click the **Browse** button. The Modify Location dialog box appears.

7. Select your desired folder location as directed by your instructor, then click **OK**. If you are not changing your file location, click **Cancel**.

8. To verify that the new location you have selected is now the default folder location, you can view the Open dialog box.

9. On the Ribbon, click **File**, then click **Open**. The Open dialog box appears, using the path you specified.

TAKE NOTE✱   Specifying the folder you want to open by default in the Open and Save As dialog boxes can be helpful if you usually keep all of your Microsoft Project files in one location.

10. Click **Cancel** to close the Open dialog box.

11. **SAVE** the project schedule.

PAUSE. LEAVE Project open to use in the next exercise.

In this exercise, you specified the folder that you wanted to open as the default in the Open and Save As dialog boxes. This can be quite helpful if you tend to keep most or all of your Microsoft Project files in one location. Like many other Microsoft Office applications, you have the capability within Microsoft Project to make choices about how you work with this application. By selecting these preferences, each person who uses Microsoft Project can personalize the software to fit his or her needs.

■ Working with Templates

THE BOTTOM LINE
A template provides the basic structure of a new project schedule. It may include information such as resources, tasks, assignments, views, tables, and more.

➔ CREATE A NEW TEMPLATE BASED ON A CURRENT PROJECT SCHEDULE

USE the project schedule you created in the previous exercise.

1. On the Ribbon, click the **File** tab, then click **Save As**. The Save As dialog box appears.
2. In the *File name* box, key **Music Video Template**.
3. In the *Save as type* box, select **Project Template**. Notice that Microsoft Project takes you to the location where templates are saved.
4. Find the file in which the Lesson 17 solutions folder is located, or find another location as directed by your instructor.
5. Click the **Save** button. The Save As Template dialog box appears.

   The *Don Funk Music Video 17* file contains both baseline and actual values, and you do not want to include these with the template.

6. Select the **Values of all baselines**, **Actual Values**, and **Fixed Costs** check boxes. You are indicating that these items should be removed from your template. Your screen should look like Figure 17-3.

Figure 17-3

Save As Template dialog box

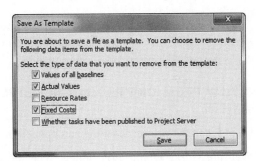

7. Click the **Save** button. Microsoft Project creates a new template based on the *Don Funk Music Video 17* file.

   Based on the options you selected in the Save As Template dialog box, Microsoft Project removes the data you chose not to include with the template. However, the task list, relationships, resources, and assignments are conserved as entered in the original *Don Funk Music Video 17* file. Thus, if Southridge Video has a similar project in the future, you could start with this template and modify it to fit the new project.

TAKE NOTE*

When you first save a template from a current Microsoft Project file, you are working in the template (note the .mpt file extension in the title bar). Any changes you make before saving and closing this file will remain in the template.

TROUBLESHOOTING

When you create a new project file based on a template, you may need to adjust more than the project start date to preserve the task relationships and schedule logic. For example, if the template contains hard constraints with dates prior to the current date, Microsoft Project may not be able to properly schedule tasks.

8. Make sure the *Music Video Template* file is in the active window. On the Ribbon, click **File**, then click **Close**. If prompted to save changes to the *Music Video Template*, click **Yes**.

9. On the Ribbon, click **File**, then click **Don Funk Music Video 17**. Microsoft Project reopens the *Don Funk Music Video 17* file, just as you left it.

10. **SAVE** the project schedule.

PAUSE. LEAVE Project open to use in the next exercise.

In this exercise, you saved your current project schedule as a template. A *template* is a Microsoft Project file format that lets you reuse an existing project schedule as the basis for a new project schedule. Templates can include any of the types of information you might expect to find in a Microsoft Project schedule, including task and resource lists, assignments, customized views, tables, and filters.

As you saw in this exercise, you can save any Microsoft Project file, at any time, as a template to use in the future. When saving a template from a current file, you usually exclude baseline and actual values, as these would not be useful as part of a template. You can also exclude things such as resource cost rates and fixed costs, if there is a need to protect this information as confidential.

■ Working with the Organizer

↓ **THE BOTTOM LINE**

The Organizer is a feature in Microsoft Project that enables you to reset custom elements or to copy elements (such as views, reports, tables, etc.) from one project schedule to another.

⊕ **COPY A CUSTOM VIEW FROM ONE PROJECT SCHEDULE TO ANOTHER USING THE ORGANIZER**

USE the *Don Funk Music Video 17* project schedule you opened in the previous exercise.

1. **OPEN** the *Adventure Works Promo 17M* project schedule from the data files for this lesson.

2. **SAVE** the file as *Adventure Works Promo 17* in the solutions folder for this lesson, as directed by your instructor.

3. On the Ribbon, click the **View** tab. In the Window group, click the **Switch Windows** button, then click **Don Funk Music Video 17**. The *Don Funk Music Video 17* project schedule is brought into the active window.

 Other Views ▾

4. On the Ribbon, click **Other Views**, then click **More Views**.

5. Select **Music Video Schedule View**, then click **Apply**. Your screen should look similar to Figure 17-4.

You'd like to copy this custom view to the Adventure Works Promo 17 project schedule using the Organizer.

Figure 17-4

Don Funk Music Video 17 schedule with the Music Video Schedule View applied

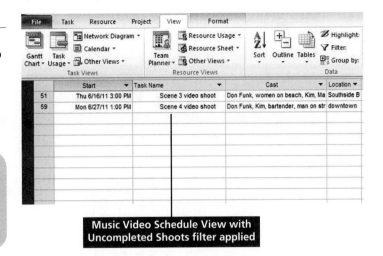

The *Adventure Works Promo 17M* file for this lesson is available on the book companion website.

Music Video Schedule View with Uncompleted Shoots filter applied

Organizer

6. On the Ribbon, click the **File** tab, then click **Organizer**. The Organizer dialog box appears. Your screen should look similar to Figure 17-5.

Figure 17-5

Organizer dialog box

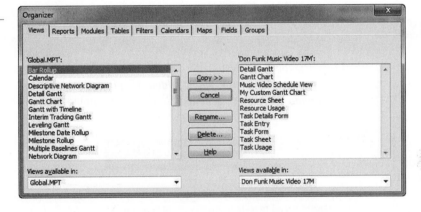

7. Click several of the tabs in the dialog box to get an overview of the available options.

Notice that each tab of the Organizer dialog box is structured in the same way: elements such as views and tables appear on the left and right sides of the dialog box. The elements on the left are from one file, and the elements on the right are from another file. By default, the elements from the Global.mpt file appear on the left side of the dialog box, and the corresponding elements from the active project file appear on the right.

TAKE NOTE*

The global template is a Microsoft Project template named Global.mpt.

Selecting an element on the left side of the dialog box and then clicking the Copy button will copy that element to the file listed on the right, and vice versa.

8. Click the **Views** tab, if it is not already selected.

9. In the *Views available in* list on the left side of the dialog box, select **Adventure Works Promo 17**. The names of the views in the *Adventure Works Promo 17* file appear on the left. Note that the *Adventure Works Promo 17* file does not contain the Music Video Schedule View.

10. In the list of views on the right side of the dialog box, click **Music Video Schedule View**. Your screen should look similar to Figure 17-6.

Figure 17-6

Organizer dialog box with the Views tab selected, showing views in both projects

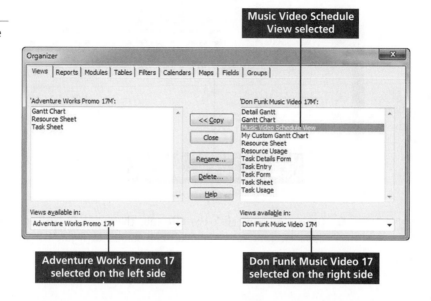

11. Click the **<<Copy** button. Microsoft Project copies the Music Video Schedule View from the *Don Funk Music Video 17* project schedule to the *Adventure Works Promo 17* project schedule. Your screen should look similar to Figure 17-7.

Figure 17-7

Organizer dialog box with Music Video Schedule View in both project files

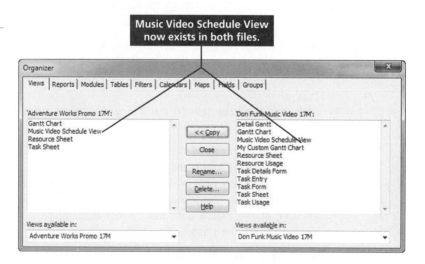

TAKE NOTE ★ Notice that the two arrow symbols (>>) beside the Copy button switch direction (<<) when you select an element on the right side of the dialog box.

12. Click the **Close** button to close the Organizer.

13. **SAVE** both project schedules.

PAUSE. LEAVE Project open to use in the next exercise.

In this exercise, you used the Organizer to share a table between two Microsoft Project files. The *Organizer* is a feature you use to organize elements between Microsoft Project files so that they can be shared, edited, and reset. The names of the tabs in the Organizer dialog box indicate the elements you can copy between project schedules.

One feature of Microsoft Project that you can work with via the Organizer is the global template, a Microsoft Project template named Global.mpt. The *global template* provides the default views, tables, and other elements in Microsoft Project, and it includes the following:

- Calendars
- Filters
- Forms
- Groups
- Import/export maps
- Ribbons
- Reports
- Tables
- Modules (macros)
- Views

At first, the specific definitions of all views, tables, and other elements are contained in the global template. The first time you display a view, table, or similar element in a Microsoft Project file, it is copied from the global template to that file. From then on, the element resides in the Microsoft Project file. If you customize that element in the Microsoft Project file (for example, you change the columns displayed in a table), the changes apply only to the Microsoft Project file, and not to the global template.

It is possible to use Microsoft Project extensively and never need to use the global template. If you do need to work with the global template, however, there are two primary actions you can accomplish with it:

- You can create a customized element, such as a custom table, and make it available in all project schedules with which you work by copying the custom view into the global template.
- You can replace a customized element, such as a custom table in a project schedule, by copying the original, unmodified element from the global template to the project schedule in which you've customized the same element.

Note that customxized data maps, modules, and toolbars are not normally stored in individual Microsoft Project files, unlike other elements with which you work via the Organizer. Instead, these elements are stored in the global template, and they are available for all Microsoft Project schedules with which you work. If you want to share a data map or module with another Microsoft Project user, you need to copy it from the global template to a Microsoft Project schedule, then send the project schedule to the other user.

When using the Organizer, if you attempt to copy a view, table, or other element from a project schedule to the global template, Microsoft Project alerts you if you will overwrite that same element in the global template. If you choose to overwrite it, the customized element (such as the Music Video Schedule View in this exercise) will be available in all new project schedules, as well as any other project schedules that do not already contain that element. If instead you choose to rename the customized element, it becomes available in all project schedules, but it does not affect the existing elements already stored in the global template. You cannot share or copy any Visual Report templates with the Organizer.

SKILL SUMMARY

IN THIS LESSON, YOU LEARNED:	TASK
To define general preferences.	Specify the default path for use in the Open and Save As dialog boxes.
To work with templates.	Create a new template based on a current project schedule.
To work with the Organizer.	Copy a custom view from one project schedule to another using the Organizer.

■ Knowledge Assessment

Fill in the Blank

Complete the following sentences by writing the correct word or words in the blanks provided.

1. The filename of the global template is _____.

2. A(n) _____ is a Microsoft Project file format that lets you use an existing project schedule as the basis for a new project schedule.

3. The _____ allows you to share elements between Microsoft Project files.

4. A template is saved to be used in the _____.

5. The names of the _____ in the Organizer dialog box indicate the elements you can copy between project schedules.

6. The _____ _____ provides the default views, tables, and other elements in Microsoft Project.

7. Actual data and _____ data should be removed from a file when creating a template.

8. The _____ tab in the Options dialog box enables you to specify where you want your files to be saved.

9. The _____ button on the Organizer allows you to erase elements from the designated file.

10. When working in a newly created template, the _____ file extension will be displayed on the title bar.

True/False

Circle T if the statement is true or F if the statement is false.

T | F 1. Your Microsoft Project files must always be stored in the default file folder.

T | F 2. When you create a template, you can choose not to include information such as baseline and actual values.

T | F 3. The two primary actions you can accomplish with a global template are to create a customized element and to replace a customized element.

T | F 4. You can share custom views, field reports, and other custom information with any other Microsoft Project file.

T | F **5.** You can save a Microsoft Project file as a template only if a baseline has not yet been saved.

T | F **6.** You must save templates in the default folder.

T | F **7.** The Global.mpt file contains all the views, tables, and other elements that have been added to the file.

T | F **8.** Templates can include information such as task and resource lists, assignments, customized views, tables, filters, and macros.

T | F **9.** It is not possible to overwrite elements in the global template.

T | F **10.** The Organizer enables you to reset custom elements in a project schedule.

■ Competency Assessment

Project 17-1: Copy the Critical Tasks Report to the Office Remodel Project Schedule

You want to copy the Critical Tasks report from the global template for use in the Office Remodel project schedule. Use the Organizer to do this.

GET READY. Launch Microsoft Project if it is not already running.
OPEN *Office Remodel 17-1* from the data files for this lesson.
SAVE the file as *Office Remodel Critical Tasks Report*.

The *Office Remodel 17-1* file for this lesson is available on the book companion website.

1. On the Ribbon, click **File**, then click **Organizer**.
2. Click the **Reports** tab, if it is not already selected.
3. Make sure that in the *Reports available in* box on the left side of the dialog box, Global.mpt is selected. Make sure that in the *Reports available in* box on the right side of the dialog box, Office Remodel Critical Tasks Report is selected.
4. In the list of reports on the left side of the dialog box, click **Critical Tasks**.
5. Click the **Copy>>** button.
6. Click **Close**.
7. **SAVE** the project schedule, then **CLOSE** the file.
   PAUSE. LEAVE Project open to use in the next exercise.

Project 17-2: HR Interview Template

Because your department is currently in hiring mode, you want to save the HR Interview project schedule as a template so that it can be used by anyone in your department to develop an interview schedule. You do not want to save baselines, cost rates, and fixed cost data in the template.

OPEN *HR Interview 17-2* from the data files for this lesson.

The *HR Interview 17-2* file for this lesson is available on the book companion website.

1. On the Ribbon, click **File**, then click **Save As**.
2. In the *File name* box, key **HR Interview Template**.
3. In the *Save as type* box, select **Template**.
4. Locate and select your Lesson 17 solution folder (or do otherwise as directed by your instructor).

5. Click the **Save** button.

6. In the Save As Template dialog box, select the **Values of all baselines**, **Actual Values**, and **Fixed Costs** check boxes.

7. Click **Save**.

8. **CLOSE** the file.

PAUSE. LEAVE Project open to use in the next exercise.

■ Proficiency Assessment

Project 17-3: Copying a Base Calendar

Your Adventure Works Promo project will use the same base calendar as the Overnight Beach Filming calendar you used in the Don Funk Music Video project. Use the Organizer to copy the base calendar to the Adventure Works project file.

OPEN *Don Funk Music Video 17-3* and *Adventure Works Promo 17-3* from the data files for this lesson.

The *Don Funk Music Video 17-3* and *Adventure Works Promo 17-3* files for this lesson are available on the book companion website.

1. Activate the Organizer from the File tab.

2. Place the Don Funk Music Video file in the left portion and the Adventure Works Promo in the right portion of the Organizer.

3. Switch to the Calendars tab.

4. Copy the Overnight Beach Filming calendar from Don Funk to Adventure Works.

5. Close the Organizer.

6. Close the Don Funk Music Video file.

7. Activate the Change Working Time dialog box in the Adventure Works Promo project. Verify the Overnight Beach Filming calendar is there.

8. **SAVE** the file as *Adventure Works Overnight Filming*, then **CLOSE** the file.

PAUSE. LEAVE Project open to use in the next exercise.

Project 17-4: Restoring a Customized Table to the Default Settings

While you were working with the Litware project schedule, you accidentally customized the default Usage table, rather than making a copy of the default table and then customizing the copy. You want to restore the customized Usage table by replacing it with the default "factory settings" Usage table from the Global.mpt file.

OPEN *Litware 17-4* from the data files for this lesson.

The *Litware 17-4* file for this lesson is available on the book companion website.

1. Change the view to the Task Usage view.

2. Activate the Organizer dialog box.

3. Activate the Tables tab.

4. Make sure that the Global.mpt table list is on the left side of the dialog box and that the Litware 17-4 table list is on the right side of the dialog box.

5. Copy the Usage table from the Global.mpt list to the Litware 17-4 list.

6. Select **Yes** when you are alerted that you are about to replace the Usage table, then close the Organizer.

7. Activate the new Usage table from the Tables list on the View menu.

8. **SAVE** the file as *Litware New Usage*.

PAUSE. LEAVE Project open to use in the next exercise.

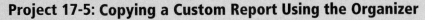

■ Mastery Assessment

Project 17-5: Copying a Custom Report Using the Organizer

You have several custom views and reports already defined in the HR Interview project schedule. You want to copy the Custom Critical Task Report from the HR Interview schedule to the Gregory Weber Biography schedule.

OPEN *Gregory Weber Biography 17-5* and *HR Interview 17-5* from the data files for this lesson.

The *Gregory Weber Biography 17-5* and *HR Interview 17-5* files for this lesson are available on the book companion website.

1. Use the Organizer to copy the Custom Critical Task Report from the *HR Interview 17-5* project schedule to the *Gregory Weber Biography 17-5 project schedule*.

2. **SAVE** the project schedules as *HR Interview Custom Critical* and *Gregory Weber Custom Critical*, then **CLOSE** the files.

   PAUSE. LEAVE Project open to use in the next exercise.

Project 17-6: Defining General Preferences

You want to set some more preferences for how Microsoft Project looks and works for you. In a separate Word or WordPad document, explain the steps you would follow to set the following preferences. Use any Microsoft Project file with which you are familiar to explore these options. DO NOT make the actual changes in the file; just explain in a separate document how you would set these preferences.

1. Use the Options dialog box to:

   • Set the number of Undo levels to **25**.

   • Have Microsoft Project prompt you for project information for new projects.

   • Have Microsoft Project automatically save your active project every 10 minutes, prompting you before saving.

2. **SAVE** the Word document as *Defining General Preferences*.

   CLOSE Project.

INTERNET READY

In this lesson, you learned how to save your project schedule as a template for use in other projects. Many Microsoft Project experts have saved their project schedules as templates and shared them on the Internet for public use. Search the Internet to find Microsoft Project templates that may be useful to you—at work, at school, at home, or in your community. Microsoft offers many templates from the Project home page, but many other sites offer templates also. Download several templates and save them to your local drive. Explore what information has been provided with each template, such as general resources (HR Manager, Line Supervisor, etc.) and task durations, as well as what information was removed by the author before saving as a template (baselines, cost rates, etc.). If possible, post one of your own project schedules (saved as a template) to the Internet to share with others.

■ Circling Back 3

Mete Goktepe is a project management specialist at Woodgrove Bank. He is managing a project schedule for a Request for Proposal (RFP) process to evaluate and select new commercial lending software. This process entails determining needs, identifying vendors, requesting proposals, reviewing proposals, and selecting the software.

Now that Mete has established the foundation of the project schedule, he will begin using some of the more advanced features of Microsoft Office Project to fine-tune the tasks and resources and to format the project schedule.

→ Project 1: Sharing and Importing Data into the Project Schedule

Acting as Mete, you need to prepare some of your data to share with stakeholders. You then must import some additional tasks and add them to the project schedule.

GET READY. OPEN *RFP Bank Software Schedule 3* from the data files for this lesson.

SAVE the file as *RFP Bank Software Imported* in the solution folder for this lesson, as directed by your instructor.

The *RFP Bank Software Schedule 3* and *RFP Additional Tasks* files for this lesson are available on the book companion website.

1. Switch the View to the Gantt chart view.
2. Switch the Table to the Entry table.
3. Adjust the table and bar chart so that only the Task Name and Duration columns are visible in the table.
4. On the Ribbon, click the **View** tab, then click **Entire Project** in the Zoom group.
5. Click the **Task** tab, click the **Copy** button in the Clipboard group, and then select **Copy Picture**.
6. In the Copy Picture dialog box, select **For printer** and click **OK**.
7. Launch either Microsoft Word or WordPad.
8. Paste the snapshot into a new, blank document to send to your stakeholders. You will finish the memo to the stakeholders later.
9. **SAVE** the document as *RFP Bank Software Memo*, then **CLOSE** the document.
10. **SAVE** the project schedule.
11. On the Ribbon, click the **File** tab, then click **Open**.
12. In the File type box, select **Excel Workbook**.
13. Locate and double-click the *RFP Additional Tasks* Microsoft Excel workbook in the data files for this exercise.
14. In the Import Wizard, select the following options:
    Map: **New map**
    Import Mode: **Append the data to the active project**
    Map Options: **Tasks, including headers**
15. On the Task Mapping page of the Import Wizard, select **Sheet 1** from the Source worksheet name list.
16. Click **Finish**.
17. **SAVE** the project schedule.
    PAUSE. LEAVE Project and the project schedule open to use in the next exercise.

Project 2: Working with Contours, WBS Codes, and Interim Plans

Next, you want to apply a work contour to one of Kevin Kennedy's assignments. You will then add Unique ID and WBS columns to help you track and analyze your project data. After that, you will update the project to reflect some progress made and set an interim plan.

GET READY. SAVE the open project schedule as *RFP Bank Software Interim* in the solution folder for this lesson, as directed by your instructor.

1. On the Ribbon, click the **View** tab, then click the **Task Usage** button.
2. On the Ribbon, click the **Tables** button, then select the **Usage** table.
3. Press **Ctrl + Shift + F5** to activate the Go To dialog box. Key **14** in the ID box, then click **OK**.
4. In the Task Name column under task 14, right-click the resource named **Kevin Kennedy**.
5. From the shortcut menu, click **Information**. Click the **General** tab, if it is not already selected.
6. In the Work contour box, select **Front Loaded**, then click **OK**.
7. Click the timephased field that intersects Kevin Kennedy's assignment on task 14 and June 6, 2011. Key **2.38**, then press **Tab**.
8. In the timephased field for June 7, 2011, key **2** and press **Tab**.
9. In the timephased field for June 8, 2011, key **0** and press **Enter**.
10. On the Ribbon, click the **Gantt chart** button. Click the **Other Views** button in the Task Views group, then click More Views. In the More Views dialog box, select **Task Sheet** and click **Apply**.
11. Right-click the Task Name column heading. On the shortcut menu, click **Insert Column**. Key **UNI**, then press **Enter**.
12. Right-click the Task Name column heading. On the shortcut menu, click **Insert Column**. Key **WBS** and press **Enter**.
13. Auto-fit each of the columns you just inserted.
14. On the Ribbon, click the **Tables** button, then select the **Tracking** table.
15. Click the **Act. Start** field of task 10, key **5/27/11**, and press **Tab**.
16. Click the **Task** tab, then click the **100% Complete** button in the Schedule group.
17. Click the name of task 14. In the Act. Dur. cell, key or select **8d**, then press **Tab**.
18. Select the name of task 15. Click the **100% Complete** button on the Ribbon.
19. Click the **Project** tab, click the **Set Baseline** button, and then select **Set Baseline**.
20. In the Set Baseline dialog box, click **Set interim plan**, then click **OK**.
21. On the Ribbon, click the **View** tab, then click the **Other Views** button and select **More Views**. In the Views list, click once on **Tracking Gantt**, then click the **Copy** button.
22. In the Name box, key **Custom Tracking Gantt**, then click **OK**.
23. Make sure that Interim Tracking Gantt is selected in the More Views dialog box, then click **Apply**.
24. On the Ribbon, click the **Format** tab, then click the **Format** button in the Bar Styles group. From the drop-down menu, select **Bar Styles**.
25. Click the **Insert Row** button. In the new cell directly below the Name column heading, key **Interim**. In the same row, click the cell under the Show For... Tasks column heading, then select **Normal** from the drop-down list. In the Row field, key or select **2** from the drop-down menu.

26. Click the cell under the From column heading and select **Start1** from the drop-down list. Click the cell under the To column heading and select **Finish1** from the drop-down list.

27. Click the **Interim** name cell. On the Bars tab, in the Pattern box under the Middle label, select the **third option**. In the Color box, select **green**. Click **OK**.

28. Click the name of task 16, then press **Ctrl + Shift + F5**.

29. **SAVE** the project schedule.

   PAUSE. LEAVE Project and the project schedule open to use in the next exercise.

⊙ Project 3: Creating a Resource Pool and Copying a View from Another File

You have decided to create a resource pool, using another project from within the bank as an additional sharer file. While you have the additional sharer file open, you will copy a view from the file using the Organizer, and you will apply this view to your project.

The *Check Processing Rework* file for this lesson is available on the book companion website.

GET READY. SAVE the open project schedule as *RFP Bank Software Organizer* in the solution folder for this lesson, as directed by your instructor.

OPEN the *Check Processing Rework* project schedule from the data files for this lesson.

SAVE the newly opened file as *Check Processing Rework Pool* in the solution folder for this lesson, as directed by your instructor.

1. Make sure that the RFP Bank Software Organizer file is in the active window.

2. On the Ribbon, click the **View** tab, then click **Resource Sheet**.

3. Click the **File** tab, then select **New**.

4. Click **Blank Project**, then click **Create**.

5. On the Ribbon, click the **File** tab, then click **Save As**. In the Save in box, locate the solution folder for this lesson, as directed by your instructor. In the File name box, key **Bank Resource Pool**, then click Save.

6. On the Ribbon, click the **View** tab, then click **Resource Sheet**.

7. On the Ribbon, in the Window group, click **Arrange All**.

8. Click the **title bar** of the RFP Bank Software Organizer window.

9. On the Ribbon, click the **Resource** tab, then click **Resource Pool**, and then click **Share Resources**.

10. In the Share Resources dialog box, under Resources for 'RFP Bank Software Organizer,' click **Use resources**. In the From list, select **Bank Resource Pool**, if it is not already selected. Click **OK**.

11. Click the **title bar** of the Check Processing Rework Pool window.

12. On the Ribbon, click the **Resource** tab, then click **Resource Pool**, and then click **Share Resources**.

13. In the Share Resources dialog box, under Resources for 'Check Processing Rework Pool,' click **Use resources**. In the From list, select **Bank Resource Pool**, if it is not already selected. Under the *On conflict with calendar or resource information* label, make sure that **Pool takes precedence** is selected. Click **OK**.

14. **SAVE** the Bank Resource Pool project schedule.

15. Expand the RFP Bank Software Organizer project schedule to fill the active window.

16. On the Ribbon, click the **File** tab, then click **Organizer**.

17. Click the **Views** tab, if it is not already selected.

18. In the Views available in list on the left side of the dialog box, select **Check Processing Rework Pool**. In the Views available in list on the right side of the dialog box, select **RFP Bank Software Organizer**, if it is not already selected.

19. In the list of views on the left side of the dialog box, click **My Custom Gantt Chart**.

20. Click the **Copy>>** button, then close the Organizer.

21. On the Ribbon, click the **View** tab, then click the **Other Views** button and select **More Views**. In the More views dialog box, click **My Custom Gantt Chart**.

22. Select **task 16** and press **Ctrl + Shift + F5** to see the new formatting.

23. **SAVE** and **CLOSE** the *RFP Bank Software Organizer* file. **SAVE** and **CLOSE** the *Check Processing Rework Pool* file. **SAVE** and **CLOSE** the *Bank Resource Pool* file. **CLOSE** Project.

Glossary

A

actual cost The cost that has been incurred so far (after the indicated total work has been completed).

actual cost of work performed (ACWP) The actual cost incurred to complete each task's actual work up to the status date. Also known as actual cost in earned value terms. Used in earned value analysis.

actuals Values of a project's work completed, such as actual duration, actual cost, and actual work. Usually recorded in a Microsoft Project file.

allocation The portion of a resource's capacity devoted to work on a specific task.

assignment The matching of a specific resource to a particular task to do work.

AutoFilter A quick way to view only the task or resource information that meets the criteria you choose.

automatic scheduling A task scheduling mode that automatically schedules a task depending on the task relationships, constraints, resource calendar, and project calendar.

availability Determines when and how much of a resource's time can be assigned to work on tasks.

B

base calendar Can be used as both a task and project calendar and specifies default working and nonworking times for a set of resources.

baseline A collection of key values in the project plan, such as the planned start dates, finish dates, and costs of the various tasks and assignments. A baseline allows you to begin the tracking phase of project management.

baseline cost The total planned cost of a project when the baseline was saved.

bottom-up planning Developing a project plan by starting with the lowest-level tasks before organizing them into higher-level phases or summary tasks. This approach works from specific to general.

budgeted cost of work performed (BCWP) The portion of the budgeted cost that should have been spent to complete each task's actual work performed up to the status date. This value is also called earned value (EV) because it is literally the value earned by the work performed. Used in earned value analysis.

budgeted cost of work scheduled (BCWS) The value of the work scheduled to be completed as of the status date. Microsoft Project calculates this value by adding all the timephased baseline values for tasks up to the status date. Also known as planned value (PV). Used in earned value analysis.

C

calendar A scheduling tool that determines the standard working time and nonworking time (such as evening or holidays) for the project, resources, and tasks. Calendars are used to determine how tasks and the resources assigned to these tasks are scheduled.

chart A view or part of a view that presents project information graphically, such as the Network Diagram.

consolidated project A Microsoft Project file that contains other Microsoft Project files, called inserted projects; also called a master project.

constraint A restriction that you or Microsoft Project sets that controls the start or finish date of a task.

contour Determines how a resource's work on a task is scheduled over time.

Copy Picture Enables you to take a snapshot of a view. With Copy Picture, you have several options when taking snapshots of the active view: (1) you can copy the entire view that is visible on the screen, or just selected rows of a table in a view, or (2) you can copy a range of time that you specify or show on the screen.

cost Refers to how much money will be needed to pay for the resources on a project.

cost performance index (CPI) The ratio of budgeted to actual cost, or EV (BCWP) divided by AC (ACWP). Used in earned value analysis.

cost rate table Resource pay rates that are stored on the Costs tab of the Resource

Information dialog box. For a given resource, you can enter up to five cost-rate tables.

cost resource A resource that doesn't depend on the amount of work on a task or the duration of a task.

cost variance (CV) The difference between the budgeted and actual cost of work performed. Used in earned value analysis.

crashing Action to decrease the duration of an activity or project by increasing the expenditure of resources, without altering the basic sequence of activities.

critical path The series of tasks whose scheduling directly affects a project's finish date.

current cost The sum of the actual and remaining cost values.

D

data maps Allow you to specify how you want individual fields in the source program's file to correspond to individual fields in the destination program. Once you set up an import/export map, you can use it over and over again.

deadline A date value you enter for a task that indicates the latest date by which you want the task to be completed. However, the deadline date itself does not constrain the task.

deliverable The final goal of a project.

dependency A need or a condition that exists between two elements; not to be confused with a task relationship.

discretionary dependency Situation in which the first element does not necessarily have to be complete in order to start or complete the second element. Also known as a soft logic or preferred dependency.

duration The amount of working time required to complete a task.

E

earned value (EV) (variable) The portion of the budgeted cost that should have been spent to complete each task's actual work performed up to the status date. This value is called earned value because it is literally the value earned by the work performed. Also known as budgeted cost of work performed (BCWP). Used in earned value analysis.

earned value analysis (process) Used to measure a project's progress and help forecast its outcome. It gives you a more complete picture of overall project performance in relation to both time and cost. Earned value can be used on any project in any industry to objectively measure project performance.

effort-driven scheduling A scheduling method in which the duration of a task increases or decreases as you remove resources from or assign resources to a task; here, the amount of work needed to complete the task does not change.

elapsed duration The total length of working and nonworking time you expect it will take to complete a task.

Entry table The default table in the Gantt chart view, used for entering basic data in a project.

export map Specifies the exact data to export and how to structure it.

external dependency An element from outside the project that must occur before an element in the project can start or be completed.

F

fast-tracking A schedule optimization method in which tasks are done in parallel that were originally planned, or normally completed, in series.

field The intersection of a row and a column in a table. A field represents the lowest-level information about a task, resource, or assignment. Another name for a field is a cell.

filter A tool that enables you to see or highlight in a table only the task or resource information that meets the criteria you choose. Filtering doesn't change the data in your project plan— it merely changes the data's appearance.

fixed consumption rate A resource consumption rate in which an absolute quantity of the resources will be used, no matter the duration of the task to which the material is assigned.

fixed duration A task type in which the duration value is fixed.

fixed units A task type in which the units value does not change.

fixed work A task type in which the work value is held constant.

flexible constraint A constraint type that gives Microsoft Project the flexibility to change start and finish dates of a task.

No constraint date is associated with a flexible constraint.

float The amount of time a task can be delayed before it will delay another task or the project end date. Also called slack.

form A type of view that presents detailed information in a structured format about one task or resource at a time, such as the Task Form.

free float The amount of time a task can be delayed before it will delay another task. Also called free slack.

free slack The amount of time a task can be delayed before it will delay another task.

fully allocated The condition of a resource when the total work of its task assignments is exactly equal to its work capacity.

G

Gantt chart view A view in Microsoft Project that consists of a table (the Entry table by default) on the left side and a graphical bar chart on the right side.

ghost task A task relationship between project files. A ghost task is similar to a link between tasks within a project file, except that external predecessor and successor tasks have gray task names and Gantt bars. Ghost tasks are not linked to tasks within the project file, only to tasks in other project files.

GIF (Graphics Interchange Format) An image format used for storing images and pictures.

global template A template that provides the default views, tables, and other elements in Microsoft Project, and includes calendars, filters, forms, groups, import/export maps, menu bars, reports, tables, toolbars, VBA modules (macros), and views.

group A way to reorder task or resource information in a table and to display summary values for each group according to various criteria you can choose. Grouping goes a step beyond sorting in that grouping your project data will add summary values, called "roll-ups," at customized intervals.

H

hyperlink A portion of text that contains a link to another file, a portion of a file, a page on the Internet, or a page on an intranet.

I

import map Specifies the exact data to import and how to structure it.

inflexible constraint A constraint type that forces a task to begin or end on a certain date, completely preventing the rescheduling of a task. Inflexible constraints are sometimes called hard constraints.

inserted project A Microsoft Project file that is inserted into another Microsoft Project file.

interim plan A snapshot of current values from the project plan that Microsoft Project saves with the file. Unlike the baseline, an interim plan saves only the start and finish dates of tasks, not resource or assignment values. You can save up to 10 different interim plans during a project.

L

line manager A manager of a group of resources; sometimes also called a functional manager.

link A logical connection between tasks that controls sequence and dependency.

M

macro A recorded or programmed set of instructions that carry out a specific action when initiated.

manually scheduled A task scheduling mode that ignores all task relationships, constraints, and calendars; it does not move as related information about the task changes. This is the default scheduling mode.

mandatory dependency Situation in which the first element must be started or completed before the second element. Also known as a hard logic dependency.

mask When working with outline or WBS codes, the mask, or appearance, defines the format of the code—the order and number of alphabetic, numeric, and alphanumeric strings in a code and the separators between them.

master project Another name for a consolidated project.

material resource Consumable items used up as the tasks in a project are completed. Unlike work resources, material resources have no effect on the total amount of work scheduled to be performed on a task.

maximum units The maximum capacity of a resource to accomplish tasks. The default value for maximum units is 100%.

milestone Represents a significant event reached within a project or imposed upon the project. Milestones are often represented as a task with zero duration.

N

negative slack The amount of time that tasks overlap due to a conflict between task relationships and constraints.

Network Diagram A standard way of representing project activities and their relationships in a sequential format.

nodes The boxes that represent tasks in a Network Diagram. The relationships between tasks are drawn as lines connecting nodes.

noncritical task In Microsoft Project, by default, it is defined as a task that has slack (float) greater than zero. In project management terms, it is defined as any task that is not on the critical path.

note Supplemental text that you can attach to a task, resource, or assignment.

Notes field A tab on the Information dialog box (for tasks, resources, and assignments) where you can place text, pictures, hyperlinks, or documents.

O

OLE A protocol that allows you to transfer information, such as a chart or text (as an OLE object), to documents in different programs.

optimizing Adjusting the aspects of a project plan prior to saving a baseline, such as cost, duration, and scope (or any combination of these), to achieve a desired project plan result. A desired result may be a target finish date, duration, or overall cost.

Organizer A feature you use to organize elements between Microsoft Project files so that they can be shared, edited, and reset. The names of the tabs in the Organizer dialog box indicate the elements you can copy between project plans.

outline number A numeric representation of the outline hierarchy of a project. Outline numbers are numeric only and are generated by Microsoft Project.

overallocated The state of a resource when it is assigned to do more work than can be done within its normal work capacity.

P

phases A group of closely related tasks that encompass a major section of your project.

planned value (PV) The value of the work scheduled to be completed as of the status date. Microsoft Project calculates this value by adding all the timephased baseline values for tasks up to the status date. Also known as budgeted cost of work scheduled (BCWS). Used in earned value analysis.

planning Developing and communicating the details of a project before actual work begins.

predecessor A task whose start or end date determines the start or finish of another task or tasks. Any task, except the last task in a project, can be a predecessor for one or more tasks.

predefined contour Describes how work is distributed over time in terms of graphical patterns. Some options are Bell, Front Loaded, Back Loaded, Double Peak, and Turtle. Predefined contours work best for assignments where you can estimate a probable pattern of effort.

program office A group that oversees a collection of projects (such as producing doors and producing engines), each of which is part of a complete deliverable (such as an automobile) and the organization's strategic objectives.

progress bar The bar in the Gantt chart view that shows how much of each task has been completed.

project calendar The base calendar that provides default working times for an entire project.

project plan A model of a real project— what you want to happen or what you think will happen. The plan contains tasks, resources, time frames, and costs that might be associated with such a project.

project triangle A popular model of project management in which time, cost, and scope are represented as three sides of a triangle. A change to one side will affect at least one of the other two sides.

R

recurring task A task that is repeated at specified intervals, such as daily, weekly, or monthly.

remaining cost The difference between the current cost and actual cost.

remaining duration The amount of time required to complete an in-progress task.

report A predefined format intended for printing Microsoft Project data.

resource calendar Defines the working and nonworking time for an individual resource. A resource calendar applies only to people and equipment (work) resources—not to material resources. When you establish resources in your project plan, a resource calendar is created for each resource.

resource leveling The process of delaying a resource's work on a task to resolve an overallocation. Depending on the options you choose, resource leveling might delay the start date of an assignment or an entire task, or split up the work on a task.

resource manager A manager who oversees resource usage in project activities specifically to manage the time and cost of resources.

resource pool A project plan from which other project plans gather their resource information.

resources The people, equipment, supplies, money, and materials used to complete the tasks in a project.

risk An uncertain event or condition that, if it occurs, will have an impact, either positively or negatively, on your project. In a project, negative risk decreases the likelihood of completing the project on time, within budget, and to specification.

S

schedule performance index (SPI) The ratio of performed to scheduled work, or EV (BCWP) divided by PV (BCWS). Used in earned value analysis.

schedule variance (SV) The difference between the budgeted cost of work performed and the budgeted cost of work scheduled. Used in earned value analysis.

scheduling formula The formula Microsoft Project uses to calculate work: Duration × Units = Work.

semi-flexible constraint A constraint type that gives Microsoft Project the flexibility to change the start and finish dates (but not the duration) of a task within one date boundary.

sequence The chronological order in which tasks occur.

sharer plans The project plans that are linked to the resource pool.

sheet A table view that presents task or resource information in rows and columns, such as the Task Sheet.

shortcut One or more keys that you press on the keyboard to complete a task.

slack The amount of time a task can be delayed without causing a delay to a task or the overall project. Slack is also known as float.

sort A way of ordering task or resource information in a view by the criteria you specify. You can sort tasks or resources using predefined criteria, or you can create your own sort order with up to three levels (a group within a group within a group).

split An interruption in a task, represented in the Gantt bar by a dotted line between the two segments of the task.

sponsor The individual or organization that provides financial support and supports the project team within the larger organization.

stakeholders All people or organizations that might be affected by project activities, from resources working on the project to customers receiving the end result of the project.

status date The date you specify (not necessarily the current date) that you want Microsoft Project to use when calculating earned value numbers.

subproject Another name for an inserted project.

subtasks The detail tasks that fall below a summary task.

successor A task whose start or finish is driven by another task or tasks. Any task, except the first task in a project, can be a successor to one or more tasks.

summary task A task that is made up of and summarizes all of the detail tasks that fall below it. You cannot directly edit a summary task's duration, start date, or other calculated values.

T

table A spreadsheet-like presentation of project data, organized in vertical columns and horizontal rows. Each column represents a field in Microsoft Project, and each row represents a single resource or task.

task Represents the actual individual work activity that must be done to accomplish the final goal of a project. The tasks contain the details about each activity or event that must occur in order for your project to be completed. These details include the order and duration of tasks, critical tasks, and resource requirements. Also known as a schedule activity.

task calendar The base calendar that is used by a individual task. It defines working and nonworking times for a task, regardless of settings in the project calendar.

Task ID A unique number that is assigned to each task in the project. It appears on the left side of the task's row.

task priority A numeric ranking between 0 and 1000 of a task's importance and appropriateness for leveling. 1000 is the highest task priority.

task relationship Controls the start or finish of one task relative to the start or finish of another task. There are four types of relationships in Microsoft Project: finish-to-start, start-to-start, finish-to-finish, and start-to-finish.

task type Determines which of the three scheduling formula variables remains the same if the other two values change.

Team Planner view A view that displays task assignment information, unassigned tasks, and resources in graphical form and allows you to make resource assignments or replacements.

template A Microsoft Project file format that lets you reuse an existing project plan as the basis for a new project plan. Templates can include any of the types of information you might expect to find in a Microsoft Project plan, including task and resource lists, assignments, customized views, tables, filters, and macros.

Timeline view A view that appears above the Gantt chart view by default and displays tasks from the task list in a timeline form. Tasks must be placed on the timeline for them to appear.

timephased fields Task, resource, and assignment values distributed over time.

timescale The band across the top of the Gantt chart grid that denotes units of time.

top-down planning Developing a project plan by identifying the highest-level phases or summary tasks before breaking them into lower-level components or subtasks. This approach works from general to specific.

total float The amount of time a task can be delayed without delaying the project end date.

total slack The amount of time a task can be delayed without delaying the project end date.

tracking The collecting, entering, and analyzing of actual project performance data, such as work on tasks, resource costs, and actual durations.

U

underallocated The work assigned to a resource is less than the resource's maximum capacity.

Unique ID An identifier that Microsoft Project uses to track the order in which you enter tasks and resources.

units The capacity of a resource to work when you assign that resource to a task.

V

variable consumption rate A resource consumption rate in which the amount of the material resource consumed is dependent upon the duration of the task.

variance A deviation from the established schedule or budget.

view A window through which you can see the various elements of a project plan in a way that is helpful to the viewer. There are five different formats that can make up a view: chart, sheet, form, diagram, and usage.

W

work The total amount of effort a resource or resources will spend to complete a task.

work breakdown structure A graphical or textual representation of all the work required to complete a project.

work breakdown structure (WBS) code A numeric representation of the outline hierarchy of a project. You can change WBS codes to include any combination of letters and numbers that you desire.

work resource The people and equipment that do work to accomplish the tasks of the project. Work resources use time to accomplish tasks.

Credits

Index